IT'S NOT PHYS

Part one: What's it all about then?

John Z Langrish, MSc, PhD, FDRS.

[Part two: Memes and Me: the memetics of design is published separately]

Newton by Blake

In this work Blake portrays a young and muscular Isaac Newton, rather than the older figure of popular imagination. He is crouched naked on a rock covered with algae, apparently at the bottom of the sea. His attention is focused on a diagram which he draws with a compass. Blake was critical of Newton's reductive, scientific approach and so shows him merely following the rules of his compass, blind to the colourful rocks behind him.

Gallery label, October 2018

ITS NOT PHYSICS

Heaton Mersey: IAS

Independently Published

ISBN 979 8 499335 85 7

Copyright ©John Langrish 2022

jlangrish@aol.com

Contents

Chapter 1. Prelude   1

Chapter 2. The Dream Years 1937–1940   9
    Removal Day...At Home...Patterns
    in the Fire (PIFs)...Words...Activities
    ...Reading...Pattern Recognition

Chapter 3. Thinking at School   21
    Clarendon Rd School...The War...
    Junior School...The Wireless...Pattern
    construction...Interlude...Sermons...
    Barton Bridge and Trafford Park

Chapter 4. Grammar School 1946–1953   45
    Eccles Grammar School...Scouts...
    Form 2L...The Wireless...School Sports
    ...Sixth Form...Interlude: New things and
    purpose...Brenda...The year 1953

Chapter 5. Patterns: Their Acquisition,
Recognition and Effects on Actions   65
    Purposive Pattern Recognition (PPR)...
    Pattern Formation...Some disadvantages
    ... Prevention of further PPR... Either/Or
    (E/O)...Patterns in the fire

Chapter 6 Manchester University 1953–1959   83
    Chemistry Department...The OTC...
    Social life 1...Finals...MSc by Research
    ...Roman Catholicism...Polymer research
    ... Part time earnings...Social Life 2...
    Polymer research 1957 -1959

Chapter 7. Politics   137
        Politics...Election 1945...Committees
        ...Scientific planning...Elections 1950,
        1951 and 1955...CND...Politics and
        religion

Chapter 8. Marriage and King Ted's 1959–1961   153
        Sheffield...Teaching chemistry...
        Getting Married...The Twins...
        ICI and Crumpsall

Chapter 9. Crumpsall and ICI 1961-1967   167
        Crumpsall...Liberal Party...Working
        At ICI...Cyril Lord Carpets...Foundry
        Resins...The Pilot Plant...Injection
        Moulding and Langrish House...
        Supersoft foam pillows...The Polymer
        Lab...The move to Stockport

Chapter 10. Langrish – village and family   199
        Langrish Village...Langrish Family...
        Talbot-Ponsonby

Chapter 11. LSS: 1967–1970   209
        LSS and F R Jevons...The Queen's
        Award for Innovation...The Sussex
        Study SAPPHO...Strange animals and
        evolution... Three remarkable women
        ...What is culture?...Wealth From
        Knowledge and Causation...Wrong way
        round evolution... Correlation of Parts
        ...The Reverse Paley Argument...The
        pushmi-pullyu debate... Lectures...
        Research Funding...Scientific
        techniques

Chapter 12. MBS: 1970-1974   245
    Manchester Business School...
    Scientific Techniques...The Scientific
    Confidence Trick...The Saver Seven...
    The New Building...The MSc. in
    Structure and Organisation of Science
    and Technology...Modules...
    Dissertations – Taxonomy...
    Dissertations – Industrialised building
    ...Contract Research...Zero growth and
    new idea points...Small Ideas...Small is
    Beautiful...Derek Medford...Ken Hill...
    The Sloan...Mensch Cycles...The
    Lloyds Arms

Chapter 13. UMIST Man. Sciences 1974–1977   275
    Technical Colleges...Management
    Sciences...The MACS Course...
    Interdisciplinary Team Projects...
    Publications...The Four Sided Triangle...
    Technological Determinism...Iowa State
    University (ISU)...The Swinging Sporran
    ...Institute of Advanced Studies (IAS)

Chapter 14. From Darwin to Dawkins   313
    Darwinian Change...Salford
    Conference 1995...Dawkins...
    Different kinds of memes...Purposive
    Pattern Recognition (PPR)... So, what's it all
    about?...Newton and the Secret

Index   328

Preface

In about 500 BCE, Heraclitus of Ephesus said:

"You cannot step into the same river twice, for fresh waters are ever flowing in upon you."

If you want to describe a river, do you talk about its banks, changing slowly or do you discuss the water, changing rapidly but subject to events such as floods, droughts and human interventions. A similar problem arises when writing an autobiography.

When my granddaughter, Daisy, heard that I was writing my autobiography, she asked, "Is it sequential or is it a bit of this and a bit of that?" In academic terms, the question becomes, narrative or thematic? I don't like either/or type questions; the answer is usually both and something else as well.

The main structure of this book is provided by its 'banks', the institutions that framed my life. There are chapters on home, primary school, grammar school, university, and King Edward School, where I taught chemistry. Also ICI where I was a technical officer and then back to university with three chapters on the Faculty of Science, the Business School and UMIST. This takes my life story up to 1977, a convenient point to end part one. The rest of the story forms another book, Part Two of my autobiography. It is as though the river of my life joins a new river, Manchester Polytechnic, itself the product of three institutions becoming one and then flowing into being the Manchester Metropolitan University (MMU).

The present book, Part One, is subtitled, 'What's it all about then?' It started as an attempt at recording the history of my mental life but that turned out to be like describing a river without mentioning its banks. Part Two is subtitled, 'Memes and me: the memetics of design'. It records my life from 1978 and the development of my thinking about thinking leading to the idea that it is useful to classify our idea patterns into three kinds of memes: recipemes, explanemes and selectemes.

The overall title, It's Not Physics, is a partial answer to the question, What's it all about then?

Dividing my life flow into two, mirrors a real division. In the first half I was married to Sandra and we nurtured twin daughters, Suzanne and Nina. In the second half, I was married to Helen and we nurtured our son Tom. In the first half I worked with scientists and became an expert in technological innovation. In the second half I worked with art and design people and became an expert in design research. The first half saw me become senior lecturer in the management of innovation. In the second half I was Dean of the Institute of Advanced Studies and visiting Professor of Design Research.

The final chapter of this present book, describing how an evolutionary theory of innovation became a memetic theory of design, provides a bridge between the two parts. Some themes run through several chapters and in the case of my involvement in politics, it seemed better to put things together in chapter 7. Two other chapters that are not part of the sequence are chapter 5 on patterns and chapter 10 on the Langrish family tree and the village of that name.

A river can be enjoyed at many places along its course. The same goes for this book. View the Contents page and pick a spot to contemplate.

Acknowledgements

"Any new thing that appears in the made world is based on some object already in existence." ... George Basalla (1988). The same might be true for ideas. My ideas are based on things said by family, friends and colleagues, by written words and by words heard on the radio. Harry Rothman gave many ideas; Bill Evans taught me that engineering could be fascinating. Philip Steadman exposed me to Victorian ideas about design evolution. My many postgrad students were the source of lots of my ideas, from my first, Carol Goldstone, to my last, Elif Kocabiyik - too many to name but Chris Rivlin gets a mention for getting me to read Dawkins and Mark Hinnels for selling me his Apple LC computer (memory counted in kilobytes!). The exchange of ideas needs institutions that organise conferences and journals. So many thanks to the organisers of the British Society for the History of Science, The Royal Society, the Design Research Society, the Design History Society, the Design Management Institute etc. Important roles were played by academic entrepreneurs, people who seized the opportunity to do something different. In particular, the late F R Jevons created an interdisciplinary environment and the late John Holden saw the need for postgrad education in design before art and design had acquired first degrees. Entrepreneurs provided the opportunity for me to exchange ideas overseas. Aziz Fouad got me to the USA. Kazimir Poznanski got me to Poland and the Russian, Vadim Goncharov, through his Task Force on Innovation enabled me to visit iron curtain countries before the Wall came down.

Ideas about values and how to do things came from Grandfather Fairclough, my parents and Sandra, Helen, Suzanne, Nina and Tom. Thanks to David Rigby for encouraging me to finish this book and to call it 'It's not Physics' (It started life as 'Memes and Me: The autobiography of a mind'). Thanks also for encouragement from Greek design historian, Artemis Yagou. Finally, thanks to Julia Yates for home-made soup and help with publication.

Chapter 1. Prelude

Good things can sometimes emerge from disasters. Joseph Schumpeter called this process 'creative destruction' and compared it to biological evolution. The city of Lisbon rose from the remains of a disastrous earthquake in 1755 and modern Germany emerged from the disaster of World War II. This process can be accompanied by cycles of pessimism leading to optimism and back again.

The twentieth century started as a time of optimism. Both emotionally and rationally, people in the UK just knew that better times were ahead. Exciting new things were happening. Flying machines got themselves invented. A new visual experience - Art Nouveau – was around. Electricity began to change the streets, factories and homes where people went about their lives. Oilcloth, in the form of Linoleum – Lino for short – transformed the wooden floors of people's houses.

1901 saw the death of Queen Victoria, symbolising the end of an era. 1901 also saw the birth of George Arnold Langrish who arrived just in time to be able to describe himself as a Victorian - more about him later. 1906 saw the election of a radical government, suitable for the times. The new Liberal Prime Minister, Campbell Bannerman, was unusual for the UK in that he had been against the Boer War – against the militarism that had typified the Victorian Great Britain. His government expanded free compulsory education. His Chancellor of the Exchequer, Lloyd George, introduced the first old age pensions, paid for by a penny stamp stuck on a card every week. Optimism was part of the Zeitgeist. It was not to last.

Good things and bad things happen to people in what seems a random manner. Statistics, being what they are, have the result that some people experience more than their fair share of disasters and others have more than their fair share of the opposite. Why is there no word in English for the opposite of a disaster?

1914 saw the end of British optimism – not to return until 1951. Disaster struck, in the form of what became known as the Great War – the war to end all wars – who could be so stupid as to start another such disaster? When stupidity was discovered not to be the only cause of war – evil is not just stupidity; it has to be resisted - the Great War had to be renamed as the First World War, which became the 1914-18 war (later in the USA, where they had enough sense to try and keep out of it)

At the family level, disaster struck the Langrish family on the 20th December 1910 with the death of George William Langrish, aged 36, leaving my father, George Arnold, his younger brother, Norman and a baby girl Edna to be looked after by their mother, Alice Mary née Jordan.

Widows' pensions paid by the government did not arrive until 1925 and in 1910 a widow with three young children was faced with poverty. My grandmother partly solved this problem by taking in a lodger.

Another source of income was my father who at the age of twelve was sent out to work – in a coal yard, holding sacks open whilst strong men shovelled coal into them. The lodger turned out to be more than just a paying guest. He fathered a child, my aunt Elsie, the only relative to have heart problems. The young George, bringing home money to a house with0 two growing children, a baby and a 'lodger', could not stand it and left as soon as possible to live in 'digs' where he lived until he got married.

When he was able, my father continued to provide financial support for his mother. The lodger left without trace to be replaced by more lodgers,

From then on, my father experienced more than his fair share of misfortune until his luck changed when I was born in October 1935. This misfortune started with the loss of his father when he was nearly ten years old, continued with the loss of his first wife in child birth and the loss of his second son, Brian, born to a new wife, Marjorie. When Marjorie became pregnant again (they didn't say 'pregnant' in those days; they said 'expecting') my father was worried. The pregnancy was a chance event – the result of the failure of a contraceptive called Volpar Gells. His first experience of being a father had seen his wife die and his son looked after by grandparents. His second had seen the baby die after only two weeks of life. What would the third bring?

Things began to stir in the council house at Grasmere Crescent, Winton (pronounced Wint'n to rhyme with Swint'n and Mont'n) and the midwife was sent for. But unfortunately, it was one of those days when daylight was obscured by a pea soup fog, the result of industrial pollution, not removed until the Clean Air Acts of the 1960s. The cleaner air was to have unexpected results. The peppered moth changed its colour back to being pale again after 100 years of being black (the reasons for this are still disputed) and the increased sunlight speeded up climate change.

Intentionality played its part as well as luck. It wasn't just the moths that changed colour; government grants to clean up the black Victorian buildings led to the discovery that Owen's College, the centre of the University of Manchester, had a red roof.

All of this was in the future back in 1935 with my mother starting to produce me and lying on the stairs where she had stopped on her way back to bed. Where was the midwife? She was lost in the fog. Those pea soup fogs were really something. Buses attempting to follow the pavement could end up in a cull de sac, the wet air was a pea green colour – hence the name – and you could not see a lamppost until you nearly walked into it.

My poor father was going crazy. He was not too sure even how to boil water. In those days he never even made a pot of tea. Then the luck changed. The fog began to lift. The midwife with bicycle and bag arrived. I was born safely and all was well. My father's luck was on the increase. What do we mean when we say, 'luck changed'? Fay Weldon, in her 1992 novel, Growing Rich, describes events taking place in the village of Fenedge.

> It was noticeable that during the next few months the luck of Fenedge changed ... It wasn't so much that good things happened as that bad things ceased happening. Or perhaps the Devil was looking the other way...

Things happening because other things stop happening is a type of causation that is ignored. For example if you were sat in a garden under an apple tree and an apple fell, you might think of Newton and gravity causing the fall. In fact, gravity was there yesterday when the apple did not fall off. The real reason that an apple falls is that its supporting twig no longer stops it from falling. However, why the apple fell at ten past two rather than ten to four could be seen as the operation of chance or because the wind had changed direction. When we are not sure, we can call it luck.

PRELUDE

My father's share of whatever luck was around continued to increase. He had a 'steady job' in the Borough Treasurer's Department of Eccles Town Hall. He avoided the call up in the Second World War, being in a reserved occupation. His two sons, Peter (the one whose mother had died) and I seemed healthy enough. Then he managed to land the job of Number Two in the Education Offices (Number One being H J Bailey, the Director of Education whose name was on the board outside every school in Eccles).

In those days, to acquire a senior job in Local Government educational administration, you had to meet two out of three requirements – a university degree, teaching experience and relevant experience. My father had no degree (few people had degrees then – even in the early 1950s only 3% of 18-year-olds went to university – and many school teachers possessed a teachers certificate but no university degree). His relevant experience was that he had worked on the educational budget in the Borough Treasurer's Department and had made important contacts with people who mattered, including the councillors who would decide who got the job.

The second requirement, teaching experience, was met through his being a qualified shorthand teacher who taught in local 'night' schools where hoards of young women who worked during the day went to learn Pitman's shorthand and typing, hoping to move out of the copy typing pool and become a secretary.

Before photocopying was invented, organisations of any size had a room filled with copy typists, bashing away at their typewriters, their eyes fixed on the document being copied – they were trained not to look at the typewriter keys – under the eye of a fierce spinster lady who sat at a desk on a dais and superintended things. Permission was needed to 'leave the room' – just like being at school. Escape from this imprisonment was by marriage or by obtaining certificates from the RSA (Royal Society of Arts) or the ULCI (Union of Lancashire and Cheshire Institutes). No wonder they went to night school to obtain precious qualifications and to meet males who were trying to obtain technical qualifications.

My father met my mother (his second wife) through teaching her shorthand. She was a very proficient person and became personal secretary to one of the senior people in

Turner Bros, the asbestos people whose head office was in Trafford Park, the huge industrial estate built at the end of the Manchester Ship Canal and connected to Monton by the Barton swing bridge over the Ship Canal - a product of Manchester entrepreneurship.

Since Manchester was not next to the sea, its exports had to go via Liverpool docks where Liverpool charged considerable docking fees. If Manchester wasn't next to the sea, then the sea would have to be moved by building a canal deep enough to carry sea-going ships directly to Manchester docks. Some 5,000 navies and five steam shovels were used in its construction.

The Manchester end of the canal was next to Trafford Park, the ancestral home of the Trafford family who sold it to a financier. It was then converted into what is claimed to be the world's first planned industrial estate. The manufacturers who moved in included Westinghouse who brought a piece of America into England. In addition to the factory, Westinghouse built a village for his workers on the American style grid system of numbered avenues and streets. The community had shops, eating rooms, a dance hall, schools, a church, and a cinema. All that remains today is Second Avenue.

Rolls Royce started out in Trafford Park where they manufactured the Merlin engines that powered the Spitfire fighter and the Lancaster bomber in the Second World War. Turner Brothers Asbestos Co moved into the Park in 1913 with a large factory and offices where my mother worked after leaving school.

My mother had had her own run of bad luck. Starting out in a 'nice' area, Monton, her father, John Scarisbrick Fairclough, earned enough money as a sales representative for Wilson's brewery to pay for her education outside the rough world of the local schools. So, she went first to a small school run by two sisters, where she learned copper plate handwriting and then on to Pendleton High School for Girls where she did very well until her father became out of work.

The school said she was very bright and could stay there for free but her father said it's not just the fees; she has to get a job to bring some money into the house. So like my father, mother had to leave school before she should have done and get to work, earning money for a family facing poverty.

PRELUDE

Her father, my grandfather Fairclough, believed in self-help. Being without a job, he did not mope around at home. Instead, he took himself off to London, leaving my mother, her younger sister Molly (christened Mary Francis) and his wife to fend for themselves with what little money my mother earned and what money he could send from London where he had some temporary work including being a strike breaking railway guard during the General Strike. Eventually he talked his way into being a sales representative for Roneo, the office equipment supplier, where he became a star salesman, sometimes obtaining large financial bonuses. However, in 1932, that was the future. 1932 was the year that my mother decided to take charge of her own destiny by marrying my father.

She did this against the wishes of her father who thought that she should be looking after her own family and not my father's family i.e. his son Peter, now living with his dead mother's parents in Yorkshire.

One lunch time, my parents to be went to the Eccles Free Church of England with witnesses and no one else where they were joined in matrimony and then went back to work. That evening, my mother told her mother that she had given up her job, was now married and was moving into my father's council house where they would be joined by baby Peter. She never spoke about this; I learned about it from my aunt Molly.

My mother, being a devout believer, had wanted a church wedding but weddings in the C of E are preceded by the reading of the bans (If anyone know just cause or legal impediment, you are to declare it now) and she was trying to keep it secret. So it had to be the 'Free'.

The Eccles Free Church of England was a monument to extreme protestant prejudice. At some time in the past, the people who ran things at Eccles Parish Church (an ancient foundation with a list of vicars or priests in charge going back to the 12th century – hence the ecclesiastic significance of the word 'Eccles') decided to 'improve' the interior of the church by adding a reredos, a decorative stone wall covering behind the altar.

Some wealthy protestant types objected to this on the grounds that it would break the commandment against idols (either the first or second depending on whether you are Jewish, Anglican or Roman Catholic). This commandment includes the words, "You shall not bow down to them or worship them". To the extreme prots, this meant that kneeling down to receive communion in front of a stone carving with representations of the gospel writers was bowing down before them and as abhorrent as the Catholic practice of seeming to pray to statues.

So the wealthy dissidents built themselves a new church, affiliated to the Free Church of England, an association of independent churches objecting to the high church tendency. It started in 1844 in opposition to attempts by the hierarchy to impose changes in worship. It became a legal entity in 1873 and still exists today (In the USA, it is the Reformed Episcopal Church). The church where my parents were married was still going when I was young. Its activities included a boys' boxing club where I learnt the smell of boxing gloves and the joy of hitting a disliked opponent smack in the face (not easy to do). Eventually it lost its congregation, became a furniture warehouse for a while and was then demolished along with streets of houses in the enthusiastic town planning of the 60s. (They thought they were building a better world – so much for intentionality).

My own introduction to formal Christianity was at the ancient Parish Church and its Sunday school in Albert St where it was a school during weekdays and a social center in the evenings and week ends. I went there to Sunday school, the Cubs, Scouts and Youth Club as well as the odd dance (not much fun without a bar). It was eventually demolished along with other important social centers including the Liberal Club and the Tory Club.

So, my father now had his son Peter at home and a wife to look after him. My mother had a husband and freedom from the responsibility of her family which moved to London to be reunited with the successful office salesman in one of those Victorian establishments – the key flats – built in blocks around splendid gardens, only three stories high but with no lift except for an outside conveyance used for moving coal into the flats and taking rubbish out of them. My mother's younger sister, my aunt Molly, was to live in that flat for some sixty years.

The new Langrish family in Winton hit some more bad luck. My mother's first born, Brian, died after two weeks. My father was declared a bankrupt as a result of becoming a partner in his brother Norman's wood yard. He didn't speak to Norman again for years and insisted on paying back the debts so there was no money to spare.

PRELUDE

Then I arrived. Friends of my father told me later that he was transformed by this event, changing from being gloomy to being a jolly good chap. He took charge of his life again and decided that living in a council house with bad memories was not a good idea. So the family moved to 9, Ellesmere Avenue, a large Victorian semi, where I lived for more than twenty years and where I started to think long enough to be able to remember some of my thoughts as described in the next chapter.

References Chapter 1.
Fay Weldon. 1992, Growing Rich p. 72. London: Flamingo.

Chapter 2. The Dream Years 1937-1940

2.1 Removal Day

My earliest memory is of removal day. I was only two years old but I remember the day well – or rather I remember remembering it so many times that the details must have changed over the years. Memories are like Dawkins' imperfect replicators or Darwin's descent with modification. But who knows which bits of a memory have been modified?

The memory starts early in the morning, stood at the front door of the Winton council house, watching the arrival of a red van. This belonged to the man from the wireless shop who was entrusted with my father's six-valve radio that was too precious to go with the furniture. The memory continues with my mother taking me to get the tram from Winton to near Ellesmere Avenue. My father and brother were to follow with the removal people.

Trams (street cars in the US) were a much-used form of transport. Running on rails and powered from an overhead electricity cable, they were slowly being replaced by buses. There are people who write about the 'ever increasing' pace of technological change. If such people looked outside electronics and read some history, they would know that the normal pace is slow; stop; start again. The first trams were pulled by horses. Then came steam, soon to be replaced by overhead power. Horse-drawn transport still survived, however. Even in the 1950s, horse drawn carts were visible on the streets of Manchester, moving slowly alongside trams, trolley busses and the internal combustion engine. Trams eventually disappeared from the streets but then made a comeback. In Manchester now, the modern transport system known as the Metro is still being expanded. Trams run through the streets again.

The tram that I traveled on in 1937 was quite different from the modern versions. Its body was mainly constructed from wood and the seats were wooden with an ingenious construction that allowed the back to be moved so that passengers could face forward when the tram swapped its front for its back. There were driver's cabs at both ends to avoid having to have turntables. I remember playing with one of these movable backs until stopped by my mother. Later, at 9 Ellesmere Avenue, I remember men unloading a truck and one of them waving my 'potty' (made of metal – the technology changes but the name remains - from pot to metal to plastic; it's still a potty.). I also remember being embarrassed by this.

2.2 At Home

During the next three years, from being aged two to being five, I turned into 'me'. All those millions of neurons in my brain got used to forming connections with each other and those neurons that did not find themselves part of a repeating pattern just died of neglect. I spent most of the time inside my head. In fact, I was told later that my mother had been very worried because I was not talking until I was two and then I spoke in complete sentences. My aunt Molly claimed that my grandfather had said, "John was too busy thinking to bother with talking until he was ready".

I spent part of the day running around a very large garden (large enough for another house to be built there many years later). My brother, Peter, being six years older, was at school and there were no other children at that time in Ellesmere Avenue. For mental company, I created a world of imagination and dreams. I used to like going to bed because I knew that I was going to have wonderful dreams with only the occasional bad dream involving men who looked like dustbin-men or coal-men who came and took my mother away. I don't remember the content of the nice dreams - just a vague memory of a pleasurable pattern with hints of fairy tales. In fact, I did not have a word for the pattern of dreaming.

I spent the days in the company of my mother. My father was at work but came home from the Town Hall every day for his lunch. My brother had lunch at school (known as school dinners, supervised by dinner ladies). My days were spent mainly in the garden or in the large room known as the kitchen where my mother was kept busy preparing meals - midday lunch and the early evening meal (known as tea) plus breakfast for the four of us and a late evening 'supper', consisting of home made cake or buns and sandwiches.

She also did most of the laundry - washing, drying, ironing and, in some cases, repairing. The washing took place in a large cellar containing an electric water heater, a washtub and a mangle with huge wooden rollers for squeezing water out. There was also a remnant from earlier days, a coal fired copper boiler with an open top, formerly used for washing clothes and sheets. The cellar had a channel in the floor leading to a grid for disposing of water. There was no electric washing machine in the house until after I had left home. There was however, an evolutionary link between the old and the new. This was a metal washing tub with a water heater fitted.

Drying the clothes was a problem. Several items were pegged onto an outside line that was held up and tightened by a wooden clothes prop. The problem was that we lived near a railway and the smoke from many house chimneys plus the coal smoke from the railway added up to floating black blobs of soot, known as smuts. When the weather was damp and windy, these smuts could float through the air, sticking to the partially dry clothes. My mother had no alternative then but to wash the clothes again. The house was shared with a cat called Smut because it was black.

At some point, my mother must have rebelled and insisted that most of the washing went to the laundry. Items were collected weekly by a laundry van that took away sheets and some underclothes plus my father's collars in a special collar box. In those days, middle class men wore shirts with detachable collars to make the shirts stay clean longer. My father's work collars were made of celluloid, stiff, white and shiny.

On top of all that activity, my mother had the struggle of keeping the house clean. This involved a never-ending battle against a fine dust deposited everywhere from the coal fires. There was a Hoover vacuum cleaner and once a week we had a cleaner to help but the three males did little cleaning apart from applying 'black lead' to the coal fire metal surround and occasional Hoovering.

My father and brother were responsible for the coal fires. This meant lighting the fire in the morning, filling up the coalscuttles, taking out the ash and cinders every day and chopping wood into chips for fire lighting. In the evening a shovel-full of burning coal would be taken from the kitchen to the so-called dining room where the wireless was listened to, the piano played, books read, card games played on a folding card table and so on. The dining room was never used for eating. Visitors were entertained for tea in the front room, kept for special occasions.

The coal fire in the kitchen was part of a 'range' with large and small ovens, a water heater and a device for swinging a kettle onto the top of the fire. Different metal shutters controlled the flow of hot air from the fire. The flames could be directed backwards under the hot water tank or sideways round the ovens or just allowed to flow up the chimney, depositing soot that required the occasional visit from a chimney sweep.

This system was a remarkable tribute to the ingenuity of the Victorians and it was used to produce my mother's homemade sausage rolls - deliciously warm, straight from the oven. In addition, the kitchen contained an electric cooker. The basic design had been adapted from early gas cookers and is still the basis for many of today's products with four hot plates on the top. The main difference is the removal of a separate toaster. Oven toasters have been replaced by the pop up toasters invented in America.

2.3 Patterns in the Fire (PIFs)

In the winter, we used to sit round the coal fire. The glowing coals were a source of patterns. Sometimes you could see a face in profile, shining in the centre of the fire. At other times, there was an animal, a castle, a forest or anything else that the imagination could conjure up. Sometimes different people saw different patterns and with some effort could persuade others to see the same pattern. "Look, just to the right under the big piece of coal there's a face".

Patterns in the fire became an idea - a pattern of thought resting on electrochemical circuits in the brain. (Pattern recognition is discussed in chapter 5.) This thought pattern became a nucleus for further development and many years later I was able to use 'PIFs' as a term for discussing competing theories. Different people could see different patterns in the 'coals' of history, science, economics etc. Speculative theories may be patterns that only exist in a mind; they may have no correspondence with reality just like castles in the fire.

In the other half of the Victorian semi lived two sisters, Mabel and Winnie Elmore, their bed-ridden mother and a resident servant called Gertrude. Gertrude was young and pretty and I fell in love with her. One day her father came to visit her and I asked him if I could marry Gertrude when I grew up. He smiled and gave me a shilling - a lot of money in those days. When the war came, Gertrude, like many other domestic servants, left to work in a munitions factory. The only remaining live-in servants that I knew were rather elderly. My mother's aunt Eleanor had one; Captain and Mrs. Bell at no. 21 Ellesmere Avenue had a servant and so did Aunt Grace. (The aunts were aunts of my mother whose parents both came from large families - Myles and Faircloughs)

2.4 Words

I used to go next door sometimes and one day, in their garden, someone was talking about a dream. That was when I learnt a new word. I said "Is it a dream when the world changes?" That's how I know it's possible to think about something without having a word for it. I could think about dreaming without having a word for that pattern of thought. Learning the word, 'dream' did not change how I felt about dreaming.

Some people claim that thinking needs words but I know that's not always true. I sometimes think in terms of 'patterns' that don't have words or have words that I can't remember, like recognizing a face but not being able to put a name to the pattern. In the same way, I could think about dreaming without having a word for the pattern.

Now, of course, it is most unlikely that I can remember that event so far back. Most people that I have asked about early memories seem to have difficulties in remembering anything before they were five and when they do, they tend to wonder if they are remembering a photo of an event such as a birthday party. However, my pre-five years old memories include mental events as well as occasions. I do remember remembering them over and over again because they made a big impression on all those neurons busy sending electrochemical signals to each other.

Later in life when I read that you could not think if you did not have words, I would re- remember that occasion. I could think about something as a pattern – a collection of feelings that added up to – to what – it didn't need a word. When forced to use words, the best I could do was 'when the world changes'. This was so significant that I remembered it. It was also significant because it shows that I was thinking about thinking - but not necessarily in words.

Children learn new words all the time. What was unusual in my case was the self-realisation of learning a new word and remembering the event. I was not just thinking; I was thinking about thinking and thinking about my thinking about thinking. This causes problems. If it is 'me' that does the thinking, then what is doing the thinking about thinking? Many years later, I would discover that philosophers had written about this problem but back then it was the start of a chain of thought that is continued in the next chapter.

Another memory concerns the word 'cloud'. Someone must have caused me to look up by saying, "Look at that cloud". When I looked up I saw the telephone wire that crossed over our garden. (We didn't have a 'phone then so the wire was going somewhere else.) 'Cloud' became a word that meant a wire going over the garden. Some time later, my father is in the garden with a ball. I say, "See if you can throw the ball over the cloud." He laughs and I can't see what was funny; the 'cloud' isn't very high up. So, I look higher up and realise that the word means that stuff up in the sky.

One of Steven Pinker's books (2007) is called 'The Stuff of Thought' with the sub-title of 'Language as a Window into Human Nature' and it might be that remembering my thinking about words gives a window into my nature. In addition to being mistaken about 'cloud' and not knowing the word, dream, two other words have got themselves remembered - pictures and church.

One afternoon my mother said 'we are going to the pictures'. To me, pictures were things that hung in frames on peoples' walls; I didn't know about the cinema. We went through Eccles near its boundary with Salford to reach the Regent cinema. (It still exists - as a Wetherspoon's pub - with a foyer exhibiting photos of Eccles cinemas, all six of them and all gone except the Regent). We went inside and up a grand staircase lined with framed pictures of people who were actually film stars but how was I to know?

Then we went through a curtain into a dark space and I discovered that we had come to see moving pictures - not those framed things on the stairs. When the cinema was first invented, it needed a new word and 'moving pictures' got itself into circulation, becoming just 'the movies' in the USA and 'the pictures' in England, plus that strange singular 'a movie'. We also had 'the flicks' but that term was not used at 9, Ellesmere Avenue, being regarded as too 'common'.

On another occasion, my mother said, "We are going to church" and I asked, "What's church?" "God's house" was the answer. Now I was familiar with the pattern represented by 'X's house'; it meant a building where 'X' lived. So off we went to Eccles Parish Church and sat on a bench seat (a pew, but I didn't know that word). I looked around and saw a strange wooden structure towards one end of this place called church.

The structure was actually part of the organ but how was I to know that? Pointing to the wooden structure, I said to mother, "Is that where God lives?" Her reply wasn't sufficiently memorable for me to remember it.

2.5 Activities

There were some days when instead of being at home we went out. I can even remember going out in a pram but I was soon old enough to be able to walk with my mother to the shops in Eccles, nearly a mile away. Fortunately, my mother did not have to carry vast amounts of shopping. Most requirements were delivered. Every week, a lady from T Seymour Meads would call and sit in the middle room, known as the dining room even though we never ate there. Armed with a red notebook and pencil she would take the order for the week to be delivered by lorry.

Greengroceries were delivered by Mr Knowles from his shop in Eccles. He lived two doors away from us at No. 13 (Victorian house builders were not superstitious about 13). He was the only person in Ellesmere Avenue with a car. There was a bread van that called to see what my mother wanted and if we ran out of something, there was a nearby corner shop at the end of the 'dog entry' - so called because it was shaped like a dog's leg.

There were other trips out with my mother. We used to visit her friends and relatives, most of whom had a supply of things to occupy a young child so that I could continue to live in my own world of imagination. One special trip was going to Belle Vue, an entertainment centre with zoo (opened in 1836), funfair, concert hall, sports' stadium etc. Mother would pack a bag with our lunch including a thermos flask with weak sweet tea. Travel involved the No 9 Salford bus into Manchester, and the Hyde Road tram to Belle Vue. If we were there at the right time we could see the chimps' teas party. This involved some chimps dressed as humans, pouring something from a teapot into mugs and drinking the result (which might not have been tea but the chimps seemed to enjoy it). Many years later, I was to recall this ability when I read Dennett's "Apes can ape but they don't get to compare notes" (2003). Those chimps could have only learnt to use a teapot by imitating humans and then imitating each other.

Whilst my mother was busy with housework, she made sure that I had something to do. In cold weather, I would sit at the kitchen table with some toys or something vaguely educational. I remember a device that was rather like a picture frame with a transparent front that could be written on. There were various items that could be placed under the front and then drawn over. My earliest attempts at drawing letters and numbers were by tracing over appropriate cards in the frame. This might be one reason why I was never able to draw without tracing. Both my father and brother had some skill in drawing plants and trees but not me.

In fine weather, I was running around the large garden. In my imagination, I turned the 'real world' into something else. It was dreamtime again - only I was wide-awake. The back door to the house led into a porch with another door leading via a step to the path. I used to stand on this step, holding on to the door and pretending that I was getting into or out of a train. I had a similar trick inside the house where a door from the kitchen led up a step into the hall. I used to pretend that the hall was a removal van and I would carry a small chair from the kitchen into the hall and then back out again until my mother got cross and demanded that I close the door.

Much later in life, I discovered Richmal Compton's (1933) Just William books and was delighted to discover someone like me. In one of the stories William is described as a scruffy boy who seemed to be beating a hedge with a stick when in fact, he was a knight fighting off the enemy or a sailor disposing of an invading pirate.

Also later in life (aged perhaps eight) there was a memorable day spent with two other boys from school trying to dam a stream. The day was memorable because when we had to go home for tea, I realized that I had managed to spend a long period of time without imagining I was doing something else. That was so unusual that I remember remembering it. I had been preoccupied with the task of stopping the water flow but no matter how many stones were piled up and how much earth and clumps of grass were put between the stones, the dam still got washed away. I did not need to pretend I was doing something else.

2.6 Reading

During the pre-war dreamtime, I learnt to read. Once a week, a children's comic called Chicks' Own was delivered. This had pictures of assorted animals pretending to be human and having adventures. It was aimed at helping children to read. The words of the story were printed with hyphens between the syllables – like Per-cy Pig does some ex-er-cises - but I had to wait until my mother was free to read the words.

Waiting for my mother to read to me gave me the motivation to want to read and so she taught me phonetics – d for dog etc. Once started, I could soon read Chicks' Own and then on to books. I remember one called something like Three Little Pups and I got stuck on a word beginning with c and h. C for cat and h for hat didn't help so I asked my father who was doing the Telegraph crossword. The word was 'chips'. It's strange how little things like that stick in the memory or rather in the memory of a memory of a memory.

Whilst I was growing up in my private dream world, disasters were threatening the rest of the family but I did not notice. My father had an attack of colitis that made him very weak and loosing weight. Apparently, he was packed off to a convalescent home in the country where he found that a bottle of Guinness was the only thing that did not make him sick. He then recovered.

My brother was involved in a nasty road accident on his way home from cubs. He ran from behind a bus into the path of a car driven by Hilda Baker who was to become a famous comedienne. She had not been trained to do emergency stops (like my father, she had a driving license but had never had to take a driving test). My brother's head ended up between the car and a lamppost. He was in hospital in a coma for weeks and my poor mother was distraught. She was told that even if he did recover, it was likely that he would suffer from fits or be partly paralysed. She went to see him every afternoon. Then one day when she was visiting, he sat up and said, "Mummy I want to go home". So good luck was fighting back. In fact, the accident had an unexpected side effect. My father was able to sue the driver and a sum of money was placed in court until Peter was 21 by which time he was married with a son, Vernon, and living with the parents of his wife, June. The money plus some from his own grandmother helped him to move to a place of his own at the side of the Bridgewater canal just before it reached an amazing aqueduct that swung a portion of the canal over the Manchester Ship Canal.

In the dream years, there were no other children living in Ellesmere Avenue and I only met other children when my mother took me to visit families - relatives and friends - where I would encounter others of about my own age. I didn't enjoy these rare occasions because I had no idea what I was supposed to do with other people of similar age.

Being able to read fueled my imagination and more neurons formed circuits. Having no other children to play with meant that I had to invent an imaginary friend. Every child in books did things with other children so why shouldn't I? Some adult asked me what was the name of my friend. Of course he didn't have a name – what use was a name? Nevertheless, I realized that I had better invent one and I came up with Forrit. The adult had more sense than to ask any more but he looked puzzled. When I'd been in a shop with my mother, I had heard a woman say to a small child, "You're for it" (a Lancashire expression meaning retribution will fall later). My brain had turned those words into a pattern meaning, "I know you, and you are called Forrit". I've never been good with names – unless they make a pattern. Concepts I remember because those neurons oblige with appropriate electro-chemical patterns but names – my neurons don't know what to do with names. When I was in the infants' school, I must have been the only child who did not remember the names of many of the other children. So when asked for a name, on the spur of the moment, my brain came up with Forrit.

2.7 Pattern Recognition

I have mentioned patterns a few times and I am convinced that pattern recognition is an important activity of our brains. Before patterns can be recognised, they have to be constructed so that they are available for re-cognising, that is re-knowing. You cannot re-know something unless you already know it. Therefore, the patterns that we know have to start with a germ of a concept that is capable of further development. Once established, that is once a neuronal circuit is available for re-activation, then other patterns can be added to it if they 'fit'. This is discussed in more detail in chapter 4.

A very early example of the construction of a pattern, capable of growth and extension, happened before I went to school. This was the effect of a 'loud speaker' that sat on top of a cupboard in the kitchen. It was connected by a wire to a radio in the dining room. A corridor ran from the kitchen into the hall and separated the doors to the kitchen and to the dining room. When I walked down this corridor, the noise from the kitchen speaker got less but as I neared the dining room, I could hear the noise from the radio. Volume went through a minimum at some point between the two rooms and I remember walking backwards and forwards to find the spot where the volume was lowest.

It may be rather fanciful to see this as the start of a pattern to become important in later life. I don't like 'either/ors'. Nature v nurture, supply v demand, push v pull are all the wrong sort of pattern for me. Faced with opposite pairs, my brain finds patterns that involve 'and' or 'both' or a spectrum flowing from one to the other with perhaps a minimum or maximum in the middle.

Once a pattern has been constructed, it becomes easy to recognise but this has the side effect that it reduces the possibility of constructing new patterns that don't fit. Patterns fixed in early life are like patterns of speaking and hard to change. The patterns that we call music have to be constructed before we can recognise them.

A lifelong love of music started in those early years. At some time before my arrival, my father had decided to catch up on his lost childhood by learning to play the piano with the help of a private tutor. He used to play bits of Mozart, Beethoven and Schubert plus unsuccessful attempts at Chopin. He sometimes played in the evening after I had gone to bed and I can remember lying there, enjoying the familiar patterns of the few pieces that he played.

This enjoyment would be interrupted by my mother's voice. "Arnold! John's in bed. Stop playing". This made me cross. Much later in life when I heard these pieces played on the radio, they sounded wrong. The pattern that I knew contained my father's mistakes and failures to play the difficult passages properly. It took time before the proper pattern emerged to replace the pattern constructed from my father's playing.

In those pre-school years, in addition to learning to read, my father introduced me to simple sums and before I went to school, I could add and subtract. Somewhere there is a blue hardback note book in which my father set exercises for me to do during the day when he was at work. They are dated between February and April 1941 so we have some documentary evidence to support my memory. I had become five years old in October 1940 and should have been at school but apparently my being ill delayed the start of school. Years later, I was told that I had been kept off school because of 'swollen glands'. This was a good example of confusing symptom and cause.

My solitary dreamtime was ended by two events, the arrival of some other children in Ellesmere Avenue (I didn't know what to make of them) and starting school, as described in the next chapter. Before moving on, there is a little diversion.

Kanizsa Triangle

The brain tries to be helpful by sorting sensory inputs into patterns that we recognise. In this case, it constructs a white triangle that actually is not there. The brain tells the mind that there are borders round the white triangle - but they are phantom borders.

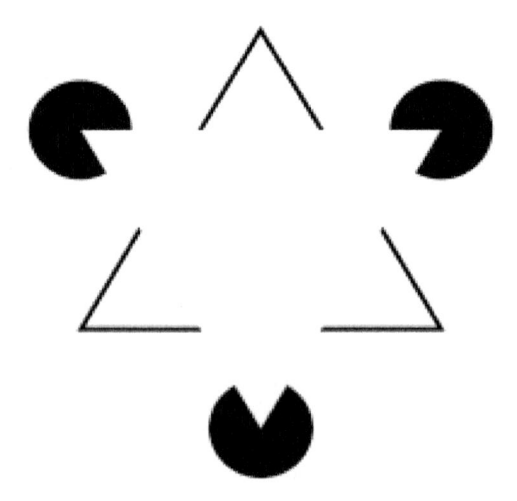

References Chapter 2.

Richmal Crompton. 1933. William the Pirate. London: Macmillan.
Dennett, Daniel. 2003. Freedom Evolves. New York: Penguin.
Steven Pinker, 2007. The Stuff of Thought: Language As a Window Into Human Nature. Allen Lane.

Chapter 3. Thinking at School

3.1 Clarendon Rd School

1941 was a memorable year for two reasons - starting school in Eccles and Hitler's war. I became five years old in October 1940 but didn't start school then because I was ill - or so I was told. Apparently, I was suffering from swollen glands; this being an example of confusing symptoms and causes. The swollen glands were the result of infection by bacteria but the family doctor, one Dr McCauley, had qualified in the previous century and still thought of swollen glands as the cause of a fever, rather than being a symptom.

Eventually I recovered and one day I walked to Clarendon Road School with my mother who deposited me with a strange adult. The school had a separate infants department (for children up to the age of 8) with its own headmistress, Miss Shaw, and separate entrance, playground and hall.

I don't remember much about that first visit but people are different and another person who went to the same school has remembered his first impression of the outside. Paul Morley, best known for writing about music, has written an autobiography (2013), The North, a mixture of his own early life and facts about the north of England.

Before he came to Eccles, Morley's father had worked as a warder in Parkhurst Prison and Paul remembers waving goodbye before his father disappeared through massive wooden doors into "a clanking dark inside I didn't want to imagine". So, when he arrived at the school he compared what he saw with a pre-existing pattern - the outside of a prison. In his own words, "It looks as if what goes on inside involves straight jackets, solitary confinement and random forms of punishment and it perhaps scared me because the only building I could compare it with in my young mind was Parkhurst Prison. … Being sent on my own into this giant brick building by my mother triggered five-year-old hysterics."

To me, the school could not have looked like a prison because I had never seen one. Manchester's Victorian prison, Strangeways, is surrounded by a huge wall and inside is a tower, taller than the factory chimneys that used to dominate the landscape.

To me the predominant features of Clarendon Road Primary School are the red bricks and large windows. Several schools look that way. They were constructed in the years before the First World War, following changes in education brought in by the reformist Liberal government of that time. What we have here is one building, two young minds and two quite different responses. The fact that different people have different patterns in their minds and therefore respond differently to attempts at social engineering and advertising should be born in mind by planners, architects and marketing people.

After that first occasion, I went to school every day on my own. The journey to and from school crossed a main road but this was not a cause for concern because there were very few cars (petrol was rationed). Delivery vans and buses that used the road made a noise so I suppose my mother wasn't worried. But this is odd because my brother had been hit by a car and nearly died, staying in a coma for weeks before he suddenly sat up in his hospital bed and said to my mother, "Mummy, I want to go home". It could just be that taking a child to school in these days just 'wasn't done'. Bullies called one unfortunate boy a cissy because he was brought to school every day by his mother. Doing 'the right thing' was an important guideline for my mother.

At school, I stayed in my first class for a few weeks. Then, when it was discovered that I could read, write and do sums, I was moved into the next class with older children. Since they all knew each other, I was an outsider but this did not bother me; I was happy to live inside my head. There was a wide range of ability amongst the pupils and the teacher often gave out work on printed sheets with different sheets for different abilities. We wrote the answers on a slate because being wartime there was a shortage of paper. I remember being given a sums sheet and seeing a strange sign, the dot over dot division sign. This was new to me; I only knew the x sign for multiply. The teacher had to explain what it meant and then I had some more patterns to think with. I remember little about the children in that class or about the teacher but I do remember finding out about division.

There are a few other school things that I remember from that time, all to do with activities rather than people. Once a week, we had music in a music room where we banged, rattled and blew various noise-making instruments in time to the teacher's piano playing. We sometimes had to paint things and I realized I was rather hopeless at making any sort of mark on paper. There were three making activities that I enjoyed. One was making a ship from matchboxes, glue and paper; another was making a 'pot' from some kind of plasticine. We rolled out a thin sausage shape that was then coiled into a flat base. More sausage shapes were then added to make the sides.

A third activity that I enjoyed was paper weaving. We were given pieces of coloured paper with vertical slits through which we could insert paper strips with a different colour. This could produce a repeat pattern of squares or any other pattern that you chose. The word 'pattern' came to mean something on wallpaper, tiles, curtains, dresses, ties etc. My mental pattern of a pattern was thus restricted to something that repeated itself. Sometimes, I would sit and contemplate wallpaper or bathroom tiles to detect the repeat.

But of course, the word pattern is not restricted to those repeat patterns that originated with weaving. Carpets were said to be plain or patterned. In those days, only posh people had wall-to-wall carpets. Most houses that I visited had lino floorings with a rug or two and possibly a carpet, covering the centre of the floor. These carpets did not have repeat patterns, just a central design, originating in Persian carpets but they were still patterns. This meant that the meaning of the word 'pattern' had to be extended (the pattern of patterns had grown). The first carpets were hung on the wall not the floor. Patterns are crucial to my ideas about how we think and are discussed later in chapter 5.

Away from school, I attempted to improve my drawing ability by copying some of my brother's sketches. I learned that drawing 'match stick men' was easy, starting with a head and using the ratio 1:2:3 for the head, the body and the legs. I also drew aeroplanes, ships and tanks in battle scenes. I still have some of those childish drawings in a notebook, produced from somewhere by my father during the wartime shortage of paper.

The most interesting drawing in this notebook is the outline of a large head with my imaginative attempt to show the brain at work. At the cinema I must have seen films that showed a 1930s style telephone exchange, creating a pattern that went into my sketch as a little matchstick man listening to messages that came from the nerves.

He then pulled levers to cause movements in the limbs. In the days before electrification, railway signals were moved up and down by wires attached to large levers that were pulled by a man operating them in a signal box. So my sketch of a brain box had telephone messages coming in and signal control going out.

The problem with the little man in the head model is the disturbing fact that this little man must have his own little man in order to do what he does and this very little man must have …Many years later, I would discover that this was known as the homunculus problem but back then when I drew the man in my head I thought of this as another example of something going on forever. I knew the pattern without having words such as infinite regression.

My first example of something going on forever came to me from one copy of Chicks' Own. This had a picture of Percy Pig reading Chicks' Own with a picture of - Yes - Percy reading … I remember that I looked very carefully at the comic trying to see how many versions of the same picture appeared. Another example could be found in my parents' bedroom where there were mirrors in a dressing table and on the front of a wardrobe. By standing in the right place, it was possible to see one mirror in the other mirror. This produced the image of a line of mirrors going on as far as the eye could see. I was familiar with the pattern of an infinite regression long before I had any words for this experience.

3.2 The War

Some of the most memorable events from this period were connected with the war. 1941 was a dark year for the UK - both literally and metaphorically. After dark, all lights had to be concealed. Heavy curtains covered windows and street lights were out. My father was in the ARP (air-raid precautions) and took his turn going round the streets shouting, "get that light out". He also spent some nights at the Town Hall helping to operate a 'report centre' that included being on the roof to look out for signs of fire in the town. This was before America entered the war and we expected to be invaded.

In the hope of confusing advancing Germans, all signposts were removed or turned to point the wrong way. Then there were the tank traps. Large cylinders of concrete appeared at strategic road junctions. In the event of invasion, they were supposed to be rolled into the road and turned upright to obstruct passing tanks. I was aware of the physical manifestations of all this but not too sure what it was all about.

In 1941, things seemed bleak. Britain was the only power resisting German take over. But then here was a significant victory for British forces; the top German battleship, the Bismarck, was sunk by an attack from air and sea. This so impressed Miss Shaw, the head of the infants, that she summoned the school into the hall to tell everyone that this was a turning point. To mark the significance of the event she opened a tin of sardines that she had been hoarding and gave it to the school cat. Tins of food were in short supply and my mother built up a secret hoard that occupied two drawers in a chest of drawers. The tins were hidden under a layer of clothes.

Eccles lies on the northern side of the Manchester Ship Canal and the opposite side is occupied by Trafford Park formerly the home of the de Traffords but turned into a major industrial centre, following the construction of the Manchester Ship Canal. It was a target for German bombers but some of them dropped their bombs a little early causing damage to Eccles instead.

We lived at No 9, Ellesmere Avenue, a cul de sac with houses numbered from 1 to 23 - no even numbers. Bombs destroyed Numbers 1,3,5 and 19 but no one was killed. During the height of the bombing raids, we slept in the cellar and when the air raid siren sounded, we got out of bed and sat at the bottom of the cellar stairs. This was the safest place to be as was obvious to me from my morning walk to school when I could see bomb damaged houses with the outside walls mainly gone and inside rooms destroyed. But most of these semi detached Victorian houses had the inner joining wall still there and clinging to this wall were the stairs.

This meant that being in a cellar under the stairs was a good place to be. When numbers 1 and 3 were destroyed, I heard that they did not know that their house had gone until they came out of the cellar. The night that 1, 3 and 5 went, we faced a damaged house when we emerged the next day. Both front and back doors had been blown off their hinges by the blast. All the windows at the side of the house had gone and the main rooms were covered in soot shaken down the chimneys. Also we had no water supply.

All this was quite exciting. I went with my brother and father, carrying buckets to get water from a pipe in the nearby factory that had its own water supply. Our windows were covered up with some semi transparent material to keep the rain out. We ate bread and tinned stuff - possibly Spam and tinned pilchards.

One large bomb exploded in the graveyard of Eccles Parish Church causing the East window to be demolished and several graves to be disrupted including one for the son of the Stephenson who had been responsible both for 'The Rocket' and the construction of the Liverpool -Manchester railway. This explosion took place during evening service inside the church. Fortunately, the needs of the 'blackout' had resulted in a thick curtain covering the ancient stained glass window, preventing people from being cut by flying glass.

Another side effect of this curtain was that much of the glass remained in large pieces and some years later, the pieces were put back together to recreate the window but with several pieces of white glass where the original had been destroyed. The general opinion was that the window looked much better with some white in it.

The news of the bomb in the graveyard spread round the school and after school some of us went in search of what were called 'skelingtons'. We didn't find any and we were chased away by the Verger, a Mr Jones, who looked after the church during the day, spending part of his time in a café above a shop where he kept an eye on the church door. This row of shops facing the church included Bradburn's 'Original Eccles Cake Shop'.

The aftermath of bombing raids included bits of metal lying about. This was shrapnel and was collected by some boys. At school we were warned not to pick things up. They might be unexploded bombs or even booby traps, designed by the fiendish Germans to stick to children's hands.

After the war, some workmen discovered an unexploded incendiary bomb in the eaves of our house. It had landed in a birds' nest and was still there, nestling in the bones of some dead chicks. If that bomb had got itself through the roof into the house then hopefully the bucket of sand and the stirrup pump jet of water would have extinguished the fire. But being in the cellar, we wouldn't have known about it.

Air raids were very noisy with lots of bangs and whistling sounds. The anti-aircraft guns provided some protection against air raids. The main effect of these guns was probably to scare the German bomber crews with the result that some dropped their bombs on Eccles before reaching Trafford Park. A secondary result was bits of metal from the exploded shells falling on the protective helmets of people out at night or simply landing on the ground to be collected by children the next day.

Another air raid protection was the anti aircraft barrage balloons, one of which was placed in a field in Ellesmere Park where a small crew looked after a large balloon that held a suspended steel wire. This was supposed to stop the Germans from flying low. Some of the crew were women who in my memory were wearing trousers but this could be an addition from wartime news films and documentaries.

A further bit of excitement was provided by the Home Guard, training in the Avenue. They crawled through gardens approaching the shell of no. 5, later to be demolished but then still having its front wall intact. Some of the Home Guard soldiers climbed up the front of this building and in through a window. I couldn't see why they didn't go through the front door.

3.3 Junior School

When I was seven, I moved from the infants into Standard One of the Junior School in a different part of the same building. Its head was a Mr Marsden. The school had five 'standards', reflecting the time when pupils moved up a class on reaching a certain standard, rather than being in classes determined by age. The old standard system had gone but the names remained and there was still some flexibility to the age division so that I was usually the youngest in the class.

Also when I was seven, I was allowed to join the junior section of Eccles Library, an Edwardian building endowed by the Carnegie foundation. It had a junior section upstairs so as not to get in the way of adults using the main library and of course to protect the young from 'unsuitable' books. (One result of this protective policy to children was that I was about thirteen before I discovered 'the facts of life'.)

My father believed in the importance of a network of contacts, maintained through his work in the Borough Treasurer's office in the Town Hall where he looked after the council spending on libraries, schools, parks etc. He knew the Borough Librarian, a Mr Lambert, whose name was on the board outside the library and the branch library in Winton. He used this contact to get me into the library before I reached the official age of eight. I became an avid reader and remember being annoyed at the rule 'no books over meals'. I could be in the middle of a gripping story when I had to stop in order to sit at the table for a family meal.

Another of father's contacts was a local taxi firm. Every Friday, he went in a taxi to pay the out-workers, gardeners, gravediggers, road menders etc. He sat in the back of the cab wearing his bowler hat as a badge of authority and the workers queued up to receive their wage packets, ingenious devices that enabled the contents to be counted before they were opened. In holidays, I sometimes accompanied my father. Some of the older workers queuing for their pay touched their hair as a mark of respect. I guessed that this action was a substitute for raising their cap when they were hatless.

He used the taxi contact to take his family on a wartime holiday. We went by taxi to a guesthouse in Derbyshire. This involved travelling up a hillside pass in cloudy weather. My father said that we would soon be in the clouds instead of under them. This seemed to me to be an exciting prospect but I was soon disappointed. The clouds turned out to be the same as fog i.e. wet stuff that hindered visibility.

It was on this holiday that I saw a fairy sat on a tree. This shows the power of prompting on perception. We had been walking through fields with toadstools growing in rings. The adults talked to me about fairy rings. Then in a wood, there was something on the end of a branch. My brain decided that it was a fairy, looking like those fairies in children's books.

Being eight years old was a turning point. In addition to the library, there was Sunday school and the Cubs both of which met in the Albert Street Church School (now demolished) I had started going to Sunday school when I was five. I was taken there by my brother, Peter, one of the few things we did together. Being six years older meant that he had left primary and secondary schools before I had arrived there. After Sunday school, Peter sometimes took me to Barton where there were two swing bridges over the Ship Canal. One bridge carried the road into Trafford Park; the other was an aqueduct, carrying the Bridgewater canal over the Ship Canal. This feat of Victorian engineering was said to be one of the seven modern wonders of the world.

Queen Victoria had opened the Manchester Ship Canal in 1894, connecting the port of Manchester with the sea at Liverpool and allowing the export of cotton goods and machinery together with the imports of world trade including rubber from Brazil wheat from Canada, cotton from Egypt and sugar from the West Indies. Peter and I enjoyed watching ships from foreign parts guided by tugboats as they passed through the two bridges. Many years later, ocean-going ships became much larger and the use of the canal declined. Manchester docks, like many other docks including Cardiff's, became a trendy place for residence and leisure.

An important event provided those neurons with some new circuits, patterns of a ladder and of conflicting emotions. The government organised a huge waste paper collection, using school children. Points were awarded for the amount of paper brought into school and the points were rewarded with a cardboard army rank badge. Bringing in lots of newspapers got you a badge with three stripes - a sergeant. My father got involved and cleared out old papers from the Town Hall plus books and things from people he knew. All this I carted to school over several days and was eventually rewarded with the badge of a general, presented to me at school assembly. Becoming a general in 'the Book Brigade' required bringing in 150 books.

My mother must have told her father about this via her weekly telephone call (from a call box - Trunks please - London Archway 2725) and my grandfather Fairclough, being someone given to grand gestures, sent a telegram saying, "Congratulations on your promotion - to General John" The local telegram office must have had a spy for the Eccles Journal because a reporter appeared at the front door, asking for the general. He was not pleased to find a small boy.

This incident helped to form the pattern of a ladder up which I could climb, gaining approval on the way. Once formed, patterns can grow and expand to include new inputs. The initial pattern was extended by my discovering similar patterns so that I discovered a ladder in cubs/scouts.

In the cubs, you could be a seconder then a sixer, in charge of six cubs. Then there was the possibility of being a senior-sixer, a rank that I eventually attained. I learnt about the rank of senior sixer from a publication known as POR - policy, organisation and rules. This added another pattern to the climbing ladders one. It gave me the idea that in any organisation, knowing the rules could help in climbing ladders. Patterns can also expand by association with other patterns. The waste paper pattern was associated with a sense of approval, providing a motivation to climb ladders when I found them.

Another result of the waste paper collection was a history book amongst the pile collected by my father. This had a hard-back red cover and some rather lurid coloured illustrations. These had a strange fascination for me - people dying from the plague, being hacked to death in battles or living in squalor. I was not allowed to keep this book - it wouldn't be right since it was given for the war effort. But it did have two effects.

The first was the start of an interest in history. I am not alone in starting with a fascination for the lurid. A friend, Mark Sykes, who was a history teacher, admitted that he also first became interested in history from pictures of violence. The other effect was the realisation that it was possible to have conflicting attitudes in the brain. Normally, I was a sensitive child. I could not understand how small boys could pull living frogs to pieces. I was even upset by flowers being thrown out - poor flowers with no water, I thought. So it was a surprise to find that violence had a strange fascination - as long as it was in books or American comics. In real life, I still try to avoid killing flies; persuading them out of the window is a better option.

At the cinema, I watched the news of the war provided by Pathé or British Gaumont. Towards the end of the war there were scenes of bodies hanging from a line covered in snow and swaying in the wind, I hid behind the seat until these distressing scenes had gone.

As a family we went to see Snow White. Full-length colour films were unusual in those days and records were sold of the music, including 'Hi Ho, It's off to work we go', the marching song of the seven dwarfs. One scene had the skeleton of the person who had not killed Snow White. It was in a cage and had an outstretched arm that was just short of a jug of water. This also caused me to hide. So it is a puzzle why violent pictures in a history book did not upset me. This made me realize that there was a pattern that later I might call conflicting emotions. At the time it did not need a name; it was a feeling that I recognised and, of course to re-cognise something you have to already have the pattern available. Patterns have to be constructed before they can be re-known - recognised.

A major result of going to school was discovering how to get on with other children. This was a difficult process but did not worry me - I was still content with being inside my own head. One thing that I discovered was that you were supposed to be either United or City - Manchester's two top-level football teams. I picked Manchester United to follow because at that time they were above City in the League tables.

I also took an interest in Lancashire's county cricket team and even kept a scrapbook with newspaper cuttings of match reports. Since I already had the pattern of a ladder, it was easy to add a similar new pattern, the pattern of a league table with some things higher than others depending on the results of events. This did not have to be restricted to sporting events; I extended the pattern to books and how often they were read.

I had been transferred from a bedroom next to my parents' room to a large attic on the top floor of 9, Ellesmere Ave. (The houses in Ellesmere Avenue are all marked on the 1899 Ordnance Survey map - along with most of Victorian Eccles as I knew it.) The attic was much larger than the main bedroom of a 1930s semi and my father fitted a bookcase to the wall of my new room. This had two shelves on which I arranged my growing collection of books. The top shelf was 'the first division' and the lower shelf was the second. The left end of the shelves represented the bottom of the division and the right was the top. Whenever I read one of these books, they moved position. Any book in the second division that was picked out for reading was replaced on the upper shelf.

The top floor of the house contained another large attic and this became my playroom. Running round the floor was my Hornby clockwork railway. This was a magnificent example of the model railway that my parents had acquired from a church sale. The vicar of Eccles (Rev Burket) had a son who had been killed in action as a pilot. The things that had been kept from his childhood were sold including a clockwork model railway. There were three different engines and many trucks, carriages etc. One of these was a snowplough that spun round when pushed by an engine. There were points, crossings and station platforms so that an elaborate system covered the floor.

I also had some other toys that were from an earlier generation. There were soldiers in various uniforms from World War I and a toy farm that included a milkmaid. There was a field hospital with stretcher-bearers and nurses. These toy people became invested with lives in my imagination. They were all listed in a book as though they were real people. The soldiers could be promoted and the presence of nurses and a milkmaid allowed for romance and marriage. This had the effect of providing me with a pattern in which I was in control of other people.

My father became involved with many of my activities at home. Partly it was an excuse for him to experience some of the boyhood things missing from his own childhood and he must have enjoyed helping me. His 'help' included allowing me to press out the pieces from cardboard books of model aeroplanes. He then did the difficult task of gluing them together to make a Spitfire, a Lancaster bomber etc. One day a real Spitfire appeared on Monton Green where for a small sum of money you could climb up a ladder and sit in the cockpit (a strange word).

3.4 The Wireless

Another of my father's helps consisted in the construction of a Morse code tapper board. In the early days of wireless, my father had been an enthusiast, making his own radios from kits. The attic still held boxes full of radio parts, some of which he used in a circuit constructed on a breadboard. The board was the base for a battery leading to a three-way switch set to 'off' or lamp or buzzer in a parallel circuit that led to the Morse tapper and back to the battery. The wire connections were all neatly hidden under the board and provided me with a pattern of serial and parallel circuits plus on/off. Similar patterns crop up in school electricity and in logic circuits etc.

Another remnant of my father's early radio activity was some headphones (the first sets did not have powerful amplifiers and needed headphones) Attached to his modern set, they allowed for the detection of strange broadcasting stations from foreign parts. We kept a log to record these foreign stations. Making lists of things observed provided a pattern that was later extended into recording the numbers of railway engines and much later the results of scientific measurements.

The main use of the radio was for simple enjoyment. In the days before television, the Light Programme of the BBC provided entertainment in the form of variety shows, descended from the Victorian music hall and half hour comedy series.

Starting in 1939 and continuing through the war, the BBC attempted to provide some cheer through ITMA - It's that man again - starring Tommy Handley and a cast of characters with their own catchphrases. These included the charlady, Mrs Mopp ("Can I do you now, sir?"), the German spy Funf ("this is Funf speaking"), the upper class odd-job men, Cecil and Claude

("After you, Claude—no, after you, Cecil") and Mona Lott ("It's being so cheerful that keeps me going").

The show continued after the war and for no particular reason, a silly jingle has stuck in my memory

>Living in the jungle,
>Living in a tent,
>Better than a prefab,
>NO RENT.

The formula continued with other shows such as Take it From Here, with Dick Bentley, Joy Nichols and Professor Jimmy Edwards and Much Binding in the Marsh starring Richard Murdoch and Kenneth Horne in a pretend airfield. The ITMA tradition of repetitive catchphrases continued. Kenneth Horne used to say, "Not a word to Bessie about that".

On Saturday evenings, we all sat down to listen to Variety Bandbox. My mother sliced up a Mars bar into eight small pieces - two each for the four of us. The high spot for me was the comic turn, split between Frankie Howard and the Australian, Bill Kerr. Howard, of course, survived into television. Kerr was billed as the man from Wagga Wagga with his catchphrase of "I'm only here for four minutes". He told jokes from his 'Bumper Fun Book' but he managed to mix up the punch lines. Later he joined Tony Hancock in the radio version of Hancock's Half Hour.

3.5 Pattern construction

The most important help from my father (apart from teaching me to do long division) was his encouragement of stamp collecting. I started in the usual way with an album arranged alphabetically in order of country. Then my father got people at work to save stamps from overseas and these were soaked to float the stamps from their envelopes followed by drying on blotting paper before being attached by paper hinges into the album.

I soon needed a larger album and then he came into his own by making use of one of his contacts. Part of his job in the Treasurers department involved obtaining special loose-leaf binders for bills etc. Important documents were stored in solid binders that needed a key to open. The covers had a panel with Eccles Corporation embossed in gold letters, the product of a local printer who, of course, counted as a contact. My father managed to obtain two versions of this binder, one each for his two sons, with Stamp Album printed on the cover and a supply of specially printed pages suitable for a stamp collection - plus of course the key to open and close access to the binding. I still have mine.

He then went further. Having acquired a copy of the Stanley Gibbons World Catalogue (there were far fewer stamps to list back in the 1940s), he wrote in spaces for most of the stamps that I might acquire. So then the initial pattern of stamps divided into countries became subdivided into issues. If you acquired all the stamps in an issue you then had a set. Over the next few years, I obtained a used copy of every stamp issued for India in the reign of George VI.

This meant that I had acquired a new classification system to add to the ladder. Any collection of things could be sorted into groups within groups. This mental sorting activity has remained part of my way of thinking.

My mother was also very important in the formation of patterns in my young brain. Most Sunday evenings we walked to Eccles Parish Church with the sound of a full peel of bells as accompaniment.

Interlude

This is not a conventional autobiography, starting with my parents and ending near the end of my life. What happened to me is the background to the emergence of some ideas. Patterns have already been mentioned. The sound of church bells provides an excuse to bring in another theme - technological change, how it happens and why. Why did anyone go to the trouble of finding how to make large bells? How did they do it? Why did anyone want to hang them in towers? Etc.

Now, of course when I was walking to church, the 'whys' did not concern me. At that age, my mental attention was focussed on things in the present. There was not much mental space for wondering about historical causes of things. I knew that we were fighting Adolf Hitler and that he was responsible for dropping bombs on us but I did not wonder why.

Nor did I wonder where those bells came from or what they were for. I knew that there were bell ringers and they went through a door at the side of the church tower to climb up some steps to reach something called the belfry. I knew that they rang on Sundays and on one day in the week when the ringers had a practice.

That was enough. I was not one of those children who are supposed to go around asking 'why?' If there are children who say things like, "Daddy why are trees green?" then I never met any. (The answer is because leaves are green, why, because they contain chlorophyll and that's green, why?)

The curiosity about causes came later so why am I mentioning it here? Because it's an interesting literary device used both in some novels and some science books. In the 1930s, John Dos Passos provided an account of the USA. He used the form of a novel, interspersed with newspaper headlines and potted biographies of famous American capitalists. The fiction is constructed by introducing different characters first, with a chapter each, and then allowing them to meet later on.

A similar form is used by Fay Weldon in her Shrapnel Academy in which we meet different characters who are all heading to a military establishment where they stay in rooms named after famous military people, giving an opportunity to introduce some non-fiction in the form of the lives of those people.

Joseph Wambaugh in his The Onion Field uses a three-step process. This starts with someone being killed in an onion field but the reader is not told who was killed, why or by whom. This is followed by accounts of the lives of different people leading to their meeting each other, culminating in the death in the onion field.

Konrad Lorenz uses this circular three-step process in a book aiming to describe comparative behavioural research. His book was assembled posthumously from The Russian Manuscript, written when Lorenz was a POW in the hands of the Russians. It starts with a discussion about science books. Lorenz points out that most science textbooks introduce a general principle and then follow with examples. However, this has a disadvantage, "the reader is led in the opposite direction to that originally followed by the research concerned". (Remember it's a translation from German).

He points out that research leads to "the abstraction of governing principles from a great number of individual concrete facts that must first be observed and accepted". A textbook, in contrast, presents principles first and then examples "that back up that particular abstraction". A danger in that approach is that the 'deadliest sin in research' is formulating a hypothesis and then looking for examples that support it. [Lorenz was a friend of Popper]

Lorenz suggests that a readable book is different from a textbook and should make use of examples first but also some mention of the principles has to come first producing a circular process. He uses this format in the book that follows and I have tried to use a modified version of this approach by giving examples of patterns etc. first and leaving a general approach until later with some circularity thrown in.

Now, back to going to church where I became familiar with the words of the Book of Common Prayer (BCP) and still love those words even though the Church of England has almost abandoned them.

One of the bible readings, known as lessons, contained the words, "Blessed are the wise". This struck me as being very significant. I knew that I thought differently from other school children. When we went in a gang to the pictures, they did not seem able to follow a plot. Even those who could read library books took ages to get through a book that I might finish in a couple of days.

Also, I had worked out for myself how to say the nine times table. Each answer was one less than the preceding one. I extended this to the eight times table by taking two from the one before (adding eight is the same as adding ten and subtracting two) There was a large chart in the classroom with all our names down the side and numbers one to twelve across the top. When someone could say a particular 'times table', they had a star placed on the chart. I was the first to have all the stars filled in and was surprised that others could not see the patterns in the numbers, relying on memory instead. So I thought that "blessed are the wise" applied to me. Fortunately, this did not make me feel superior - just different.

I was fully aware that others were much better than me at remembering things, being able to draw and other practical things. In retrospect, activities at home seemed more important than school. I read a lot - not just fiction - I devoured animal and nature stuff such as the Romany books and The Wonders of …

Games became important - draughts then chess, one of the few activities I shared with my brother. Card games provided an entry into strategic thinking and trying to anticipate what opponents were trying to do. What could have become a lifelong interest stopped when I was a post graduate student, spending nearly all my time playing bridge in the students' union. I decided that this was one addiction too many.

Looking at cards provided one of those early experiences that I remember remembering. Young children with educationally minded parents are given shape sorters, supposed to help them learn the differences between circles, squares and triangles. Children of my age discovered these patterns without the use of educational aids.

I knew that there was a pattern called a diamond. This is a four-sided figure with points above and below. It differs from a square because a square has lines at top and below. A quarter of a pack of cards has red diamonds on it and one day it struck me (why struck?) that a diamond was really a square turned round a bit. So I got a diamond and turned it round until it had a line at the top and below. Was it then a square? Try it for yourself. You might find that it is really a square but some kind of optical illusion is making it seem rather squashed in. Anyway, this gave my brain one of those patterns of thinking that don't have a name but may be re-cognised. This pattern is somewhere between 'things aren't always what they seem to be' and 'first impressions may be wrong'.

Between being at school and at home, there was 'playing out'. This involved other children and fortunately I learned something about relating to other minds. I had three particular friends that I played with and was welcome in their homes. Two of these came from large families - the Biggs and the Barnes. Spending time in homes with lots of people was a new experience. The third friend, Peter Mann, lived on the other side of the Manchester Liverpool railway (the first modern railway. Its first victim had been Huskinson who was hit by a train at the opening ceremony and died in Eccles vicarage)

To get to Peter's house, I had to go down the dog-entry that led to a bridge over several rail tracks, passing the engine sheds and goods yard where wooden trucks were shunted into lines for dispatch to other places. Then it was along a side road leading to the main road that had to be crossed to reach his house.

On the way was a derelict house; another victim of bombing and this provided a site for imaginative games. One day with some others, I was on the top floor of this shell of someone's home when I fell through the floor. As I was disappearing into the floor below, my friend's sister, Eileen Mann, grabbed my hair - a somewhat painful way of preventing a nasty accident. From that day, I was more careful. My danger-warning brain circuits had acquired a new pattern.

Friendship with Peter Mann provided reinforcement to the ladder/rules pattern originally constructed from the senior-sixer/POR pattern in the cubs. Peter had formed a club from his friends. It was well organised and even had a set of rules. One rule said that you couldn't be a member of any rival clubs. I discovered that the girl who was treasurer to the club did belong to another club and used this to replace her as treasurer - climbing up the ladder through knowing the rules - but not a nice thing to do.

As treasurer, I became guardian of a shiny tin with the money from subs paid by members. Since then, I have been treasurer of many organisations, being surprised by the fact that many intelligent people have no clue to the meaning of a balance sheet - they have never constructed that particular pattern.

On Sunday afternoons, brother Peter and I went off to Sunday school in the ancient Albert Street School. Sometimes the school went to church and I remember two sermons that were inflicted on us.

Sermons

Trinity

One Trinity Sunday the Sunday school was escorted from the Albert Street School to church where we were subjected to a sermon from an enthusiastic young vicar who started by asking us what we did on Saturday evenings. He managed to find someone who said their family went to the pictures. He then asked what they did after the cinema. Someone replied that they went for fish and chips. In the late 1940s before TV reached the north, the cinemas were packed and showed films continuously so on a Saturday many families waited for the football results on the radio and then went to an early showing of a suitable film, selected from the many cinemas advertising on the front page of the Eccles and Patricroft journal. After the cinema, a visit to the local chippy was a possibility. Fish, chips, peas, bread and butter and a pot of tea were served in a room at the side of the main take away shop and would be considered a special treat by children fortunate enough to be taken out to the pictures.

Having established some sort of interest, the visiting vicar then got on to his theme of the nature of the Trinity. He was using analogy. Father, Son and Holy Ghost were like fish, chips and peas. One meal - three items was like one God - three aspects. (This was before the church changed the Ghost into the Spirit.)

Self Control

Another sermon that I remember remembering was also an analogy. This time comparing self-control with the brake on a van rolling down hill. I remember this because it got me thinking - and it still does. There is something very odd about self-control. Where is the self in all this? If the self has to be controlled, who is doing the control? The self seems to be controlling itself so who or what is in charge. The preacher was claiming that gravity was pulling the van down hill and the van if it was aware would want to stop. The van needed help - a hand to pull on the hand brake. Enter the analogy - God the hand brake. If we called on God for help, he would help us overcome the pull of evil desires. To me, there seemed something wrong with this. The so-called evil desires were my desires weren't they? They weren't some external force like gravity.

The Victorians had a solution to this problem. Evil desires were an external force stemming from the Devil. The Bible recorded how Jesus himself had been tempted by the Devil. More scientifically minded Victorians did not go for the Devil. Instead they had a split self. This elusive self had two components, our bestial nature, inherited from our evolutionary past and our civilised self that was supposed to subdue the animal. A modern primatologist, Frans de Waal (2006) calls this 'Veneer Theory" - the idea that we are biologically brutish and "morality is but a recent coat of varnish over our true natures".

In this quote, the Victorian 'brutish' has become 'fact'. De Waals believes that chimps have morality. They have a theory of mind and they can be cooperative. So animal nature versus self-control just will not do. This still leaves me wondering about the self.

3.6 Barton Bridge and Trafford Park

After Sunday school, Peter sometimes took me to Barton Bridge to watch the ships on the Manchester Ship

Canal. As its name suggests the Ship Canal carried ocean going ships bringing cotton from America, grain from Canada and exporting the products of the industrial revolution. Someone said that Barton Bridge was one of the Seven Wonders of the World and I wondered what the other six were.

I later discovered that the original seven wonders of the classical world had been destroyed. Only the remains of the pyramids are still there. Since then, many lists of seven wonders have been compiled and Barton is no longer a listed wonder but it now has listed building status and the site is a conservation area.

There are two Victorian bridges at Barton, the road bridge and an aqueduct carrying the Bridgewater Canal over the Ship Canal. Both swing from a central point on an island in the centre of the ship canal. This island also contains a brick control tower that sends up a signal when the bridges are about to close.

The aqueduct is most impressive, a huge metal structure that seals off a stretch of canal water and then turns through 90 degrees. In the background there used to be the two high chimneys of a coal-fired power station, now demolished. To one side there was a structure that in the early days of the war had contained a machine gun crew to protect the bridges against an attack by German paratroopers. In 1941, England had expected to be invaded.

Also on one side was an air raid shelter that stood there for several years after the war was over and was used by courting couples with nowhere to go. The swinging road bridge was of strategic importance because it connected the workers living in Eccles with the factories on the opposite side of the ship canal in the industrial estate of Trafford Park.

The story behind the canal and Trafford Park had it that a group of Manchester businessmen were complaining about the port fees charged by Liverpool. In some cases, it was cheaper to import raw materials via Hull on the East coast. One chap is supposed to have said, "It's a pity that Manchester is not by the sea". This produced the reply, "We can't move Manchester but we could move the sea".

They then decided that they needed to meet with civil engineers who knew about modern canals and politicians who knew how to get a bill through parliament. Such a meeting took place in 1882 but a long political campaign had to be fought to overcome resistance from those with a stake in existing forms of transport - the Liverpool to Manchester railway and the Bridgewater canal.

In 1887, work began on what was a mammoth undertaking. Manchester is sixty feet above sea level. So even with the help of locks, building a canal to connect the sea with inland docks involved digging a trench that was wide enough to allow ocean going ships to pass each other in opposite directions and was thirty six miles long, almost the length of the Panama Canal. The construction involved some 12,000 workers to dig and remove the earth. Steam shovels and a light railway assisted the process. The canal was officially opened in 1894 with the two Barton swing bridges attracting much attention.

The canal cut through the northern side of Trafford Park, the ancestral home of the de Trafford family who trace their ancestry back to Anglo Saxon times before the Norman Conquest. (The family name continues; Sir John Humphrey de Trafford was born in 1950.) The arrival of the canal opened up commercial opportunities and the site was sold to a property developer. The hall became a hotel and the artificial lake was used for pleasure boats. Manufacturing industry then moved in. Slowly at first but then a rush including a piece of America when the electric firm of Westinghouse set up a British subsidiary to take over a slice of the park with American style street names. Most of the original village has gone but Eleventh Street and Third Avenue were still there when I last looked. Westinghouse became Metropolitan Vickers.

By 1903 some 12,000 people were working in the park and it could claim to be the first planned industrial estate in the world. My mother worked in the park as secretary to one of the directors of Turner Bros Asbestos, a position she gave up to marry my father. The first Rolls-Royce cars were made in the park and their Merlin engines powered both the Spitfire fighters and the Lancaster bombers in the war. The Park played an important role in supplying material for both world wars and in 1945 was employing about 75,000 people.

1945 saw the end of the war - VE day followed by VJ day. I learnt about the end from someone in school and I don't have any memories of celebrations apart from a very vague one of a large bonfire on the site of a factory demolished after an air raid. The main event of 1945 for me was my September arrival in Standard IV. This was the class from which some pupils departed to Eccles Secondary School or Winton Senior School, with the rest staying at school in Standards V and VI. (In those days before the 1946 education act, there were many all age schools taking pupils from age 4 into a nursery class and pushing them out from the Senior section at age 15.)

The form teacher for Standard IV was Miss Berry. In later years, I realized that she had been trained before World War I when teaching mixed age and mixed ability children was considered important. (It was not until the 1970s that a pendulum swing brought back an emphasis on diversification as it was then called.) The class was often divided into different groups with different tasks and she had an amazing system of handicapping, so that everyone had some motivation to do their best.

We sat in rows and columns and for tests; the ones at the front had a start of 6 out of ten, whilst the ones at the back started with zero out of ten. At the end of the week if you had more marks than the one behind you then you swapped places. Also at the end of the week the marks for each column were added up to give a winning team, allowed out early at 'play time'.

In addition, there were question and answer sessions run like a race with the better pupils starting against one sidewall of the classroom and the others one or two columns ahead. On answering a question correctly, you moved forward one until someone reached the opposite wall of the classroom.

One day I was told that I had been entered for the 'Scholarship' exam. In fact, it wasn't the Scholarship anymore; it had become the 11 plus, a new test that decided on where you went to school when you were eleven. Children who would be eleven years old at the start of the next school year took this test. Since my birthday is October the 26th, I would have still been ten at the beginning of the autumn term. However, in those days, the educational system was not so obsessed with age and there was provision for schools to recommend people of my age to take the exam.

I think that my parents were taken by surprise and had been planning for me to take the entrance exam for Manchester Grammar School (MGS) a year later. (In those days, schools didn't go in for consulting parents). So one day, I turned up at Eccles Grammar School and took the three papers - English, Arithmetic and the new IQ test.

Eventually, I was asked to go for an interview with the headmaster, Mr Harold Fairweather, MA, FRGS, and it was decided that I was OK despite my age. So, I was only ten years old and the youngest in my class when I started Grammar School education.

References Chapter 3.
John Dos Passos, 1937, USA. New York: Modern Library.
Konrad Lorenz, 1948/1991,The Natural Science of the Human Species: Introduction to Comparative Behavioural Research, The Russian Manuscript. MIT Press. P xxix
Paul Morley, 2013, The North (And Al.ost Everything In it). London: Bloomsbury.
Frans de Waal. 2006. Primates and Philosophers: How morality evolved. Princeton UP.
Joseph Wambaugh, 1973, The Onion Field. New York: Delacorte Press.
Fay Weldon, 1986, The Shrapnel Academy. London: Hodder and Stoughton

THINKING AT SCHOOL

Chapter 4. Grammar School 1946-1953

4.1 Eccles Grammar School

In 1946, not long after the end of the war, I was prepared for my Grammar School days. This required a green school blazer with a badge on one pocket. There was also a green school cap and other items including gym and games kits, pencil case, school bag etc. The badge was the Eccles coat of arms, containing a symbolic representation of Eccles Parish Church, cotton flowers and an embroidered attempt at portraying Nasmyth's steam hammer. In 1836 James Nasmyth opened a factory in what then was the countryside, where the Liverpool Manchester railway crossed the Bridgewater canal in Patricroft, a district that became part of the borough of Eccles in 1892. Eccles itself was absorbed into Salford in 1974.

In the summer before I started at Eccles Grammar School, my father indulged his love of teaching by trying to introduce me to some French and algebra that he knew would be useful in my new school. I discovered that the French classed all nouns as either feminine or masculine and learnt the difference between le, la and les. So I was well prepared for the first lessons in French.

My father's introduction to algebra turned out to be extremely useful because the maths teacher for my form in year one turned out to be incapable of keeping discipline and therefore left most of his class regarding algebra as some kind of mystery - what were all these xs for? I had grasped two essential patterns for doing algebra; the first was that $7x$ meant 7 times an unknown quantity and you didn't need your 7 times table to do anything with it because you could add $7x$ and $5x$ to get $12x$ in the same way that seven oranges and five oranges added up to 12 oranges and it did not matter what size the oranges were.

The other pattern that I constructed was about the meaning of the deceptively simple equals sign $=$. In arithmetic, when doing sums, $=$ meant that you had done a sum and here was the answer. $7 + 6 - 4 = 9$ meant that 9 was the answer. If you had that sort of pattern in your brain, how could you cope with $5x - 3 = 17$? And how on earth did you get to $x = 4$? Fortunately for me, my father's efforts had replaced equals as 'the answer' by equals means 'the same as', quite a different pattern and one that resonated with an existing pattern - the scales. In those days, the corner shop at the end of the dog entry still weighed things on scales. For example, biscuits were picked from a tin and sold by weight; the same for sweets - sold in small bags of 2 ounces plus a coupon from the ration book. So, a two-ounce weight equalled a bag of sweets.

All this meant that at the end of my first term when we had the Christmas exams, I was the only person in my class capable of solving a simple algebraic equation. I did this by trial and error. Guess what number x might be and try it out. Then try another number until you find the right answer. So another pattern was born and I could use it later in life when it became the engineers' 'suck it and see' or more impressively it could be 'randomised empiricism'. Much later, trial and error became survival of the fit - not fittest - fit as fitting in. Mutations only survive if they fit into everything else.

In January 1947, one term after joining the Grammar School, there was a record-breaking fall of snow. We had to dig our way out of the house because doors would not open and paths were buried under the snow. Throwing snowballs and building snowmen were fun and everyone helped with clearing the gutters and grids to allow melting snow to escape. It was not until March that the last of the snow melted and then there was flooding from the arrival of water from the hills. None of this stopped me from going to school.

Eccles Grammar School was a small three-form entry co-educational school. It had been built as Eccles Secondary School. My brother had attended this school but had left before I arrived. In his day, although the school was run by local government, it charged fees and pupils had to buy their own textbooks. Entrance was by exam and the highest scoring applicants were awarded scholarships, money to help with the fees, books and uniform costs. These top pupils formed an 'A' stream that was fast-tracked to take the School Certificate exam a year earlier than the norm. Two more forms were made from pupils without scholarships but passing the entrance exam. My brother was one of the latter and our father had paid fees for his education.

By the time that I went there, the national education system had changed. Secondary education was free and the School Certificate had become the GCE - the General Certificate of Education. The Scholarship exam had become the Eleven Plus.

4.2 Scouts

My first year at the school was mainly uneventful; things outside school were more memorable. It was not just the snow. Being eleven meant that I had to leave the cubs and go up to the Scouts. The 2nd Eccles Group (Eccles Parish Church) at that time had no Scouts, only the cubs. The adults who had run the Scouts had been in the air force and were waiting demobilization so I had to join the 13th Eccles (St Andrew's Church) group. This was run by a very energetic chap, Jack Cartwright who was unmarried and lived with his mother. Today, a Scoutmaster who still lived with his mother would be regarded with some suspicion by worried parents but in those days it caused no comment. One of the first things that happened was the Gang Show. I had to march up and down singing,

> We're riding along on the crest of the waves,
> And the sun is in the sky,
> All our eyes on the distant horizon,
> Look out for passers by.
> We'll do the hailin'
> While other ships around the sailin'
> We're riding along on the crest of the waves
> And the world is nigh.
> (There was also an unofficial version that started with,
> "We're riding along on the chest of the slaves")

Then there was the annual camp. This was 1947; the war only just over and rationing was still in place. Ordinary families had little money to spare and we paid sixpence or a shilling a week, marked onto a camp card until we had paid for the cost of two weeks away. Any extra money was kept for us as 'spends'.

This was my first time away from my parents and it was a transforming experience. Prior to the camp I had been what was known as 'faddy', meaning refusing to eat certain kinds of food. My poor mother used to try and hide vegetables in mashed potatoes but I would pick them out and try

A thick slice of bread with marg and jam was not my idea hard not to eat them. Rice pudding made me feel sick and so on. As a result I was rather thin and pale. However, at camp the food was so awful that I was starving. Breakfast was porridge with a spoonful of treacle. I would eat the part of the porridge surrounding the treacle and then give away the rest. A thick slice of bread with marg and jam was not my idea of food; nor were tinned pilchard and more thick bread. When I returned home to my mother's home baking - treacle tart, sausage rolls, scones, cake etc. - I just ate and ate, putting on so much weight that I was called porcus at school where we were beginning to show off our newly acquired Latin.

After that experience, for future Scout camps, I always took with me a tuck box, containing chocolate and other goodies. It was not until I was about fourteen that I decided I had to loose weight. I gave up throwing sugar into drinks, breakfast etc. and by using exercises from one of my mother's magazines, I managed to reduce my stomach fat.

My first scout camp was in a field by a river not far from Lancaster. We were given a day out, taken to the seaside and left to our own devices. I went with some others to a 'chippy' and gorged on fish and chips - delicious. Then we went on the boating lake where the combination of seasickness and a greasy, full stomach resulted in my being violently sick.

Despite the food problem, I enjoyed that camp. It was sunny and we could play in the river, wander about fields and just be boys.   There were some older boys who had a tent to themselves. They had different interests, mainly focused on girls in the nearby village. I wondered why they wanted to talk to girls. I had discovered the word 'misogynist' and claimed that I was one. Girls? Not for me - an attitude soon to change - but also another example of conflicting emotions. Rather like 'Just William' I didn't want to play with girls (remember Violet Elizabeth Bott) but at the same time a pretty face could produce a strange feeling. Being away from parents and school was good for me.

4.3 Form 2L

At the end of the school's first year, there was an exam and the top pupils went into form 2A, the fast track equivalent of the earlier scholarship class. The rest of us went into 2S or 2L. S for science and L for Latin. My father thought that Latin was needed to gain entry to university so I had to go into 2L. He was only partially mistaken. When I came to consider applications to universities, I discovered that Oxford and Cambridge still demanded Latin. They also insisted that applicants complete their two years National Service before entry. Universities in those days had separate admissions system (it wasn't until later that the central UCCA system was devised).

When the Victoria University was founded from existing colleges in Manchester, Liverpool and Leeds, it was rumoured that the academics were against the Latin entry requirement but the Northern industrialists who were putting up the money insisted that a 'proper' university had to 'have the Latin'.

My stay in 2L was short, lasting only for one term. At the Christmas exams I came top in most subjects - but not in French or Latin where I was hampered by my inability to acquire a vocabulary. Despite understanding the grammar better than most, remembering the French or Latin words for their English equivalents made translation into foreign a nightmare. I must have done well in the exams at the end of the first year and should have gone into the A stream but the school had decided against this on the grounds of my youth. However, after the yearly Christmas exams I was moved into the fast track A stream. Since I was already a tear younger than the others, this meant that when it became time to take O level GCE, I would be two years younger than the norm.

Despite only being in 2L for a few months, it was a memorable time. For a start, it was the end of misogyny. I became friendly with a very pretty girl, June Greenwood and she suggested that we go to the pictures together. This set a pattern where my female friends decided what needed to be done - not that I was reluctant, just ignorant.

At the cinema we held hands - June's idea, not mine, and I discovered the joy of physical contact. Holding hands with June was a never to be forgotten experience which sadly did not survive my move to 2A.

Also in 2L I acquired two good friends, Cedric(Donegan) and Tom(Pendlebury), and we went on bike rides together. Some time earlier, I had been given a secondhand bicycle and brother Peter had taught me how to ride by holding the saddle as I pedalled through Ellesmere Park. One day, he left go and I found myself on my own. Not knowing how to stop, I ended up in a hedge. When I could ride properly, I was given a brand new BSA bike with drop handlebars and a three speed gear - more sporty than the sensible 'sit up and beg' first bike. Many years later, in Holland,

I found myself riding a borrowed old style bicycle and realised that 'new' is not always 'better'.

My new friends, Tom and Cedric, accompanied me on cycling excursions to fun places like the seaside towns of Southport and New Brighton plus a Cheshire lake, Pickmere, which far from being a nice country spot was the site of a fun fair with slot machines, a ghost ride and the added attraction of hiring a rowing boat on the lake.

The bike ride to New Brighton via Birkenhead involved going through the Mersey Tunnel. This had been described as a first when it was built, being the longest underwater tunnel in the world. Bicycles are no longer allowed in the tunnel but then it was free wheel down hill followed by use of a low gear to struggle up the other side.

The first part of the ride to Southport went down the East Lancashire road (known as the East Lancs - its original official title had been The Liverpool-East Lancashire Road). This had been another marvel when opened by King George V in 1934. It was Britain's first purpose built intercity road, connecting Liverpool and Manchester partly as a response to high unemployment but also in imitation of Hitler's road building in Germany. Technological trajectories seem obvious when viewed in hindsight - petrol and diesel powered road transport just had to overtake other forms of transport but this was not so obvious in 1930. The road when first built had lay-bys with water taps for the use of steam powered vehicles. Steam power was still in evidence during the fuel shortage of WWII and I have memories of the red glow coming from the cabs of steam lorries passing down Monton Road.

When built, the East Lancs Road had cycle lanes kept separate from the road by grass and also walking lanes. Both of these were still there when we rode to Southport or New Brighton; though they had to be removed when eventually the road was widened. These days, cycling on the East Lancs would not be a fun experience.

The road from the East Lancs to Southport went through Ormskirk. Map reading had taught me that a cross on a square represented churches with towers. A cross on a circle meant a church with a steeple. The church in Ormskirk seemed to be unique in having both a tower and a steeple. Its north wall is supposed to date from 1170. The tower was added to accommodate a peal of bells but the existing spire was retained giving the church its unusual appearance

Another memory from 2L is the General Science course consisting of lessons in chemistry, physics and the only formal lessons in biology that I ever attended. The biology part of the General Science curriculum was only for one lesson a week. This means that I had about 12 biology lessons before being transferred into the A stream where science was chemistry. Anything else that I know about biology is self-taught.

School notebooks for science and geography had lined pages facing blank pages. These blank pages were used for maps in geography and for the apparatus used in so-called experiments in chemistry and physics.

I remember the first physics lesson, given by Dickey Derbyshire. We were given a new notebook and instructed to add our names, subject etc. This was memorable because of the embarrassment I suffered through asking what 'physics' was short for. The puzzled teacher needed me to add, "maths is short for mathematics so physics must be short for something". Many years later I remembered remembering this episode when I was wondering about the evolution of words. Where did the word come from?

I discovered that the word 'physics' began to be used in English around 1580 when it was just transferred from the Latin 'physica', a plural word in Latin - hence the 's' ending in English. This word came from the Greek physika, φυσική, as used by Aristotle.

The philosopher, William Whewell, in his History of the Inductive Sciences (1837), added two new words. He wrote,

> As we cannot use physician for a cultivator of physics, I have called him a physicist. We need very much a name to describe a cultivator of science in general. I should incline to call him a Scientist. Thus we might say, that as an Artist is a Musician, Painter, or Poet, a Scientist is a Mathematician, Physicist, or Naturalist.

In school biology I had to draw things (done by tracing of course) and I still have the notebook that shows how birds are adapted to different environments. Their claws are the way they are depending on whether the bird hops around trees a lot, spends time on the ground or drops out of the sky to snatch its food. Similarly, birds' beaks are the way they are depending on whether they eat seeds, insects or other birds. The odd thing is that no mention of evolution was made. Despite the fact that Charles Darwin had been influenced by the differences between birds on different islands, this was not mentioned. It was just a fact - that was the way birds are with no discussion of why they were made that way.

Although, I knew no formal biology, from an early age I had been interested in 'nature', being an avid reader of books such as the series of Romany books with titles such as Out with Romany Once More. These were written by George Bramwell Evens who also appeared on Children's Hour, in a BBC radio broadcast, 'Out with Romany', in which he was supposed to be a gypsy who travelled in a horse drawn caravan.

Romany gave out snippets of information about the countryside such as the song of the Yellow Hammer, 'a little bit of bread and no cheese'. He claimed you could cook a hedgehog by wrapping it in clay - when cooked the skin and prickles were supposed to peel off with the clay. When he died in 1943, the BBC attempted to replace him with Nomad the Naturalist who lived on an island. The Radio Times provided a map of the island and I tried to be interested but Nomad was no replacement for Romany.

My interest in nature included collecting birds' eggs. I went with father, on bikes of course, into country lanes where you could find birds' nests in the hedges. My brother also helped me to find eggs in the park where he was working. I was only to take one egg from a nest and I learned how to make two pinholes in an egg and then blow out the contents. The pride of my collection was an ostrich egg that someone at school swopped for - well I've no idea what for.

No mention of change cropped up in my nature books and change was missing from my biology lessons. Things were the way they were - like church bells. The question of where do new things come from had to wait until later.

I continued with activities outside school including being a patrol leader in the Eccles Parish Church Scouts. This became possible when Cyril Page returned from the RAF and pulled me out of the St Andrew scouts to join the reformed scouts in the cellar of the church school.

I rejoined the Sunday School - not for any religious reasons but hoping to meet a girl called Beryl Webster. I did not manage to meet Beryl but I stayed involved with Sunday school until many years later when I became the superintendent of the church mission Sunday school.

After school, there were several school activities and three in particular were important for me. These were the Chess Club, the school choir and the debating society. Chess was once a week and included sticky buns and tea. It also provided opportunity to meet people and I became friendly with a girl named Eileen May Harrison who lived in Worsley. We used to go for walks in Worsley Woods (now partly demolished to make way for Motorways). There was an annual chess competition and one year I was the winner, adding my name to a trophy.

In the days before television, evening entertainment was provided either by visiting the cinema or listening to the radio, known as the wireless.

4.4 The Wireless

Food rationing continued after the war was over and so we still had to share one Mars Bar between the four of us whilst listening to Variety Bandbox with Frankie Howard and Australian Bill Kerr alternating as comedians. Howard, of course, survived the advent of television to become a star. Kerr was billed as the man from Wagga Wagga with his catchphrase of "I'm only here for four minutes". He went on to play supporting parts in various comedies including Hancock's Half Hour, originally a radio series with Hancock, Kerr and Sid James.

I purchased a record of one of the 'Half Hours'. This episode was famous for having a silence that gained a laugh. It was set on a Sunday afternoon. In those days, shops were closed on Sundays and pubs closed at 2.0pm so Sunday afternoons were notoriously boring for many people. The BBC radio specialised in sound effects. A team of people was employed to produce doors opening, cars starting etc. They managed to get the sound of boredom by having the noise of newspaper pages being turned and then silence before Hancock says, "What time is it?" This is then repeated, more newspaper turning then more silence.

Why does Sunday boredom seem funny? One theory of laughter involves those neuronal circuits in the brain building up a voltage that is supposed to make something happen. The absence of an expected result is felt as a surprise and the voltage has nothing to do except discharge itself in the form of laughter or at least a smile.

Bill Kerr's act on Variety Bandbox gives another example of surprise producing laughter. He used to tell jokes that he read from his 'Bumper Fun Book'. The surprise came from his getting the jokes wrong. When you are listening to a comedian on the radio, you do not expect the joke to be mistold.

In the days before television reached the north in October 1951, radio comedy was very popular. Richard Murdoch and Kenneth Horne featured in 'Much Binding in the Marsh' (BBC from 1944 to 1954) and Jimmy Edwards (The Professor) starred in 'Take it from Here' together with Dick Bentley and Joy Nichols.

Another popular form of radio was the variety show. The radio variety shows had evolved from Victorian Music Hall turns and included the voices of Anne Ziegler and Webster Booth. Larry Adler showed that the humble mouth organ could be elevated to a 'serious' instrument, the harmonica. A Polish couple, Rawicz & Landauer, played piano duets and I remember them every time I hear Litolff's Scherzo, one movement from a forgotten piano concerto but converted by them into a piano duet.

In the days before the invention of gramophones, popular classical orchestral pieces had been rearranged for piano. My father played versions of themes from symphonies using an ancient book of music, The Star Folio. I had a few formal piano lessons and one of my pieces was a version of Finlandia, not really suitable for piano but I enjoyed the crashing chords.

Commercial radio did not become legal until 1973. Before that there were pirate radio stations in the North Sea and for those with long wave sets there was Radio Luxembourg, broadcasting with English adverts. Older people still remember its children's program, the Ovaltineys, and its song "We are the Ovaltineys, Little girls and boys...". I continued to drink Ovaltine for many years as a bedtime drink.

In the absence of commercial competition, the BBC had a near monopoly of radio broadcasting. This meant that popular culture was much more uniform than it is today. When we came home from school, we might play cricket on a bomb site or indulge in other outdoor pursuits (weather permitting) but suddenly, children would vanish. It was time for the latest episode of Dick Barton, Special Agent. Barton together with Jock and Snowy had nightly adventures involving the BBC's special effects team making the noises. The series lasted from 1946 to 1951.

An unsuccessful attempt was made to resurrect Dick Barton as a TV series in 1979 but it failed because crude visual representations of fights are no match for the special effects team's sounds of fist hitting flesh.

4.5 School Sports

On Wednesday afternoons, our year went to the changing rooms (one for boys and one for girls) and got into our sports gear. Then we walked down the road to the school playing fields. It was cricket in summer and football (soccer) in winter (hockey for the girls). Being younger than most and not having played much sport before, I was rather hopeless. I had played a form of cricket on the bombsite left by the demolition of No. 19 Ellesmere Avenue but this had not added the right neuronal patterns to my repertoire.

Running around a muddy field in the rain was not my idea of fun. The school sports pavilion did not have any showers and we had to go back to the school changing rooms to cram into the hot showers and return to normality.

After a few years of this, I found a way out. Someone decided we could have cross country running as an alternative. I joined a group of like minded youths and on Wednesday afternoons, we would run away from the sports field, down a lane out of sight of the school where we had stashed bags with ordinary clothes. After changing, we went to a snooker hall underneath the Princess cinema (now demolished) warm, dry and more fun than running.

Then we went back to our stash, changed back into running gear, found a few puddles to splash our running shoes and legs, then run very rapidly back to the school fields. This was fine until a new sports master arrived at the school and he announced that he was going to come with us on our run. Disaster!

We set off to do a run through the fields at the side of Ellesmere Park. No sign of the new master - relax - but then he appeared - on his bike - not fair. After that we ran along the canal towpath for the Bridgewater canal, never knowing when the bike would arrive, so we became reasonably proficient at running a few miles. Then further disaster. The school head, for some reason, said the school had to enter a team in the schools northern counties cross country championship. There was one youth, Dave Leighton, who was a proper runner, being a member of Winton Harriers and possibly capable of winning the school competition. So we had to have a team to support him.

The five-mile race started with the teams lined up on one side of a field. The other side of the field had a gate leading to a country path. The good runners ran very quickly across the field, trying to get through the gate before the others. The rest of us went more slowly and found ourselves in a crowd trying to avoid each other as we went down the path.

Other runners hemmed me in on all sides and then suddenly the crowd in front just vanished. There was a ditch and not knowing it was there I just tumbled into open space, landing on top of another youth whose spiked shoes were uppermost. When I clambered out, my leg was bleeding from contact with those spikes. I staggered on then noticed the school head, shouting at me to hurry up. Eventually I finished in about position 120, not too bad given some 300 starters. Dave Leighton came third and the Head was not too pleased with his school's performance.

Every year, the school held a sports day on the playing fields and everyone had to turn up to watch the various events and cheer on their houses. There were four houses - Normans, Tudors, Stuarts and Saxons. I was a Stuart. I noticed that the entrants in various races wore sports clothes but the rest of the school was in school uniform. The girls seemed to take an interest in the male athletes, posing about in their white shorts, looking more glamorous than those wearing the boring grey uniform trousers.

When I was in the sixth form, I thought, "Next year I'm going to be one of the white shorts crowd". So I trained for the half mile by running distances that were about a mile to gain stamina and also by practicing sprinting so that my body had the pattern of sprinting to use for the finish.

On Sports Day my training paid off. I tucked myself behind one of those 'proper' runners who was a member of Winton Harriers and we soon left the others behind. As we came round the bend to approach the finishing line, I was energised by the sight of Stella Meadowcroft just beyond the finish. She was also in the Stuart House and was jumping up and down shouting, "Come on John". Stella was a curvaceous blond with a pretty face. The combination of sprinting practice with Stella's shouting resulted in my shooting past the runner who was expected to win and ultimately getting my name on a cup for the half-mile winner.

4.6 Sixth Form

After four years at the Grammar School, I should have taken the GCE O level exam but the socialist government had decided that I was too young to be subjected to this pressure and I was denied being able to say that I had passed in several subjects. The experience of being denied the opportunity to take the C\GCE turned me against the kind of socialism that tries to make the world a better place through force. The school was sensible and knew that I would have easily passed these exams. So I moved into the sixth form.

In those days, the sixth form was where pupils spent two years preparing for GCE A level. Although the law said I was too young to take exams, it also said that I was old enough to be employed. This meant that in the summer before starting in the sixth form, I could take a summer job.

My father used his contacts to get me an interview at a local firm, Lankro Chemicals, founded by a German chemist, Dr. Wolf. This gave me my first sight of industrial chemistry but no job. However, I managed to be taken on by the Co-op Dairy. This was a large operation run from an old mill near Barton Bridge. In those days, having milk delivered to your house was still popular and if you used the Co-op then you got the 'divi' - a share of the profits given to members of the Co-operative Society.

The Co-op Dairy was a distribution centre for a large area of Eccles and parts of Swinton. There were four means of transport depending on the economics of distance. Each delivery required a driver and a youth (e.g. me). The area near to the dairy used horse-drawn milk floats. After two hours we would stop. The horse would be given a nosebag and we sat behind the horse to eat our sandwiches. The next inner circle of delivery used electric milk floats. These used large batteries manufactured by a local firm, Chloride Batteries, and recharged every night. The next circle used conventional petrol lorries and the outer circle used diesel to cover the larger distance from the dairy.

The other source of employment money was Christmas post. Every Christmas I turned up at Eccles Post

Office delivery centre and signed on for hourly paid employment. This started with clocking on, using a device that printed a time on your card. You were then given a round, a pile of post covering a few streets and off you went into the December cold and rain. On returning to the Post Office, the skill then was grabbing some inside work such as stacking letters to be passed through a franking machine.

I carried on working at the post office every Christmas during my six years in the University Chemistry Department and discovered there were some different opportunities. My favourite was getting on to the railway run. This involved loading a van with bags of mail and going with the driver to Eccles railway station where the bags had to be placed on a trolley and taken down a lift to the platform below street level. The lift was a remnant of Victorian technology using water pressure to power its movement. It was claimed that the lift had never been converted to electricity because the railway company LMS had signed a fifty-year contract with the lift supplier.

There was then a long wait for the train that was often late. Fortunately, the platform had a staff room with heat radiating from a coke stove. Toast and tea were sometimes available.

Another alternative to walking around with a heavy sack of mail was the parcel post. Parcels were defined as postal items too large to go through a letterbox but small enough to be easily carried by hand. During the year, uniformed postmen in the familiar small red vans delivered parcels. But at Christmas time there was a huge increase in the number of parcels, as nearly everyone seemed to be sending presents by post. This extra delivery required the use of an old technology - the handcart.

For Christmas deliveries the post office dragged out its old basket topped red handcarts that required two people to push and deliver. One year, I worked on parcels with another Grammar schoolboy, Alan Dyer. Because you had to knock on doors to make a delivery, you met people in a way that you didn't when pushing Christmas Cards through letterboxes. Sometimes these meetings produced a tip, a mince pie, or some other tangible recognition.

On one occasion, a woman who turned out to be a remarkable German invited Alan and me in for a cup of tea. It transpired that she came from a family of Prussian landowners and had admired Hitler at first but then turned against him. She had married an English major in the army of occupation and followed him back to England. She claimed to have trained as a paratrooper and had been awarded the iron cross by Hitler. She also claimed that she could sense the presence of a Jew in the same building as herself. I was paid to help her son with his reading and we stayed in touch until she discovered that I was engaged to marry a Jewish girl.

In my last year at school, I won an essay competition organised by International Rotary who offered a prize for the best essay on "The Contribution of Science to International Understanding". In this essay I did the obvious stuff about travel and communications being massively improved, making the world a smaller place. I also tried to point out that radio; air travel, film etc. were not entirely the product of something called 'science'. My awareness of the difference between science and technology goes back a long way.

My school chemistry text books, following examination requirements, used to have separate sections on industrial chemistry and I was never very interested in the manufacture of something - that was not science; that was something else. Examinations might ask for a description of the manufacture of sulphuric acid and I would have to learn the details but this was not science. It did not tell me why it was made that way or how the process had been discovered, invented, borrowed or whatever.

A new question slowly emerged to be added to the question about the secret of life. The question of where do new things come from became a background to my future academic life. Schopenhauer claimed that man was 'the metaphysical animal' who by nature seeks an explanation of the reality in which he finds himself. In my experience, most people just accept reality as it unfolds. They might complain but explanations often don't go much further than what happened yesterday. "My back hurts because I sat in in a draught". "My pigs are ill because that horrible woman looked at them." "Those tomato skins have upset my digestion". I felt that my desire for explanations made me different from most other people. An explanation for new things was a particular need.

4.7 Interlude: New things and purpose

In the 6th Form at Eccles Grammar School, we all did RE (Religious Education) projects. At the time, I thought that individual projects were an excellent approach to education. I later realised that they also had the advantage of involving less work for the teacher. In part of a project on "the purpose of life" I went and asked various clergymen what was the purpose of life. They all attempted an answer but I was not very impressed by what they said; so I turned to philosophy and there I found the German philosopher, Schopenhauer (1898). A rough translation of his view of the purpose of life was a hollow laugh. He compared human life with lambs gambolling in a field whilst in the corner the slaughterer sharpened his axe. As I have always been in favour of the human equivalents of gambolling, this view has an attraction but at the same time, I have always suspected that there is something called "the secret of life". I used to think this secret was hidden in a library somewhere. If it is, it is well hidden; but I have not stopped looking. If there is a purpose then new things might be purposeful.

Where do new things come from? I touched on the origin of church bells - where did they come from? As I learnt from Professor Joad on the radio Brains Trust, "It all depends on what you mean by …" Asking where new things come from sounds like a meaningful question. The answer might even be part of the 'secret of life' that I was searching for. In fact the question is rather silly. If new things come from somewhere else or something else, then they cannot be new can they? They have just arrived from some place else. Or in Joad mode, it all depends on what you mean by 'new'.

If new things come from somewhere else, that just pushes the answer further away. As with those who maintain that life itself originated in some other part of the universe but are unable to say how it got to this other place. This is understood by sceptical children who faced with the claim that God made things, will reply, "So where did God come from then?"

New things must be made from things that are there already. There isn't anything else for them to be made from. This idea can be emphasised by calling it WIT - what is there already - the source of anything new. The newness comes from a new combination of WIT. Something that is 100% new cannot be recognised. You would not know what it was.

R B Campenot (2016), writing about the history of our knowledge of animal electricity claims that when faced with something new "scientists attempt to relate the unknown to the familiar". So that early anatomists seeing nerves thought that they were seeing hollow tubes, like the familiar veins and arteries. And like the blood vessels they had to be carrying something. Since electricity was unknown then, the hollow tubes were thought to contain animal spirits. When electricity had been discovered and wires forming circuits had become familiar, the nerves were again related to the familiar - they became continuous 'wires'. In fact, our nerves are not continuous. They are constructed from individual cells, neurons, separated by gaps. The nerve impulse is transmitted across the gaps via chemical neurotransmitters. Nerves were known to disectionists in the time of Aristotle. The first known neurotransmitter, acetylcholine, was not identified until 1921. It takes time for the new to become familiar.

I became interested in where do new things come from at a very early age. I remember (or, rather, I remember remembering) at the age of three or four asking my mother where babies came from. To her credit, she was not fazed by this question and proceeded to explain something about the female body without actually getting into details. As a result, I was left with a weird impression that stayed with me until me early teens. My mother and most of her friends were slightly overweight and wore low cut dresses that revealed a cleavage. She had talked about women having breasts and a womb so I had concluded that babies grew in the womb and then escaped via the visible cleavage between the breasts. Another example of relating the new to the familiar and getting it wrong!

The arrival of a new baby used to be the cause of debate amongst the curious. Planned or a mistake? Accident or design? I remember my brother coming home one day and announcing that he and June were getting engaged. My father erupted with, "Daft blighter; should have been more careful". My mother tried to be conciliatory asking for details.

The question, 'Accident or Design?' has been addressed to the appearance of new things in general - not just babies. I once thought of writing a book with that title but then I discovered that it had been done already. Also, there are titles having the same dichotomy such as Butler's 1887 Luck, or Cunning as the Main Means of Organic Modification? (Like several writers, including George Bernard Shaw, Butler was dismayed by the implications of what he saw in natural selection and was in favour of 'cunning' or what today is termed 'intentionality'.)

Once our earth contained people capable of wondering where things came from, someone would have the idea that accident or chance was important. In the 1st century BCE, the Roman poet Lucretius tried to show that things were the result of natural causes and not the intervention of the Gods. His account included a place for 'fortuna' i.e. chance. Lucretius took some of his ideas from Empedocles, a Greek thinker and poet, who writing around 450 BCE described the construction of everything from the four elements of earth, air, fire and water. (See Fairbanks 1898)

He also went back to the beginning of everything with an imaginative account of bits and pieces floating about until some things stuck together and survived. Most things that stuck together such as oxen heads and human bodies, did not survive. Once the two sexes had sorted themselves out, life as we know it could begin. This can be seen as an early example of natural selection without the imperfect replication needed to create evolution. Empedocles' pattern of bits and pieces floating about could be taken as a description of the classical world of idea patterns. Descriptions, theories, practices and stories from Mesopotamia, Babylon, Egypt, India, Persia, Greece, Rome and elsewhere were swirling around and influencing each other. Patterns that fitted into the others managed to survive and perhaps get copied.

4.8 Brenda

One important accidental result of working on Christmas post was my meeting Brenda, a grammar school girl in a different form from myself. After delivering post in the afternoon, those of us who had managed to be signed on for evening sorting were sent out for an hour's break. On the other side of the road from the post office was a branch of Redmans, a grocery store with a corner selling pies, sandwiches and mugs of tea. We sat on tall stools at a counter with our feet on a metal rail and we chatted.

That is how I met Brenda. Later we met again at a school dance and I escorted her home by bus to Peel Green where she lived in a shop run by her mother. We arranged to meet again for a trip to the cinema and we were close friends for three years.

When she was old enough, Brenda left school. She also left home to live in the nurses' home in the grounds of Hope Hospital, just outside Eccles, over the border into Salford. In 1953, I left school to go to university and our friendship did not survive.

Brenda, in the words of my mother 'got into bad company' and became pregnant. Some people thought that I must be the father of the baby girl who appeared. To protect myself I had to carry around a cutting from the Eccles and Patricroft Journal in my wallet. In those days local papers worked on the principal of print as many names as possible. Young potential journalists were sent to the magistrates' court to record who had been prosecuted. My cutting recorded that one, David Barker, had been ordered to pay maintenance to Brenda. I only remember the name, Barker because I knew that his nickname was 'woof'.

The baby girl was adopted by her grand parents and grew up thinking that Brenda was her sister. Such an arrangement was not uncommon then. The guitarist Eric Clapton thought his grandmother was his mother, his real mother having gone to Canada. Brenda eventually married a respectable mining engineer and went to live in Yorkshire. I have no idea if and when the daughter discovered who her mother was.

4.9 The year 1953

1953 was an important year both for the world and for me. At the international level, it saw the death of Stalin, the coronation of Queen Elizabeth II, Eisenhower becoming President of the United States and Tito as President of Yugoslavia.

1953 saw two major advances in the search for the meaning of life and what was it all about. Watson and Crick announced the double helix structure of DNA in the journal Nature and Stanley Miller published an account of the synthesis of amino acids in the journal Science. Miller flashed electricity through a soup of simple chemicals that he thought represented 'primitive earth conditions'. Since life needs proteins and proteins are made from amino acids, the two papers together could be compared to a toolbox and instruction manual for the software and hardware of life.

At the personal level, the summer of 1953 produced my GCE A level results - 80% in chemistry, 80% in physics and

85% in Maths. These results were good enough to gain me a place in the Chemistry Department of Manchester University. I learnt later that there had been over 600 applications for this course. The expansion in university education was to happen later. In 1953 only 3% of 18-year-olds went on to university. I was still only 17 when I attended the university freshers' conference to start my new life.

References Chapter 4.
Butler, S. 1887. Luck, or Cunning as the Main Means of Organic Modification? London: Trunber
Robert B. Campenot. 2016. Animal Electricity: How We Learned That the Body and Brain Are Electric Machines. Harvard University Press.
Arthur Fairbanks, ed. 1898.The First Philosophers of Greece. London: K Paul, Trench, Trubner & Co pp. 157-230
Arthur Schopenhauer, 1819 (2011) The World as Will and Representation, Volume 2, xviii.
William Whewell, 1837, History of the Inductive Sciences, London.

Chapter 5. Patterns: Their Acquisition, Recognition and Effects on Actions

Why a chapter on patterns? Because it's part of the answer to, "What's it all about?"

In earlier chapters, patterns have been mentioned a few times. This chapter leaves my life story on one side to provide a discussion of patterns and their importance. It is the first of two chapters about what goes on in our brain/minds. The second chapter arrives later and is concerned with memes but since I did not discover memes until much later in life, it seems sensible to place the discussion of memes and memetics in Part 2.

5.1 Purposive Pattern Recognition (PPR)

I am convinced that pattern recognition is one of the most important activities of our brains. We are so used to this ability that we hardly notice it. We take it for granted. Every waking second our brain is bombarded with a massive input of potential information. Our eyes, ears, nose, fingers, toes, tongue and other body parts are sending signals to our brain but most of these inputs do not reach our consciousness or if they do, they may be forgotten almost immediately. Most of this input we don't even notice.

Life forms use energy in doing what they do. They must replenish this energy - usually in competition with other energy seeking life forms. This means that they either become very efficient in energy consumption or die. Signal detection uses energy. If every incoming signal were detected and acted upon, the energy cost would be enormous. Short cuts are needed and the main method of saving energy is to ignore most of the signal inputs and to collect some of them into a group that, for lack of a better word, can be called a pattern. Essential features emerge and are organized into recognisable patterns with associated meanings. That is, patterns can convey information.

Cognitive philosophers have been debating what is meant by 'information' but most agree that something is only information if something else can decode it. Morse code exists in patterns of sound, light or writing but it only becomes information to someone who knows the code and the problem with codes is how does the recipient get to know the code?

To recognise is to re-cognise, to re-know. You can only re-cognise a pattern if it is there already. So where did it come from? As Thomas Wedgwood put it in his 'Essay on Vision',

> The far greater part of what is supposed to be perception is only the body of ideas which a perception has awakened.

This 'body of ideas' that has been acquired to be there already may come from learning and memory or it might in some way be built in, inherited as Chomsky's universal grammar is supposed to be, or as some people say, 'hard wired', implying that somehow it gets passed on from one generation to the next.

The acquisition of patterns is one of those short cuts used by the brain to save time and energy. The neuroscientist Daniel Bor (2012) uses the word, 'chunking', for the ability to retain an overall impression. Chunking is described as holding data not as a series of individual items but as a linked whole. Bor gives the example of the star chunk known as Orion, which provides an easily recognisable pattern even though most people do not remember the precise position of the stars or even their number. Another example is what I call 'the man in the room'

Ask a man who had been in a room for half an hour what colour were the walls. He had been 'looking' at the walls but in most cases after leaving the room he will have no idea what colour they were. (It's different with women). Similarly, he won't be able to say much about the things that were in the room. And yet, if he were to go in that room again, he would recognise that he had been there before. He has remembered a pattern, an overall impression but is very unsure about the detail.

Daniel Bor provides an example of 'drawing together of information' that resonates with my own brain circuits because it concerns meeting a friend in a pub. He writes that this meeting is not experienced as a "series of disjointed features but as a unified whole combining his appearance with the sound of his voice, knowledge of his name, favourite beer and so on - all amalgamated into a single person-object".

The one part of his list that does not resonate with my experience is 'knowledge of his name'. That brain activity is highly faulty in my own case and it's not just age, even when at school. I had difficulty in recalling people's names.

Bor claims that when we recognise unified wholes, we use two important brain parts, the lateral prefrontal cortex and the posterior parietal cortex. These areas are much larger in human brains than in animals and form many connections between themselves and other parts of the brain. It seems reasonable to accept the idea that a greater number of potential connections makes it possible for the human brain to be better at 'amalgamating' different sense inputs together with memory to produce the feeling of pattern recognition.

Pattern recognition involves memory. Bor's bunching could be described as collecting, and remembering a collection is 're-collection. Pattern recognition is pattern recollection.

Once we are capable of re-cognising patterns from a link between some sensory input and an awakened body of ideas that convey meaning, what do we do with this ability? Can we say that it has a purpose in the same way that a kneecap serves the purpose of protecting a sensitive joint? The purpose of pattern recognition is to make things happen. Sensory inputs of sound, sight and smell are chunked together into a pattern that might convey the information, 'predator approaching'. This results in action – flee, fight, or hide.

This ability is not restricted to human life. Nearly all life forms contain signal-detecting systems that can make things happen. Signals may be from their environment - light causing a flower to open - or water causing roots to grow towards the water - or they may be from inside - pain makes things happen.

The ability to extract a pattern from incoming signals exists even in very simple life forms. Many organisms that inhabit the sea can detect nutrition gradients. If they can convert sugar into energy, they might also have the ability to detect a gradient in dissolved sugar. This gradient (i.e. more sugar at one end of a line) can signal the organism to move up the gradient in the direction of the source of the dissolved sugar. One sugar molecule can have no effect on directional movement. There needs to be enough sugar in a stream of increasing concentration to enable the directional movement.

The ability to detect this gradient can be regarded as the recognition of a pattern, like the pattern formed by a line that is thicker at one end. Molecular gradients are important components of many biological systems. It's not just simple organisms tracking energy sources; neuronal activity and ovulation make use of molecular gradients.

This ability of a nervous system to construct patterns out of incoming signals gives a competitive advantage to the pattern constructor. It enables it to do something. In the case of detecting a gradient, the part of the nervous system that has done the detecting then has to act on another part to set in motion the muscles that make the organism move along the gradient to its source where it then must do what is needed to absorb the source of energy. Pattern recognition leads to activity so it can be described as purposeful, though not in any sense of being conscious of that purpose. That is why I use the abbreviation PPR to stand for purposive pattern recognition.

Over a billion years, some nervous systems acquired specialised parts that can be described as brains and brains are rather clever at PPR. Once brains existed, simple light detecting cells could become more sophisticated - an eye without a brain to process the incoming signals would not be much use. Plant life uses light detection for many purposes but is has not acquired eyes because plants don't have brains.

The brain of a frog is comparatively small and has a limited set of patterns at its disposal. One of these is that it can detect the presence of flies near to its face. This triggers the frog into sticking out its tongue, moving its head and eating the fly. One interesting part of this ability is the fact that it only works with moving flies. A frog could starve surrounded by flies as long as they didn't move. It has a movement pattern detector, as do most living things that have eyes attached to brains.

Incoming eye signals are detected and remembered long enough to be compared with the next input. Small differences between then and now are interpreted as movement. Hens have an unusual way of doing this. If you watch a hen moving it seems to be moving its head backwards and forwards as it walks. In fact, it keeps it head still, moves its legs, leaving the head behind and then jerks its head forward to catch up with its legs. This has the effect of taking two snapshots of then and now, allowing it to detect the movement of an approaching fox and then flying away.

By the time that brains had improved to the stage where they found themselves in the heads of humans, they became able to acquire many more patterns than the few known to frogs and hens.

5.2 Pattern Formation

In earlier versions of writing about patterns, I used the word 'formation', to signify the process that happens before a pattern can be re-cognised, but this word was quickly replaced by 'construction'. Neither of these words is a very accurate description. Construction, assembly or formation imply that you start with bits and then put them together. In fact, what happens is that brains have the ability to extract a pattern from all those inputs. We only 'see' the essential parts; the rest can be ignored, saving energy.

A demonstration of this pattern extracting ability is provided by tests for colour blindness. When I became employed by ICI Dyestuffs Division, one of the first things that happened was a test for what was then known as colour blindness, (now known as colour vision deficiency). An organization that sells colour needs to know that its employees can tell the difference between different colours.

The test involved my looking at the pages of a book, each page of which had a mixture of different shaped blobs printed in different colours and I had to detect a number within the blobs - one number per page. For example, on one page I could extract the pattern that I recognised as a 2. The large 2 contained mainly red blobs and the surround had mainly green blobs but these were mixed with various other colours and there was no obvious line surrounding the 2.

Someone with difficulty in distinguishing red from green would not have been able to extract the 2 from out of all those blobs but people with normal colour detecting abilities could see the 2; the rest of the page being ignored. I did not construct the 2 out of its parts; I extracted the number from a confused mixture. (Apparently, red/green vision deficiency is inherited but mainly from mother to son. Knowing this is not much use to sufferers)

The important difference between construction and extraction is not understood by some of those engaged in trying to persuade computers to imitate brains. Most computer programs for pattern recognition rely on construction, that is sticking bits together.

Ray Kurzweil (2012) as inventor, entrepreneur and then Director of Engineering for Google has succeeded in developing word recognition programs, speech recognition technology and other forms of pattern recognition. He has extended his experience into writing about the human mind. In a book, How to Create a Mind, his chapter 3 is called 'A Model of the Neocortex: The Pattern Recognition Theory of Mind'. PRTM for short is based on the claim that the neocortex, the wrinkled, thin outer layer of the brain, contains millions of neural pattern recognisers. When given a stimulus, such as the letter A, these pattern recognisers break down the A into bits - a horizontal line, three angles and three sides - before recognizing an A. The A is then combined with other letters that have been recognised by different circuits to produce a word - APPLE. He claims that this is a hierarchical procedure, moving from shapes to letters to words and then to sentences. This may be how Kurzweil's technology works but I do not believe that brains do that. When I recognize the word Apple, I do not start with the horizontal line in A, I would probably 'see' an A in Apple even if the horizontal line were missing. Even If the lower half of the letters were obscured, I could still recognize the word. We extract the essential features of Apple; we do not construct it from its bits.

Both rooms and people can be said to 'make an impression' on a viewer. This is a form of pattern formation. An example –

I was at school with a boy called Elgar Howarth. As his name suggests, he came from a musical family and grew up to be a well-known conductor and a force for taking brass bands more seriously. Some fifty years after I had last seen him, I went to a concert where he was conducting. As he walked onto the stage, I looked very closely to see if there was anything I recognized. Then it clicked - the way he held his head slightly forward was just how I remembered him at school. He was taller than other boys and developed a slight stoop to bring his head down a bit. The same stoop was apparent fifty years later.

In addition to extracting a pattern from too much input, the human brain has another trick; it can recognize a pattern when there is too little input. Some circuits sort out boundaries and can even insert lines where they don't exist, as in the Kanizsa triangle illusion. (See Chapter 2)

This ability is not pattern acquisition; it only works after the pattern first exists. The brain obliges us with a triangle where there isn't one but it can only do that because it has already established the circuits that recognise triangles.

One of those TV quiz programs has a competition where competitors must give names to pictures of famous people where the pictures are revealed only gradually. Many faces are recognized when only half completed. This is only possible because a pattern of the face has already been acquired and remembered. So, how was this pattern acquired in the first place? Could it have been inherited? In the case of one particular person's face, this could not have been known to us at birth but maybe we inherited the ability to acquire such patterns.

It's just not possible for the genes alone to carry all the information needed for pattern acquisition. What the genes convey is the propensity for certain things to develop. The case of language is a good example. There is language and languages. A normal child born of French parents but brought up in England inherits the propensity to acquire language, but it does not inherit French, English or any of the thousands of languages that exist. The pattern of whatever language it acquires depends on its upbringing but the upbringing rests on a foundation of ability to acquire.

You cannot bring up a chimp to speak English. For a start it does not even have the necessary body parts to be able to speak anything. It can make noises, and these can convey information to other chimps. It can squeak but it cannot speak. Humans start with the propensity to speak. However, they do not speak until they have learnt how to do it and you cannot learn to speak if you don't inherit the propensity in the first place.

Similarly, the propensity to acquire, re-cognise and make use of patterns must be inherited and then developed in the early years of our life. Once a pattern has been acquired, memory becomes important and memory is consolidated through repetition and familiarity.

One way in which new patterns can be acquired is by being like an existing pattern. Very young babies learn to recognize the pattern of 'mother' from which they extract the pattern of mother's face. They then can accommodate other faces. Brain scans on young babies have shown that when shown various shapes, ones that are oval with a slight hint of facial features cause brain activity to take place, suggesting that they have extracted a basic pattern of face essentials that can be used to accept new faces into their mental repertoire.

I came to think in terms of PPR because of research carried out by a Jordanian PhD student, Maria Abu Risha (1999). She interviewed professional graphic designers and asked them how they made visual choices. How did they decide what images to use? Their answers were mostly in terms of things like 'intuition', 'you just know it's right; 'it's not scientific' and so on. In my terms, this is B type thinking as opposed to P type or old brain not new brain. In terms used by Kahneman (2011), this is fast thinking as opposed to slow methodical thinking.

Later, I was able to place PPR in a Darwinian framework of memes (Langrish & Abu Risha, 2009) but this is for discussion in Part Two of these memoirs.

5.3 Some disadvantages

PPR helps life forms to survive and multiply but life is extremely complex and in complex systems, gains in one part of the system can sometimes be offset by disadvantages in other parts of the system. Three disadvantages that follow from the ability to recognise patterns are now discussed.

5.3.1 Prevention of further PPR

An acquired pattern is available for making sense out of new incoming sense data. If made use of, it becomes established and may be thought of as a pattern receptor, acting as a trawl of incoming data to catch things that can fit into the established net. The disadvantage with this ability is that once established the receptor takes priority over alternative patterns and the brain loses the ability to construct new patterns.

This loss of ability can be detected in animals. It is well known that some animals can learn by association. Pavlov's dogs and swans getting ready to be fed following the chiming of a cathedral bell are well known. What is less known is that this ability may hinder further acquisitions. In an experiment with dogs, red lights were a signal that food was coming. In the Pavlov tradition, the dogs then started to salivate before the food arrived. Red light means food, so salivate. Later the dogs were shown both red and green lights before food. As long as both colours were displayed the dogs salivated but when shown a green light on its own, nothing happened. In the words of Richard Byrne (1995), "With an adequate predictor of the food already learnt, there is nothing further to learn, and the redundant cue is ignored" This is a further example of how brains take short cuts in the interests of energy economy.

Individuals develop their own personal set of patterns like Slater's personal constructs that claimed to detect differences between the concepts used by different people when categorising things. Differences between individuals can cause much confusion in academic circles when different people have established different patterns that prevent them from seeing another person's pattern of thought.

For example, historian Perry Anderson (2012), the author of an essay, 'Gandhi Centre Stage', had to defend his piece from its critics by writing to the London Review of Books. He attacks his critics for their inability to look with much care at any view out of step with inherited convictions, as too upsetting to be fully registered.

What Anderson calls 'inherited convictions' are, in my terms, firmly established pattern receptors. Different patterns that do not fit the receptor are 'out of step' and fail to be 'fully registered'. They may also be 'upsetting', leading in Anderson's words, to "the persistent resort to euphemism and evasion wherever awkward questions are at issue".

Another example is from the history of our pattern recognition when viewing the brain. We now know that brains are made up of cells called neurons (the neurons are very similar whether in worms, insects or humans) but it took time for neurons to be recognised.

When people started looking at living things through microscopes, they discovered cells. Cells come in different sizes and shapes but most are roughly round. Microscopists learnt what cells looked like. They extracted a pattern that was roundish. When they looked at the brain, however, they did not recognise any cells; they saw a dense fibrous mass, called the reticulum.

This recognition was associated with a theory – the reticular theory of brain anatomy which asserted that the brain has no separate components – it's just a mess.

We now know that brains are made of large numbers of neurons (bees have about a million neurons in their brains, whilst snails get by with about 30,000)

The first person to make a name for himself by showing that the brain was made from identifiable bits was the Italian Camillo Golgi (1843-1926) who developed a staining technique using photographic chemicals. The technique did not work very well which was good luck because only a few neurons got stained with silver, enabling them to stand out from the tangle of all the other neurons. It could then be seen that brains are made of long thin things with lots of sticky out bits looking like the roots of a seedling. These structures are so different from the cells in the rest of living things that Golgi refused to accept that these neurons were cells. He continued to think in terms of the reticular theory.

It was left to the Spanish scientist, Santiago Ramon y Cajal (1852-1934) to find the modern view of neurons – that they are cells and they convey signals in one direction. Golgi and Cajal shared a 1906 Nobel Prize but Golgi still did not accept that neurons were cells – it seemed obvious to him – you only had to look at them through a microscope – they didn't look like cells, did they?

In the history of science, there are many examples of scientists being unable to 'see' the pattern of something new; their old pattern is too firmly entrenched. Max Planck (1949) put it well,

> A new scientific truth does not triumph by convincing its opponents and making them see the light, but rather because its opponents eventually die, and a new generation grows up that is familiar with it.

The last part of that quotation is often left out. I have included it because it shows that - as any schoolteacher knows - some patterns take time to be acquired through repetition leading to familiarity. But once a pattern has been established, it becomes harder to acquire a new one that does not fit with the existing one. This disadvantage is not just restricted to academic debate; it applies in the case of the design of artefacts, electric kettles for example. "No, it doesn't look like a kettle"

The first electric kettles looked like previous kettles. They had a wide base, a curved handle and a long spout. The difference was the connection to the electricity supply but they still announced what they were and what you could do with them. Then designers pointed out that whilst the form of a kettle was fine when it obtained heat from an outside source - a coal fire, a gas burner or an electric hotplate - it could be improved when the heat source was an internal electric heater.

There were two important implications that came from transferring the heat source to the inside of the kettle. The first was energy saving. If the shape were changed to having a narrow base instead of the traditional broad base, then less water would be needed to cover the heating element, saving the energy used in heating up more water than needed. The second was that the kettle did not need to be made of metal. A plastic kettle became possible because it only had to withstand the heat from boiling water instead of having to resist the heat from an outside source. Thus, the idea of a plastic jug-shaped kettle occurred to designers working for the kettle manufacturers who decided to carry out some market research. When faced with prototypes of jug kettles, a typical response from a potential buyer was, "No, it doesn't look like a kettle".

Then a small company, Redring, who manufactured energy efficient water heating systems, decided to diversify into the jug kettle as another example of heating efficiency. They did not know about the market research. At first, sales were poor. Then pictures started to appear in periodicals and newspapers, and it became possible to see the kettle being used in other people's houses. The jug kettle became familiar and other manufacturers brought out their own version. Many people put away their chromium plated old style electric kettle and replaced it with the new plastic jug kettle. In the UK today an old style electric kettle would be a curiosity.

A similar story is that of England's most successful small car - the Austin Mini. It used a novel design, involving a space-saving transverse-engine with front-wheel drive layout, allowing more space to be used for passengers and luggage. To obtain even more space, the wheel size was reduced, and this had the advantage of giving the Mini excellent road holding ability when cornering. It was still recognizable as a car but it was odd looking. There is more to pattern recognition than just identification. Once recognized, a pattern leads onto other patterns such as desirability.

At first, the Mini sales were disappointing; it was not the sort of car that most people wanted to buy. Size was seen as a pattern of status, and many decided that for the same money they could buy the larger and more conventional Ford 100E Popular or Austin A40. Then photographs appeared of prestigious people with the Mini. In particular, the husband of Princess Margaret, Lord Snowdon, owned one and when the Beatles appeared with a Mini, there could be no doubt. The pattern of the Mini changed from being seen as small and odd to being prestigious and affordable.

The disadvantage of one pattern preventing the acquisition of a different pattern can be overcome but the recognition of patterns has other disadvantages including what I call the Either/Or problem.

5.3.2 Either/Or (E/O)

Once a pattern has been recognised, other things happen. A specific pattern may be categorised into a class of patterns and the simplest classification system is dividing things into either this or that, abbreviated to E/O. The ability to sort our impressions into different kinds with associated feelings is obviously very useful (e.g. good – move towards or bad – run away) but it comes with a disadvantage. We tend to apply E/O to situations that are much more complex than a simple two-part division allows for. In complex systems, E/O can be replaced by this and that and something else. The nature/nurture division is a classic example, illustrated in studies of bird song

Each bird species has its own distinctive 'song'. It is tempting to use E/O to wonder whether this song is built into its inheritance (nature) or acquired through imitating other birds of the same species (nurture). In fact, the answer is very complicated. There is enormous variation in the way that birds acquire their distinctive 'song'. Some species are well known for their ability to imitate almost anything - from the human voice to the click made by an old-style tape recorder, set to record their sounds. Other species produce chicks that can only produce a very poor version of their song when hatched in solitude; they need to learn from other members of their species.

In the 1950s, the British ethologist, William Thorpe, determined that if the chaffinch is not exposed to the adult male's song during a certain critical period after hatching, it will never properly learn the song. He also found that in adult male chaffinches, castration eliminates song. Subsequent research has shown connections between mating and singing. As with many birds, only male canaries sing. The females are silent until given an injection of testosterone when they burst into song.

One possible explanation is that bird song enables females to select males of their own species. If some male in the wild had an unusual genome that encouraged variation in the song pattern, then its chance of mating would be reduced. However, if birds are kept in captivity and selected by breeders for attractive plumage then song innovation is not selected against. In fact, this is what happened to a bird species, studied by Kazuo Okanoya (1996) of Tokyo's Riken Institute.

The Bengalese finch has been bred in captivity for centuries. It is a domestic version of the wild white-rumped munia. After centuries of breeding, the captive species is now much more attractive to human buyers than the wild variant and in addition, the domesticated bird has a much more elaborate variety of songs.

Life is much more complex than allowed for by simple E/Os but even humanities students can take the tempting short cut of dividing things into two. History professor, Colin Kidd (2013), reflecting on 15 years of teaching the 18th century Enlightenment at the University of Glasgow, recalled,

All too often students would assign writers to one of two camps, the party of enlightened progress or the party of anti-Enlightenment reaction … they were so bedazzled by the term 'Enlightenment' that they couldn't resist framing the complex debates of the 18th century as a clash of two rival armies.

Instead of taking the easy option of E/O, it is often necessary to consider the three alternatives of both, neither and more than. 'Both' includes seeing a spectrum stretching from E to O. 'Neither' includes the case of something else being more important. The case of 'more than' is interesting. Sewall Wright (1967), the evolutionary biologist, wrote,

The Darwinian process of continued interplay of a random and a selective process is not intermediate between pure chance and pure determination, but in its consequences qualitatively different from either of them.

The consequences of 'more than' can be described as 'emergent properties'. An example is provided by the properties of table salt, sodium chloride, NaCl. An E/O question such as which is more important in causing the properties of sodium chloride the sodium or the chlorine, is answered by a 'more than'. Sodium is a metal that explodes on contact with water (much to the delight of school chemistry students in the days before health and safety took over). Chlorine is a poisonous gas. Combining the two together to produce sodium chloride results in emergent properties such as crystallinity, a special taste and being essential for life, none of which could be predicted from the separate properties of sodium and chlorine. In such cases it's the interaction between the E and the O that is important. As is the case with nature and nurture: - it's never nature versus nurture; It's both; it's more than; it's the interaction between the two that matters.

5.3.3 Patterns in the fire

Back in the days of sitting around coal fires, people saw patterns in the fire and sometimes different people would see different patterns. Something similar happens in academic debate when dealing with causation and explanation in a complex system. When different academics 'see' different patterns in the past then we have the makings of an academic controversy. This can be a result of looking at different parts of the 'fire' or seeing different patterns in the same part of the fire.

History (meaning what historians write) provides many examples of this phenomenon. Take, for example, the English Civil War in which Cromwell's forces beat the royalists and the King lost his head. (The English were always fighting each other with interludes when they fought the French or the Scots but only one war is known as The Civil War)

Different historians have seen different patterns in the Civil War. Some looked at different records of the past, using official documents to examine the political history whilst others looked at what individuals wrote about their experience in the war.

Some historians could see different patterns in the same records. Before the 1950s, the civil war was seen as a military contest between the landed gentry and the aristocracy, list of battles, generals and military strategy were what it was about. After all, it was a war – wasn't it? Then historians started seeing different patterns. Economic historians argued about whether the gentry were getting richer or poorer before the war. Marxist historians such as Christopher Hill (1958), saw the war as a bourgeois revolution overthrowing an out-dated feudalism. Historian, Hugh Trevor Roper (1951) (famous in more recent years for authenticating a forged diary supposed to be Hitler's own account of WWII) forced a controversy with others that became known as 'the storm over the gentry'. It was as though two people looking at a fire were claiming, "My pattern is better than yours".

More recently, it was argued that the idea of 'the gentry' was too simple; members of the same family were on opposite sides of the war. The role of religion was given greater emphasis and these days no historian would claim to see a grand theme in the civil war. Such grand themes turn out to be PIFs, useful but concealing the complexity.

Blair Worden (2012) writing about Trevor Roper in History Today concludes, 'what we have lost is an explanatory framework for it (the Civil War), indeed for much else. Trevor-Roper and his fellow contestants may have thought wrong but they thought big'. In other words, PR works by selecting some essentials from a much larger set of inputs. When we look at the detail, the pattern disappears.

In the UK, the Clean Air Act of 1956 started the process of removing most domestic coal fires and an alternative to PIFs might now be useful. 'Patterns in the clouds' could be a better phrase. When two people are looking at the clouds they may both see different patterns but sometimes it is possible for one person's pattern to be communicated to the other. For example, in Emma Darwin's novel (2007), The Mathematics of Love (p 118), two characters are sitting outdoors together,

> and when I said that a cloud that was drifting towards us over the clearing looked like a witch on a broom stick, he tilted his head on one side and said, 'Or a dragon, if you look at it this way.' 'Or a swan. Look, it's stretching its wings up like it's about to land.' We watched the swan till it started to break up altogether.

'Castles in the clouds' has been used as a metaphor for seeing patterns that are in the mind and not 'really' out there. For example, Candida R Moss (2014) a historian of early Christianity, discussing the use of words such as Jew, Christian and pagan, points out that Christianity as a word did not exist in the time of the Apostle Paul. Although, we think we know what we mean when talking about early Christianity, our mental patterns will not be the same as the reality of those early thinkers. In her own words, "if we slacken the ties that bind rhetoric to reality, we run the risk of describing castles in the clouds."

She criticises another historian for describing the Apostle Paul as a "Jewish convert to Christianity". Paul, on the road to Damascus, certainly changed his mind about something but the modern usage of 'conversion' is a PIF or pattern in the cloud. He changed from seeing Jesus as a false prophet and an enemy into seeing him as the Messiah, long prophesised in the scriptures. He did not give up being a Jew and the word 'Christianity' had not yet been invented. So, he could not have been a 'convert'. He stayed with his Jewish mental patterns but added the arrival of what had been prophesised.

Why, then does Moss claim that 'we run the risk' when we follow this form of analysis? What is the danger in looking for castles in the air? It is simply that on close inspection, so many concepts turn out to be individual versions of what is seen in the clouds. Communication becomes imperilled. For example, take the word 'Christianity'. The patterns that exist in different peoples' minds, when given this word, are clearly different from each other. To Richard Dawkins the word conjures up patterns of believing in nonsense and assaulting children with this nonsense. An extreme Protestant in Northern Ireland sees different patterns to those seen by a follower of the Ukrainian Greek Catholic church. The differences are associated with patterns of political identity (anti Republicanism and anti Moscow, respectively) as well as being divided by the importance of the Bishop of Rome (the Anti-Christ and the Pope respectively)

The danger lies in the fact that this form of analysis paralyses communication of abstract concepts. In the days before TV, the BBC had a program called The Brains Trust, in which a panel attempted to answer questions sent in by listeners. One regular member of the panel was a philosopher, Professor Joad, who often started his response by saying, "It all depends on what you mean by ...". (Joad was removed from the panel in 1948 because of his being fined for attempting to travel on a train without a ticket. In those days the BBC saw itself as a guardian of morality)

Questioning meaning can lead to failure to provide an answer. The opposite danger is that ignoring individual differences in patterns of meaning can lead to two people talking over each other's shoulders as semantic confusion takes over.

Moss summarises the problem with, "if there's one thing worse than a romanticist who cannot be quiet, it's an expert who cannot say anything at all"

Epictetus the Stoic is supposed to have claimed, "Man is disturbed not by things but by the views he takes of them". We could not get through the day without using PPR but it helps to be aware that this ability can cause problems.

References Chapter 5.
Abu Risha, Maria. 1999. Purposive Pattern Recognition. PhD thesis, De Montfort University.
Anderson, Perry. 2012. Gandhi Centre Stage, LRB 5 July 2012 p 3. Letter LRB 13 Sept 2012 p 4
Bor, Daniel. 2012. The Ravenous Brain: How the New Science of Consciousness Explains Our Insatiable Search for Meaning. New York: Basic Books.
Byrne, Richard. 1995. The Thinking Ape: Evolutionary Origins of Intelligence. Paperback. Oxford U P. p 51.
Darwin, Emma. 2007. The Mathematics of Love. London: Headline.
Hill, Christopher. 1958. Puritanism and Revolution: Studies in Interpretation of the English Revolution of the 17th Century. London: Macmillan.
Kahneman Daniel. 2011 Thinking, Fast and Slow. Allen Lane. p236 intuition as recognition.
Kidd, Colin. 2013. Book Review in London Review of Books. 5th Dec.
Kurzweil, Ray. 2012. How to Create a Mind: The Secret of Human Thought Revealed New York, Viking,
Langrish, John Z and Abu-Risha, Maria. 2009. Purposive Pattern Recognition: The Nature of Visual Choice in Graphic Design. In: DRS Conference 2008, Sheffield Hallam University, UK. Available from Sheffield Hallam University Research Archive (SHURA) at: http://shura.shu.ac.uk/461/
Moss, Candida. 2014. Between Pagan and Christian - book review of Jones, Christopher P. 2014. Harvard UP in THE 10th July p 51,

Okanoya, Kazuo. 1996. The Bengalese finch: a window on the behavioral neurobiology of birdsong syntax. Annals of the New York Academy of Sciences, 10.11

Planck, Max.1949. Max Planck, Scientific Autobiography and Other Papers, trans. F Gaynor, New York 1949, pp. 33-34.

Trevor-Roper, H R. 1951. "The Elizabethan Aristocracy: An Anatomy Anatomized," Economic History Review pp. 279-298. https://en.wikipedia.org/wiki/Hugh_Trevor-Roper 1953. "The Gentry 1540-1640." Economic History Review 1, 1-55.

Worden, Blair. 2012. History's Heroic Age. History Today. April p. 72.

Wright, Sewall. 1967. Quoted in Moorhead, P. S. and Kaplan, M. M. (eds.) Mathematical challenges to the neo-Darwinian interpretation of evolution, Philadelphia: Wistar Institute Press. P 117.

Chapter 6. Manchester University 1953–1959

6.1 Chemistry Department

In October 1953, still just aged 17, I turned up for the Manchester Freshers' Conference, held in the original buildings of what had been Owen's College before it became The Victoria University of Manchester. I was enrolled onto the three-year course for the BSc Honours in Chemistry. I have only one firm memory of that freshers' conference. I met up with someone who suggested we went for a pint in a pub. It was illegal for people under the age of 18 to go in a pub so this became my first visit and started me on a path that combined beer and good conversation on many occasions.

The building that housed the chemistry department where I was to study was attached to the rear of the original Owen's College and had been a brewery in Victorian times. When opened, it had been the newest and largest chemistry department in the UK. There were spacious laboratories that made use of the open spaces available from the original brewery. These old laboratories were named after important Manchester chemists, Roscoe, Schorlemmer, Perkin, Morley and Schunck. (Roscoe was more than a chemist. He had been an MP and he also founded extra mural education in the university).

The corridors had photos of chemists from the past. One of these included Chaim Weizmann who became the first President of Israel. Photos of more recent members of staff included three Nobel Prize winners, Walter Haworth (1937) Robert Robinson (1947) and Alexander Todd who had been a student of Robinson and was Manchester's professor of organic chemistry at Manchester from 1938 to 1944 when he was poached by Cambridge. He went on to gain a Nobel for Chemistry in 1957 and to become Lord Todd in 1962.

Before leaving the Nobels there has to be a mention of the Polanyis. Michael Polanyi provided me with an inspirational model of how to be an academic. Like Roscoe, he was a 'been there; done that; move on' type of person. He was one of those émigré Hungarian intellectuals described by Leó Szilárd as The Men from Mars and he made important contributions to different branches of chemistry before deciding that understanding knowledge was more important than chemistry. In 1933 he left Germany, becoming first a chemistry professor, and then a social sciences professor at Manchester.

Polanyi's elder brother, Karl, was another 'man from Mars' who was an unorthodox economist and political analyst. Two of Michael Polanyi's students and his son John won Nobel Prizes in Chemistry. The academic link between father and son was provided by Ernest Warhurst who had been supervised by Michael and who in turn was the supervisor of John's PhD, completed in 1952 the year before my arrival. For some reason, I had thought that Hungarian men tended to be small but John Polanyi was tall being easily visible in a crowd.

Ernie Warhurst gave lectures in physical chemistry and quantum theory. I enjoyed his lectures but did not always understand them. The Schrödinger equation for an electron trapped in a box gives a very small probability that the electron will be outside the box. I could not see that. It is not much of a box if the electron can be outside it. Later I discovered that the small probability of escape could be described as tunneling.

Lewis and Barnes are Australian astrophysicists. They attempt to explain their subject to the non-specialist. Commenting on the concept of existing outside the box, they say, (2016 p 81)

> This quantum tunneling sounds like a fudge, something that quantum physicists made up at a party after a few too many Chardonnays. But it is a real phenomenon and is regularly observed in the laboratory.

Their explanation of tunneling uses analogy with a high-walled prison yard. The prisoners do not have enough energy to escape over the wall but they keep trying despite the amazingly low probability of escape.

> In a typical uranium-238 nucleus, for example, the alpha particle will bang its head against the wall a trillion trillion trillion times over a few billion years before successfully tunneling to the outside. (P 81.)

(U-238 decays into thorium with a half-life of about 4.5 billion years.)

So in 1953, I settled down to the life of a chemistry student living at home. The laboratories - for both teaching and research - together with the sloping floor lecture theatres, had been very suitable for Victorian ideas about chemical education, with a strong concentration on the practical side of chemistry. The sloping floors enabled students to see practical demonstrations given by lecturers at the centre of the tiered theatres. Chemistry had been something that you DID and there was an expression - thinking with your hands - that even became a book, Penser avec les mains (Rougemont 1936)

Prior to the 1950s the main employment for chemistry graduates outside school teaching had been working as an analytical chemist in quality control. Making sure that raw materials consisted of what they should consist of and that food had not been adulterated had been a skilled job but there was now a new type of analytical chemistry replacing hands-on skills with the automatic read-outs from new instruments.

New techniques such as vapour phase chromatography, atomic absorption and mass spectrometry drew graphs for the chemist whose skill now lay in the interpretation of graphs rather than practical chemical analysis involving things such as persuading a liquid to become a pure solid with a fingerprint melting point.

The Victoria University of Manchester's chemistry department along with its physics department where Rutherford had 'split the atom' had been a major international centre. There is a photograph from the 1887 meeting of the British Association for the Advancement of Science, in Manchester, showing Wislicenus, Quincke, Schorlemmer, Lothar Meyer, Mendeleev, Schunck, Joule and Sir Henry Roscoe. (Four Germans, one Russian and three Brits). With the exception of Quincke, all these are known figures in the history of science. Quincke was a German physician who is known in the history of medicine. (Quincke's edema, Quincke's puncture and Quincke's pulse).

However in 1953, times were changing. The science buildings were old and it was another ten years before the new 1960s buildings were in use. When I was still at school, the chemistry teacher, Johnny Ball, had advised against applying to the 'new' universities (i.e. those opened after 1918). I remember his saying he would not support an application to study chemistry at Sheffield University. And yet the next northern university chemistry department to have a Nobel laureate was Sheffield with George Porter who won the 1967 prize for flash photolysis.

Nonetheless, back in 1953, we knew we were where the action had been and assumed it was still there. One major change involved the status of practical chemistry. In the Christmas of 1953, I went to my first chemistry department Christmas party. It was a tradition that second year students had to provide an event at this party and in my first year this took the form of a funeral for the practical exam, just abolished as far as being part of finals was concerned. There had always been a practical exam as part of 'finals', the series of exams that determined what class of degree was obtained. The practical exam was now abolished.

A year later I was in the second year and we had to decide on a theme for the Christmas event. I suggested the discovery of a traffic light dye - something that changed colour. I had no way of knowing then that I would be working for the Dyestuffs Division of ICI. The synthesis of dyes, pharmaceuticals and other chemicals was another source of employment for chemistry graduates and had been particularly important in Germany where teams of chemists had turned out new chemical compounds.

The German industry set up research laboratories and asked the universities to supply them with trained synthetic chemists. This led to the invention of a new degree, the PhD, a junior doctorate that released students into industry more quickly than the six years needed to get a proper doctorate - the D.Sc. Even in 1949 half of all PhDs gained in England were in chemistry. Who would have guessed that the Germans would take the PhD to America where it became the standard requirement for an academic post in any subject?

My own vague thoughts about the future were focussed on my desire to teach. This coupled with the knowledge of my own lack of practical capabilities meant that I hoped I would become a university lecturer - if I could avoid national service.

My first year in the chemistry department was spent with lectures and practicals together with enjoying the social side of university. Three mornings a week were spent in a large laboratory where we did analysis and so called experiments that were not really experiments at all because they had 'right answers' based on an educational theory that the best way to learn something was by direct experience. The experiments were designed to demonstrate some aspect of chemistry but as far as I was concerned they were hoops to be jumped through. The so called experiments had to be written up and then given a mark recorded in an official notebook by the person looking after the laboratory - often a student 'demonstrator' in the days before the word demonstrator took on a different meaning.

I had a friend, Paul Freeman, who had a very direct approach to these experiments. Their only purpose was to get a good mark in that book. He was one of several students who came from Burnage Grammar School. He lived in a council house and like others had been able to achieve social mobility through the Grammar School. He was friendly with another former Burnage product who was now a postgraduate student and lent Paul his own practical book from his time as an undergrad.

This meant we could just make a few measurements, write up the results by copying from previous work and then disappear into 'Caf' where we would meet and chat to non-chemists over coffee. Some years after graduating, I met Paul Freeman again. He had stopped being involved with chemistry and said he had given up on academic chemistry when he realised that he would never win a Nobel Prize. It is a tribute to his teachers at Burnage Grammar School and to those photographs in the Chemistry department's corridors that he had ever thought that a Nobel was possible. In 1953, Paul was a self-assured young man with useful contacts.

Some of our fellow students were two years older, having completed their National Service before university. With the benefit of two years experience, they were amused by Paul and referred to him as Skipper Dan. Even so it was very useful for me to know someone who had contacts.

6.2 The OTC

Paul persuaded me that we should join the university's OTC - the officer training corps and officially a branch of the TA, the Territorial Army. We were paid for turning up every Wednesday in our khaki uniforms and shiny boots. We learnt to march, fire guns, read maps, look after truck batteries and so on.

We then had to specialise and Paul and I joined the signals section where we learnt how to lay a landline and to operate a two-way radio set - over and out. I saw enough of the army to realise that the last thing I wanted to do was spend two years of my life doing the so-called national service. There were different ways of avoiding this fate and I decided to try them all. I joined the Anglican Pacifist Fellowship and no one seemed to notice that I was also a member of the TA. I had a vague idea that I would either get out of national service through being a conscientious objector or failing that I would go in the army as an officer.

Another possibility was to train as a science teacher. There was a national shortage of science teachers and the government was considering granting exemption to science graduates who wanted to teach. What actually happened was that I stayed in the chemistry department for another three years after graduating and then became a science teacher. So I did not have to spend two years of my life in the army.

Being in the TA was a good substitute for the real thing. I experienced ABT, arms basic training. This involved being able to fire and maintain rifles, Bren guns and Sten guns as well as throwing hand grenades. The Bren and Sten were light machine guns used by the British army in various conflicts including the Korean War. The 'en' part of their names came from Enfield, the site of the army's factory where they were made. St stood for the initials of the designers of the Sten. Br stood for Brno, the Czech town where the original Bren had been designed. These two weapons represented two different approaches to technology with different ideas of 'betterness'. The selecteme for the Sten was ease of manufacture. The regular army corporal who instructed us in using the Sten claimed that it was little more than a drainpipe with a spring. He also said that in a fight between a native with a poisoned blow dart and a soldier with a Sten, the native would win if he were more than 30 feet away. We were allowed to fire a Sten at a life size cardboard figure. My first attempt pulled the gun to the left so the cardboard was untouched. My second attempt had me clutching the gun to prevent it spraying to one side. Instead it shot up over the cardboard figure. The poisoned dart would have won.

The Bren was completely different. Its ruling selecteme was accuracy and it was based on a Czech gun that had been the winner of a competition organised in the 1930s. Its major problem was that its barrel overheated. This was solved by having a spare barrel and a mechanism that allowed for the speedy replacement of the hot barrel by the spare. A corporal with a stopwatch timed our attempts at barrel replacement and surprisingly, I turned out to be the fastest. The corporal was complimentary and made reference to my skill with 'the maiden in the boat'. This had a sexual significance that was lost on me at the time.

The regular army staff that had been seconded to the TA specialised in army obscenities. For example, in map reading a six-figure map reference is used. Three numbers refer to the horizontal distance and three to the vertical. But which is which? The army way of remembering was, "You have to go along with a girl before you can get up her". East West before North South.

Demonstrating competence with weapons required visits to the army rifle range at Holcombe Brook, on the edge of the Pennines to the north of Manchester near Ramsbottom. One weekend, the army captain borrowed a chef from the nearby army barracks. This chef had been with the army in India and was responsible for my experiencing the sensation of curry for the first time.

In addition to firing guns at targets, we had to man the targets. This involved being in concrete trenches below ground level and sending up targets to be shot at. We then had to report the results via a phone attached to a landline. We also took part in exercises involving charging about on Holcombe Moor whilst army staff threw firecrackers around to create noise and smoke.

In the summer, there was a one-week exercise that qualified us for an annual bonus. Paul Freeman and myself avoided the charging about aspect of soldiering by manning a signals truck situated in a country field. A truck was needed to carry the heavy two-way radio - alpha bravo etc. - over and out. On the second day, an umpire chap arrived, discharged a firecracker and said, "Sorry chaps but you are now dead. Switch off the radio." So we sat in the sun with some beer that we had brought with us.

Paul discovered that instead of spending time in a field in Wales, we could earn our annual bonus by spending time in the real army along with national service new recruits. So one summer we found ourselves in Ashton barracks doing the arms basic training course. Northern towns have army buildings dating back to the time when the powers that be were worried that the workers might be inspired by the French revolution. A two-pronged defence was adopted. The army and the Church would defend the middle classes against the workers. This required barracks for the army and churches for the clergy. Ashton barracks was a relic of that concern. (The need for vicars in industrial towns led to the establishment of a new university in Durham, about as far North as you can get in England. Durham University still has more Professors of theology than anywhere else.)

My experience in Ashton showed me that the two years national service was to be avoided. It also showed me how people can hide themselves in large organisations. There were two soldiers who had been transferred to Ashton but not all their paper work had arrived. They found themselves a small room and during the day they did ironing for others at a fee. When they went for a walk, they carried a pot of paint to pretend they were busy. Fortunately for them, pay details had been transferred so that they could attend pay parade on Fridays. I was reminded of this when I worked for ICI and found people doing their own thing including one who was making a central hearing system for his own home.

6.3 Social life 1

The university cafeteria that we escaped to was housed in a former church - eventually to be demolished and replaced by Staff House which itself was also demolished much later. (One of the many interesting things about growing older is being able to have witnessed the construction of a new building and also its eventual demolition. This was true of several buildings that I knew, including the university's Maths Tower and some high-rise buildings, designed to house people from the vast slum clearance program but ending up having to be cleared themselves.)

Caf was an important part of the social scene for some of the chemistry students. There were few female science students but many female Arts students and they managed to join forces in Caf. For exclusive male company there was the Men's Student Union. (There was a separate building for the Women's Student Union).

Students today would be amazed if they could time-travel back to the Men's Union. It was modelled on a Victorian gentleman's club. It had a billiards room where snooker was usually played. This was guarded by a 'servant', who if asked would go to the bar on another floor and return with a tray of drinks for the 'gentlemen'.

Beer was consumed in half-pint mugs with handles. Drinking beer in pints was regarded as a habit of the lower orders. Halves had the advantage that buying rounds was much easier. When four people are playing snooker doubles, they can each buy a round of drinks consisting of halves with little effect - and of course beer in those days had a lower alcohol content than the modern student drinks.

The union building contained a hall known as MDH - Men's Debating Hall - This was used on Wednesday afternoons by amateur student jazz groups. It was also used for entertainment. I remember one St. David's day going to see Harry Secombe, one of the stars of the radio comedy series, The Goon Show. I know it was St David's Day because Secombe started his act by eating some daffodils. The Goons were first broadcast in 1951 with Secombe playing the character, Neddie Seagoon. It became an instant success with many including Prince Charles. To others, it was just silly. I liked its surrealist humour and even bought a record of a Goon song, 'I'm walking Backwards for Christmas' and think I can remember the words –

> I'm walking backwards for Christmas,
> Across the Irish Sea,
> I'm walking backwards for Christmas,
> It's the only thing for me.
> I've tried walking sideways,
> And walking to the front,
> But people just laugh at me,
> And say, "it's a publicity stunt!".
> I'm walking backwards for Christmas,
> To prove that I love you.

This was released by Decca and reached the charts in England but failed in America. It was not until Monty Python that British surrealist humour caught on in parts of America.

On some days, as an alternative to Caf and the Students' Union, I took myself off to the Arts library as a means of escape from practicals. The 1930s depression had seen some money for new buildings (in the same way that some American universities have 'New Deal' buildings from the 1930s). The original Christie library became the science library and a new arts library appeared. Also, the Arts faculty had acquired a new building. This had an impressive front leading into a hall that contained a Jacob Epstein bust of Samuel Alexander, Manchester's first professor of philosophy. Both the Arts building and the library gave the impression that they had not been finished and it was not until the expansion program of the 1960s that they were considerably enlarged.

Back in the 1950s, science books and journals remained in the Christie and arts literature was crammed into the unfinished new library which had some small rooms, known as 'the stacks'. One of these was devoted to philosophy and I decided to explore these books. I already knew a little as described in an earlier section. Joad, Russell and needed some company. Amongst the books in the philosophy room I discovered a book with an intriguing title, The Nature of Existence vol 1. (Published in 1921 by Cambridge U. P.) Could this be the secret I had been looking for?

It turned out to be a very odd attempt to show that matter and time were not what we thought they were. I did not understand the argument but I remembered the name of its author for future use so that when I met an Arts student in Caf I could contribute to a philosophical discussion. "What do you think of McTaggart?" was a question designed to baffle anyone who thought that chemistry students were ignorant of non-scientific matters. Fortunately, I never met anyone who had heard of McTaggart. One philosophy student claimed that I was joking and assured me that there had never been a philosopher called McTaggart, which is sad because John McTaggart did exist and was a Fellow of Trinity College, Cambridge. Being a philosopher, McTaggart allowed himself to get carried away by use of logic. This led him to an intriguing slant on orthodox Christianity. If God is omnipotent, he could have created us with better nature and nurture so that we did not sin. In which case we should not have to apologise to God for our sins; they are his fault for allowing them to happen. (The standard response involves free will but after that too much logic creates chaos)

Through Paul Freeman and another chemistry student, Mike Hall, I was able to meet many non-chemists and I was curious about what was taught in other subjects. For example I found out that first year economics was easier than school sixth form physical chemistry. They both use the pattern of dynamic equilibrium but chemical equilibria have to correspond to reality whilst economic equilibria seem to live in a theoretical no man's land where there are more exceptions than patterns with predictive power.

Being curious about other subjects led me to some interesting areas. I remember talking to someone who had just taken an exam in the philosophy of education as part of the one-year post graduate certificate in education, taken by graduates intending to work as school teachers. I was able to look at his exam question paper and I partly remember one of the questions, something like "Contrast the educational philosophies of Plato and Rousseau as given in The Republic and in Emile."

I had heard of Plato but I was only vaguely aware that Rousseau had gone on about 'the noble savage' so I went to the library to find out about Emile. It turned out that the book was part fiction - an account of the upbringing of the eponymous Emile - and partly Rousseau's educational ideas. The one bit that I remember (or perhaps remember remembering) concerned the idea that normal education taught children to lie. Adults tell a child not to do something. The child does it anyway and then tells lies to avoid punishment.

Rousseau's way round this was original if extremely impractical. Emile is told not to go outside the garden gate; so of course he does go outside. Waiting for Emile is a gang of ruffians paid to scare the wits out of Emile without hurting him. Emile dashes back inside the house and says to his father something like, "You were right. I should not go outside the gate".

In modern terms, this approach to controlling the population might be described as nudging and could be contrasted with Plato's society where everyone has his or her place and education is training for a pre ordained role. In Plato's republic, the only people allowed to do any serious thinking are philosophers, which is why of course Plato has remained popular with philosophers for 2,000 years.

Another focus for curiosity was Eng. Lit. How could English students do a degree in English? My cousin Elizabeth Maslen became a Professor of English at London's Queen Mary College where she taught courses on twentieth-century literature. She could have told me about teaching English literature but in her mind people seemed divided into different categories. I was clearly in a box marked 'family' and you don't do academic talk with family. So I had to rely on Caf where I did meet an Eng. Lit student who gave me a copy of Way of All Flesh. This was a set book and students might have to write essays about it.

I could see two reasons why this book might be singled out for discussion. One was its evolutionary background. The book starts not with the birth of its hero, Ernest, but with his grandparents. The second reason for this book being notable was its concentration on what Ernest was thinking rather than on what happened to him. He became a Church of England curate but due to a stupid mistake he gets stuck in prison. Now, you might expect that having a curate in prison would be some kind of unpleasant adventure. But Butler tells us about Ernest's thoughts during his time in prison where he loses his religious enthusiasm.

Much later on I became interested in Butler's other writings. He understood the implication of Darwin' s ideas and tried to find ways round them. I never got round to +finishing The Way of All Flesh and I discovered that Butler's own life was more interesting than the life of the fictional Ernest.

Sam Butler opened up a sheep farm in New Zealand and when it became clear that sheep farming could be very profitable, he sold the farm for a large sum and returned to England where he spent the mornings in the reading room of the British Library and then off to the pub. The desk that he used in the library was near to the one used by Karl Marx when writing Das Capital.

Back in Caf, the conversation sometimes turned to music and one day I was asked who my favourite composer was. I replied 'Vivaldi'. In those days, Vivaldi was just being rediscovered. I only knew about him from a series of concerts on the BBC's Third Program and when the questioner said, "Oh, The Four Seasons?" I could reply that I preferred the concerti - a piece of one-upmanship.

Motivated by more musical one-upmanship I decided that I must find out about Sibelius' fourth symphony. Many people were aware of his second and fifth symphonies but his fourth was not played. So I purchased a record of the symphony and played it. Just noise! It seemed obvious why it was not popular. However I persevered in listening to it until I could actually whistle the various themes. This provided an example of what many years later, I would call pattern construction. Humans are very good at pattern recognition. Patterns may be musical themes, faces, scientific theories or whatever but recognition is re-cognition that is re-knowing something that we had to learn in the first place. So how do we construct the patterns so that later we can re construct them?

Repetition is one obvious answer. Playing the fourth symphony over and over turned 'noise' into tunes that could be whistled.

Sam Butler was interested in repetition. He thought about the violinist playing a sonata apparently without conscious effort - the result of much repetitive practice. Butler then extended this pattern of thought into thinking about the evolution of different organs and he came up with the interesting idea that the degree of conscious control over parts of our bodies depended on how long they had been evolving. In evolutionary terms, hearts came before lungs - fish have one but not the other. Hearts do their own thing; they are not under conscious control but lungs can be controlled if needed though most of the time they also do their own thing. Butler compared this to musicians who reduce their conscious effort after much practice.

By far the most important result of meeting people in Caf was getting to know a medical student, Jeanne. We were an item for three years. She came from Horwich, a Lancashire town originally devoted to textiles but then growing with the advent of a railway works. The first mills had been water powered using the streams that poured down from the westward spur of the Pennine hills. The tallest hill is Rivington Pike where in 1927 my father had gone to witness a total eclipse of the sun. The Pike looks down on a stretch of land developed by Lord Leverhulme who had restored an ancient tithe barn attached to Rivington Hall.

In the 1930s depression Leverhulme had used some of the unemployed to construct terraced gardens on the slopes of the Pike. During university vacations, Jeanne lived at home and we went for walks in the area.

By the 1950s the gardens were almost gone but still known as the Chinese Garde. The barn had acquired new owners and was used for concerts and parties. Jeanne and I with friends celebrated our 21st birthday at a jazz dance in the tithe barn (these days it is called Rivington Hall Barn and nearly 60 years after my 21st I went there for the wedding celebration of one of my brothers grandsons.)

In her first year at university Jeanne lived in St Gabriel's Hall, founded in 1920 by the Sisters of the Cross and Passion. In the 1950s some families still hesitated before allowing their daughters to leave home before marriage. Teacher training colleges for women tended to be out in the countryside, away from any unseemly nightlife. The nuns zealously guarded the young women residents of 'Gabs'. Comings and goings were supervised and a tall wall surrounded the hall. After her first year she moved out of hall into a shared house.

Jeanne and I continued to meet in Horwich and in Manchester and I continued to devour books from various libraries. I don't remember how I came across An Experiment with Time, by J W Dunne (1875–1949). Originally published in1927, it went through various editions and was being talked about in the 1950s. Dunne claimed that when asleep, the mind was freed from being trapped in the 'now' of the body. It could wander into the past - down memory lane - but it could also travel into the future. The results of its travels were expressed in the brain as dreams.

To test his ideas, Dunne persuaded his friends to keep a record of their dreams. Some claimed that they did not dream but they discovered that keeping a pencil and paper by their bed and writing down their thoughts on first waking up showed that they had been dreaming. Apparently most dreams are forgotten within a few minutes of waking unless they are actively re-membered.

I decided to try out Dunne's experiment and I kept a record of my dreams for a few weeks. One of these involved sitting at a table having coffee with Jeanne and two of her friends. Nothing very unusual about that BUT the place was not Caf; it was somewhere strange. Two weeks later, Jeanne decided to go for a swim at the McDougal Centre. In addition to being the place that I knew from the TA, the McDougal housed a swimming pool and gym plus a café. I went to meet her after the swim and we had coffee with some friends - just as it had been in the recorded dream. This is probably an example of seeing what you are looking for but it has stuck in my memory. Another aspect of Dunne's book that has stuck is his strange ideas about time. As those cosmologists with a sense of humour, Lewis and Barnes (2016), put it,

"The nature of time has puzzled many people for a long ... uh ... time". Things pass at a speed or time passes slowly so we need a sort of meta time to measure how fast time is passing. This causes problems and Dunne took this timing of time to an infinite regress ending with something that sounded like God.

Through Jeanne I was able to catch a glimpse of life as a medical student. The dissection room was fascinating;

rows of bodies in various stages of disassembly, the smell of formaldehyde, white coated figures digging into the bodies and looking at notes for comparison with what they could see. What remained of flesh was grey coloured so that the bodies seemed to be non-human - more like leather dummies. This may have had the result that some of those students became medics who saw patients as symptoms rather than people.

The students all had their own human skeleton and they had to learn the names of every bone in the body. As there are 206 bones in adults this took some doing. Apparently infants have more bones than adults - some of them fuse together during development.

One memorable occasion was a visiting lecture on family planning, given in the Medical School by Marie Stopes who was famous for her advocacy of birth control and her book Married Love. She was also known in Manchester for being the first woman lecturer in the Faculty of Science. She had left Manchester to open a family planning clinic in North London. This offered a free service to married women. Stopes was particularly concerned with less affluent women. Too many children and not enough money caused misery for some. She was attacked by sections of the medical establishment as well as the churches but she defended herself. She gained publicity by chaining a copy of her second book, Wise Parenthood, to the altar rails in Westminster Cathedral.

Some of the male medical students were quite appalling in their attitude to Stopes' visit. They seemed to think that a woman giving a lecture on family planning was a huge joke. One of her concerns was with the use of spermicides. She claimed that these contained cumulative poisons such as mercury that could be absorbed into the body. She phrased this as, "Don't put things in the vagina that you would not put in your mouth". This, of course, produced roars of laughter.

The contraceptive pill was still in the future and Stopes advised the use of what was known as the Dutch cap. However, this was not very reliable. The annual report of the Sheffield Family Planning Clinic in 1961 claimed that the cap had reliable results with women who had been married for some years but was less so with the newly married. The failure of contraception is an example of causation by 'stopping the stoppage'. Something happens because whatever had been stopping it from happening has itself been stopped. I was the result of the failure of a spermicide - Volpar Gels - and my lovely twin daughters were the result of the failure of the cap.

Another memorable lecture that I attended was the annual public lecture by the Beyer Professor of Zoology, H Graham Cannon. He was one of the last reputable zoologists to come out openly in favour of Lamarck. His research interests were in experimental embryology and functional morphology, which is relevant because embryologists might be justified in believing that too much attention goes to genetics. Way back in 1957, I heard him present his annual lecture on the topic of Lamarck was right.

Cannon was not alone in having an unusual version of evolution. Manchester's Professor of Anatomy, F Wood Jones, had a theory that the universe was purposeful. His ideas anticipated what became known as the Goldilocks theory - the universe was 'just right'. Wood Jones was also known for his Arboreal Man theory that the ancestors of Homo sapiens were upright tree dwellers. Both Wood Jones and Cannon were Fellows of the Royal Society, meaning that their scientific work was highly regarded.

Cannon started his lecture by claiming that there was something odd about the legs and necks of giraffes having both been elongated to the same length. This was presented as an example of coordination that could not be explained by the principle of accidental changes. At that time I knew next to nothing about evolutionary theory but I did know a few things about probability and I could not understand Cannon's problem. It seemed to me that if you produced a large number of random changes in giraffes, most of them would lead to disaster. After a long time, the only giraffes left would be those that 'worked'. (I had by then picked up the notion of pragmatism as 'truth is what works'.)

Having legs and neck the same length 'works' because it enables the giraffe to drink without having to kneel, leaving its powerful legs free to fend off any attacking lion. As a small boy, standing next to giraffes in Manchester's Belle Vue Zoo or in London's Regent's Zoo, I had marvelled at the size and power of those enormous legs.

The other thing that I picked up from Cannon's lecture was an analogy with Le Chatelier's principle, which concerns chemical solutions reacting to change in such a way as to minimise the effect of that change. Cannon seemed to be suggesting that living organisms also had the power to resist changes in their environment in a way that powered evolution. I later discovered that this idea had been developed by Cannon's American namesake, Walter Bradford Cannon, who called it Homeostasis. I did not follow this but then I might have been more interested in Jeanne who had invited me to the lecture.

One summer I was invited by Jeanne's family to go with them on a camping holiday in France. Jeanne, her two younger sisters and her parents made six people with me and we all went to France in Mr Wright's Ford Consul. It had two bench seats; so three of us sat at the front and three at the back. The Wright family slept together in one tent and I had a very small tent to myself. We visited the usual tourist spots in Paris and the Rhone valley. Some of these I had visited before on a school cycling holiday, staying at Auberge De Jeunesse.

I was particularly impressed by the Pont du the three-tiered Roman aqueduct. In those days, it was still being used to carry road traffic across the river. It just seemed amazing that something built to carry water to Nimes some two thousand years ago still had enough strength to carry a Ford car. We went swimming down stream in the river where the view of the aqueduct from below was even more impressive.

Another memorable tourist attraction was a Son et Lumiere display at the Popes Palace in Avignon. There is something rather special about the evening air in Provence - as long as you avoid the mosquitos. And when you add lights moving round a 14th century gothic palace accompanied by a commentary from loud speakers, you have an almost surreal experience.

The final part of our French expedition was spent staying with the family of a French girl who had been an exchange partner with Jeanne. When still at school, they had both stayed in each other's homes and they had remained friends. Fortunately, the French family lived in a large house with enough room for the six of us. The house was at the end of a valley in a small village, centred round a square with a pump used by some of the villagers for their water supply.

The bedrooms were equipped with bowls and jugs of water used for washing and shaving. The used water was thrown out of the window into a gutter in the street below. During the wartime occupation, German soldiers had only visited the village on two occasions when they were looking for escaped Brits. Apparently, the French underground had organised routes via the Pyrenees into Spain to enable British airmen and escaped prisoners of war to get out of France - but not by this valley.

6.4 Finals

Back in Manchester I went into my third year culminating with 'Finals', six examination papers that determined what class of degree was awarded. Between each exam spread over two weeks, I revised in the reading room of Manchester's Reference Library. This was situated at the top of the building under an impressive dome that magnified sound. Even turning over the page of a book produced a sound that bounced back from the roof. This meant that library silence was kept, providing an atmosphere conducive to study.

When this got oppressive, I would escape to the basement of the building. In addition to the Library Theatre the basement held a café and in those days smoking was allowed. The café was used by students including sixth form schoolgirls and various attempts at chatting up could be observed but not for me. A coffee, a quick smoke and back to the serious business of trying to get some things hammered into my memory banks.

I had a particular problem with remembering names. Even at primary school, I did not remember the names of the other children. This causes problems with a subject like chemistry, containing thousands of names. In organic chemistry many of the common names have now been systematised by the International Union of Pure and Applied Chemistry, (IUPAC). What I knew as acetic acid (the acid in vinegar) is now known as ethanoic acid with the 'ethan' part of the name telling you that its molecules have two carbon atoms.

The dicarboxylic acids caused me particular problems. They form a whole series of acids with two acid groups per molecule. In those days they all had common names - oxalic acid, malonic, succinic, glutaric acids and many more. I could never remember which was which. Today they have systematic names ethanedioic acid, propanedioic acid, butanedioic acid and so on depending on the number of carbons between the two acids.

Those parts of chemistry that required understanding were easy to remember. Show me a concept that makes sense and I can repeat it when needed. Tell me a name of something or someone and its retrieval seems to be a matter of luck unless it is anchored to something else.

For example, in the 1930s there was an evolutionary theorist, Ronnie Fisher. He was an important person in the so-called modern synthesis, putting selection and mutation together. Not only did I have papers written by him but also I knew one of his granddaughters, Emma Posey, who was a PhD student of mine. She gave me a biography of Fisher written by her aunt. Despite all this, being able to say his name seemed to be a matter of chance until one day it hit me. His initials were RAF; not Ronnie Fisher, but Ronald Aylmer Fisher - RAF. From that day I never forgot his name again.

After finals were over, there was the wait for the results. We were all told to turn up on a certain day. When I arrived I was told that I had been picked out for on oral exam. I sat in this room opposite the external examiner who had a book in front of him. Reading upside down I could see my name in a list underneath a red line. This meant that I was being interviewed to decide which side of the red line represented my destiny. I knew that I had done badly in a couple of papers where memory had let me down. I also knew I had done well in other papers but I had a horrible feeling that the redline suggested I was on the border between a second class degree and a third.

The examiner asked me some chemical questions which happened to be in areas of chemistry that I thought were very boring and I didn't know the answers. He then asked what I was hoping to do. So I told him that I had a place to take the post grad certificate in teaching but this was conditional on my getting at least a two two (later known as 'a Desmond' after Bishop Desmond Tutu). So I was awarded a lower second class honours degree in chemistry. I need not have worried. I later found out that the border had been between the lower and upper divisions of the second class.

After the degree results, much to my surprise, I was told that Professor Gee wanted to see me. Geoffrey Gee was the Professor of Physical Chemistry and head of the chemistry department. He had previously been Director of Research at the British Rubber Producers Research Association and had been working with polymers since the late 1930s at a time when there were still scientists who did not believe that large molecules were possible and before the advent of the thermoplastics that made such an impact after World War II.

Prof Gee offered me a chance to do an MSc. In those days the MSc was a research degree; the idea of 'taught' Masters took time to catch on, though officially they existed as Method 2 in the university regulations. He told me that they had a grant from the Ministry of Supply for one year's work on reaction kinetics, to be supervised by Huw Pritchard. I said what about my degree result; I thought you had to have at least a 2.1. His reply cheered me up. He said that I had obtained very high marks in the physical chemistry paper, that they had not observed any correlation between overall degree performance and research ability and that the 2.1 requirement was needed for a scholarship but I would be paid from the Ministry of Supply grant. So, obviously I said, "thanks very much, yes".

6.5 MSc by Research

Later that year (1956), when I enrolled as a research student, I was given a laboratory notebook engraved in gold letters proclaiming "Department of Physical Chemistry" together with the university crest. Its motto was arduus ad solem - the way to the sun is difficult - and to make the point, it had a sun behind a mountain with a snake in the foreground.

Way back in the 1950s, the English title of Professor was mainly a job title rather than an honour. It signified that someone was head of a university department. Before the expansion in university education, Professors in England were entered in Who's Who? The Chemistry department was slightly unusual in having two departments and therefore two professors. I discovered that at postgraduate level, there was a Department of Physical Chemistry headed by Professor Gee and a Department of Organic Chemistry headed by Professor E R H Jones.

There was not much contact between the two departments. The physical chemists referred to the organicists as 'cooks' and in return the physical chemists were regarded as 'number crunchers'. The divide between physical and organic chemistry was much worse in Germany where according to one chemist of the same age as myself, the professors of physical and organic chemistry at The University of Tübingen, "took pains not to encounter each other".

I don't think that Professors Gee and Jones avoided each other but I do not remember seeing them in the same room together. Jones appeared in the latest organic textbook as the developer of 'the Jones oxidation'. He was poached by Oxford who needed a new chemistry professor and I remember his turning up at the chemistry Christmas party where he told us that he had just returned from Oxford where he had been taken into a room with a chap dressed in robes who read some Latin to him, tapped him on the shoulder and told him that he was now a honorary MA. This was needed because in those days Oxford had not got round to accepting that degrees existed outside Oxford, Cambridge, Trinity College Dublin and the ancient Scottish ones.

Jones was replaced at Manchester by an Australian, Arthur Birch who also had a chemical reaction in the textbooks - 'the Birch reduction', discovered in 1944 when Birch was working in Oxford. Jones went on to become Sir Ewart Jones.

People who thankfully gave up chemistry at school might not be interested in the difference between physical and organic chemistry but this difference resonates with an important difference in the social sciences - the divide between the so-called quantitative and qualitative branches. Both physical chemistry and quantitative social science involve measuring things and measuring involves numbers. Both organic chemistry and qualitative social science involve classification into different kinds of things and finding patterns in how they relate. The difference is not restricted to the presence or absence of numbers. It is more a question of how you view the world.

The physical view, or 'P' for short, rests on a deterministic assumption coupled with a belief in 'consistent causation', that is repeating the causes that determine something will lead to a repeat of the result. The organic or qualitative view of the world is also the view of classical biology; so I use 'B' for short.

The major difference between the two views can be summarised as variety and complexity. The P view aims ultimately for 'a theory of everything'; it doesn't like 'exceptions to the rule'. The B view welcomes diversity. There are more than one hundred species of grass. Even so, the discovery of a new species would be welcomed with interest. Its discoverer would get to name it and botanists would be interested in a new way of surviving and reproducing.

Similarly, an organic chemist is half way to earning a PhD by synthesising a compound not known before. This is not too difficult as the number of possible organic compounds is infinite. (Think of the largest known molecule and then add another methyl group etc. forever.)

The social scientists' use of qualitative and quantitative can be misleading. Numbers alone are not enough to make a P view. That's why we have the apparent paradox of 'numerical qualitative' used to describe the use of numbers in a non-deterministic setting. Organic chemistry, like baking a cake, uses quantities in its recipes. This does not turn it into physical chemistry. There are times when organic chemistry can turn to the techniques of physical chemistry but its use of numbers is still different. Recipe numbers tell you what to do. Deterministic numbers fit into equations with predictive power.

The social science division of research into quantitative and qualitative is partly a product of their ignorance about ideas outside their narrow disciplines. My division of world views into P and B is similar to the ideas of two Austrian economists, writing in the 1930s. Both Mises and Hayek contrasted the physical sciences (e.g. physics) with the natural sciences (e.g. biology and sociology). Writing later (1967), Hayek claimed that the natural sciences deal with complexity and don't aim at "specific predictions of particular events"; they aim to make "pattern predictions". I found myself in the fairly new physical chemistry research building. This was in Brunswick Street, somewhere near where the library extension has now been built. It was a single story building with a long corridor and laboratories leading off. These were rooms with one or two researchers plus a partitioned area used as the office by a member of staff. There was also a glass blowing facility with two glass-blowing technicians who made specialised equipment for researchers. Most of the labs had two benches with an upright metal stand on which was fixed a 'vac line'. This was an individually constructed piece of glassware that could be evacuated i.e. have the air pumped out to make a vacuum.

Three main kinds of pumps existed in the laboratories. Simple water pumps had been known for centuries and most school science labs had several of these attached to cold water taps above sinks. Water from the tap goes through a nozzle with the same effect as pinching the end of a garden hose. As the water rushes through a tube it pulls some air with it and a side tube has air sucked out of it, turning it into a device for pulling air out of whatever container the teacher or pupil wants to be evacuated.

The second kind of pump is a piston pump containing a cylinder with a device for moving a piston up and down inside the cylinder. This kind of device can be used for either pushing as in a steam locomotive or for pulling as in a pump. Again, such devices have been around for centuries. The big change was in the use of electricity to power the moving piston.

The third kind is a mercury diffusion pump in which mercury is heated to produce a flow of vapour that like a water pump, sucks gas though a side tube to produce a vacuum. A so-called vacuum is not, in fact, completely empty. There is always something inside a vacuum such as gas coming from the walls of its container. There needs to be a measure for how much of a vacuum you actually have. Since you can't measure how much nothing you are dealing with, the opposite measure is used, what is the pressure inside the so-called vacuum?

The invention of the barometer enabled pressure to be measured and compared with the air pressure that surrounds us. In a U tube containing a liquid, with air on only one branch of the tube, the air pressure on one branch will support a column of liquid in the other.

If the liquid is water, then a column about 34 feet high can be supported. The actual height varies from day to day and is used to predict changes in the weather. Since a barometer with 34 feet of water (10.3 metres) is obviously impracticable, another liquid was needed and mercury being both liquid and of high density, was the obvious choice.

Air pressure will support a column of mercury that is about 760 mms high, less than three feet. Many English homes used to have an ornate barometer hanging in the hall. These had a mercury column and a clock face that showed the pressure instead of the time. My home in Eccles had one of these and every morning, my father used to tap it, making the pointer move. Pressure going up was supposed to signify better weather and vice versa.

The Italian, Evangelista Torricelli, invented a mercury barometer in 1644 and a unit of pressure is named after him, one torr being the same as one millimeter of mercury i.e. 1/760 of normal air pressure. (A standard atmosphere is defined as 760 mms of mercury)

The research that I found I would be doing required a very low vacuum, that is one that was nearly empty. The remaining pressure in my vacuum line had to be 10^{-5} mms of mercury, (1/100,000 mms or nearly one ten millionth of atmospheric pressure). So, how did one measure such a low pressure and how was it possible to attain it?

Herbert McLeod made the measurement of low pressures possible through the invention of the vacuum gauge in 1874. This is filled with mercury and the pressure can be read visually from a scale. (Today, an electronic device would be used).

The required low pressure was obtained by using two pumps, in series. In the morning, I would switch on a conventional electric pump that would remove any air in the line and then light the Bunsen burner that heated the mercury in the mercury diffusion pump. After waiting a few minutes, the gauge would show 10^{-4} and then the anxious wait to see if it would reach 10^{-5}. If not, there must have been a leak.

In the 1950s, Acts of Parliament regulating Health and Safety lay in the future (apart from individual Acts for factories, mines, railways etc.) and there was an almost macho approach amongst chemists. If the vac line had been left open so that it contained air, then switching on the vacuum pump in the morning sometimes caused a fuse to blow in a box in the corridor. This was because there were many other devices connected to the electrical input and when first switched on, the pump had to struggle to cope until some of the air had been removed. My supervisor climbed a ladder to the box and replaced the fuse with a brass nail. "That'll be OK," he said.

Lack of attention to safety caused more serious problems. One research student, name of Brian Pedley, was washing out a flask in a porcelain sink but he had forgotten that the flask contained sodium wire, used for drying organic solutions. The resultant explosion cracked the sink and Pedley lost two fingers. He still went on to become a Professor of Chemistry at Sussex where he used bomb calorimetry to determine the heats of reaction of metal hydrides, halides and organometallic compounds. These are very reactive substances and extremely susceptible to moisture and air; so great care had to be taken in purification and sampling. His earlier loss of fingers must have been a reminder to be careful.

Down the corridor was Morton Litt, a visiting American post-doc who had a PhD in polymers from the Polytechnic

Institute of Brooklyn. He was probably the first American that I knew and he seemed very strange to the Brits who had never come across a name like that. Sometimes in the afternoon, there would be a bang and Morton would stagger into the corridor with blood and broken glass on his forehead, followed by a cloud of smoke. He had been using a flame to collapse a narrow glass tube, sealing off a sample of an organic compound. This was supposed to be frozen solid by a thermos filled with liquid nitrogen but after lunch, the solid could have started to melt resulting in an explosive vapour trapped in the tube - bang. There were some other more serious accidents that occurred later and for many years a bang would produce a reflex action in my body - heart beating etc.

Physical chemists tend to be people who are fascinated by numbers, including the study of probability. Thinking about probability was historically the domain of gamblers who needed to know the odds for and against events taking place. Documented thoughts on the probability of throwing a pair of dice to give two sixes cropped up in 17th century France.

The American, Morton Litt, followed this tradition through being fascinated by the British Football Pools. In the 1950s most forms of gambling were illegal or tightly controlled. There was no national lottery and no betting shops but every Saturday evening many Brits (including my father) settled in front of their radios to listen to the football results, hoping that their forecasts would make them a small fortune.

Littlewoods football pools had been founded in 1923 by John Moores of Liverpool. The most popular version was the treble chance that required the forecasting of eight matches that would be draws (ties). The cost of a single entry was very low so multiple entries were possible.

For example, you could pick ten matches that looked like draws and cover all possible combinations of eight by entering 45 lines. (Eight from ten is the same as two from ten - the two that are left out - and that is 10 times 9 divided by two because each pair crops up twice.)

In 1957 someone called Nellie McGrail from my present home town of Stockport, made the newspapers by winning over £100,000 (in the days when one thousand pounds was a very good annual salary and you could buy a house for five hundred pounds)

Gambling in the USA was even more restricted than in the UK and Morton Litt decided to study the English football results from the previous year. He claimed to have discovered that matches played between teams in the centre of the league tables had a higher proportion of draws than other matches and he used this idea to select his ten potential draws.

However, he did not win any money. His forecasting method was wrong because of a classic mistake - what I would later call 'confusing a symptom with a cause'. He had used league tables from the end of the season and obviously when all matches have been played, teams in the middle of the table have more draws. If they have more wins they are at the top of the table and if they have more losses they are in the lower half of the table. Being in the centre is a symptom (a result) of having more draws. It is not a predictor (a cause) of future draws.

This is also an example of the failure of causation to be consistent. If you discover some causal pattern from past data, there is no guarantee that this pattern will continue into the future. Physics works by assuming consistent causation but the human world is rarely as simple as physics.

Millions of molecules moving about randomly produce overall patterns and these patterns are consistent. This is the essence of physics and my MSc research topic was an example of what I would later call 'P type' science. Its title was "Some kinetic studies on the thermal decompositions of cyclopropane and cyclobutane". It had a theoretical prediction needing experimental testing.

This prediction was within the general area of reaction kinetics, concerned with the speed at which chemical reactions take place. The more specific area concentrated on what happened at low pressures when the effect of molecules bumping into each other was reduced. Most chemical reactions involve two reactants turning into something else. For example, sodium hydroxide plus hydrochloric acid goes to sodium chloride plus water. Such reactions are known as bimolecular because two molecules are involved. My research involved unimolecular reactions in which one chemical turns into another without any intervention other than energy. This makes them simpler than the normal type of reaction, ideal for P type experiments that like to make things as simple as possible; the fewer the number of variables the easier it is to control the experiment. The experimental aim was to test a prediction made in 1953 by N B Slater (published in The Philosophical Transactions of the Royal Society vol. 246A p 57).

The speed of chemical reactions varies between a very rapid reaction, producing a sudden outburst of gas, affecting the ear as a bang or in extreme cases death, to reactions that are so slow that you don't notice they are happening such as iron slowly rusting, i.e. reacting with oxygen from the air to form iron oxide.

In the case of one particular reaction, its speed normally depends on two factors, the concentration of the reactants (i.e. the pressure in the case of a gaseous reaction) and the temperature. My study kept the temperature constant and examined the effect of pressure on rate. It then kept the pressure constant and looked at the effect of temperature on rate. In most chemical reactions, the speed depends on how often molecules can collide with each other. In a simple A + B bimolecular reaction, molecules of A have to bump into molecules of B. This depends on how much A and B is present (concentration) and how fast they are moving about (temperature). In the case of unimolecular reactions, there is no B molecule for A to bump into.

The unimolecular reaction takes place through the structure of the molecule changing from one form into another (isomerisation). This used to be explained in terms of the chemical bonds that hold the molecule together, being like vibrating springs breaking when the vibrations got too fast. A more modern account would involve electron orbitals and quantum theory but the result is the same. If the molecule gets enough energy, it rearranges itself into a different form, known as an isomer.

Given enough energy, a molecule of cyclopropane turns into a molecule of what used to be called propylene but is now known as propene. Similarly, cyclobutane may turn into butylene (butene). In a unimolecular reaction, the A molecules can acquire energy through bumping into each other but at pressures of nearly 10^{-5} the molecules are moving through almost empty space and have a reduced chance of colliding. This means that the 'vibrating springs' holding the molecule together can be studied in isolation, all the other variables having almost been removed, a classic P type experiment.

Slater's theory, as is usually the case with theories, was an advance on previous theories and involved some rather complicated maths. This caused problems for the professional typist who produced the final version of my thesis. In those days, photocopying and word processors lay in the future. Since four copies of the thesis were needed, carbon paper copies were used. A typing error could not be easily corrected so the page and its carbon copies had to be done again. Imagine trying to produce chemical formulae with subscripts and maths with Greek symbols on an old fashioned manual typewriter. Research students produced hand written versions of their thesis and then had to pay a typist who charged a fee per page with an extra fee for pages of mathematics.

Slater's theory predicted what would happen to the reaction rate at very low pressures. Being able to obtain accurate measurements had proved difficult in the past. Even something apparently simple such as keeping the reaction at a constant temperature was not easy and I had to spend some weeks wrapping glass wool round a two litre Pyrex reaction vessel and adjusting various heating coils to produce a temperature profile that was constant within 0.05 degrees. (Imagine an oven with the same temperature, top, centre and sides and keeping it at that temperature to an accuracy of five hundredths of a degree)

Many branches of science are subject to division of labour between theorists who produce explanations that come with predictive power and experimentalists who find ways to test the theories and this was the case with my MSc, designed to test the predictions of Slater. However it is often the other way round with experimental results demanding a theoretical explanation. For some reason, the theorist gets more credit than the experimentalist. This was the case with Tycho Brahe (1546 -1601) who spent half his life gathering data on the motion of the planets but had to wait for Isaac Newton to see that he had been observing parabolic motion. Watson and Crick famously gained the Nobel prize for their double helix model of DNA but this needed the data gained by Rosalind Franklin who did not share in their Nobel prize.

Slater's prediction concerned the rate of unimolecular reactions at low pressures. The rate of reaction is usually measured as the rate constant, k. When A turns into B, the rate (speed) could be measured as so much B produced in a litre in a minute. The amount of B is proportional to how much A you had to start with. If you start with twice as much A then you get twice as much B. In fact, the amount of B is equal to a constant, k, multiplied by the amount of A.

In practical terms, measuring the speed at which heated cyclopropane turned into propylene meant measuring the amount of propylene you were getting. The more propylene, the faster the reaction. This was where Slater, the theorist needed Huw Pritchard, the experimentalist who was excited by the latest scientific techniques. Several new techniques had emerged from wartime science used in solving practical problems such as getting enough of the right uranium isotope to be able to make a bomb.

To test Slater's theory I had to use three new techniques. Analysis of how much propylene was being produced required the use of a mass spectrometer and an electronic computer. Better results were obtained through using a special form of cyclopropane made from deuterium, a hydrogen isotope with heavier atoms. These three methods had only become possible in a university setting some years after the end of the war in 1945.

The concept of mass spectrometry is fairly simple; making it work had been much more difficult but in 1956 commercial machines were available. My research used a MS2 made by Metropolitan Vickers (Metrovick or just MV). MV were an innovative company situated in nearby Trafford Park and they sold about 120 MS2s between 1948 and the 1960s (A Quayle. Organic Mass Spectrometry vol 22 1987 569 – 585 Recollections of mass spectrometry of the fifties in a UK petroleum laboratory)

There are three main parts to a mass spectrometer, a basher, a spreader and a catcher.
The molecules of a substance are bashed by charged particles and turned into several fragments. The basher is known as an ioniser because the resultant fragments are ions.
These ions are then spread out by being passed through magnetic and electronic fields resulting in a spectrum of charged particles. The amount of separation depends on the mass of the particles. Lighter ones travel further and heavier ones are deflected sooner, producing a spectrum of mass; similar to a rainbow that is a spectrum of light frequency. Having spread out the particles you then need a method of catching them and measuring the quantities of the different masses.

In the 1930s the first spectrometers used a photographic plate as detector. The fact that charged particles have an affect on a photographic plate was first noticed in 1896 when it was not known that particles were involved so the agent responsible for the blackening of a photographic plate was given the name of X rays. That did not sound very scientific and serious people called them cathode rays before J J Thompson showed that they were charged particles called electrons. Medical uses for X rays were found before people knew what the rays were. In other words, use came before understanding and X rays are not 'applied science' because the so-called application came before the science.

The first use of mass spectrometry was in separating elements into their constituent isotopes. The gas, neon, is an element but its atoms exist in at least two forms with different mass. MS was used to separate out the stable isotopes, ^{20}Ne (neon with 10 protons and 10 neutrons) and ^{22}Ne (neon with 10 protons and 12 neutrons). Mass spectrometers were used in the Manhattan Project for the separation of isotopes of uranium in the creation of the atomic bomb.

Mass spectrometry was first developed commercially as an analytic device. Westinghouse sales literature for its mass spectrometer proclaimed it to be "A New Electronic Method for fast, accurate gas analysis". To do this required an efficient way of measuring the quantities of the different ionic fragments. The photographic plates used in early work were replaced by an induction device. Charged particles induce a current in a metallic coil. The strength of this current measured by an ammeter gives an indication of the quantities of the different masses. This meant that in practice I fed a sample into a MS2 spectrometer from Metrovicks in Trafford Park, adjusted a dial that gave the mass and then read a number indicated by the swinging arrow of an ammeter. The process was then repeated for a different part of the spectrum. The numbers were converted into holes in a punched tape that was kept in a tin the size of a pipe tobacco container. The tape was then taken for processing by the University's computer housed in a building next to the Physics Department.

Slater's prediction tuned out to be correct and the results were published in the Journal of Physical Chemistry. (J. Langrish and H.O. Pritchard. 1957) as "The Thermal Isomerisation of Cyclopropane". In those days before the arrival of photocopying, extra copies of published papers were printed. New papers could be discovered by consulting Current Chemical Papers or Chemical Abstracts. Researchers then sent postcards to the authors of new papers requesting copies. My paper obtained fifty four such cards from around the world. My MSc thesis required diagrams of the apparatus. Jeanne produced these for me. Examiners approved the thesis and I attended a graduation ceremony in December 1957.

6.6 Roman Catholicism

Friendship with Jeanne resulted in my considering becoming a Roman Catholic. I had first discovered that there were people called Catholics when I was little. I had asked my mother what they were. I remember her taking a deep breath - she had not expected this one - and coming up with an answer that was so odd it stuck in my mind. She said that Catholics were different because they did not keep the commandment that was against idol worship and said, "thou shalt not bow down before them". (The words as given in Exodus 20 are "You shall not make for yourself an image in the form of anything in heaven above or on the earth beneath or in the waters below. You shall not bow down to them or worship them."). Apparently, these Catholics did not know this because their churches had people kneeling before statues of saints.

My mother had some experience of the importance of not 'bowing down". She had married my father in secret but had wanted a church wedding. If their marriage had been in the Church of England then for three weeks, the imminent wedding would have been announced in church. To avoid this publicity they got married in the Eccles Reformed Church of England. This was a church founded by some wealthy dissident members of Eccles Parish Church when that church had installed a reredos behind its altar. Since this was decorated with images of Mathew, Mark, Luke and John it meant that people kneeling at the altar to receive communion would be bowing down in front of images as forbidden by the commandment. Therefore, the dissidents had felt it necessary to build a new church without a reredos and in so doing they provided the opportunity for my mother to have a secret wedding.

This can be seen as an example of contingency in historical causation. Otherwise known as the minimalist view, it goes like this –

If something happens, it happens.
If it makes something else happen,
Then something else happens.

Whilst I was still at school, I learnt a little more about Catholicism. No.21, Ellesmere Avenue acquired a new family, the Nagles, who were Roman Catholics. Living with them was Mrs Read, the mother of Mrs Nagle. Mrs Read was bedfast and consumed a lot of library books. She got into a little trouble with the library because she kept writing in their books. Whenever the word 'Catholic' appeared on its own in a book she would write Roman in front of it. That was because she had been brought up in the catholic wing of the Church of England, the high church Anglicans who believed that they were part of the universal Catholic Church but not accepting that the Bishop of Rome had some special authority. So Mrs Reed was catholic but not Roman Catholic hence her objection to library books that confused the two.

I was always attracted by unusual arguments and I was fascinated by the idea that the Church of England was the true Catholic Church in England and the Romans were usurpers. So I got to know about the Oxford movement and the Tractarians. I also found out a little about Henry VIII and discovered that the idea that he was some kind of protestant was just plain silly.

Henry provided the opportunity for a good argument. Someone suggesting that of course Henry VIII was a protestant could be shown a coin out of my pocket. English coins have the letters F D after the name of the sovereign. They stand for Defender of the Faith a title given to Henry and his successors by the Bishop of Rome. He earned this for writing an attack on Protestantism. Once you started to doubt the authority of the church the next step would be doubting the authority of the king and that most definitely would not do. Henry was a catholic who had fallen out with Rome. It also was not true that he wanted a divorce. He wanted a declaration that he had never been married in the first place because his bride had been the widow of his brother and "Thou shalt not marry your brother's wife" was one of those restrictions in church law.

To begin with, I had no objection to becoming Roman in order to marry Jeanne. I saw an advert in a newspaper that promised twelve weekly pamphlets on being a Catholic to be sent by post in 'a plain brown envelope'. These were produced by the Catholic Truth Society (CTS) and Mrs Read would have scribbled all over them. The CTS approach seemed quite reasonable to me except for the section on contraception which was stated to be against something called 'Natural Law'. This seemed to mean contraception wasn't natural but then knives and forks and clothes aren't natural. It could be claimed that the whole of civilisation was about doing better than nature.

I had a long chat with Jeanne's mother, Mrs Wright. She claimed that they didn't accept the infallibility of the Pope. They thought he was just a good man. I got the impression that having produced three girls and a son, they had decided it was time to ignore the ban on contraception. I suspect that in the late 1950s many Catholics in England expected the Church to relax its ban on contraception. (With the arrival of Pope Paul VI in 1963, it seemed that things might change - the vernacular mass - what next. BUT in 1968 the supposedly modern Pope reconfirmed that contraception was a mortal sin.) The mental problems of young Catholics from the 1950s to the 1970s are described in How Far Can You Go? (1980) A novel by David Lodge. (Published as Souls and Bodies in the United States). If you thought that this was just history then take note that in the present century it was still necessary to publish a serious book, How Far Can We Go? A Catholic Guide to Sex and Dating. 2011. By Brett Salkeld and Leah Perrault. Paulist Press.)

Back in 1955, Mrs Wright tried to tell me about catholic practices. She thought that as a protestant I would be uneasy with what went on in catholic churches. I tried to explain that the C of E was not simply a protestant church and I told her about a Manchester church, St Benedict's, that had a sign outside giving times of mass, stations of the cross on the inside and a red lamp signifying the reserved sacrament. This church was part of the Church of England but was most definitely not a protestant church. I think this puzzled her but it didn't matter because I had arranged to meet their parish priest.

When I met the priest to discuss being received into his church, he explained that the first step was baptism. This threw me and I protested that I had already been baptised and somewhere there was a certificate to prove it. He said it was called conditional baptism and was just to make sure I had been properly done. I said that the church claimed that anyone could carry out a baptism. If a baby in hospital seemed in danger of dying then a nurse could baptise the baby. The priest quite reasonably pointed out that I was not a baby and was not in danger of dying. The next step after baptism would be confirmation and that needed a certificate of baptism - hence I had to be baptised even though conditionally.

I thought "No way. This would be a betrayal of my upbringing. My mother, Sunday school teachers and vicars had made sure that I was a Christian. I was not going to be baptised again." So I told the priest I would think about it.

Back in the 1950s the Roman church was very rigid in its attitude to other Christian churches. Pope Pius XII was not for change. He had excommunicated members of the communist party and he also excommunicated a bishop who had advocated the vernacular mass and relaxation of the ban on contraception. If you were a Roman Catholic in England, you were not allowed to attend other churches services. This meant that if your mother had been a non-Catholic, you would need special permission from a bishop in order to attend her funeral.

I began to feel that the poor old Church of England needed some defence and I began to read about church history. I discovered that when Henry's daughter, Mary, became Queen she restored relations with the Pope who sent a legate, Cardinal Pole, to supervise the return of England to the Roman flock. The Archbishop of Canterbury, Thomas Cranmer refused to cooperate and ended up being burnt at the stake. Pole then replaced him as Archbishop. Six new bishops were appointed and those clergy who would not accept the authority of the Pope were disposed of BUT - and it was a big but - priests who had been appointed during Henry's break with Rome were not re-ordained. No one baptised in Henry's time had to be re-baptised. In other words, Cardinal Pole accepted that Henry's Church of England had still been part of the Catholic Church. If it had been OK to be baptised after Henry broke with Rome, then why was it not OK for me to be baptised in the modern C of E?

I discovered a few more items of interest. There had been a bishop of Rome who did not want to be Pope. He claimed that you could not be more bishop than a bishop. Also at one time there had been three people all claiming to be Pope - one in Rome, one in France (at Avignon, the home of that superb Rhone wine, Palais des Papes) and a compromise one in Scotland. The idea that the Pope could be infallible when declaring a doctrine had only been established in the reign of Queen Victoria. When this happened, some bishops in Europe had objected and had taken their followers away from Rome, forming the Union of Old Catholic Churches. These bishops recognised the Church of England as being part of the Catholic Church and participated in the consecration of Anglican bishops.

Armed with these arguments, I had an interview with a priest from the Holy Name, a magnificent church built and looked after by the Jesuits and situated almost opposite the Student Union building. The Holy Name is another example of something happening for one reason but now being useful for a different reason. It was built to provide for the needs of a large immigrant Irish population who emigrated to Manchester and lived in rows of terraced houses. The houses are gone, replaced mainly by university buildings and the church is now officially part of the Catholic Chaplaincy to the university. It was originally hoped that the Holy Name would be the Catholic Cathedral for Manchester but when England allowed the restoration of the Roman hierarchy, the deal was 'no two bishops in the same city'. So the Romans got a bishop of Salford instead. Liverpool is the only place in England with both an Anglican and a Roman Catholic cathedral but that is because the Romans have an archbishop of Liverpool so there is still only one bishop of Liverpool.

The priest was not very helpful but in the church itself I discovered a pamphlet headed "The Validity of Anglican Orders". This addressed the question of whether Anglican priests were 'proper' priests or not. Being written by Jesuits, regarded as the brains of the church, I expected a good argument against my Cardinal Pole position but was surprised by the cunning way that it was avoided. The pamphlet started with the statement that the Church of England was founded by Queen Elizabeth. What Cardinal Pole did or did not do became irrelevant. The main argument that Anglican orders were valid then became a matter of the apostolic succession. This held that true priests had been ordained by bishops through the laying on of hands and these bishops had been made bishops by laying on of hands going back to the original apostles.

The pamphlet seemed to agree that the succession and the words used in the Anglican ceremony were probably satisfactory so what was wrong? It turned out to be something to do with intent. The bishops did not have the correct intention. At that time I did not understand what this meant but many years later I came across an example of intentionality that did make sense.

There was a member of the Reform Club that I knew and I followed with interest his efforts to obtain an annulment. He was divorced but in the eyes of the church he was still married to his ex wife. "What God has joined together let no man put asunder." The way out of this was for the church to declare that God had NOT joined them together in the first place. This is known as an annulment and one way of obtaining this is through a demonstration of wrong intention.

His ex wife signed a document in which she stated in effect that she had crossed her fingers behind her back when making the marriage vows, She had no intention of having children and she had not become a mother. After about four years he managed to obtain an annulment. In a similar argument, bishops making a priest do not have the intention of making the sort of priest that the Roman church wants. Their priests have the power to change the essence of bread and wine into the true body and blood of Christ. Bishops ordaining an Anglican priest are unlikely to believe in transubstantiation as it's called and so they have the wrong intention.

This all seems very silly but I still had to be baptised if I wanted to marry Jeanne. The problem was solved by her being pursued by the son of the leading Professor of medicine. Her medical student friends all persuaded her that the son of a medical prof was a much more suitable boyfriend than a chemist from Eccles. So after three years together we parted. But before then Jeanne did the diagrams for my Master's thesis that was approved by examiners in 1957. This takes us back to the chemistry department.

6.7 Polymer research

December 1957 was a turning point in my life. The three year relationship with Jeanne came to an end when she moved up the status ladder by becoming the girlfriend of the son of a senior medical professor. My MSc thesis with diagrams drawn for me by Jeanne had been approved in time for me to attend the December degree ceremony in the Whitworth Hall. The results of my research had been written up as a paper that was to be published in the Journal of Physical Chemistry. What was I to do next?

I had already decided that theoretical research into the speed of chemical reactions was a bit of a time waster. If people needed to know how quickly chemicals A and B turned in to chemical C, they could just measure it. Of course, one could be curious about how it was that A and B turned into C; just what was going on when that reaction happened? I was not very curious about what was happening when cyclopropane turned itself into propylene. If you banged it, the atoms in the molecule rearranged themselves into a different form.

However, in the next room in the physical chemistry block there was something that was worth being curious about. Down the corridor from Huw Pritchard's domain was the home of Dick Colclough (pronounced coll-kley) who had a vacancy for a PhD student. He was looking at stereo specific polymerisation and this was very curious. In effect, 'stereo specific' means that there is a catalyst system that can tell the difference between right and left handed gloves and then tie all the right handed ones together in a line and all the left handed ones in another line. The catalyst systems being studied were organo metallic compounds with names like ferric butoxide. In the human body, the catalysts known as enzymes are also organo metallic compounds.

In the 1950s, polymers were exciting. They were leading to new plastics, synthetic fibres, paints, adhesives and so on. This meant there were jobs in industry for polymer scientists. Stereo specific polymers were particularly exciting. 1957 saw the introduction of a new plastic by the Italian firm Montecatini. This was polypropylene using a catalyst system discovered by G Natta who was awarded a Nobel Prize in 1963. The polypropylene oxide molecule has a methyl side chain and the special properties of Natta's polypropylene are due to the methyl groups all being on the same side of the polymer chain. Commercial polypropylene is the product of a stereo specific polymerisation.

So there were two good reasons for grabbing the chance to work for Dick Colclough; the possibility of its leading to a job in industry and the fact that it was intellectually exciting were both good reasons. My MSc entitled me to qualify for a research student grant from Lancashire County Council but this source of money was means tested. As I was still aged under 25, the student grant was reduced on a sliding scale dependant on my father's income. This meant that I needed another source of income. It seems appropriate at this point to insert an account of my part time earnings.

6.8 Part time earnings

As described in an earlier section as soon as I was old enough, I worked on the Christmas post and then in the summer I delivered milk from the Co-op dairy. Through the sixth form and on to university I continued to work on the Christmas post and I had a variety of summer jobs.

These included working for Swinton Parks Department as a garden labourer. One year I spent a fortnight in charge of a bowling green. This involved using a long flexible bamboo pole to remove the worm casts that had appeared overnight. Then I had to use a large wire brush to remove leaves and to align the grass leaves. The grass was then mowed.

When people arrived wanting to play bowls, I charged them the fee and gave out tickets from a device similar to that used by bus conductors. A side handle was rotated producing the ticket and the total money received was added up at the end of the day. In the afternoons there were various jobs such as sweeping the paths and hedge cutting with a hand powered-trimmer - there was no electricity at the bowling green. When it got dark, the green was closed.

My most interesting summer job was being a ward orderly in Eccles and Patricroft Hospital, a small hospital subsequently demolished as being a remnant of the past.

In the 1950s the National Health Service was only ten years old and still resembled its pre war organisation. 'Eccles and Pat did not have the team of administrators characteristic of hospitals today. A local accountant came to the hospital twice a week to sort out the money and the hospital organisation seemed to be carried out by the matron, the chief medical officer and the ward sisters.

The original cottage hospital had been opened in 1883. It had a south facing iron veranda where patients used to be wheeled out to get some 'fresh air'. Though, south facing meant facing Trafford Park industrial estate, which in those days emitted noxious chemicals and smoke.

The male surgical ward had about twenty beds with occupants mainly for routine operations - varicose veins, haemorrhoids, hernias etc. In addition, the hospital had an accident and emergency section with some men needing admission to the surgical ward. I saw a number of motorbike accident cases with head damage and I resolved that if I ever had a son, he would not be allowed to ride a motorbike. Crash helmets were rare in the 1950s.

I also remember some suicide attempts involving large quantities of Aspirin tablets. After the stomach pump, two of us had to walk them up and down to keep them awake. Going to sleep could be fatal. On one occasion, the night staff had kept someone awake for a few hours then put him in a bed for the day staff to take over. When we got to him it was too late. The ward sister was furious. "They just kept him alive so they wouldn't have the trouble of sorting out a death. They knew he wouldn't survive 75 aspirins."

The senior ward sister had a smiling pretty face that hid a ruthless interior. One morning we had been giving bed baths to men recovering from operations. After we had finished I was surprised by her saying, "I've seen enough willies today. My husband will have to hold his own tonight."

Thursday was tonsils day. About six frightened children were stuck in a small side ward and put in bed. No parents were allowed in. In the 1950s parents were people who got in the way. The children were injected with a sedative and turned into an assembly line with beds lined in the corridor leading to the operating theatre. They were anaesthetised by the old method of gauze and ether and moved one at a time onto the operating table where it was my job to hold their heads whilst the surgeon used what looked like a miniature guillotine to extract the tonsil. I then tipped their heads to one side to allow blood to escape. Whilst the next child was replacing them it was my job to apply a mop and bucket to move blood from the floor.

With my student grant reduced by means testing, I needed more money and this came from private tutoring and lecturing in an evening class. In the 1950s, ten year old children in state schools took an exam, known as the eleven plus. It was supposed to assess children to find the most appropriate type of school for their secondary education. There were supposed to be three types of school in every area - grammar, technical and modern. In practice it became seen as an entry test for the grammar schools and people thought that their children either passed or failed the eleven plus. This produced a lot of anxious parents, some of whom decided to spend money on tutors who claimed to help children to pass the exam. I was well placed to meet this demand.

My father got hold of past exam papers and the marking system that produced a standardised score i.e. the mark for a test divided by the average mark for children of the same age. There were three papers, arithmetic, English and the so called intelligence test, also known as reasoning. A combined score of 120 would gain entry into a Grammar school in most places but there was considerable variation between different towns and the numbers of potential pupils also varied with the year, depending on the birth rate.

These tests had been used everywhere in England since the Education Act of 1944 established Grammar Schools. At first the organisers were puzzled by the fact that on average girls did better than boys. You couldn't have more girls than boys going to the Grammar School, so they were assessed separately. The higher scores of girls were explained as 'earlier development'.

The tests were supposed to test 'innate ability' and not the skill of teachers. You were not supposed to be able to teach intelligence. In fact, familiarity with the type of test made a noticeable difference. My friend John Larkin still remembers being faced with a page of anagrams to solve. Problem was he did not know what the word 'anagram' meant so he couldn't do that page. Sickness had kept him away from school when they had looked at some old papers and he had just never come across anagrams. When he retired he taught himself classical Greek so presumably he would have benefitted from an academic education but the eleven plus failed to spot his ability.

Several children were brought (one at a time) to the door of 9 Ellesmere Avenue where I found that I could increase their scores by around six. If they started with 113 then after a few old papers and a discussion of strategies, they would reach about 119. After that there was little improvement.

I also did some tutoring away from home usually in response to adverts in the Eccles and Patricroft Journal. On one occasion, responding to someone wanting a maths tutor for two girls, I arrived at a door in Ellesmere Park to be greeted by a young girl. 'Hello', said I with an attempt at a smile. The girl fled into the house and then I realised that I had spoken to the mother, not a child. It turned out that the mother (about five feet tall) was the daughter of a well-known composer and resented having to live in the North surrounded by uncouth people like me.

The two girls were being educated at home, presumably to avoid contamination. The Law said that, with some exceptions, all children had to go to school. If children were being educated at home, they had to be inspected. The last inspection of these two girls had said they were not being taught maths and hence the advert. The father was a supplier of alternative health products such as oil of evening primrose.

Another mother living in Ellesmere Park wanted a tutor for two sons. She had been an officer in the ATS (Auxiliary Territorial Service), the 'women's army'. She was probably aged about forty with dark hair and a seductive body that I found to be very attractive. After lessons she sometimes got me to stay and share a drink - beer not tea - and I wondered ... but fortunately nothing happened beyond conversation.

A major source of income was teaching for one evening a week at the Eccles Technical School. This occupied the Grammar School building but was separately organised with its own head and secretary. My father taught shorthand at this 'night school' and he also knew the head through his work in the education office. My MSc and my father's influence got me the job of teaching science to a Preliminary Craft Course, a route into craft training designed for people who had left school with no paper qualifications.

One of the items on the syllabus was heat transfer - conduction, convection and radiation. I thought that I was clever by explaining all this by analogy with passing a message. Conduction was sending a verbal message down a line of people. Convection was one guy leaving the line, bumping into someone and passing on the message.

Radiation was the chap at the end of the line using a walky-talky to talk to the other end of the line.

In the exam, there was a question about heat transfer and two of the students wrote about - guess what - sending messages. I had discovered that not everyone could make the transition from one kind of thinking to another as needed to understand an analogy.

6.9 Social Life 2

With Jeanne gone and some extra money from teaching, I was able to expand my social life, mainly in search for a new girl friend. I had some very good friends in the youth club attached to Eccles Parish Church and there were girls to meet at university either as part of the daily social scene or at the Saturday night dance. In addition to seeking a new girl friend, I was heavily involved in the life of Eccles Parish Church. I was a sidesman, a member of the Church Council, an Assistant Scout Master, a Sunday school teacher and a member of the church youth club. Then there was politics - member of the Young Liberals and vice-chairman of Eccles CND. Some of these activities are discussed elsewhere under religion and politics.

The focus of my university social life had moved from Caf to the new students' union. Building a new union had meant abolishing the original separate men's and women's unions. I had attended a meeting of the men's union to discuss the new arrangements. A two-thirds majority in favour of change was required and the opposition to joining the two unions together was led by a medical student, Stan Hindle. By one of life's coincidences, Stan was to turn up again many years later, attempting to oppose the admission of women into the Heaton Chapel Reform Club.

The architects designing the new student building had a problem in that they did not know whether the two unions would be formally combined or that there would be a need for single sex premises. This produced some interesting compromises. There were two halls incorporated in the design, known as LDH and MDH. The letters could stand for Lady's and Men's Debating Hall or preferably for Lesser and Main. As it turned out, the necessary two-thirds majority was obtained and the idea that the Men's Union should be like a gentleman's club became part of history.

One remnant of the old system was the men only bar on the first floor. There was a much larger general bar but a separate men's bar was quite common in the 1950s. For example, The College Arms that stood opposite Owen's College had a side entrance leading to a men only vault. Some years later 'men only' became illegal and the student bar moved to the basement of the building.

The Union provided a home for various student societies. I joined Gram. Soc. - the society for lovers of classical music played on the latest equipment. In those days sound reproduction involved separate turntables, amplifiers and different speakers (bass and tweeters). Gram Soc. provided talks and concerts using their expensive Hi Fi equipment, financed by subscription and by a grant from the Students' Union.

In order to qualify for a grant, societies had to produce annual accounts and few students knew how to do accounts so I became Treasure of Gram. Soc. As a committee member and guardian of the money, I joined the small party that accompanied the visiting speaker for lunch. Speakers were usually well known writers or performers who were intrigued by the idea of presenting records to students. They included the music critics from Manchester based papers. One person we did not get was Evelyn Rothwell, the oboist married to John Barbirolli, the conductor of Manchester's orchestra, the Halle´. She wanted a fee that far exceeded our budget. Gram. Soc. also participated in a Manchester festival. We gave a concert in the Library Theatre, sharing the event with a Manchester poet.

The first week in October every year saw the Freshers' Conference and I would join the group of society organisers trying to persuade new students to join their society. Some lecherous males used this event to search for convent girls wanting to celebrate their new freedom.

Some years later, I was persuading new students to join another society, the Anglican Fellowship. To join the Fellowship, I signed a standing order. In those days, bank direct debits had not been invented and standing orders carried on until cancelled. This produced some odd results. When I was treasurer of the Design Research Society, I found that some people who had joined the society in the 1960s were still paying subscriptions through a standing order. The sub had been increased four times since they joined but they did not notice and their original address no loner worked.

A similar situation existed with the Anglican Fellowship. In the late 1960s, the Anglicans joined forces with some other religious societies to form the St Paul's chaplaincy but they had to keep going with the Fellowship in order to receive the subs from people like me who had not noticed that I needed to cancel my standing order. The new chaplaincy included a church area but I much preferred the Victorian church that had been used by the Fellowship (now demolished).

In 1957 I learned to play bridge and I joined an informal group of students who met in the lounge on the first floor of the Union where we played bridge, drank beer (in halves) and ate snacks. Among these students was Sandra who I had first met in Caf. She was to be my wife but of course I did not know this at the time. I have a strong memory (that is I remember remembering) of an odd mental experience. I was walking along Brunswick Street and on the other side of the road I saw Sandra. I said to myself, "If there were a Law that I had to get married then that's the girl I would marry".

We began to go out as a foursome, Sandra, myself, a chemistry postgrad, Mike Hall, and a girl called Anne whose parents ran a fish and chip shop in Nottingham. One of our outings was a trip by bus to visit Bramall Hall. In those days, Bramhall was considered to be posh and I had no idea that one day I would be living there. We went to the cinema in Cheadle where there was a cinema café serving afternoon tea. These days most old cinemas and their restaurants have been demolished though Stockport has its restored cinema, the Plaza, with art deco splendour, a waitress-served café and an organ that rises from the floor.

My friendship with Sandra became more serious and I was invited to meet her mother in Crumpsall, North Manchester. In the 1950s, Crumpsall housed a thriving Jewish community including the family of Sandra and several of her relatives. It had been an independent township with Council offices on Crescent Road but in 1890 Crumpsall found itself absorbed into the expanding City of Manchester. When I first met Sandra's mother at 2, Limestead Avenue, I could not have imagined that one day I would be living there. In 1957, my priority was my PhD and finding out about stereo specific polymerisation.

6.10 Polymer research 1957 -1959

In my final year as an undergraduate, there had been several optional courses. One of these that I had NOT taken was on Polymer Science. Since I was hoping to do a PhD in that subject it seemed a good idea to acquire an up to date textbook. I was pleased to note that my new supervisor, Dick Colclough, had a mention in the book that I bought. In a section on metallic catalysts, the book mentioned the use of stannous chloride discovered by R O Colclough. My research topic was around another metallic catalyst, ferric butoxide.

My knowledge of polymers was very basic. I knew that certain chemicals had simple molecules known as monomers and these monomer molecules could be strung together into long chains of polymers. For example, vinyl chloride is a gas, made up of small monomer molecules. These monomers can be persuaded to link up into a long chain of polyvinyl chloride (PVC). The word 'polymer' means 'many parts' in Greek. In addition to the well known synthetic polymers produced by the chemical industry - polystyrene, polyvinyl acetate etc. our bodies contain many, natural polymers. Proteins, for example, are special forms of polypeptide, folded into a particular three dimensional shape. What I didn't know was how these monomers were persuaded to stick together in chains. How did the process of polymerisation come about?

My new book told me that there was a three-stage process - initiation, propagation and termination. These terms are somewhat self-explanatory, they describe how a monomer gets activated and joins on to another monomer passing on the activation, a process that propagates until it is terminated. This polymerisation process can be thought of as linear - all those monomer molecules sticking together in a line. What the book was rather vague about was the three dimensional aspect of the polymer chains. If you got a lot of paper clips and fastened them together to make a chain it would not sit there in a neat line; it would become coiled and tangled. Similarly, polymer chains have a shape in three dimensions. In natural polymers - the ones in the body - their shape is of crucial importance but the first synthetic polymers - plastics and fibres emerging from a factory - had properties that did not seem to depend on shape.

This was changed in the early 1950s when the Italian chemist, Giulio Natta , produced polypropylene with a particular shape that he called 'isotactic'. Polymer molecules can be visualised as chains of monomers but in addition they can have side chains or pendant groups, sticking out from the main chain. Polypropylene has methyl groups sticking out. Isotactic means same configuration and that means that the methyl groups are all on the same side of the main polymer chain. The importance of this particular shape is that the chains can pack more closely together, producing a stronger, higher density plastic than would be the case if the chains were separated by random methyl groups.

In 1957 Natta's plastic was put into production by the Italian firm, Montecatini (founded in 1888) and in 1958, Natta came to Manchester to give a lecture organised by the University and the Manchester branch of the Chemical Society. The lecture took place in a large, tiered lecture theatre, part of the original Owen's College and attended by several industrial chemists as well as university types. The question that interested everyone was just how did you persuade the monomers to stick together in such a specific shape?

The answer lay in the nature of the catalyst that induced stereo-specific polymerisation. Rumour had it that Natta had stolen the basic catalyst from the laboratory of Karl Ziegler who had managed to make high density polyethylene in Germany. Natta had managed to modify the Ziegler catalyst to make it work for propylene. His research had been carried out at Milan Polytechnic with finance from Montecatini and the rumour had it that the Italian militia had guarded the laboratory to prevent anyone discovering the nature of the catalyst.

The Manchester lecture took place in the dark because modern visual aids had not been invented and lights out was the norm for seeing slides from an epidiascope or 'lantern slides' as they were known. The lecture turned out to be about the structure of stereo-specific polymers but not about the catalyst system or how it worked. When the industrial chemists found that they were not going to get answers to the important question, they used the cover of darkness to creep out of the theatre by the top entrance. When the lights came on again about half the audience had disappeared.

Ziegler and Natta were to be awarded the Nobel Prize for chemistry in 1963 but back in the 1950s that was in the future and several groups in industry and university were working on stereo specific polymerisation. Industry was hoping to find useful products or processes. University science was hoping to discover how these catalysts did what they did.

The Manchester group under Professor Gee was looking not at propylene but at propylene oxide. Propylene molecules contain a double bond, that is two carbon atoms held together by four electrons. Propylene oxide has two carbon atoms held together by a single bond and an oxygen atom. Both have methyl side groups and both can be polymerised to give isotactic polymers. So my PhD project was the stereo-specific polymerisation of propylene oxide using a ferric butoxide catalyst. The basic question was 'How does it work?' How is it that all the methyl groups end up on the same side? This is similar to a pile of gloves being stitched together so that all the right hand gloves are sewn up with the thumbs all sticking out the same way.

The approach to answering this question, the research method, was to follow the course of the polymerisation and hope that it provided some clues as to what was going on. This was a quite different type of research from my Master's research. The MSc started with a hypothesis that could be tested. The PhD if it had been successful would have ended with a new idea in need of further testing. Having a hypothesis at the end of a piece of research is quite common in science but this came as a shock to some social scientists who thought that if they wanted to be 'scientific' they had to start with a hypothesis. In particular, two social scientists Glaser and Strauss made a name for themselves in the 1960s by developing what they called 'Grounded Theory', a methodology that allowed a theory to 'steam off the page' of results.

Much later in life when I came across grounded theory, I felt like the man who discovered that he had been writing prose all his life without knowing it. My PhD was intended to be 'grounded' in the results of following the course of the polymerisation. This was to be achieved by two main routes, reaction kinetics and molecular weight determination.

As the polymerisation proceeds, the monomers pack closer together in chains. This means that the overall volume decreases and this decrease can be measured by having the reaction in a container that ends with a capillary tube - like a thermometer.

As the polymerisation proceeds, the liquid meniscus in the tube recedes in a similar manner to a falling temperature.

The position of the meniscus can be accurately measured and its change over time is a measure of the speed of reaction. The other variable of importance is the molecular weight of the resultant polymer. If the initiation step happens easily then you get a lot of low molecular weight polymer but if the initiation is difficult then you could get high molecular weight material as the polymer chains once started could grow to some length.

In order to gather this data, I first had to construct a vac-line. This involved glass tubes, valves etc. put together by glass blowing. One piece of glass tubing could be stuck to the side of another tube via a T joint. This involved a complicated operation using two hands, a mouthpiece, a solid glass rod and an oxy-acetylene welding torch. My first attempts produced an ugly, lumpy joint and it took some practice before I could produce a T joint that was symmetrical and neat.

Years later when working with artists, I could empathise the satisfaction that comes from seeing a well-finished construction. It is similar to listening to a musical instrument that you have played yourself. The enjoyment of listening to a Mozart piano sonata is enhanced when you can feel it in your own fingertips. The contemplation of a hand made glass T joint produces a similar satisfaction. It took about two months to construct the complete line. All the joints had to be tested for tiny air holes. When finished, the line had to hold a vacuum and leaks had to be identified and removed.

This was done using a sparking device that gave off visible blue sparks. If near a pinhole the blue line of sparks would converge on the hole. More heating and blowing got rid of the hole. The construction was delayed by my preference for going to the union and playing bridge.

Then, one night, my construction was completely destroyed by an explosion that wrecked the laboratory and brought out the fire brigade. I shared the lab with another PhD student, Tony Jagger, who was working on polymerisation catalysed by aluminium trihydride, AlH_3. This compound explodes if it touches water and was stored in an airtight container kept in a dry box.

Dry boxes have dry air inside and two large gloves connecting the outside with the interior so that things inside the box can be moved about. A Perspex screen allows the user to see inside. (Perspex is the trade name for a transparent plastic, polymethacrylate. Like Hoover and Biro it is one of those trade names that became the collective noun.) The dry box in our laboratory had an extra screen a short distance away from the main screen as protection against the screen exploding. The protection did not work!

Inside the box, Tony had been carrying out a distillation. You may remember from school chemistry that distillation uses a water filled Liebig condenser to cool down the distilling gases. The water went in and out of the box via rubber tubes fastened to the condenser but one of the tubes must have come unstuck.

Imagine the scene. The box designed to keep air out also keeps water in. As the box fills with water the bottle containing the AlH_3 begins to float. Then it tips over and the stopper falls out. Water rushes in, meets the AlH_3 - BANG. Both screens splintered, producing jagged edged fragments that hurtled through the lab. On a table there had been a copy of It's Physical Chemistry, one of the thickest books around. This had a piece of plastic stuck half way through it. The clamps holding my vac line were still there but they were clamped to broken fragments.

Modern dry boxes are safer. Screens are laminated so that they craze instead of splintering. Modern safety officers would have a fit if they saw a water cooled condenser in a dry box. Tony Jagger gave up on Aluminium trihydride and finished his PhD using Aluminium trimethyl instead.

I rebuilt my vac line and carried out experiments. Following the polymerisation by measuring the meniscus required some readings to be taken in the evening. I was given three keys - to the laboratory, to the building and a large iron key to open the outside gate. Late night working was popular with some students for non-scientific reasons. In an unusual concern for safety, the building had been equipped with fire blankets designed to smother a fire. (It is best not to throw water on a chemical fire) and it was rumoured that the blankets were rather comfortable for lying on.

I realised that I needed to find out more about the catalyst. I had an idea that could be tested by using a compound, ferric acetylacetonate. Today, this compound is commercially available and is used as a catalyst in some reactions but when I wanted some, I had to make it for myself. I did this by consulting Beilstein's, Handbuch der organischen Chemi, to find instructions on how to make it. Beilstein was originally published in the 1880s by Professor F K Beilstein in an attempt to record every organic chemical that had a recorded synthesis. It soon stopped being a 'handbook'.

By the start of W War II, it had only managed to record compounds known before 1930 but this required over 200 volumes. I found the synthesis of my compound recorded in French and I was quite pleased with myself for being able to understand it and to actually make it work. Foreign languages and making things were not amongst my recognised accomplishments. So the sight of the attractive red ferric compound was very satisfying. Unfortunately it was definitely not a catalyst for persuading propylene oxide to polymerise. I had to think of something else.

Down the corridor, one of the researchers was using a molecular still and I found that I could use this device to measure the molecular weight of my catalyst. A molecular still makes use of the phenomenon of freeze drying. If you make some coffee and then want to transport it, getting rid of the water is desirable. Water can be removed by boiling but this destroys some of the coffee flavour. If you stop before all the water is removed, then you have a thick black syrup that could be bottled and sold under trade names such as Camp Coffee.

Freeze drying freezes the coffee and then subjects it to a vacuum pump. At low pressures ice does not melt; it goes straight from solid to vapour without going through the liquid phase. A brown solid 'instant coffee' is the result.

Using freeze drying in the molecular still, I was able to extract my catalyst and determine its molecular weight. It seemed that the best explanation for the molecular weight was the presence of three iron atoms in each catalyst molecule. Iron can form some rather amazing complex compounds, the best known being haemoglobin, responsible for carrying oxygen round the blood with more than a million molecules in each red blood cell.

I was fascinated by the idea that stereospecific polymers were involved in the origin of life. In the 1950s some chemists began to consider possible routes from ordinary stuff to living things. In 1953 the double helix structure of DNA was discovered. In the same year, a biochemist, Stanley Miller, sent electricity through a mixture of gases and liquids thought to have been present in the early Earth. The spark turned these simple chemicals into the basic building blocks of life, amino acids, molecules that polymerise to make proteins.

A Scottish chemist, Cairns-Smith, realised that there

was a huge gap between simple molecules and complex molecules such as DNA. It was not enough to hope for things just sticking together, they had to be arranged in a particular shape. He suggested that mineral crystals in clay could have arranged simple organic molecules into complex organised patterns. Then, these complex organic molecules could have discovered how to organise themselves and reproduce.

Erwin Schrödinger had published the idea that the organisational structure of crystals could be involved in the evolution of life in his 1944 book, What is Life? (He went on to gain a Nobel Prize for his quantum theory, now remembered as Schrödinger's cat). He knew that inheritance required the transfer of hereditary information from one generation to the next and he speculated that genetic information could be recorded in the arrangements of chemical bonds in a complex crystal.

However, Schrödinger could not point to an actual crystal that did what he suggested. Cairns Smith knew that under a microscope, there are tiny crystals in clay. These contain Aluminium and a complex arrangement of silicon, oxygen and sodium. Such crystals could have been present at the dawn of life and could have arranged simple molecules into complex molecules that were capable of reproducing themselves.

It seemed to me that similar ideas could be used to account for the organisation of simple molecules of propylene oxide into chains of a particular shape. I was able to suggest a mechanism involving monomer molecules being absorbed onto the catalyst complex in a specific configuration that allowed the monomers to combine in the required shape.

One of the monomers was then partially released leaving room for another molecule to be added to the growing polymer chain. The only record of my mechanism is contained in a PhD thesis by Brian Jackson. I was quite pleased to see, "Langrish, J. Private Communication" as a citation.

I began to gather data on molecular weight and reaction rate but the numbers did not fit into a neat pattern. So I did more experiments and flasks accumulated waiting for me to determine molecular weights - a time consuming business. National Service still existed but science teachers were exempt. I started to look at adverts in The Times Educational Supplement and I saw one for a Grammar School in Sheffield, to start in January 1960. I spoke to Dr Baxendale who lectured in chemical thermodynamics but was also Tutor for the Faculty of Science, in charge of the PhD system. He told me two things. First that it was possible to leave and finish the PhD in my spare time - if I had any. And he said something like, "A PhD is no big deal; it's a training so just get it done." Years later when I was looking after my own PhD students, Rachel Davies (now Lady Cooper, President of the Design Research Society) remembers my telling her to 'just get it done'.

In those days there was such a shortage of science teachers that a science graduate was allowed to teach without being a qualified teacher. A satisfactory year's probation would result in the granting of qualified status. I therefore decided to apply for the position of 'Assistant Master' at King Edward VII School Sheffield.

Sandra had not quite finished her degree. She had taken finals in the summer but still had to pass a subsidiary Spanish exam. Given that change was in the air, she suggested that it was time for us to be officially engaged. I said this was an excellent idea but I could not afford to buy an engagement ring.

A week later, she said she had solved that problem. Uncle Mick(Bernstein) who lived with Sandra and her widowed mother had said that I could have the ring that he had bought many years before and he only wanted what he had paid for it. The ring was later valued at several hundred pounds but Mick let me have it for £15. (In 1959, £15 was more than a good weekly wage.) The ring had an unusually large diamond but I subsequently discovered that the diamond was flawed with the flaw being hidden inside the silver mount.

One of Mick's cousins was a jeweller who I suspected had been the source of the ring. I did not discover the story of Mick's engagement that wasn't. He had never married but I did learn the story of how Mick and family had arrived in Crumpsall. Sandra's maternal grandparents had been living in Russia when Cossacks decided that weekend sport could include burning Jewish villages. The family came from near Odessa, now in Ukraine, but back then Ukraine had been split between Poland and Russia. In 1905, a pogrom had killed about 500 Odessa Jews and if you had some money, it made sense to leave. Some Jews had already left and there were relatives in Argentina. So the family packed up and left.

Mick remembered being half asleep in a waggon and looking at a swinging oil lamp being jerked by holes in the road. When they reached the sea, Sandra's grandfather had paid a bag of gold to a ship's captain who said he would take them to Argentina.

The story goes that they were put off the boat in Liverpool believing that they were in Buenos Aires. I find this a little unlikely but the story claims that they set out clutching a piece of paper with an address in Buenos Aires. They felt lost until they spotted a door with a mezuzah attached. This is a scroll containing biblical verses that can be seen on the doors of Jewish houses. It is supposed to be in obedience to the biblical injunction, "write the words of God on the gates and doorposts of your house". However, even non-religious Jews use it as a secret sign or for good luck. The family were very relieved to find that behind the mezuzah lay a Jewish couple who spoke Yiddish. They learned that they were in Liverpool, England and a better place to be in was Manchester. So they walked down the road to Manchester where there was a Jewish community in an area near to Victoria Station and Strangeways prison.

The experience of a similar Jewish immigration can be found in the novels of Maisie Mosco. Almonds and Raisins describes the period from 1905 to the 1930s and the arrival of Moseley's fascists in Manchester. The area north of Victoria Station expanded along Cheetham Hill Road and became a centre for immigrants from Ireland and from Eastern Europe. Life there in the 1930s is described in two novels, Rachel Rosing and Shabby Tiger, by Howard Spring.

In the 1930s, despite the depression and high unemployment, people who did have a regular income were able to buy one of the new houses being built all over England including Crumpsall. So Sandra's grandmother and relations moved out of Victorian Cheetham Hill into 1930s semis. Sandra's mother had married a Maurice Clyne who tragically died when Sandra was thirteen, and they lived in an old street, Trafalgar Street, before moving to Crumpsall.

So, in 1959, living at 2, Limestead Avenue were Sandra, her mother and Uncle Mick who officially was Michael Bernstein, a name probably given to him by immigration officers on his arrival in Liverpool as a young boy. There were other Bernstein's in the area though most had changed their name to Benson or Burns. Bernstein had been out of favour being both Jewish and German (In German it means amber. It became an OK name again with Sidney Bernstein's Granada

TV and Leonard Bernstein's West Side story.) Round the corner at the end of Limestead Avenue lived Uncle Izzy (Benson) who had three children Phil, Ralph and Bernice of whom more later.

After this diversion, it is time to return to the events of 1959. I put together an application for the Sheffield job. I had no teaching qualification but I obtained a reference from the principal of Eccles Tech. He had only once observed my teaching the preliminary craft course science class. By good luck he had looked in when I was giving a demonstration - I usually just talked and dictated notes. His reference said that my lessons were well prepared and illustrated with demonstrations. My application also mentioned that I had been an assistant scoutmaster, the superintendent of a Sunday school and a private tutor. I felt that these details made up for the lack of a formal teaching qualification. So into the post went my hope for the future.

References Chapter 6.
A. Hayek, 1967. Studies in Philosophy, Politics and Economics. P 12 Chicago U. P.
J. Langrish and H. O. Pritchard, 1958. The Thermal isomerisation of Cyclopropane. J. Phys. Chem. 62, 761.
G. Lewis and L. Barnes 2016. A Fortunate Universe: Life in a Finely Tuned Cosmos. Cambridge U P
UKA. Quayle. 1987. Recollections of mass spectrometry of the fifties in a UK petroleum laboratory). Organic Mass Spectrometry vol 22 569 - 585
Denis de Rougemont. 1936. Penser avec les mains. Paris: Albin Michel.
John McTaggart, 1921. The Nature of Existence. Vol 1. Cambridge U P.
Maisie Mosco, 1979. Almonds and Raisins, London: Harper.
Brett Salkeld and Leah Perrault. 2011. How Far Can We Go? A Catholic Guide to Sex and Dating. Paulist Press.
Howard Spring. 1934. Shabby Tiger. 1935 Rachel Rosing. London: Collins
Erwin Schrödinger, 1944, What is Life? Cambridge U P

Chapter 7. Politics

7.1 Politics
When she heard that I was writing my autobiography, my granddaughter, Daisy, said, "Is it sequential or a bit of this and a bit of that?" Academics might put this as either narrative or thematic but I don't like either/ors; 'either and or' is better. This book is mainly narrative. It starts in the 1930s and ends in 2021. My involvement with politics stretches from writing leaflets for the Liberal candidate in a school election of 1951 to being Treasurer of Stockport Constituency Lib Dems for 24 years, ending in 2014. It follows that writing about politics is best done out of sequence. Hence this chapter.

Politics is one of those words that conjure up different thought patterns for different people. What are the first three images that come to your mind after 'politics'? Ask this question to other people and you will get lots of different answers.

I don't remember when I learnt the politics word. My first awareness must have been via the cinema. During Saturdays I was allowed to go with other friends from school to children's matinees at the Crown cinema. Whatever the occasion, there was always a news program and being war time, I became familiar with Churchill, Stalin, Roosevelt and of course Hitler but they weren't politicians, they weren't even 'world leaders'; they were just people in the news.

Politics is supposed to be a way of resolving differences. If everyone agreed on what was needed and on how to get it, then we would not need politics.

Young children have to learn that disagreement is a fact of life. This starts with disagreement over ownership, 'That's mine!' Later, there are disagreements over what is or is not a fact. To begin with, children accept what they are told by mother, teacher, older sibling, priest etc. as 'true'. This knowledge builds up as neural patterns in the brain and one consequence of this is resistance to ideas that don't fit in with the existing patterns. As the Jesuits are supposed to have said, "Give us a child until it is seven and it's ours for life."

I have a strong memory (that is I remember remembering my remembering) of perhaps the first time that I was shocked to find that not everyone agreed with what I thought was true. There was a local decorator, name of Percy, who had been employed to add wallpaper and paint to some of our walls at 9 Ellesmere Avenue. He wore voluminous white overalls with many pockets containing different sized brushes, a cig packet, matches etc. For some reason I found myself talking to Percy about the war. I knew that Churchill was a good guy and Hitler was the bad guy responsible for the bombs that dropped on Eccles.

Percy had different ideas. He claimed that the war was Churchill's fault. We had started the war -- not Hitler and we should have left Hitler to destroy the Communists who were a bigger threat. This was so contrary to what I thought was the case that I have remembered the shock. Later I was to discover that Percy's view was similar to views held by the Edward who was almost crowned King Edward VIII.

7.2 Election 1945

The end of the European war in 1945 was followed by a general election and my introduction to party politics. The cinema newsreels, the newspapers and the BBC news gave me a vague idea that something important was happening and I began to take an interest in parliamentary politics. I discovered that there were three parties - Conservative, Labour and Liberal. The three candidates wanting to become MP for Eccles were featured in the weekly Eccles and Patricroft Journal.

The national scene was covered by the News Chronicle, delivered every day. Both these papers seemed to be in favour of the Liberals and I decided that though they were not likely to win, a sense of fairness or sympathy with the underdog made me into a Liberal supporter. So in 1945 I wanted the Liberals to win. In fact, they were nearly annihilated and the Labour victory brought Clement Attlee to the Prime Minister's residence in 10, Downing Street.

Former Liberal voters tended to split two ways. Those who supported the idea of public ownership of railways and coalmines voted Labour and those who feared socialism voted with the Conservatives. The few Liberals who were elected to parliament benefitted from local pacts with the Tories.

After the 1945 victory, Labour set about establishing a socialist state in a country that was virtually bankrupt. The means of transport and coalmines were nationalised; a health service and a new education system were introduced. These changes had an impact on my life. Instead of my father having to pay the doctor for home visits when I was ill, medical care was now free.

The school that my brother had attended changed its name from Eccles Secondary School to Eccles Grammar School. The change meant that no fees were charged and textbooks did not have to be purchased. The locomotives on the railway changed their signs from LMS (London Midland and Scottish Railway Co.) to British Rail. Second class coaches disappeared, leaving only first and third class options. (Egalitarian tendencies did not stretch to the abolition of privileges for the rich)

New faces appeared on the cinema news. There was Clem Attlee, the Prime Minister who looked to me like a solicitor and Sir Stafford Crips, the Chancellor of the Exchequer who looked like an undertaker or someone from a horror film. Then there was Herbert Morrison, Attlee's deputy and expected to become Attlee's successor. To me he seemed a funny little man, which of course he wasn't.

In his autobiography, Morrison (1960) described the early days of the new government. With the coalmines being nationalised, he asked for the plan of how they were to be run when owned by the state instead of by private companies and private individuals. He discovered that there was no plan. He was told that the senior Labour Party people had believed the establishment would never allow nationalisation. They had imagined that the army would be used to prevent the removal of ownership from the existing elite.

Nonetheless the mines were taken into public ownership through the establishment of the National Coal Board. The mines continued to be managed by the existing managers (who of course had not been the owners) and much later I acquired a pattern that meant, "It doesn't matter too much who owns something; it's how it's run that counts". Companies are supposed to be owned by their shareholders but chief executives run the companies and in many cases award themselves huge bonus payments for no discernable reason.

7.3 Committees

In the late 1940s, the pattern called politics extended its meaning from elections to a vague sense of something to do with committees. I remember my father telling my mother over tea that he had been presenting the annual budget to the education committee. Part of his job in the Treasurer's Department of the Town Hall involved looking after educational spending. He seemed pleased with himself, the reason being that he had included a small but controversial item picked on by the councilors whilst they had not noticed his inclusion of a more important change in the annual allocation of funds known as the budget. So politics began to mean getting you own way in a committee by slightly devious means. (The distraction technique was known as 'the bicycle shed syndrome'. This meant getting the committee to argue about a small sum of money whilst not noticing the proposed large expenditure on something else.)

Politics as involving committees was important later in life when I became an officer of various organisations in university and Liberal circles. A foretaste was provided when I worked for ICI. I heard the head of an ICI research department saying that he had been asked to apply for a university position but he wasn't going to do that because he couldn't cope with university politics. The idea that universities could be more political than industry seemed strange at the time but was confirmed later.

I gained an idea of political parties from reading a William book that brother Peter had brought home from a library. Many years later I was able to find a secondhand copy of this book, William the Bad, originally published in 1930 (my copy is a ninth reprint 1939.). This collection of short stories includes a political fantasy, 'William, Prime Minister' (p. 60). In this story, Henry, the thoughtful member of William's 'Outlaws', explains the different parties -

> There's Conservatives an' they want to make things better by keepin' 'em jus' like what they are now. An' there's Lib'rals an' they want to make things better by alterin' them jus' a bit, but not so's anyone'd notice, an' there's Socialists, an' they want to make things better by taking everyone's money off 'em an' there's Communists an' they want to make things better by killin' everyone but themselves.

Although published in 1930, Henry had apparently not heard of the Fascists but this was rectified by a later story - William and the Nasties (In William, the Detective 1935) - in which the outlaws pretend to be 'Nasties' supporting 'Him William' - This story was censored out of later reprints along with another story containing a description of William's dog, Jumble, killing lots of rats.

7.4 Scientific planning

The Attlee government was the first (and only) socialist government of the UK. (Future Labour governments were not socialist in the dictionary sense of socialism as the public ownership of the means of production.) The basic philosophy of 1945 Labour was that scientific planning by the state should replace the wasteful competition of free market capitalism. In the post war period many people were prepared to believe that government planning would work.

The opposition to central planning was expressed in a 1944 book, The Road to Serfdom, by an Austrian, F A von Hayek (1899-1992). The English version of this book sold over a million copies and claimed that in a complex system such as a nation, central planning does not work. The only way that central plans can be made to work – in the sense of the plan being realised – is if people are forced to follow the plan instead of the plan following people's needs. Hayek warned of "the danger of tyranny that inevitably results from government control of economic decision-making through central planning". He argued,

> The abandonment of individualism, classical liberalism, and freedom, inevitably leads to socialist or fascist oppression, tyranny and serfdom.

The late fifties and early sixties were a time of scientific optimism. In 1950, 1935 was only fifteen years in the past and yet people who had lived through those years knew that much had changed for the better. The new antibiotics could cure diseases that killed children in 1935. The luxury of expensive silk stockings had been replaced by the ready availability of lower priced 'nylons'. Chipped grimy metal washing bowls were replaced by shiny red plastic ones, churned out by injection molding machines.

There were many such changes and they had one thing in common; they were believed to be the product of 'science'. So, scientific planning seemed in accordance with the optimism of the age.

Anyone who suggested that complexity could not be planned was regarded as either silly or hopelessly right wing like John Jewkes, the Stanley Jevons Professor of Political Economy at Manchester University and author of Ordeal by Planning (1948).

And yet there were doubts. I remember standing in a queue with my mother, waiting to get our new ration books. These contained coupons that had to be exchanged for items that were rationed. Sweets, sugar and meat remained in the rationing system until the early 1950s. Standing in the queue was a young woman who was complaining about having to waste time in this way. She consoled herself by saying, "Well I suppose it's fairer this way - better than the rich having everything and the poor starving". This impressed me and later when I knew more, that conceptual pattern became the idea that liberty, equality and fraternity were strange bedfellows; you couldn't have equality AND liberty. Politics was about trying to find a balance between the two and I thought that the Liberals were about right.

When I was fourteen, my life was affected by a socialist decision that convinced me that socialism was wrong. In a mistaken pursuit of equality, the Labour government decided that school pupils had to be 16 years old before being allowed to take the GCE exams. Because I had gone to the Grammar school a year early and been in the fast A stream, I was two years too young and prevented from taking the 'O' level exams that I knew I could pass. Fortunately, the school was sensible and allowed me to go into the 6th form to study for 'A' levels in the same way as would have happened if I had passed the GCE 'O' levels.

With this experience I was able to replace the simple Just William account of the political parties by a different description. Both Liberals and Labour could be seen to be compassionate but Labour believed in compulsion where Liberals believed in co-operation. The Conservatives believed in competition even though this meant that there had to be losers with survival of the fittest supposedly leading to progress.

The Attlee government nationalised transport, steel production, the coalmines and implemented a national health scheme. The succeeding Conservative governments shared some of that belief in central ownership and although road transport and steel production were returned to private ownership, the railways and coalmines remained in the hands of the state. The 'mixed economy' became popular with some things better run by the state for the benefit of all and other things being best run by profit – oriented companies. In that era in the UK, anyone who supported Hayek or Jewkes was regarded as weird. It was not until the era of Thatcher and Reagan that Hayek became respectable again. Jewkes (1958) pursued his anti central planning stance by attempting to show that important inventions came from individual efforts rather than organised planning

I was vaguely aware that the traditional right/left way of sorting political attitudes was much too simple. Central planning versus free market did not have to coincide with forcing people versus leaving room for people to make their own mistakes.

During my six years in the Chemistry department, I had a thirst for knowledge outside the sciences. I used to skip chemistry practicals and spend time in the Arts Library. Also I purchased Pelican books, serious paperbacks published by Penguin with a distinctive blue cover. One of these was Eysenck's Uses and Abuses of Psychology (1964). This contained a questionnaire, designed to show your place on a matrix of political ideas. I was already aware that putting political opinions into a left - right spectrum was far too simple.

Eysenck's approach was to add another dimension, tough - tender, to produce a matrix with tough-left being communist, tough - right being fascist and most results of the questionnaire being nearer the centre. Tender left could be democratic socialist; tender right might be 'one-nation Toryism'. It struck me that a better approach might be a triangle with three extremes. Extreme Conservative was fascist and extreme Labour was Communist. So where was Liberal? Since the Liberal view emphasized the importance of the individual and was suspicious of state interference, it followed that the extreme Liberal point of the triangle was Anarchist. This was a much better idea than thinking of the Liberals as being in a soggy middle ground. Especially so when both Labour and Conservative were occupying the middle ground. Obtaining some policies that were different from the other two parties began to happen with the arrival of Jo Grimond in 1956 but took time to get across.

7.5 Elections 1950, 1951 and 1955

Party politics became interesting again in 1950 when there was another general election. The Grammar School thought that its pupils should learn something about voting by having an election but without the political parties. Some parents might object to the inclusion of party politics in school activities and we had to vote for people who gave speeches at lunchtime and had supporters who made posters etc. I vaguely remember supporting one of the candidates who of course didn't win. (Most of my life I have voted for people who didn't win)

After five years of war followed by five years of attempts at socialism and with some rationing still in place, it might have been the case that the population would have thrown out the Labour party. In fact, Labour obtained a 2.6% lead over the Conservatives in terms of total votes cast. However, in the British 'first past the post' system, each constituency elects its own Member of Parliament and it is the total number of MPs that matters. The way that the constituency boundaries are drawn favours the Conservatives. There are industrial centers with large numbers of Labour supporters electing one MP. The Conservative vote is more evenly spread, resulting in more MPs. The 1950 Labour lead in votes produced a majority of only five MPs, making it very difficult for the Labour government to control parliament. So in 1951 there was another election.

This time the school did allow party politics into its mock election and I supported the Liberal cause by composing some leaflets using ideas from the local Eccles and Patricroft Journal. One of the arguments against voting Liberal was that they didn't have people with experience in government. In fact, they did have people who had been in the wartime national government and in pre war coalitions. The Liberal candidate for Eccles claimed experience as a member of the Indian parliament. (Most people were unaware that an Indian parliament had existed before independence. It was known as the Imperial Legislative Council and had some members elected by ethnic groups including five seats for Europeans)

Another argument against the Liberals in the 1950 election had been that they only had candidates in about half the seats so they could not get enough MPs to 'win' the election. This time the party decided it had to have candidates in as many seats as possible. People arrived in towns they had never seen before, clutching the forms and the deposit money that were needed to get them on the ballot paper. The result was a disaster. Election results for each constituency were read out on the BBC radio and in most cases, ended with the words, "The Liberal candidate lost his deposit". In those days, in order to deter 'frivolous' candidates a deposit of £150 was required. For the deposit to be returned one-eighth (12.5%) of votes cast had to be obtained and in many places the Liberal only scored around 6%. (In 1985 the threshold was reduced to one-twentieth (5%) of the vote and the deposit set at £500.)

The result of the 1951 General Election was most odd. The Conservatives (Tories for short) won the election and Winston Churchill became Prime Minister again but this result concealed the fact that Labour achieved its highest ever vote with 230,000 more votes nationally than the winners. My parents were now taking the Daily Telegraph. They used to sit on either side of the fire doing its crossword. It was a paper well known for supporting the Tories (nicknamed The Torygraph).

I remember reading its attempt at justifying the odd result by pointing out that several constituencies either had no Tory candidate to vote for or had been returned unopposed so their potential votes had been left out of the total. In Northern Ireland, there were places where the Unionist candidate could have gained thousands of votes (Unionist MPs counted as Tories) but it was so obvious they would win that no one had bothered to oppose them.

In England there were some local pacts. Bolton, for example had two constituencies East and West. When all three parties stood, Labour won both seats with the anti Labour vote being split. In 1951, there was a pact; the Tories did not put up a candidate in West with the result that the Liberal, Arthur Holt, was elected. With no Liberal in East Bolton, the Tories won that seat Given other examples like these, the Telegraph was able to claim that if all the Conservative supporters in the country had been given the chance to vote then the total would have exceeded the Labour total so things were OK - Yes? Well no; even a schoolboy could see that the number of votes did not translate into seats and the Tories had a massive advantage.

In the Telegraph during the run up to the election, I remember reading a slightly humorous piece that suggested you should vote the opposite way to your instinct. If you thought the Unions had too much power then you should vote Labour because they would find it easier to control their excesses. On the other hand if you thought that the banks and industry had too much power, you should vote Conservative for the same reason.

Although Churchill was 77 in 1951, he stayed as Prime Minister until 1955 when he handed over to Anthony Eden. During that period, I actually became a paid up member of the Liberal party through one of those historical contingencies. I was always looking for ways to earn some money - tutoring for the eleven plus exam was one source of income. My father got me involved in a local election. Voting required polling stations with people who were paid to hand out the ballot papers and make sure things were in order. Then there were people who were paid to count the votes. My father managed to get me employed for both these activities. At the count I sat with others counting the votes for one ward of Eccles council. After the count, the candidates for that ward made short speeches and the Liberal, Alan Cooper, was most impressive. He had come a close second and promised that he would be back.

I found out that there was a branch of the Young Liberals that met in the Liberal Club. So I joined and delivered leaflets for Alan Cooper who won the election in the next year. He went on to lead a Liberal group on Eccles borough council (abolished in the 1970s local government re organization that made Eccles part of Salford). The Libera Club was a splendid Victorian building (since demolished to make way for a motorway) and the Young Liberals met in a room upstairs. One meeting was a joint debate with the Young Communists. (The connection between Eccles and Communism went back to Engels establishing a factory there.)

I used the Lysenko controversy to attack the Soviet system. In terms of nature versus nurture, Marxists were in favour of nurture - changing society could change people. Lysenko took this belief into agriculture. He claimed that the right environment could obtain greater increases in crop yields than other biologists believed possible. Under Stalin, Lysenko became director of the Institute of Genetics and president of the Academy of Agricultural Sciences.

By 1948, standard genetics was outlawed and some geneticists suffered arrest and deaths from undisclosed causes. This lent support to the Just William claim that communists killed hose that disagreed with them. My using this in a debate shows that even then, I was interested in evolution and science policy.

I was a 2nd year chemistry student during the 1955 General Election and I watched the results on television in the students' union. The Tories with their new leader, Sir Anthony Eden, slightly increased their majority. The voice of Richard Dimbleby made the event seem serious but in fact, little changed until after the event when Labour replaced their leader, Clem Attlee, with Hugh Gaitskell and the Liberal leader, Clement Davies, was replaced by Jo Grimond. Davies had been leader of the party from 1945 to 1956 and I had heard him speak at a Manchester meeting. Davies was known as a 'very decent chap'. He spoke about world peace, fair shares for all, co-operation and other 'nice' things but he lacked dynamism.

The new ideas and dynamism were to come from Grimond. Jo Grimond was well connected being married to a daughter of Lady Violet Bonham Carter. His brother in law, Mark Bonham Carter, was a Liberal M P, winning the Torrington by-election in 1958, a ray of hope for the beleaguered Liberal Party. Grimond's father-in-law was Asquith, Liberal Prime Minister from 1908 to 1916.

The Liberal revival of the early 1960s took place after I had left the chemistry department and my further Liberal activities are described in Chapter 9.

7.6 CND

During my six years in the university chemistry department, I was not involved with student politics, neither the local student union variety nor the national variety in the Federation of Liberal Students. (My student committee experience came from being Treasurer of Gram Soc.) I did become part of a new national organisation - the Campaign for Nuclear Disarmament (CND) formed in 1958. A research student from down the corridor, Bill Taylor, involved me in the organisation of a meeting to be held in the Free Trade Hall. This was a major event with speeches from philosopher Bertrand Russell, the historian AJP Taylor, Cannon Collins, known as the 'Red Dean', and a former American general.

My role was to escort AJP from his dinner to the Free Trade Hall. (At that time I didn't know that in the 1930s he had been a lecturer at Manchester University so he obviously could have found his own way). I found him in the dining room of the

Wellington Inn. This was in the upper half of an Elizabethan building, known as The Shambles. One end of the building had a shop and an office. The other end had Sinclair's Oyster Bar. It was the last surviving building of Manchester's Tudor city centre. It had been part of a butchers' market before some of the buildings were removed in Victorian times, with the rest being destroyed during the bombing of 1940. (The building has since been split in two and moved twice to make way for developments such as the Arndale Shopping Centre. It now resides next to Manchester Cathedral)

AJP was at a table with the remains of what had been a luxurious meal including an empty wine bottle. With him was an attractive woman, possibly the Hungarian historian who became his third wife. That was when I realised that it was possible to be an academic and still have enough money to enjoy some of the finer things of life.

The Free Trade Hall was full to capacity for the meeting and an overspill meeting was organised in the nearby Friends Meeting House. In spite of the success of the event, it hardly got a mention in the newspapers and I began to suspect that the news was not as free as it was supposed to be. CND was ignored by the media until the Swaffham Rocket Site sit in. TV could not resist the sight of middle aged, middle class people, sitting in a road and being politely removed by policemen. After that, CND became a familiar news item with the black and white semaphore ND symbol becoming well known.

I joined the Eccles CND branch and became the token 'other'. I was the only Anglican and the only Liberal in the group and they made me the Vice Chairman. The others were Quakers, Communists or Christian Socialists. I helped to run a stall on Eccles Saturday Market where I sold books, gave out leaflets and argued with people.

The Eccles CND organised marches and after I was married and living in Crumpsall, Sandra and I took our twins in their pram on a 'Ban the bomb' march. I noticed a photographer recording the faces of the marchers. I was told this was Special Branch who thought that CND was a Russian Communist plot. It was, of course, ludicrous to imagine that a load of Quakers, socialists and middle class people were crypto communists. It was just coincidence that my daughter Suzanne became a member of the Communist Party.

In those days, there was concern about the effects of Strontium-90, a radioactive isotope produced by the fission of uranium and plutonium in nuclear reactors and in nuclear weapons. Large amounts of Sr-90 were produced during atmospheric nuclear weapons tests conducted in the 1950s and 1960s.

CND campaigned against testing nuclear weapons in the air and by the early 1960s they were shown to be correct. Through analysis of residual radioactivity in soil, water and even polar ice, it was shown that Sr-90 had been dispersed worldwide, producing a cancer risk that is still with us. (The U.S., the Soviet Union and the United Kingdom continued testing nuclear weapons in the atmosphere until 1963, when a limited test ban treaty was signed but France and China continued with atmospheric testing.)

7.7 Politics and religion

Neuronal pattern circuits in the brain are entangled with many other circuits. Think of one thing and associations with other things take place. In my case, thoughts about politics and religion are associated at a basic level, meaning that political ideas are rooted in idea patterns about fairness, helping others, and making best use of my talents to make a better world. These values were originally acquired via my religious mother and then expanded by more formal religious influences. A major influence was the parable of the talents. (A talent was both a unit of currency and something you were good at.)

In this parable an unfortunate servant is entrusted with a talent when his master goes away. On his return the master asked what has been dome with the talent. The servant is then cast into the outer darkness, not because he had spent or lost it but because he had not done anything with it. This idea is repeated in the Anglican Book of Common Prayer that used to be used three times on Sundays. It contains the General Confession, including the words "We have left undone those things that we ought to have done." It is not enough to avoid bad things. If you are talented you have to use those talents. The reformers of the liturgy got rid of the general confession and replaced it with a 'modern' prayer that does not mention sins of omission - nothing about doing the right thing. Leaving things undone did not seem to matter until the present century when 'the service of the word' included a confession containing the words, "we are sorry that we did not ...".

The branch of English Christianity that emphasised the positive side of religion was the Congregational. It preached the social gospel -Thy kingdom come on earth - and its members were often involved in politics, particularly the Liberal party. For example, John Ashworth was a Congregational elder and Liberal chair of Bramhall Urban District Council before Bramhall became absorbed into Stockport. The Minister of Heaton Moor Congregational church used to place 'vote Liberal' posters in his house window. (The 'Cong' building was eventually sold to the Egyptian Cooptics.)

As mentioned above, I was inspired to join the Liberal party by Alan Cooper and he provides a convenient link between my political and religious activities. At the time of Alan's election to the Town Council, I was a member of the church youth club that met in Eccles Parish Church's Albert Street Church School (since demolished). The club had a competition to design a new church newspaper and as I was rather keen on the idea of politics as Christianity in action, I wrote the lead story with the headline 'From Church Council to Eccles Council'.

Alan Cooper was a member of the Parochial Church Council of St. Andrew's church and his politics were influenced by his religion as well as by his study of nineteenth century politics. St Andrew's was a daughter church of Eccles Parish, being split off when Victorian expansion meant that the old church could not cope with the population explosion.

It was opened in 1879 after being built with money raised by local people including the treasurer, Henry Boddington, Chairman of Boddington's Brewery. This gives another example of a combination of influence. Brewing families tended to support the Tories and the C of E. Chapter 9 has more on my political involvements. St Andrew's church is now a Grade II listed building.

References Chapter 7.
Richmal Crompton. 1930. William Prime Minister. In William the Bad. Newnes
Richmal Crompton. 1935. William and the Nasties. In William, the Detective.
H J Eysenck. 1964. Uses and Abuses of Psychology. Pelican.

F A von Hayek. 1044. The Road to Serfdom. New York. Routledge.
John Jewkes, 1948. Ordeal by Planning. Macmillan.
J Jekes, D Sawers, R Stillerman. 1958. Sources of Invention, Macmillan.
Herbert Morrison: An Autobiography. 1960. London: Odhams Press.

POLITICS

Chapter 8. Marriage and King Ted's 1959-1961

8.1 Sheffield

In the summer of 1959 I was a single man, living with my parents in Eccles and trying to finish a PhD. Two years later, I was married with two lovely twin daughters, teaching chemistry at King Edward School, Sheffield and spending the weekends with my family in Crumpsall, North Manchester.

The change started when, before finishing my PhD, I applied for a teaching job advertised in the Times Educational Supplement, the TES. I received a letter inviting me to go for an interview at the school. In those days, the railway line from Manchester to Sheffield went through the Woodhead tunnel under the Pennines to Sheffield Victoria station. Both the station and the tunnel were eventually closed. The present route from Manchester to Sheffield takes longer than the old one. (Not all change is for the better).

There was a bus route past the school and I arrived in time for an interview with the deputy head. He seemed impressed by two things. My MSc was a plus. In those days, post grad degrees were rare. Many of the teachers had MA after their name together with Oxon or Cantab but MAs from Oxford or Cambridge were not post grad degrees awarded for research or further study; they could be purchased after three years by upgrading a BA honours degree to an MA.

The other important thing in my application was having been a scoutmaster. The school had two scout troops and B Troop was currently without a teacher in charge. I said I would be very happy to be scoutmaster for B Troop.

In addition, the deputy head seemed relieved by the fact that I was free to start in January. I did not have to give notice of departure to anyone. The school had already gone for one term with a missing chemistry teacher and obviously did not wish to wait for another term whilst someone gave in notice.

A few days later I received a letter offering me the position of Assistant Master at the school. I accepted and then I was invited to stay for a weekend with the head of chemistry, who was also the Senior Science Master, Mr G Mackay, Mac for short.

8.2 Teaching chemistry

The teaching of chemistry was highly organised and Mac gave me a complete set of lesson plans for the classes that I would teach. These plans had been duplicated on the school's office Banda machine. In the days before photocopying became available, the office Banda was a feature of most schools. A so-called spirit duplicator, it used stencils that could be made by hand or by typewriter and allowed teachers to prepare hand-outs, exam papers, notes for parents and so on.

Before going to Sheffield, I had equipped myself with some new fashionable cavalry twill trousers and a pair of blue suede shoes. Mac took me to his tennis club where some boys guessed that I must be the new Chemistry chap and dashed off to tell their friends about my blue suede shoes. Sheffield was a little behind Manchester in its appreciation of new things. Despite the success of Elvis Pressley's version of "Blue Suede Shoes", in Sheffield the schoolboys believed that suede shoes were only worn by what they called 'queers'.

In order to teach in Sheffield, I needed somewhere to live. Travelling daily from home in Eccles was not a good idea. I had two options, a place suggested by a Quaker I had met in Eccles CND and the parents of Tony Hyde, a PhD student who knew that they had been thinking of having a lodger. Mac took me in his car to visit the two and I settled on lodging with Mr and Mrs Hyde during the week but going home at weekends.

Another important event in December 1959 was Sandra's graduation. She had finally passed the subsidiary Spanish exam and was able to attend a graduation ceremony. This was reported by the photographer of Manchester's Evening Chronicle, a paper that no longer exists. That evening, the front page of the 'Chron' had a pic of Sandra throwing her hat in the air. When she had been in the sixth form of school, she had gone to a modelling agency and acquired a certificate that said she had qualified as a model. She certainly knew how to pose for a photograph.

Now in possession of a degree, Sandra managed to find a teaching job in Sheffield so that she could join me after Easter in 1960. I moved to Sheffield, living with the Hydes, taking the bus to and from school and coming home at weekends.

One evening, I arrived in Sheffield just after ten o'clock and popped in a pub for a pint. Much to my surprise the pub had stopped serving. In those days there were strict licensing laws and Manchester pubs stopped serving at 10.30. Sheffield, however, stopped supplying alcohol at 10.00p.m.

Most evenings I used the Hyde's front room to prepare lessons for the next day and to mark homework. Sometimes I went to Sheffield University Students' Union and there I saw an advert for a place in a student bed-sit. It turned out that four students had been sharing a floor in a Victorian house but one of them had left to get married. Living there seemed more fun than lodging with the Hydes; so I moved and spent the weeks in student style, eating at the Union or cooking fry-ups, playing cards and consuming cheap beer.

I had not had the benefit of teacher training but I had the lesson plans provided by the school and I had my own experience, including a memory of a new teacher arriving when I was at school. He announced himself as Mr Truman but he did not command attention. I had a vague memory of reading about some people who would not be photographed and would not tell you their names because bad people could make spells against you if they knew your name. So, don't tell the schoolboys your name.

For first lessons with pupils who had done some chemistry, I got two youths to give out pieces of paper. I then told the class to write their names and the date on the paper and answer some questions that were already on the blackboard. I explained that I needed to know what they knew and what they didn't know. The result was that the class did not find out anything about me but spent a lesson period in thinking and writing.

For boys who had not yet been introduced to chemistry, there was some fun. They were shown how to use a Bunsen burner to heat up some gauze held on a tripod. They then heated a small heap of ammonium dichromate, an orange substance used in 'volcano' fireworks. When heated, it gives off sparks and gas whilst turning into a strange green mass that is actually chromium dioxide.

All this had to be written up in their new chemistry notebooks with a writing page facing a blank page on which they had to draw and label the Bunsen burner, tripod etc. and describe what happened. All this took some time and the writing was finished as homework. (In a modern classroom, this would be a demonstration by the teacher. Letting boys heat dichromate on their own would not be allowed today.)

I taught chemistry to the second and fourth streams of years 2, 3 and 4. The first and third streams were taught by Mr Vernon who was also the secretary of the school's branch of the AMA, the Assistant Masters Association, a sort of teachers' trade union that did not approve of trades union. He said I should join in order to protect myself. Chemistry was hazardous and I might find myself being sued for damages to some child. The AMA provided free legal assistance. They also provided a savings scheme. For a small sum per month, I could obtain a £1,000 mortgage when I wanted to buy a house. In 1960, a Victorian terraced house could be purchased for half that sum; so I signed up.

In the end of year exams my second and fourth streams did better than the corresponding streams taught by Mr Vernon and the head of the school, Mr Clapton, could see that I was doing a good job. He therefore accepted my claim that I should be doing some sixth form teaching for which there was an allowance - an addition to my salary. Teaching A level chemistry was more interesting than early years science but I enjoyed the challenge of communicating some chemical concepts.

Chemical formulae provide a stumbling block that makes some people think that chemistry is not for them. When I was a school boy we were taught 'combining power' and did some strange exercises involving swopping numbers so that to find the formula for sodium oxide we wrote Na - 1 and O - 2, giving them their combining powers. We then exchanged the numbers to get Na_2O. This meant little or nothing to most pupils but some just learned 'how to do it' without thinking what it meant - if anything. I had already noticed in junior school that some children knew how to do long division without any understanding of division. It was just a sum and that was how you did it. The equals sign meant 'here is the answer' but that caused confusion when they arrived at algebra where the equals sign means 'the same as'.

My way of teaching chemical formulae was to provide a visual accompaniment to my explanation. I got two small boys to stand at the front with one hand in pocket and one hand waving about. They joined hands to form a hydrogen molecule written as H_2. They were joined by another hydrogen molecule to give two molecules, $2H_2$. I then found a fat youth to lay on the floor with his arms and legs waving in the air. He was a carbon atom, written C and having four bonds. After

some kicking and shuffling we ended up with the four hydrogen atoms holding the carbon atom by his legs and arms to give a molecule of methane written as CH_4 and the coming together written as
$2H_2 + C = CH_4$.
(Modern textbooks will have an arrow rather than an equals sign but the equals sign was used by the French chemist Lavoisier to indicate that the weight stayed the same. Lavoisier lost his head in the Revolution but that was not because he invented chemical equations but because he had been a tax collector.)

Chemistry has long been taught with visual accompaniment. Most people remember the teacher adding a small piece of sodium to water but not too many remember that this is represented by $2Na + 2H_2O = 2NaOH + H_2$.

The H_2, of course, stands for hydrogen, an explosive gas adding fun to the demonstration. Another illustration that could be carried out by the boys involved mixing flowers of sulphur with iron filings. After mixing, the iron could be pulled out with a magnet but after heating, the mixture produced a new compound, iron sulphide. This was not separated by a magnet and was supposed to illustrate the difference between physical change - mixing and chemical change - combining. There would be exam questions on the difference between mixtures and compounds. Milk is a mixture - the cream can be seen to separate. Orange juice caused problems - you cannot see that it is a mixture of water and lots of stuff but it is still water, not a compound formed from water reacting with something.

Teaching the same thing twice to different forms and then repeating the lessons the following year got me thinking. I concluded that science teaching rested on approximations designed to make things seem simpler than they really were. One way in which science simplifies the complexities of the real world is by classifying things into eithers and ors. Chemicals are supposed to be either mixtures or compounds but what about copper sulphate? It exists as blue crystals, clearly a compound but if you heat it, steam comes off and you are left with anhydrous white copper sulphate. Adding water to the white stuff turns it blue again so it's a mixture? No, it's not. The official answer is that compounds have components in a fixed proportion. In mixtures, the proportions can vary. Blue copper sulphate has 'water of crystallisation', represented by the formula, $CuSO_4$ $5H_2O$ but other forms exist with less water - sounds like a mixture?

The fact is that dividing things into either this or that makes teaching easier but at the expense of ignoring either/and or both either, or and something else. Nature or nurture is too simple. What about nature AND nurture or, nature, nurture and something else. Matt Ridley has a book entitled Nature via Nurture.

The real world is much more complex than represented by either/or. Physicists like to think that only physics is a proper science (the rest is stamp collecting, social work or car maintenance). However, school physics is full of approximation. The oldest 'law' is Newton's law of gravity and Einstein showed that it was only an approximation. School physics includes the notion that T, the time period of a simple pendulum, is given by **$T = 2\pi \sqrt{l/g}$**. However, this formula is only exactly true for swings that are so small that the pendulum is not swinging. Similarly, the formula for the focal length of a lens is only exactly true when the lens has lost its curvature and is no longer a lens.

Chemical ideas are often explained with some visual illustrations in the form of diagrams or so called experiments. What I thought of as illustrations were officially known as experiments but to me it is not an experiment when you know what is going to happen. I began to think about how we know what we know and this developed into a formal course. My 4.2 class knew enough chemistry to pass O level with ease and I was able to obtain permission to include a few lessons on 'how we know what we know'.

The classical Greek philosophers knew that 'what we know' comes to us via our senses and our senses can deceive us. They knew about optical illusions and the power of rhetoric to fool people. So how do we tell the difference between truth and false news? I was not expecting to find an answer to a question that had been around for two thousand years.

Authority provided the answer to many questions. The church gave answers via a priest and medical knowledge came via a doctor. Science and technical answers were in books. The question of how they got in the books in the first place led to the idea that science was something that you did and what you did resulted in finding out something new. If you managed to find our something really new then you got your name in a textbook like Dick Colclough and his ionic polymerisation catalyst. (Some years later, I came across Poppers solution - falsification - Science could not prove things to be true but it could falsify things that weren't.)

The school had many out of class activities including the Scouts but my involvement as Scout Master was not enough to satisfy the system. I was told I had to contribute to the science club. The other science teachers all had interesting things for boys to do after school but I was not able to produce some tricks of interest. I did think of crystal growing. If you have enough time and patience it is possible to grow very large crystals and there could be a competition to see who could grow the largest crystal. However, this had been done already.

I wanted to get across the idea that knowing what you know was not always obvious. So I started a Flat Earth Society. Some curious bright youths were intrigued by a poster and turned up for an event to discuss the flat earth. I challenged them to convince me of the roundness of the earth. They trotted out the textbook stuff about ships sailing over the horizon but I was able to show that light had to travel in straight lines for that to work. The fact that the lower half of the ship disappears when it sails away might be due to light being repelled by the earth. Since the lower half is nearer the earth its light is repelled more and disappears.

After much scribbling and writing on a blackboard it emerged that two diagrams could be drawn. Both had a straight line and a curved line. In one, the curve was the surface of the round earth and the straight line was the path of the light. In the other diagram, the curve was the path of the light and the straight line was the flat earth. The result was the same - the lower half of the ship disappears first.

The discussion was repeated a week later. Someone could have said that other experiments showed that light did travel in straight likes. However, like the classical Greeks, the boys preferred to argue rather than think about experiments. The main argument was why we did not fall off the edge of this flat earth. If we set off in any direction we did not fall of; we went round and came back so it must be round. My answer to that was to think of a map of the world with the North Pole at the centre and the rest spread out round it. The equator would be a circle with the North Pole at its centre. You could then travel round a flat equator. OK but then if you head south you come to the edge and fall off.

Ah, but when you get half way towards the south you find you are half the size you were. The nearer you get to the south, the smaller you get so you never reach the edge and never fall off. The arguments went on and I hoped that some would realise that reason on its own does not get you to the truth.

The following year I tried something else. I had noted that all the doors in the building had metal numbers screwed on to them. The numbers were mainly painted over but still visible. The numbers started at the entrance, spread out and upwards. Some numbers were missing from the sequence and some were obviously later additions being out of sequence and much higher than their neighbours. It seemed that the history of the building might be revealed through its door numbers.

I announced the arrival of the science of portonumerology - the study of door numbers. It seemed to catch the imagination of the boys. The younger ones engaged in a competition to find the highest number. This involved trying to gain access to locked doors leading to the roof. Older boys tried to discover the system behind the numbering. They claimed that the highest number was not at the top of the school.

It had been at one time but then alterations had added new doors with higher numbers so the highest number would be the newest door. The search for unusual doors led to the need to investigate the inside doors of the Ladies. There were two ladies' toilets in the school, one for kitchen workers and cleaners, the other for 'staff' i.e. the school secretary and the personal secretary of the head. Polite requests resulted in the disclosure of the needed numbers.

King Edward VII School was formed in 1905 but the Glossop Road building is much older, being opened as Wesley College in 1838. The original building had been a boarding school with a chapel in the west wing. The interior was completely rebuilt for the new school in 1905 and it was assumed that the door numbering scheme dated from then.

The 1905 school came under the control of the Sheffield local authority and it was common practice to put numbers on everything from desks to typewriters to doors. However, as with many scientific topics, the main conclusion of portonumerology was the need for further research.

In 1959, the school recorded its best ever "O" Level results and in 1961, the year that I left, it recorded 55

Distinctions at "A" Level, 8 State Scholarships and 14 scholarships at Oxbridge.

8.3 Getting Married

Now in possession of a degree, Sandra managed to find a teaching job in a Sheffield secondary school so that she could join me after Easter in 1960. By then we were discussing wedding plans. Sandra had an uncle Chic who actually owned a chicken farm that supplied the North Manchester Jewish community with kosher chickens. When we told him that we were thinking of a small wedding, he said that Cheetham Town Hall was very good for small weddings. By 'small' he meant about a hundred and fifty people. We meant about sixteen.

Eventually we arranged a marriage in Eccles Parish Church followed by a reception in the Airport Hotel. This took place during the summer holidays of 1960. The Anglican wedding ceremony was slightly unusual with half the people present being Jewish. The traditional service involved the bride being 'given away' by her father. Since Sandra's father was dead, she was given away by her uncle Sid(Clyne), her father's brother. He had 'married out' to a Roman Catholic girl, Kitty (Clyne), and so had no problem with participating in an Anglican ceremony. Uncle Izzy was different. He came along but stayed outside the church during the ceremony.

My best man was Mike Hall, another chemistry post grad. Later I was to be best man at his wedding to Patsy. The two weddings illustrate social differences as they were. For my wedding I wore a new charcoal grey suit with a yellow waistcoat and Mike wore his only suit, which was green. Mike's wedding was much grander. Patsy's family were well to do upper middles and formal morning suits were worn. I was fitted with the required outfit from Moss Bros. This included a starched shirt with a stiff front that stuck out. I overheard one of the relatives saying, "You can tell who has had to hire their suits".

(I thought that I would never need fancy dress for a wedding ever again. My two daughters both thought that marriage was an unnecessary bourgeois capitalist institution and they never married. However, some fifty years later, weddings became more fashionable and I was off to Moss Bros again for my son's wedding.)

After the church service we all headed off to the reception at Barton. In 1928, Manchester had opened its new municipal aerodrome at Barton, just outside Eccles. In 1933, it had acquired the first wireless control tower outside London. In those days, civil air flights were the privilege of the wealthy and the airport had a hotel to cater for their requirements. Barton proved to be unsuitable for larger airplanes. It was on the edge of the area that had caused a problem for Stephenson when building the Manchester Liverpool railway. The ground was too soft to support the weight of a railway or larger planes. So Manchester had gained its present international airport at Ringway, first opened in 1938 with a KLM flight to Amsterdam.

The result was that Barton had become a remnant of the past, claiming that its control tower was the oldest tower still working and mainly looking after small planes belonging to members of flying clubs and the Air Training Corps. Small commercial flying was still there including a mail plane that came from Dublin every afternoon.

The airport hotel was still trying to maintain high standards and was a suitable host for our wedding reception. The Jewish guests must have thought our event was rather odd. Jewish weddings in Manchester were grand affairs. Ours was the usual three-course meal followed by speeches. We then went outside for photos in the hotel garden. The sun was shining and there was an interesting backdrop formed by the nearly completed motorway bridge over the Manchester Ship Canal. Ocean going ships still travelled along the ship canal between Liverpool and the Manchester docks and the new motorway had to be high enough to avoid them.

In the previous century engineers had the problem of taking a narrow boat canal over the ship canal and a swing bridge had solved that with one canal being moved at right angles to the other canal. Making a motorway into a swing bridge was rather more difficult and so it had to be a bridge, high enough to avoid shipping. Moving steel girders into place high in the air was quite a sight especially with the knowledge that two workers had died by falling from the bridge.

After the wedding, we went on Honeymoon to Spain. Cheap air travel had not started in 1960. Our journey involved trains to Spain via the channel and Paris. We spent a night in Paris before travelling to San Sebastian where we stayed for a week before going on to Madrid for a second week. This two-stop holiday had been booked by a Manchester travel agent and the first week was not in a hotel but in the apartment of a widow who had room for two guest couples.

The other couple was missing so we had the personal services of a Spanish lady who cooked our meals. At first the food seemed rather bland but we discovered that the travel agent had told our host that English people did not like spices. We assured her that we were not like that and we frequently ate hot curries in Manchester. Reassured she then cooked some superb paella. San Sebastian had a sandy beach and the weather was sunny so we lounged about.

The train that took us inland to Madrid had an armed guard, a remnant of the civil war. Reminders of the war were everywhere. Lots of people had been injured and some of them were employed selling lottery tickets. Also, there were beggars with one hand missing who would thrust their stump at you. We were booked into the Hotel Americano and we were probably the only British people staying there.

We went to the Prado museum and tried to pay the entrance fee with a large coin. This was refused. The coin was a forgery and the ticket man refused to take a large note. Fortunately, a Spanish couple in the queue moved in and paid for our entry. I was reminded of this many years later when arriving by air in Istanbul we had to have our passports stamped with an entrance visa costing £5 if you had a UK passport or $5 dollars if you had a US passport. An American on the plane had no dollars. He said he lived in London and did not need dollars. The ticket man said a US passport has to have a visa paid for in dollars. The queue became restive but by chance, I happened to have a $5 dollar note with me so I was able to pay for the American. In evolutionary theory, this sort of behaviour is known as reciprocal altruism.

8.4 Twins

After the summer break we settled down to being a married couple, living on one floor of a Victorian house in Harcourt Road, teaching in Sheffield but staying in Crumpsall for most weekends. Then, surprise! Sandra was pregnant. At weekends we went shopping for the anticipated baby. One shop offered a deal that promised to double your order for free if you had twins. We thought that having twins was likely to be inherited and we didn't have any family twins so we said 'no thanks' to the twin deal. Then, further surprise, there were two heartbeats - or three if you counted Sandra's heart.

The weekend shopping then included an up market coach built twin pram and a more sensible twin trolley that could be folded up and taken on a bus. Things for the baby were kept in Crumpsall and I thought that Sandra's friend, Pat Newman would take them to Sheffield when the time came. Pat had learnt to drive so that she could help her father by driving his van.

Sandra carried on teaching but became rather large. We used to eat most evenings in Sheffield University student union building and then walk home to our flat in Harcourt Road, known locally as the Khyber Pass because of its hilly nature.

There were alternatives to eating at the Students' Union. One was 'TV Dinners', a meat, veg and potatoes complete meal, frozen on a tray and heated up in an oven. (Microwave heaters had not yet become available and the idea of frozen meals was new). The other alternative was cooking. I produced spaghetti Bolognese using a recipe learnt in the scouts. As neither scout camps nor Harcourt Road had a fridge, I used tinned meat to the horror of Sandra who muttered things about goy cooking and traif. She ate it though.

As a special treat we could eat out at a restaurant. Near the university, there was the Bamboo. Rumour had it that until recently Sheffield had had no foreign restaurants and a Chinese student who was there to study metallurgy decided to open his own restaurant. People had told him that Sheffield did not take to foreign food but they were wrong and other places soon followed.

It was thought that the birth of twins required some extra care and about a fortnight before the birth was expected, Sandra was admitted into Nether Edge Hospital where I went to visit every evening. On the seventh of May 1961, I turned up as usual and was surprised to find that Sandra was not in her usual place. "Oh didn't you know?" said the woman in the next bed, "You've got twin daughters". After some time, I managed to find my new family - two amazing babies and Sandra all tucked up in bed. The first born who was to be called Suzanne was five and a half pounds in weight; the second, Nina, was five pounds. The hospital said they should stay there for a few days just to make sure that things were OK. Four days later, the eleventh of May, was Sandra's birthday - spent in hospital.

Whilst Sandra was recovering I ate in the Anglican Chaplaincy and the chaplain visited Sandra in hospital. One of the nurses described him as 'dishy'. Unlike most clergy he did not wear the dog collar. He had a Mao-style shirt and an ornate silver cross on a silver chain.

I assumed that when the time came, Pat would collect Sandra and babies for transport to Crumpsall where Sandra would stay so that her mother could help with the twins for a short time before they returned to Sheffield. What I didn't know was that Pat and Sandra had had one of their many fallings out. Although they had known each other since childhood, they went through periods of not speaking and this was one of them.

8.5 ICI and Crumpsall

One day, I received a message that my family was now in Crumpsall. Sandra's mother had hired a taxi and taken them from the hospital back across the Pennines to Crumpsall. The word, kidnapping, crossed my mind but I had to accept a fait accompli. My family was in Manchester and I was teaching in Sheffield. The only solution was for me to find work in Manchester so that I could be with my family. Instead of applying for advertised positions, I just wrote to people who might employ me.

I received a letter from ICI Blackley asking me to come for a chat. Blackley is a district of Manchester connected to Crumpsall by Delaunays Road as mentioned in chapter 8. I went by bus and discovered Hexagon House, the headquarters of ICI Dyestuffs Division. I had an interview with someone and I only remember one thing from that. I was asked why I didn't want to work in the Research Department. "People like you with experience in research and no industrial experience usually opt for the research department." I replied that I had read their brochure and their service department seemed much more interesting.

I was taken for lunch in ICI's hospitality suite, starting with the bar. When asked what I wanted to drink, I came up with whiskey and dry ginger. The others had gin and tonics. After a splendid lunch with lots of wine, I was taken to see the laboratories where I would work. I then saw someone from personnel, filled in a few forms and took the bus back to Limestead Avenue.

When I returned to Sheffield I told the school that I had accepted a job with ICI and I handed in my notice but I had to stay until the end of term. The result was that for two months I only saw my daughters at the weekends when I learnt how to wake in the middle of the night and give bottles to two babies at once. The week after I had accepted work with ICI, I received an invite to go for an interview with another chemical firm that I had written to. This was Ciba-Geigy, a Swiss company with factory and laboratories in Trafford Park. (Ciba stood for Chemische Industrie Basel) I wondered what would have happened if I had received their letter before the one from ICI. As it turned out, my six years with ICI were to be an enjoyable and valuable experience as described in the next chapter.

References Chapter 8.
Matt Ridley. 2003. Nature via Nurture: Genes, Experience and what makes us human. London: Fourth Estate.

Chapter 9. Crumpsall and ICI 1961-1967

9.1 Crumpsall

In the summer of 1961 I bid farewell to King Ted's and Sheffield in order to join my wife, Sandra, and our daughters, Suzanne and Nina, at 2, Limestead Avenue, Crumpsall. This 1930's semi belonged to Sandra's mother, Sadie, and her brother, Uncle Mick, aka Michael Bernstein born in Russia before the Bernstein family had emigrated as described in chapter 7.

Being a part of the North Manchester Jewish community influenced my life style. Previously, my hair had been cut by scissors in barbers' shops but in Crumpsall I went to the Electric Modern Hairdressers where in addition to the electric hair cutters they washed your hair before cutting. The shampoo was provided by a youth, presumably a boy but possibly not and giving an illustration of the word androgynous. Clothes, of course, came from Jewish tailors and had 'hand-sewn seams'.

Over time, the Jewish community had moved north; away from the city centre to Victorian and Edwardian terraces in Cheetham Hill and then into new houses being built in Crumpsall. Several synagogues were built and the community supported two newspapers, The Jewish Telegraph and The Jewish Chronicle. The Telegraph had a famous headline, "TITANIC SINKS: MANCHESTER JEW SAVED". The Jew in question celebrated his good fortune by opening The Titanic Deli where he was reputed to cut the thinnest slices of smoked salmon in Manchester.

Another famous shop was Rose's sweet shop next to Crumpsall library. It never seemed to close and it sold the largest and most expensive chocolate boxes that anyone had ever seen. Large cars on the way out of Manchester to homes further north could be seen stopping at Rose's to enable men in expensive suits to gather large boxes of goodies.

So there I was in Crumpsall during the summer of 1961, starting a new life but technically unemployed. I had managed to get myself employed by ICI Dyestuffs but the job did not start until September. I went by bus to the Employment Exchange in the centre of Manchester where I 'signed on' as unemployed. I was told that I was not eligible for unemployment benefit (known as the dole) because I had resigned from my employment. The system still had remnants of the Victorian division into the deserving poor and the free loaders. People who had been made redundant were 'deserving' but someone who had just given up a job was not deserving of public support.

Fortunately there was an appeals tribunal and it was decided that leaving my job in order to be with my wife and children was deserving and so the state paid my unemployment benefit. However, in order to qualify I had to turn up at the Employment Exchange and sign on twice a week to show that I was available for employment if something turned up.

Since I had registered as a schoolteacher and all schools were closed for the summer holidays I did not expect to be offered a job. Someone realised that this was rather silly and it was arranged that I sign on to the professional register. This was another remnant of the past class structure. As a professional, I used a different entrance, I did not have to stand in a queue waiting to sign the register and I could sit down and talk to someone.

I still had my green card that recorded my signings and this became rather useful. In order to reach the bus stop to go back to Crumpsall, I had to cross Piccadilly Gardens and these were used by assorted wine drinkers and scroungers who would try and extract money from passers by. The green card acquired the properties of a magic wand. I only had to wave it and the pesterers disappeared.

A friend of mine, a keen Christian, had a way of reconciling the biblical injunction to look after the thirsty with his reluctance to give money to alcoholics. When asked for money for a cup of tea he would offer to take the supplicant to the café over the road and buy him some tea. This offer was never accepted.

The house in Crumpsall was a little crowded with four adults and two babies. With a mother and grandmother to look after the twins, I did not get much of a look in but I was allowed to carry them up stairs and put them to bed in cots on either side of our double bed. When they were older I would read them bedtime stories or make up my own but in that summer they were still at the stage of having bottles in the middle of the night and I became quite adept at holding two bottles and two babies.

Eventually the summer was over and it was time for me to discover what happened at ICI. To get there I had to walk through part of Crumpsall to reach a bus route that took me to Blackley village (pronounced Blake-ly) on the river Irk which had been the site of dye manufacture since 1788 when Angel Delaunay, fleeing from religious persecution came from Rouen in France with the secret of Turkey Red dyeing. To connect his river based dye works with civilisation, he had built a road from Blackley to Crumpsall and that road is still known today as Delaunay's Road. The manufacturing process was not what today would be called scientific. It was partly based on throwing things in to see what happens and it was rumoured that key ingredients included milk and dung from dairy cows.

Eventually, dye making became a branch of the chemical industry and in 1865 the site became a factory for Ivan Levinstein (1845-1916) whose son, Dr Herbert Levinstein, carried on the business until it was absorbed into the British Dyestuffs Corporation which in turn was absorbed into ICI, becoming the Dyestuffs Division.

There were three major employers for people who lived in Crumpsall. There was the hospital that had started life as a workhouse, the Cooperative Society Biscuit Works and by far the largest source of employment was the Dyestuffs factory that had employed over ten thousand people and was still known as 'Levis' to people whose fathers had worked there.

The site was in two halves separated by a path and railings. On one side was the factory, making dyes, pigments and other chemicals. Amongst the residents of the factory there were rats and cats, both of which had streaks of bright colour from sacks of dyes they had explored. The other half of the site was cleaner and neater. It contained the headquarters of Dyestuffs Division in Hexagon House and the research department, built in the 1930s when it was billed as the largest chemical research department in the British Empire (which meant it was smaller than ones in Germany and the USA).

It also contained the commercial centre that included a library with financial information on ICI's customers and competitors. The research department had its own library with a translation service so that even papers from Russian chemical journals could be translated if needed.

There were two other important buildings, the Dyehouse and the Polymer and Chemical Service Department (PCSD) where I was to start work. These two eventually became combined into a new large department known as

Applied Research and Technical Service, otherwise the ARTS Department. I always thought that 'applied research' was a misnomer. The term suggests that there is something else that is being 'applied' and that this something else is more fundamental and therefore more important. This most definitely was not the case in the ARTS department. What went on was more akin to Just William's mixin' than the application of some 'scientific' principles. My work at ICI is discussed in later sections of this chapter. Before that we have a little more about my life in Crumpsall.

You might think that with a name like that it started out as the site of Crump's hall and I imagined that there had once been a Sir Roger Crump living in a hall but that is not so. Crumpsall is mentioned in ancient documents going back to 1291. Oddly enough there was a Crumpsall Hall, built around 1560. It became the home of the Chetham family and the birthplace of Humphrey Chetham who acquired wealth through buying things in London and selling them in Manchester for a higher price.

His will provided money for the establishment of Chetham's Hospital that became a famous school of music. In the same building is Chetham's Library, established in 1653 when it was the first public library in the English-speaking world. This library was used as a meeting place when Marx visited Engels in Manchester. (There are also several pubs that claim the custom of Marx, Engels and other German émigrés in Manchester.) The Chetham family moved on to grander homes and the hall became a farmhouse before finally being demolished in 1825.

Crumpsall became a township in the county of Lancashire but in 1890 the township was incorporated into the city of Manchester that was growing like a hungry amoeba, absorbing all the surrounding towns. The former Crumpsall Council office still existed at the Victorian end of Crescent Road. Further along Crescent Road was the 1930s development including the house of the Newman family.

Pat Newman was a close friend of Sandra. They had grown up together and both had passed the eleven plus exam that gave them entry to Manchester High School for Girls. Pat's father, Monte, sold jewellery at market stalls in North Wales holiday resorts. Pat had a boy friend, Arif Ghazi who came from a wealthy family in Karachi but had been educated in England.

Before we were married, Sandra, myself, Pat and Arif went on a trip to London with Arif driving his car. We left early and Arif fell asleep at the wheel, driving into the back of another car. Fortunately we only suffered minor scratches but the car was badly damaged and we had to continue our journey by train. Arif admitted that he had written off another car by driving into a tree. Arif was clearly either accident prone or just careless and his next mistake was to cause Pat to become pregnant.

They decided to get married in secret but this required a notice to be displayed for three weeks in the Registry Office where it was spotted by a friend of Pat's father. To avoid a family dispute the couple then eloped to Gretna Green, the first town you came to when you crossed the border on the road to Scotland. Although England and Scotland are almost one country - a united kingdom - they have separate legal systems and traditionally it had been much easier to get married in Scotland. For example, you had to be 21 in England to marry without parental consent but anyone aged over 16 could be married in Scotland. Arif and Pat managed to become man and wife but when the news reached Karachi his family was outraged. Apparently Arif was already betrothed to a young woman from another important family and this was meant to be a seal on a merger between two business interests. Arif's family hired a private jet and several of his relatives arrived at Manchester airport.

They proceeded to virtually kidnap Arif who was then removed from England. A well-dressed man with a brown envelope full of money visited Pat. She was told that if she kept quiet and did not try to contact Arif, she would continue to receive financial support. He also supplied the details of a solicitor who would arrange for a divorce. Some months later, a boy was born. He was named Jeremy and grew up to be a successful young man. Pat married Peter Atkinson, a Yorkshire man who was the sports sub editor of a national newspaper and they had two children.

Some forty years after these events, I received an email from Stephen Newman, Pat's younger brother. He had spotted my name on Facebook and wondered if I were the person who had encouraged him to play chess all those years ago in Crumpsall. When I knew him, Stephen had been a very bright young boy. From the sports sub ed, he acquired tickets to football matches and sold them to fellow pupils at MGS.

Passing the entrance exam for Manchester Grammar School was no mean feat, particularly since the test was not culturally neutral. That is, it was more than verbal reasoning; it had elements of general knowledge that favoured boys who came from homes full of books or whose parents paid for extra tuition.

Stephen had neither of these advantages. The Newman house had about five books, a dictionary, Singer's prayer book, printed in Hebrew and English, a couple of novels and a first aid book. Stephen went on to obtain a degree in Maths. He was evidence for the idea that there existed some form of innate intelligence. At that time, more than 20% of the boys in MGS were Jewish. Also, someone calculated that 20% of professors at Manchester University were Jewish, lending support to the idea that there was a 'Jewish gene'

Living in Crumpsall for four years provided some important influences. In addition to being in a Jewish community and working for ICI, there were two other influences. St Mary's church continued my involvement with Anglican religion. Crumpsall Liberal Club introduced me to club land and developed my political activity. Both the church and the club were on the same road, St Mary's Road, a short distance away from Limestead Avenue but culturally miles apart. Limestead was 1930s land and Jewish. St Mary's Road was part of the remnant of Victorian Crumpsall.

There were people whose parents had lived in the area and some felt rather threatened by what they saw as an immigrant takeover. The church warden at St Mary's had a flag pole in his small front garden and he displayed the Union Jack on official days like the Queen's birthday. The club was a gentleman's club run by a committee, most of whom were Conservative supporters who had left the local Con. Club when it admitted women, becoming more like a working men's club with women as associate members.

My involvement with the church included running a youth club that met once a week. I also tried to change the church magazine. Unfortunately at that stage in my life I had not learnt the value of tact and I upset the regular parishioners. When the annual meeting elected the church council for the next year, it managed to vote me out. The council, the PCC, had twenty members and more than twenty names had been proposed. Parishioners were told by their friends to vote for everyone else but not for me.

The members of the Crumpsall Liberal Club were no better. Both the club and the church were places that felt under threat from the surrounding Jewish influx. I was considered to be an anomaly. Going to St Mary's Church but living in Limestead Avenue was not supposed to happen. The Chairman of the club took me on one side and said, "Look John, we don't have Jews as members. They are very able people but they have a tendency to take things over and we like things the way they are."

One member of the club who was confused by me, thought I was Jewish but was then confronted with my helping to carry the church banner at the Whit Week walks. Coming from Northern Ireland, he was in favour of people carrying banners and the next time he saw me he gave me a fiver as a donation to the Liberal Party. Both the club and the church have since been demolished and I was told that the last vicar of St Mary's committed suicide. The Jewish community moved on and the area became occupied by a new wave of immigrants from the Indian sub continent. But back in 1961 that change was in the future.

9.2 Liberal Party

The Liberal Club had at one time owned a bowling green and there was a side door leading from a bowls room to a path that went to the green. Before I arrived in Crumpsall, the Jo Grimond revival of the Liberal Party had begun and a group of young liberals had persuaded the committee that a Liberal club ought to offer them a home. The bowling green had fallen into disuse so the bowls room was vacant and the outside door meant that the dreaded young libs could be allowed in without entering the main club.

I found myself joining the local Liberal Party and going to weekly meetings in the bowling room. The Crumpsall Ward Liberal Party had been revitalised by the young liberals and was now focussed on the election of Manchester councillors, an annual event happening every May. The ward chairman and prospective candidate was Anthony Sullivan, a Roman Catholic, part of the other main group in the area. Irish immigrants had been entering Manchester for over a century and like others they had started in the centre of Manchester, moved north through Cheetham Hill and then into a council estate in Crumpsall and Blackley.

The ward Treasurer turned out to be Phil Benson, a cousin of Sandra and the elder of her Uncle Izzy's two sons. The younger son, Ralph, went to university and qualified as a dentist but Phil was older and had left school before the grant system made university an option. He had studied accountancy and was now working for a firm of moneylenders. Jewish moneylender sounds like a stereotype with memories of Shylock in the background but, in fact, Phil was one of the nicest people I knew.

There were occasions where I attended family gatherings involving Jewish prayers. Phil would look after me and show me the place in Singer's prayer book printed in Hebrew and English. He wasn't just nice to me. I remember one time he was calling on Limestead Avenue and the noise of piano playing was coming through the wall from the other half of the semi. I made some disparaging remark about Laurence(Stone), the piano player but I was reprimanded by Phil who reminded me that Laurence had suffered from Polio and was unable to walk without assistance. As a result he spent a lot of time at the piano. The time was well spent because in addition to playing the piano in nightclubs, Laurence had managed to compose the UK entry into the "Song for Europe" competition.

The Crumpsall Liberals met nearly every week and we went door knocking, raising funds and organising social events. In May 1962, the Liberal party was doing well nationally. Jo Grimond looked good on TV and stood out from the rather jaded men of the other parties (and they were men - Ellen Wilkinson had been Minister of Education in Attlee's government but died in 1947. Shirley Williams was not elected until 1964).

The Grimond Liberal Party had some distinctive policies. One of its slogans was "People Count" and this translated into saying that people should be involved in decision-making where they lived, worked and played. Different kinds of decision fitted different kinds of places. Decisions about the manufacture of steel were best made at European level but decisions about bus stops were best made by Parish Councils. Other decisions should be at national or regional levels. Splitting the UK into regions with some devolved powers seemed a good idea and 'regionalism' became a distinctive Liberal policy.

March 1962 saw a huge boost to Liberal fortunes. This was the Orpington by-election won by Eric Lubbock. At the 1959 General Election, the Liberals had come third in Orpington and yet in 1962 the Liberals won with more than 50% of the vote. As an MP, Lubbock was unusual in having an engineering degree from Oxford and working for Rolls Royce as a production engineer. He became chair of the party's policy committee for science and technology, which is where I was to meet him. But that was in the future; In March thoughts turned to the forthcoming elections for Manchester City Council. I became the official agent for Tony Sullivan, being responsible for organising and paying for the printing of leaflets and posters. Instead of using the traditional local printer, I found a modern firm using offset litho and a typeface that turned out to be Gill sans, that is a font designed by Eric Gill and being sans serif (no twidly bits)

In the week before the May 1962 council election, I took a week's holiday from ICI and joined other Liberals in delivering leaflets and canvassing. On Election Day we ran a campaign from the front room of the Crumpsall Liberal Club where we gave out lists of people thought to be Liberal supporters who had not yet voted. Supporters with cars went and knocked them up. In the evening we were off to the Town Hall for the count. Tony Sullivan gained 2400 votes, the highest number of votes for a Liberal in Crumpsall Ward either before or since 1962.

Despite the strong Liberal vote, it was not enough and the election was won by Fred Balcombe who was destined to be a Labour Lord Mayor of Manchester. As Labour candidate he had the support of traditional Labour supporters and in addition he was well known in Jewish circles as a campaigner for the rights of Jews in Soviet Russia. His political views were not particularly left wing and I was able to ask him why he had become a Labour councillor. He grinned and said he had joined the Labour party because they were the ones who had asked him. Despite having been Mayor, Fred Balcombe was deselected in 1984 when the Left took over the Manchester Labour party and got rid of valuable people who just didn't follow the party line.

The high Liberal vote in Crumpsall attracted some attention and I was asked to become the agent for the prospective parliamentary candidate in the Blackley division of Manchester. R Michael Hammond had been the Liberal candidate at the previous general election and was hoping to take advantage of the Grimond revival to do better next time. He came from a Liberal family. His mother was a county councillor in Cheshire and a member of the Lawson family, owners of textile factories. Michael Hammond had expected to join the family firm and perhaps become a director but the decline in the Lancashire textile industry had resulted in the factories being closed and sold off, leaving him with money but no career.

The Blackley Division of Manchester contained four wards, each electing city councillors. These were Crumpsall, Higher Blackley, Moston and Lightbowne. They came together at the time of general elections to elect an MP for the constituency. In those days, electoral law recognised two people, the candidate whose name appeared on the ballot paper and the candidate's agent who was legally responsible for paying all bills associated with the election and submitting accounts to show that the limit on spending had not been exceeded. As agent, I accompanied Michael Hammond on his trips round the Constituency.

Prior to 1945, Blackley had been a Liberal area and I met several people who remembered the last Liberal MP, Philip M Oliver, who amongst other things had written a tract, Back to Balfour, published by the British Association for the Jewish National Home in Palestine. Michael Hammond, unfortunately, had no obvious Jewish connections and he was not a Roman Catholic. The third social group in Blackley was the WASPS and they tended to be Conservatives.

The area still had four active Liberal Clubs. In addition to Crumpsall, there were Liberal Clubs in Lightbowne, Blackley and Higher Blackley and they all had people who were actively engaged in local elections. I became a member of these clubs and participated with Sandra in some of their social activities such as Bingo sessions and concerts.

Between elections, the party association raises money, delivers leaflets, canvasses etc. but before the law was changed, the political party had to cease during an election. The ballot paper did not contain the names of parties, just the candidates and a description - steel worker, architect or whatever.

My involvement in Liberal politics included attending a residential training course for agents run by Pratap Chitnis, Eric Lubbock's agent at the Orpington victory. This was held in the National Liberal Club, in those days still a residential club. Staying in a London club was a unique experience. In the morning, there was a knock at my door. A servant announced that my bath was ready. He had run the water into a bath a few doors away, down the corridor.

9.3 Working at ICI

The six years, 1961 - 67, that I spent with ICI Dyestuffs Division were enjoyable and useful. They were also the years in which my daughters developed from identical twin babies into lovely human beings with their own personalities. During this time we moved from Crumpsall into Stockport but this section is about ICI.

My time at ICI was spent in three different parts of the organisation, concerned with paints, foams and sealants. ICI Dyes Division did not make any of these products; it sold chemicals to manufacturers who did make them. Its service department provided liaison with manufacture, sales and customers as well as developing new products and giving advice on their use.

I started as a Technical Officer (TO) in the Surface Coatings Section of the Polymer and Chemicals Service Department and found that I had a desk in an office, a bench in the laboratory and an Experimental Officer to look after me. ICI resembled the military in its organisation with TOs as commissioned officers and Experimental Officers as the sergeants. The TOs had their 'officers' mess', the Senior Staff Club in a large Victorian House where food and drink could be purchased by signing a chitty with money being deducted from the monthly salary.

The Club also organised social events and Sandra and myself used to watch historic films as well as going to dances. Chubby Checkers' Let's Twist Again was in the charts and doing the Twist was the latest dance craze. Living with mother in law had the advantage of providing a resident baby sitter.

The use of the term, surface coatings, instead of the older paints and varnishes, represented a change in the raw materials used in their manufacture. For thousands of years, paint has been used. Its basic ingredients are some solid stuff, some coloured stuff, ground together with a sticky binder and a liquid.

The cave paintings from 30,000 years ago used powdered rock or charcoal, ground together with water, eggs and animal fat. This was applied with animal hairbrushes or blown through a tube. Over the years various natural materials were found to be useful. Linseed oil became a vital ingredient because it was runny and sticky but on exposure to air it oxidised into a solid substance holding the paint together. Various materials, extracted from plants, were known collectively as resins and used in paints and varnishes for centuries.

During the 1914-18 World War, Germany was unable to import many of these natural materials that came from parts of European colonies. Chemists were able to analyse natural chemicals and work out how to synthesise them or to make similar compounds. The new factory-made materials were often inferior to their natural equivalents and became known as ersatz i.e. substitute.

After the war, chemists round the world were employed to make improved materials and the era of synthetic resins arrived. Of importance for paint, alkyd resins became a class of chemicals that replaced the natural resins. After an initial reluctance, the public took to the new paints. In particular, a large reduction in drying time was both obvious and popular.

I found myself undertaking a training course in paint technology. This involved making many different paints, representing both the different types of chemical used and their various applications. Paint is a strange substance. From a simple scientific perspective, it should not exist. It is runny and sticky at the same time. If you put water on a wall it runs off and its surface is shiny. If you put treacle on a wall, it sticks to the wall and its surface is rough; you can't brush treacle into a mirror-like surface. On the other hand, paint has a sticky side AND a shiny side.

The next time you paint something, pause and reflect. The back of a paint film sticks to the wall but its surface can be brushed into a shiny finish. Also, the paint that starts out as a runny substance, quickly 'dries' into a hard finish. This drying action is not just the evaporation of water or other solvent; it involves chemical reactions. For many years, paint based on natural materials relied on atmospheric oxygen to oxidise the 'drying oils' used in its manufacture. Another way of turning liquid materials into solid is by getting two liquids to react together.

This had been known for centuries in dyeing fabric. A fabric can be coloured by soaking it in a coloured substance. The coloured molecules fit between the fibbers of the fabric. The problem is that when the fabric is washed the coloured molecules can come out again just as easily as they went in. The dye molecules can be held in place by the addition of a fixative or mordant (from the Latin mordere, "to bite"). The fixative reacts with the dye molecules making them larger so that they are more difficult to remove. Modern dyes are direct dyes and do not need a mordant.

In paint, the idea of getting two liquids to turn into a solid is rather difficult to put into practice. One way is to use a special spray gun with two inlets so that chemicals A and B come together in a mixing chamber before being forced out through the spray gun. Even this method requires a skilled worker who knows that the mixing chamber has to be flushed out with solvent after use. Otherwise it becomes full of solid.

At Blackley, a particular class of chemicals was of considerable importance. Polyurethanes are made by combining a diisocyanate with another chemical, usually a polyester or polyether. A diisocyanate molecule can be thought of as a spring with hooks at either end. The reacting molecule can be thought of as a small chain with eyes at either end. When many such molecules get together the result is long chain polymers - polyurethanes - with hook and eye connections forming the links in the chains. Many combinations are possible with many different properties ranging from a solid that feels like wood to soft foam suitable for pillows.

9.4 Cyril Lord Carpets

In my six years with ICI, I developed several new combinations for new uses. One of these was a new kind of floor covering developed in response to a query from a carpet manufacturer, Cyril Lord .

In the 1960s, Britain got used to TV advertising jingles (In the north of England, Granada TV had been showing adverts since May 1956) One of those that older people remembered was an advert for Cyril Lord carpets, with the annoying message. "THIS IS LUXURY YOU CAN AFFORD - BY CYRIL LORR---DD".

Lord, 'the carpet king' was a larger than life entrepreneurial innovator whose career showed that energy and enterprise are not enough - after several ventures his company finally became insolvent in 1968. He was fascinated by new ways of making and selling carpets and I became involved when it was suggested that curtain material backed with urethane foam would be a novel floor covering.

The Blackley buildings included a busy test corridor down which passed secretaries wearing stiletto heels and also workmen with heavy protective boots, both guaranteed to wreck poor quality floors. Several test panels could be placed in the corridor and the results examined.

A surface coatings team had shown that a superior wood finish could be obtained from a two component system using a diisocyanate known as Suprasec K. Attempts at selling this system were abandoned when a Scottish firm coated a ballroom floor with half of the system, leaving out the isocyanate. They wondered why the varnish remained sticky. Cleaning up a sticky ballroom floor was a headache that convinced management that two component systems were not a good idea.

I was responsible for testing some floor panels made from curtains stuck onto urethane foam. Curtain material does not last long if you walk on it but it was hoped that foam backing would add strength and flexibility. There are two types of urethane foam - rigid and flexible. Both types have bubbles inside the foam. In rigid foams the bubbles are independent; in flexible foams the bubbles are joined together. The rigid variety is used in building panels where it adds heat retention and some sound proofing to partition walls.

Flexible foam is used in upholstery but in the 1960s it had been used to support knitted fabric in the construction of tailored coats. Knitting machines produce fabric very efficiently but knitted products are not strong enough to hold their shape. The addition of foam kept the shape in place and added some heat insulation. By simple transfer of ideas, Cyril Lord thought that adding foam to curtain material might give the qualities needed to make a carpet.

Using the traditional technological method of suck it and see - otherwise known as empirical testing - I managed to find a type of foam that lasted for a month without tearing or crumbling. If the foam was too rigid, heels made holes in it. If too floppy, the curtain lost its shape. My foam seemed to be 'just right'. A meeting was then arranged with Cyril Lord.

The meeting took place in Manchester's historic hotel, the Midland. In 1904 Charles Rolls and Henry Royce had met in the Midland to discuss the formation of Rolls-Royce Ltd. and I felt that a meeting with the carpet king might also be an historic meeting - though on a much smaller scale. The Midland hotels had been built by the Midland Railway Co. and the Midland in Birmingham had been the site of a famous speech by MP, Enoch Powell, who feared further immigration, "Like the Roman, I seem to see the River Tiber foaming with much blood".

Present at the meeting with Cyril Lord were Jack Buist, the head of Polymer and Chemicals Service Department and other senior ICI people. We sat in a corner on leather armchairs surrounded by potted plants that seemed to have ambitions to become palm trees. We were supplied with copious quantities of expensive whiskey - with water NOT ice. I could not keep up with the drinking and some of my whiskey ended up in the potted plants.

Carpets have been woven for centuries. The innovatory Lord had popularised a different way of making carpets. His factory in Northern Ireland made tufted carpets from small lengths of synthetic fibre glued into a strong base. Lord was also innovatory in selling his carpets in his own shops and advertising on television.

However, being innovatory in itself is not a recipe for success. His chain of shops began to loose money. His search for new kinds of floor coverings was a disaster. Foam backed curtain was abandoned and Lord launched a synthetic grass, 'Cyrilawn', as a competitor for Astroturf. Unfortunately, the 'lawn' was not light stable. It degraded, turning blue and emitting a slimy surface. Cyril Lord went into receivership in November 1968, with debts of £7 million. He eventually retired to Barbados where he died.

Enjoying the facilities of a top hotel was part of the ICI experience. On several occasions, I was required to visit customers in the South accompanied by a member of the sales force and this meant staying the might in London. Travelling by 1st class rail from Manchester's Piccadilly station to London's Euston, included eating in the restaurant car and arriving in Bloomsbury, an area of London I was to know well.

The Imperial Hotel Group had six hotels in the area and its newest addition was The President, aimed at American tourists and having all its rooms en suite. In the 60s many hotels had washbasins in their rooms but going to the bathroom involved a walk down the corridor. The President seemed to me to be luxurious and I enjoyed having breakfast served in my room together with the morning's paper. (Some thirty years later, the same hotel seemed rather unpleasant and the breakfast was awful.)

Travelling with ICI provided my first experience of flying. I was sent to Amsterdam and went by air from Manchester's airport, known in those days as Ringway. ICI's travel section supplied me with a new passport and some Dutch money. On my return I filled in my expense claim and to my surprise I was summoned to see Jack Buist, my boss's boss. He threw my expense claim at me and told me to write it again claiming more money. He said that my job was to entertain ICI customers and I could not do this without spending money.

In addition to keeping customers happy, my job was to find new uses for ICI products and to develop new products. A foam carpet was but one of many new ideas that I developed. None of them became a commercial success but this did not worry me. I enjoyed the fun of attempting to find new products and I learned a lot from attempts that did not work. For example, there was the foundry resin.

9.5 Foundry Resins

I was asked to examine the possibility of using urethanes as foundry resins. In a foundry, molten metal is poured into a mold where it solidifies to the desired shape. Some molds can be used many times but others - known as 'lost molds' are used once. A lost mold is made from sand held together by a binder. Heat from the molten metal destroys the binder allowing the sand to be removed as the metal solidifies. Natural resins were used as binders in ancient times. Why should anyone think of using synthetic polymers?

The answer is desirable properties. The binder/sand mixture has to be a compromise. It needs to be pliable so that it can be shaped into a mold. But it also had to be nearly rigid so that it can stand there and accept the molten metal being poured into it. It then has to loose its grip and allow the sand to be removed. A two-component system might have advantages. It starts out sticky and pliable but as the two halves combine chemically, stiffening results. Under the influence of heat, further reaction takes place producing a non-sticky brittle mass. A few laboratory experiments showed potential and a trial in a real foundry was arranged.

Accompanied by an EO and a lab assistant, I met the foundry manager. The ICI team was wearing white lab coats and this caused some amusement to the workers who demanded wafers and choc-ices. I expected that there would be a small laboratory at the side of the foundry but we were in for a shock. In order to weigh out the components of the mix we were offered scales rather like those that used to be used to weigh potatoes. For containers we were offered empty paint cans.

Mixing with sand took place on a stone floor and used a spade. Molten steel arrived in a bucket transported by an overhead gantry and the casting was a success. It was eventually decided that a two-component system was unsuitable for foundry usage and I don't think that urethanes were ever used as foundry resins. I did hear though that polystyrene was used to make lost molds. The lesson that what worked in a laboratory might not work in real life applied in other areas.

9.6 The Pilot Plant

One of the functions of PCSD was to test new materials sent from the Research Department. The surface coatings lab contained a fiendish device, a weatherometer, designed to destroy painted surfaces by throwing hot, cold and salted water at test samples, interspersed with attack from uv light. A new polyether from research gave outstanding results in the weatherometer. Its ability to protect metal against corrosion was confirmed and it was formulated in a recipe that included a carefully added amount of water. Isocyanates react with water and polyethers can absorb water from the atmosphere but by adding water to start with you know how much water is present and extra isocyanate will remove it.

Further laboratory trials confirmed the outstanding properties of the new polyether and permission was given to move to the pilot stage of production. It is one thing to make a kilogram of something in a laboratory. It is a different thing to make a ton of something. Before moving to a large scale it is customary to try things out at an intermediate size in a pilot plant.

So in the middle of winter I found myself at the Blackley pilot plant in a rather dilapidated shed supervising the preparation of this new, special paint. Pigment and filler are added to paint in a ball mill using porcelain balls in a rotating drum to stir in the pigment. The drum was open so that I could add the crucial amount of water but then I noticed that there was a hole in the roof of the shed through which snow was dropping and some snow was falling into the ball mill. A carefully controlled amount of water? With added snow? Disaster!

9.7 Injection Moulding and Langrish House

My next task involved finding out about injection moulding and this had a surprising side effect. I discovered that my Langrish ancestors came from a village of that name in Hampshire, near Peterborough. At one time, the Lord of the Manor had lived in Langrish House, now converted into a hotel. The link between injection moulding and my name was a small firm, Langrish Tooling Products that had its factory in the grounds of Langrish House.

Someone in ICI management had put two and two together to make five. A person was needed to evaluate the potential of polyurethane rubbers for injection moulding. I had worked on polyurethane coatings and on moulds for casting metal so I was given the task of investigating the potential of polyurethane rubbers. A brand new shiny injection moulding machine was installed and shared between myself and some rubber technologists investigating more conventional rubbers. The molecular roulette procedure developed in the German dyestuffs industry was followed i.e. research department produced speculative material and service department tested it.

First, I had to find out about injection moulding and how to work the machine. As the name suggests, injection moulding is a manufacturing process that injects fluid material into a mould where it is shaped and hardened.

The ideas behind the process have a long history, starting with signet rings. In ancient times important documents were sealed by pressing a shaped piece of metal into molten wax. Since metal is a good conductor of heat, the pressure from a signet ring or metal seal also cooled down the wax, impressing it into a solid pattern representing authority.

Another ancestral idea is the syringe, basically a hollow tube with a plunger. By heating the cylinder, it becomes possible to force molten material into a mould. In 1872 an early injection moulding machine was patented by the Hyatt brothers who had developed a plastic substitute for the ivory used to make billiard balls. They were able to make small objects such as combs and buttons.

The processing of modern thermoplastic polymers required further development. The plunger was replaced by a screw, enabling mixing and crushing to happen before injection into a mould. In order to find out more about injection moulding I went to a trade fair in London where I visited various displays. The good ones had a hospitality space inside the stand and I was able to combine several G and Ts with finding out about machines. Then to my astonishment I came across a small stand under the banner of LANGRISH TOOLING PRODUCTS Ltd.

In life, one thing leads to another. Finding out about injection moulding led me to discover that there was a village called Langrish in Hampshire and this led to my discovering that my great grandfather came from that part of the world. The story of Langrish village and my ancestors is given in the next chapter. Langrish Tooling Products turned out to be a small specialist firm that made the moulds for injection moulding. It was situated in the grounds of Langrish House, once the home of the Lord of the Manor but now a hotel. The house had been the home of the Langrishe family (note the e) but in 1663 it was sold in the aftermath of the Civil War (The Langrishes had supported Cromwell).

Urethane injected rubbers were not a success but management seemed to think that I was doing a good job and I should extend my experience by moving to a different section. I found myself in a newer building working for a section leader, Ron Stafford, who was in charge of flexible urethane foam development. ICI was not in the business of selling urethane foams. It sold chemicals and knowhow to people who did want to sell foams.

The big problem lay in the area of knowledge transfer. ICI could make toluene diisocyanate, TDI. Its sale force could visit people and tell them that if they had any problems, there was a crowd of helpful people at Blackley who could help.

Unfortunately, the business of persuading TDI to react with a polyester to make upholstery foam was rather complex. Blackley knew how to do it but how to transfer that know-how? Part of the answer was to transfer the brains that held the know-how. This, of course, meant moving people. So ICI invested money to help people leave ICI and set up their own manufacturing companies.

One such company occupied an old mill on the banks of a Cheshire stream that had been the site of a water mill many years before. The factory was also next to the A6, the main road from London to Scotland via Manchester. From this site large containers could carry foam panels all over the north of England.

Another ICI spin off was Viking Engineering, formed in 1956 to make the equipment needed to mix and dispense the two-part system. ICI had patented new dispensing pumps and Viking was licensed to use the ICI knowhow. The two engineers who founded Viking eventually retired and in 1989 they sold the company to Cannon. (Viking Engineering should not be confused with Viking Pumps, an American international, founded in 1919)

9.8 Supersoft foam pillows

In my new position with Ron Stafford I was in charge of an EO and a lab assistant in a laboratory that was shared with another TO and his team. After finding out how flexible foams were made I was given the task of evading a patent for polyurethane super soft foams used in pillows. Pillows had been made from feathers and straw for centuries. The first new kind of pillow was made from rubber in 1929 with the trade name of Dunlopillo, signifying that the Dunlop Rubber Company invented it. It took three years from 1926 - 29 to obtain a workable process and Dunlop's history claims that the inventor's wife's cake mixer played an important role in the development work. It took a further two years for Dunlop to be able to scale up the process to mattress size. The starting material was natural rubber from trees in Malaya and during WWII when the tress were occupied by the Japanese, a doctor's note was needed to buy a Dunlopillo mattress. (Jones 1984)

This prompted a search for a synthetic foam pillow and the advent of the new thermoplastics meant that many new kinds of filling for pillows were tried. In the late 1950s attempts were made to use polyurethane foam in pillows but the standard foam as used in seating was thought to be a little too hard for pillows.

What was needed was 'super soft' foam. Various patents were applied for by ICI's competitors. These patents covered different recipes including those with more than 100% isocyanate and some with less that 90%. I was therefore instructed to find a patentable way of making super soft foam with between 90 and 100% of isocyanate.

It seemed that this was a highly urgent project as someone else would be trying the same approach and I was leant another lab assistant. The team made lots of different foams and sent them off for testing. Various standard tests, such as compression set, indicated which foams might make pillows and we finally selected one that looked promising.

Ron Stafford was delighted with our success and he took the team for a celebratory drink at lunchtime. I knew that the only way to test a potential pillow is to sleep on it. And so a block of super soft foam was made and cutting it into shape with scissors and knife, we made something that looked like a pillow. I took the pillow home, placed it in a pillowcase and slept on it for a good night's sleep.

When I woke the next morning, I did not remember the pillow until I opened my eyes to find that my right eye had gone blind. Rubbing and washing did not help; I could not see anything with my right eye. This produced mixed emotions. Obviously I was worried - but only slightly; I had a strange optimism about my health and wellbeing. My main emotion was one that I don't have a word for, a mixture of pride and excitement; I was joining the ranks of scientists who suffered for their discoveries like Humphry Davy inhaling gases to see what happened.

Fortunately, sight slowly returned and I was able to go to work. The recipe for the super soft foam included a volatile amine catalyst and a few experiments established that it took a few days for traces of this catalyst to evaporate from the foam. Otherwise the foam seemed to be satisfactory. A patent application and technical service notes for potential customers soon followed. The notes said that foam needed to be left for two days before being used. I did not find out if anyone used my recipe because I was moved on to work in a different building known as the Polymer Lab.

9.9 The Polymer Lab

Ron Stafford's responsibility included oversight of an odd building known as the Polymer lab. This was a single storey laboratory next to one of the exits from the site. It was ruled over by a Dr Gerry Crowley and his sidekick, Walter.

What went on in this building was slightly mysterious and Ron Stafford sent me there to find out.

I was supposed to be developing urethane sealants. There was a market for something that filled up holes and cracks in walls, cars etc. The ideal material had to be pliable to start with so that it could be forced into the hole. It then had to harden to be able to resist attack by weather, fungus, animal scratching or any other adverse condition. However, it must not be too hard because it had to follow the temperature-induced changes in the size of the filled hole. The usual objections to a two-component system did not apply to sealants. Amine cured epoxy resins had been known since the late 1940s and the idea of mixing two things together had become acceptable. The unusual properties of polyurethanes - combining strength with flexibility - meant that an excellent sealant system might be possible.

I found that I had an EO to assist me and he introduced me to the secret life of the Polymer Lab which reminded me of the Phil Silvers Show, an American TV series based on the doings of a sergeant Bilko who ran a series of private enterprise get rich schemes within the US military. My EO was constructing a central heating system for his own home, using materials from the Engineering Workshop.

As central heating was only just beginning to spread into ordinary English houses, rubber hot water bottles were still popular. At one side of the lab, I noticed boxes of hot water bottles. These were supplying a small assembly line, fixing pink polyurethane foam jackets to the rubber bottles. ICI was selling a urethane rubber under the name Daltoflex and this could be used to make an adhesive suitable for gluing foam to rubber.

The Polymer Lab was responsible for product testing this adhesive. Hence the furry hot water bottles. It seemed that product testing consisted of selling these quite nice pink bottles on Bury market. I did not ask what happened to the money.

The Polymer building was situated at the top of a slope leading out of the site. There was a sink facing down the slope and this was used by a cleaner whose unofficial purpose was to keep a look out for authority. When he spotted Ron Stafford or someone looking important walking up the slope, he shouted a warning and laboratory note books suddenly appeared.

I was able to take advantage of this relaxed atmosphere. As agent for the local Liberal party, I shared an office in the Higher Blackley Liberal Club and I sometimes went there. I had an unspoken arrangement with my E O - I would not complain about his central heating system if he covered up for my absence. Anyone looking for me would be told that I was in the library. A quick phone call from my EO to the Club would bring me back to I C I.

The origins of the Polymer Lab lay in the invention of an ICI rubber, sold as Vulcaprene. This was early polyurethane, made using hexamethylene diisocyanate, HDI, rather than the more modern TDI. It existed in four forms, A, B, C and D with A having high molecular weight (that is made from long chains) and D being of low molecular weight (short chains). Vulcaprene was weather resistant which meant that it could be used in tarpaulin covers back in the days when goods were transported by rail in open trucks covered with a tarpaulin sheet. (The original tarpaulin had been tar-coated canvass used to protect goods on ships - hence Jack Tar as a nickname for sailors)

Vulcaprene rubbers were oil resistant and were used to make seals and gaskets in the aero industry where aviation fuel is a strong solvent, needing special material in pumps and seals. Thus there was a small but important market for Vulcaprene. However there was a problem; untreated Vulcaprene degraded. The high molecular weight material became lower so that A grade turned into B and then C. Experienced users were aware of this but there was an extra complication, the mention of Vulcaprene in standard specifications.

In the UK, official organisations such as the military and local government have to advertise for tenders when they wish to purchase goods or services. To ensure that low price is not the result of low quality, any contract may specify that the goods have to conform to a stated standard. The British Standards Institution (BSI) was established in 1901 to provide official standards and Vulcaprene was included in a specification for waterproofing.

The problem was that the standard required Vulcaprene B but the tests had been carried out on an old supply of Vulcaprene that wasn't grade B anymore. This difficulty was overcome by keeping some Vulcaprene B in the factory for six months before selling it. This was then labelled

Vulcaprene B6 and supplied to the manufacturer who had to meet the requirements of a British Standard specifying Vulcaprene B.

There were other problems with Vulcaprene and I found myself attending a meeting of the Vulcaprene Committee. This was for liaison between manufacture, technical service and sales. The general feeling was that Vulcaprene was a relic of the past and that customers should be encouraged to use modern polyurethane, sold as Daltoflex.

To encourage the transition, the selling price of Vulcaprene was increased. As a result, the volume of sales actually increased. At first, I thought this must be an example of Thorstein Veblen's (1899) conspicuous consumption - an increase in demand following a price increase. In fact, the increase in sales was due to customers stockpiling, something that they later regretted because the stock degraded.

I did not find out what happened to Vulcaprene because in December 1966, I left ICI - originally on a one year secondment to Manchester University but I didn't go back. Before describing this life-changing move, it is necessary to describe some other events of the early 1960s.

9.10 The move to Stockport

When Nina and Suzanne were four they started formal education at Cravenwood Road Primary School, up the hill from Limestead Avenue. I started work at 8.45 and the school playground opened at 8.30 so it made sense for me to take my daughters to school every day on my way to work. An important event was the passing of my driving test. This allowed me to take charge of the Liberal van, used for transporting teams of canvassers to outlying parts of the Blackley constituency. The van was a Bedford Workabus with steering column gear change and a roof rack containing slogans. The sides of the rack were inscribed "Blackley Division Liberal Party".

The front had "Get Ahead with the Liberals" and the rear was emblazoned with

NOT	FORWARD	NOT
LEFT	with the Liberals	RIGHT

In 1965, this van saw service in the <u>Roxburgh, Selkirk and Peebles</u> by-election, won by the 26 year old David Steel who became the MP responsible for a private members bill leading to the legalisation of abortion. Steel became leader of the Liberal Party from 1976 to 1988 when the Liberals merged with the Social Democratic Party to form a new party, the Social and Liberal Democrats with the word 'social' being quietly forgotten when it was found that some anti socialist voters would never vote for a 'social' party.

Also in 1965 Sandra and myself began to search for a house of our own. Financially I was well off. For some reason ICI had liked me and I had been rewarded with a special contract that included an annual bonus on top of the profit sharing bonus. I had invested in a regular monthly savings plan that put money into Save and Prosper's Investment Trust. I had continued to pay into the scheme that I had joined via the Assistant Masters' Association and also I discovered that because I had moved from Sheffield to work for ICI, they had a scheme that paid the legal costs of buying a house.

We nearly bought a house in Middleton but I was not sure that staying in North Manchester was a good idea so I was relieved when someone got the house before us. We then nearly bought a house in Sale but a surveyor's report looked alarming so we tried for a house in Stockport and discovered an unusual modern housing estate designed by Hampson and Kemp. Eventually we became the proud possessors of 13, The Square, an ideal first house.

It needed minimum spending on furniture. The two main bedrooms had fitted wardrobes and the landing had another built in cupboard. The fitted kitchen really was fitted. It had a double sink with waste disposal and fitted cupboards. All that we needed to buy was a table and four chairs, The open plan lounge had under floor heating and stairs that went directly upwards without any corridors. This meant that heat could circulate up stairs and bedrooms could be warmed by simply opening their doors.

To pay for the house I arranged a mortgage with the Halifax Building Society. One of the conditions of the mortgage was that part of the house had to be painted. Although the house was nearly new, for some reason the wooden fascia boards under the gutters needed painting. Since I was a paint technologist, this meant that I could make the paint. This would be the ultimate in DIY; not just borrowing a ladder and applying the paint but also making the paint myself. I decided to use a blue pigment known as Monastral Fast Blue CR. This pigment makes an attractive pale blue paint that is ideal for outside use since it is resistant to most of the things that attack paint. In that capacity it was favoured by British Rail to coat the hulls of their passenger ferries from Dover to Hull.

The Monastral pigments were a new kind of dye, chemically known as the phthalocyanines, discovered by Scottish Dyes of Grangemouth in the late 1920s and developed by ICI who acquired Scottish Dyes in 1928. At the time, phthalocyanines were an entirely new kind of chemical and a team led by Patrick Linstead at Imperial College worked out their structure. (Linstead became Rector of Imperial College 1954 - 66 and was knighted in 1959).

This new class of chemicals was discovered by works chemists who were trying to remove a blue contaminant that cropped up in their manufacture of phthalimide. Synthetic dyes are manufactured from other ingredients and these have also to be manufactured. Phthalimide is one such precursor and you don't want a stray colour to contaminate the manufacture of dyes.

Some trial and error found that the blue nuisance was the result of cracks in the enamelled iron reaction vessel, allowing the reactants to attack the iron. It could be removed by dissolving the phthalimide and filtering off the blue stuff that did not dissolve. Problem solved? Yes, but the works chemists knew their history. They knew the story of young Henry Perkin trying to synthesise quinine in his back garden laboratory. He did not succeed in making quinine but he did make an interesting mauve colour. He could have just thrown it away but being curious and also motivated by the desire to make some money, he extracted his colour and sent it to a firm of Scottish dyers who were able to make it into a dye for silk.

Perkin gave the name, mauveine, to his new dye and patented it in 1856. With the help of his brother he began manufacture, not just the dye but also the chemicals needed to make the dye. Perkin's mauve was made from aniline and that was made from nitrobenzene. The benzene needed to make nitrobenzene was obtained from coal tar, a by-product from the manufacture of town gas.

Like Perkin, the chemists at Scottish Dyes did not just throw away the intrusive coloured stuff; with the help of Imperial College the blue stuff turned out to be unlike any other known chemical and part of a new family called the phthalocyanines. The original contaminant was ferrous phthalocyanine but a copper version turned out to have a more attractive colour and after development it became the Monastral pigment.

The phthalocyanines have a structure similar to that of haemoglobin. Both molecules contain four sub units assembled round a metal ion. Compounds containing carbon, hydrogen and metals are known as organometallics and include ferric butoxide, the subject of the PhD that I never finished. I still believe that the role of organometallics in the origin of life and its maintenance is not yet understood. If I had remained in chemistry, I would have liked to find out a lot more about these unusual substances. When I contemplated the result of my painting, I liked the colour, I felt proud of having achieved something practical and also I had the feeling that my house now contained the secret of life hidden under its gutters.

The house was about two years old and cost little more than my annual salary - very different from later years when a new house might cost four or five times a good salary. This meant that even after buying furniture for the lounge, curtains and bunk beds for the girls etc., there was enough money left in my savings to supply the deposits on two second hand cars. Sandra had passed her driving test in Crumpsall and was happy with a small car, an Austin A35. I purchased a maroon Cortina estate.

Moving from Crumpsall to 13, The Square was not just a matter of moving house. Changing a complex system involves many subsidiary changes. This was discovered when the UK decided to leave the European Union. It was not just a matter of leaving the Union; there was a large number of arrangements that needed substitutes. On a much smaller scale, moving from Crumpsall left some ties to be reorganised. The girls were still at school in Crumpsall and I was still working in Blackley and helping the Liberal party there. Every weekday morning, on my way to work, I took the girls to school in Crumpsall. Their grandmother collected them from school and then I took them home to Stockport.

The largest adjustment to the move had to be made by Sandra who found that she was expected to provide evening meals and look after the house as well as having a full time job. I helped a little by taking clothes to a laundrette and using the vacuum cleaner but my attempts at cooking were rejected.

We did, however, manage to eat out once a week. A Greek restaurant in the centre of Stockport could be combined with some shopping or further afield there was the Angel Hotel in Knutsford and the Ram's Head in Disley. In the 1960s many hotels were still hotels - that is places where people could stay for the night. They were kept going partly by the continued existence of commercial travellers, salesmen who travelled around, taking orders.

The railways had spread through England long before the telephone had been available and it was not until the 1960s that long distance direct dialling became common. Hotels near railway stations were still used by salesmen and they still had small rooms designated as 'Smoking Room', 'Lounge Bar', 'Commercial Room', 'Dining Room' etc. In the 70s the hotel public rooms were turned into open plan pubs but back in the 60s we could still find dining rooms served by waitresses wearing aprons and white headbands.

Back in Crumpsall, Sandra had obtained part time evening work teaching a class of adult illiterates, sensible people who for a variety of reasons felt they needed to learn to read. One of her pupils had grown up in an Irish agricultural environment. He had missed some schooling through illness and claimed that all he had learnt at school was the Catechism. He was working for a building firm and had been offered a position as foreman but that involved filling in forms and he could not read.

Sandra found that there were no "Learn to Read" books for adults and the children's books were very boring apart from the Janet and John series. She managed to create some publicity about the lack of material for adult learners and an interview with her picture appeared in the Manchester Evening News.

I discovered that Manchester University offered a one year full time course leading to a Diploma in Adult Education - the Dip Ad Ed and I suggested this to Sandra who enjoyed the year. This diploma and her experience with teaching adults resulted in her getting employment as an Assistant Lecturer - Grade B at a Manchester college - Fielden Park College of Further Education. After our move to Stockport, she continued working there and also kept in touch with the University by signing on for a part time M. Ed.

Her income made a welcome addition to the family budget but she had a dispute with the Principal of the college and handed in her resignation. This meant that in the summer after our move, she had no job but help came from an unexpected source. Round the corner from The Square lived Mike O'Donnell and his wife and we were visited by Anne O'Donnell who was a teacher at the Stockport Convent High School for Girls. This was a small two form entry school run by nuns under the direction of the Mother Superior who did not believe in advertising to fill a vacant teaching post. "God will provide" was the answer to a possible vacancy problem.

This worked because the teachers did not fancy having to carry out extra teaching and so they usually managed to find a suitable person to fill the gap and Sandra was persuaded to meet the Mother Superior. "God moves in a mysterious way. His wonders to perform." was the response to Sandra's announcement that not only was she not a Roman Catholic but she was Jewish.

Sandra managed to teach at the convent. There were times of the day when special prayers had to be said but this problem was overcome by using monitors, keen girls eager to show that they knew how to lead the prayers.

The school provided some experience in the results of streaming. When girls joined the school at age eleven, they were randomly assigned to two classes. At the end of the first year following a series of tests, the girls were divided into two streams, A and B. The average test results of A and B were not very different but at the end of the second year a gap opened up. Either the As had got better or the Bs worse or perhaps both. Was it the effect on self confidence of being labelled A or B? Perhaps it was the result of teachers' different attitudes to A and B.

My experience at King Edward School had made me suspicious of streaming and the Convent confirmed my opinion that streaming was good for those selected as the top at the expense of those not seen as the top.

As often happens, there was an unexpected side effect of Sandra being at this school. The girls became five years old and needed to attend a Stockport School but the local schools claimed to be full. Fortunately, the Convent School had a junior section and children of teachers had free places so Nina and Suzanne started their Stockport schooling at the convent.

Eventually God ceased to provide for the Convent School. The nuns moved on and the land was sold. A friend of mine, Mike Jepson, had the contract to demolish the convent.

As a demolition contractor, Mike arranged the paper work and subcontracted the actual demolition to an Irish organiser. When Mike went to inspect the result of demolition, he found the convent building gone and the site cleared but left standing was a statue of the Virgin Mary. The Irish workers were not going to touch the BVM. So Mike had to take a hammer and break the statue himself, the only time he actually demolished anything.

Meanwhile, the girls had moved on. In total they went to six different schools before they were eleven years old. These were Cravenwood Road in Crumpsall, the Convent School, Heaton Moor Infants, Didsbury Road, Tithe Barn and Neville Road in Bramhall. Being twins seemed to enable them to change schools without problems. They always had a sister with them and being twins was a slight novelty that attracted friendly attention at a new school. At other times they were encouraged not to think of themselves as a pair. Their clothes although very similar had something that distinguished them apart. Relatives were told not to send cards or presents to "the twins"; they were to be treated as individuals.

We enjoyed living in The Square. It was so different from Limestead Avenue where all the houses seemed to belong to people who had bought them before the war and there were no other children. In contrast, most of the houses in The Square belonged to first time young buyers and there were other children to play with Nina and Suzanne. The houses were arranged in four blocks of terraces, three blocks with four houses and one block with five. No 13 was at the end of the five block, numbers 9 to 13 and this reminded me of something that had puzzled me as a small boy. There are five houses between 9 and 13 yet 13 minus 9 equal four. Something wrong? No; nine and ten pus eleven and twelve then thirteen - that's five houses even though 13 - 9 = 4. I remembered a similar problem when thinking about my school. The infants' school had four classes for 5,6,7 and 8 year olds but 8 - 5 is three. As a small boy this had puzzled me until I thought of forks - as in knife and fork. A fork has four prongs but there are three spaces between the prongs. Also, I thought about two boys, one aged five and one aged eight - three years older because 8 take away five is three BUT there are four years 5, 6, 7 and 8. Four prongs and three spaces.

The social life of The Square was a new experience. When we moved in we were asked to join the baby sitting club.

This soon got us known by the other families. Points were gained for sitting and lost when you used a sitter. There were no walls, hedges or fences separating the fronts of the houses. A grass verge kept the road from the houses and we had a petrol driven communal lawn mower, taking turns to mow the grass. Sometimes at weekends, two or three families would combine forces and have a joint meal.

I remember my 30th birthday celebration. It involved a dinner for most of my friends from The Square, held at the Old Rectory Diners Club. It was run by a man who looked like Gilbert Harding and was one of those bad-tempered chef/owners who could be rude to guests.

He was also a card carrying member of the Communist Party and this seemed surprising to his lunchtime customers who were expense account businessmen. (In those days entertaining customers was an expense allowable against tax) Someone asked him how he could reconcile being a member of the CP and making a living from capitalism. His reply was, "It's called redistribution of wealth, sir". His son was a founder member of European CND and a member of HC Reform Club.

Most of the people I knew were slightly younger than I and being thirty was something to be ignored. I thought of myself as still being in my late twenties. Thirty was old! This lasted until my thirty first birthday.

In October 1966 I celebrated my 31st birthday and this started a chain of events that changed my life. The truth of being 31 hit me like a cold shower - before I knew it, I was going to be forty. Shock horror - time to think about what I was doing with my life. I listened to older people at ICI. In the research department I knew someone who was a world expert in the chemistry of rubber additives. He'd been in the same job for years and years. So I asked him why he'd never moved. He pointed out that the head of a Dunlop factory with 3,000 workers and high responsibility actually earned less than he did. Then he added that if you didn't leave ICI when you were young you were trapped.

It finally sank in. I was 31. I was getting old! Working at ICI I was earning good money and I knew that if I stayed there I could never afford to move. I had thought of applying for a job as lecturer in polymer technology at the John Dalton College of Technology but that meant a drop in salary. So I applied for more senior jobs. I was interviewed for a post as Assistant

Principal at Stockport college of HE but fortunately was not successful. I also got interviews for jobs overseas - with the Canadian firm Uniroyal in Sarnia and with Allied Chemicals in Monaco. Finally, Sandra spotted an advert for a job as Senior Research Fellow in a strange new University Department. I sent off an application and was invited for interview.

The interview took place in Jevons' office that I subsequently discovered had at one time been used by Alan Turing of computer fame. I was faced by Jevons and Mike Gibbons who had just completed his PhD in Physics and was the first lecturer in the new department. Also present was a chap called Coates, an Oxford man who had taken a diploma in history and philosophy of science after his degree in chemistry.

This new department called itself, "Liberal Studies in Science" and offered a BSc honours degree with that name - LSS for short. The research post, funded by the Council for Scientific Policy, was for a study of industrial innovation. The salary for a Senior Research Fellow was the same as for a Senior Lecturer. I talked my way into the job and changed my life from being an industrial expert on urethanes to being an academic expert in technological innovation.

Before describing my life in LSS, the next chapter contains the story of Langrish family and village.

References Chapter 9.
Jones, Geoffrey. 1984. The Case of Dunlop. The Economic History Review. 37. pp 35-53.
Veblen, Thorstein 1899 Theory of the Leisure Class: An Economic Study in the Evolution of Institutions. **New York: Macmillan.**

Chapter 10. Langrish - village and family

10.1 Langrish Village

Not many people have heard of the English king, Stephen. Even fewer have heard of King Stephen's cupbearer, Hercules de Langrish. Stephen was the grandson of William the Conqueror (1066 and all that) but not in the direct line of succession. He only became king of England through force and he needed help in the various battles that he fought to keep his throne. One way of rewarding people on his side was the granting of land. So Hercules was given a 'tithing' in the sub-manor of Langrish in the manor of East Meon. He also acquired a coat of arms emblazoned with four rather odd looking things, like eggcups with lids on. One of the responsibilities of the cupbearer was to prevent someone from adding poison to the King's wine - hence the lids.

Today, the village of Langrish lies off the A272 west of Petersfield in Hampshire. In the 11th century it might have been called "Long rush" or something similar. That part of England had several shallow ponds, ideal places for rushes to thrive. Between 1135 and 1601, the top man in the place called Langrish (or Langeryshe or whatever) was someone called Langrish (or Langrishe or one of several other spellings - remember even Will Shakespeare spelt his own name in different ways).

Two separate events resulted in my discovering that there was a village called Langrish and that this place had given its name to a family of the same name. The discovery of the village resulted from my working on injection moulding in the early 1960s. As mentioned in the previous chapter, I found that the village of Langrish housed a firm that made moulds for forming plastic objects. My stumbling on some other people called Langrish happened in the early 1950s when I was forced to take shelter from a torrent of rain.

10.2 Langrish Family

I was walking along Deansgate Manchester, when the sky opened and buckets of rain descended. I found that I was next to a strange building that looked as though it wanted to be a Norman castle but someone had turned it into an Arts and Crafts church. The important thing about it was that its imposing entrance was open. So out of the rain I ran. I soon discovered that I had entered a library.

It was, In fact, the John Rylands library, founded by Mrs Enriqueta Augustina Rylands (someone could write a book about her, born in Cuba she married John Rylands when he was aged 74. She acquired various collections, including the library of Earl Spencer, and became the first woman to be made a freeman of the City of Manchester.)

In those days, before the development of small computers, all libraries had card indexes, stored in wooden drawers. I did not wish to be conspicuous, so I started to look in the author index. Being rather self-focussed, I started with L and much to my surprise I found that under L there was a card for one Hercules Langrishe (with an e). Sir Hercules Langrishe, Bart. M.P. had written a tract on "The Irish Question".

It turned out that this author had been made a Baronet for political services in the old Irish Parliament, abolished in 1808 by the Act of Union making Ireland part of the United Kingdom. Much later, I discovered that the inherited title still exists. Another Hercules, Sir Hercules Ralph Hume had a niece, Carolyn Langrishe who came to England and became a successful actress.

Having discovered that there were Langrishes in Ireland and there was an English village of that name, I wondered how they were connected but did nothing about it until I acquired a paper version of the Mormon Index (the IGI - International Genealogical Index, an attempt at recording all the baptisms they could find so that they could be re-baptised 'properly' to get them into heaven).

There are two ways of tracing a family tree, starting in the past and starting in the present. On the Langrish side, I knew that my father was George Arnold, born in January 1901 just before the death of Queen Victoria, allowing him to be able to point out that he was a Victorian. After he died in 1973, I inherited his silver pocket watch. This had an inscription showing that it was given to my grandfather, George William, on the occasion of his 21st birthday by his father, another George. I also inherited a piece of paper, showing ownership of a grave in Gorton cemetery. This grave had been purchased by my great grandfather, George, who sadly had to bury his only son, George William before I was born. There was only one photo of George and it showed him with a sheep dog. My mother claimed that George had been a shepherd 'down

South' but enclosures had made him unemployed and he had walked all the way to Manchester where he had worked for Bayer Peacock who made steam engines for the world.

I found that other people were exploring the family history. In particular, my cousin Irene (daughter of my father's brother Norman) had written about some old Langrish wills for her dissertation at Oxford Brookes University. Then I found that one Paul Langrish was attempting to construct a family tree for all the Langrishs that he could find. I also did my own research using the amazing Mormon index. Eventually, I was able to put together a story in two parts, the family history up to the departure for Ireland followed by what happened to the village and my ancestors.

The story starts in 1135 when Hercules Langrishe was given land, including the 'tithing' of Langrish, by King Stephen in return for his support. Hercules had the title of 'cupbearer' to the king, reflected in the four cups on the Langrishe coat of arms - still used by the Anglo-Irish branch of the family who are in Burkes Peerage as Baronets. This Hercules stopped being cupbearer when King Stephen died in 1154 but he and his descendants remained as Lords of the manor of Langrish. There are records of the Langrishe main line between 1273 and 1575 written down in 1575 following a Visitation from the College of Heralds who were responsible for recording the heredity nobility and their Coats of Arms.

Henry VIII invented the Heralds' Visitation as a legalised check on the nobility. Once invented, it carried on and in the reign of Henry's daughter Elizabeth, the visitation reached Langrish where it found that in 1273 Nicholas Langrishe, Knight, had been Lord of the sub manor of 'Langeryshe' within the Manor of East Meon. [Today East Meon is a village down the road from the village of Langrish on the A 272. It has a Norman church, All Saints, first built between 1075 and 1150. Langrish did not acquire its own church until 1871 when Langrish became a separate ecclesiastical parish around the church of St John, Langrish.]

After Nicolas, there were ten more Langrish Lords of the Manor until we arrive at another Nicolas (1473-1535). This Nicolas married Joan Stempe and they had eleven children including nine sons. At that time there were two large houses in the area. Nicholas and his son Edward lived in Langrish House and another son, Ralph, lived in Bordean House. Four of the sons, Nicholas, Peter, Martin and Richard became

Priests; The Rev Peter became Canon of Winchester but was sacked for non-conformity in 1558. (That was the year in which the Roman Catholic Queen Mary died to be replaced by Queen Elizabeth the First.) Richard was educated at Winchester College and Merton College, Oxford. He became chaplain to Cardinal Wolsey. The Rev Nicholas left a very detailed will leaving bequests to his brothers, sisters and their children. The reign of Queen Elizabeth saw the compulsory registration of births in 1560. This together with the details from Nicholas' will as starting point enabled Paul Langrish to construct his amazing record of the descendants of that family.

The second son was William and his son, another Nicholas, inherited Langrish House from Edward who died without children. This Nicholas had a son, William, who inherited the manor of Langrish but in 1610 he sold it, much to the annoyance of the other Langrishs.

Ralph and his son, Edward and grandson, Roger, continued to live in Bordean House. Paul Langrish traced the background to Roger's son, Hercules, and produced the following account.

"Major Hercules Langrishe son of Roger the playboy, married Olympe du Plessis and lived in France on their estates in the Loire Valley. He was made Chief Carver to Henrietta Maria (wife of Charles I but exiled in France) at a stipend of £200 per annum. After 18 years he returned to England, was responsible for warning the speaker in the House of Commons that King Charles was on his way to arrest the five members. Fought in the Civil War for the Roundheads; was not popular with his comrades especially Pymm and the Earl of Essex. Died penniless after spending a year in the debtors prison at Newgate. It was his son Captain Hercules who was sent by Cromwell to settle the troops in Ireland and who founded that branch of the Langrishes in that country. Three generations later another Hercules was awarded the baronetcy for his work in the Irish Government."

During the Civil War, the family supported Cromwell. There was a battle outside the village and prisoners were kept in the cellars of Langrish House. After the restoration of the monarchy the Langrishe (with an e) branch of the family kept out of the way in Ireland. Supporting Cromwell was a strategic mistake for Hercules senior who relied on money from the wife of the Charles who lost his head.

Astute readers will have spotted that of the nine sons of Nicholas, seven have been accounted for. The ninth son was Anthony and he had two sons who each had many descendants including a branch in America and a number with the hyphenated surnames 'Langrish-Smith' and 'Langrish-Dixon'. The remaining son of Nicholas, John, I have left to the last because he is my ancestor.

John Langrish (1492 - 1546) was baptised in East Meon but died in a place called Leigh near Havant, a small Hampshire village to the North East of Portsmouth and South of Petersfield. [In Hampshire not far from Mid Lavant in West Sussex north of Chichester.] So why did he move from where his family had been for some three hundred years? He lived in the reigns of Henry VII and VIII when England was recovering from the earlier Black Death and finding prosperity from producing wool. It seems likely that with family support he moved further south in search of new land. He, his wife, Rose, his son, Robert, and grandson Richard all lived in Leigh, Havant and were prosperous enough to leave wills. (A modern descendant from this branch of the family is Michael Langrish, born in Southampton and worth a mention because he became bishop of Exeter in the year 2000, though we don't approve of him because he was against the ordination of women.)

Richard married Elizabeth about 1570 and they had at least six children, one of whom was Thomas who had to move in search of a living. He became 'a gentleman of West Ashling' (A small village, west of Chichester) and left a will in which his youngest son, another Richard, is not mentioned - probably because he was born the year before his father died. This Richard moved to another Sussex village, Ardingly, where he married Elizabeth. They had five sons, the eldest being recorded by the Parish clerk as 'John Langruedge'. This John, his son, another Robert, and his grandson, George, lived and worked in Sussex. This George was baptised in 1776 and married Mary Budden in Compton (another small village north of Chichester). Their fourth son was William, born in 1814 and married to Elizabeth Philp, a domestic servant, daughter of William Philp, a carpenter. William Langrish became a shepherd in Mid Lavant, in West Sussex north of Chichester.

His son, George, born in 1849, also became a shepherd but enclosures meant that fewer shepherds were needed and he became out of work. It is possible that his mother gave him a bag of food and some money for his journey to Manchester where he found work in Gorton, then a district of Lancashire but now a suburb of Manchester. At one time he worked for Bayer Peacock who made steam engines for the world's railways ranging from the small Thomas tank engines of the Isle of Man to the giant locos of South America. I have even seen a Bayer Peacock engine in a Turkish railway museum.

The George who walked to Manchester was my great grandfather and I started my own version of the family tree by working backwards from him. Using the Mormon Index and obtaining copies of registers from County Record Offices, I found that his parents were called William and Elizabeth and I found a William married to an Elizabeth Newell in Harting on 7.10.1839. (Harting is a village to the SE of Petersfield on the B 2146.) This William was born in 1817 and was the son of John Langrish who married Mary Wells in the church at East Meon in 1813. The village of Langrish was part of the parish of East Meon until it became a parish in its own right. So I, John Langrish, had connected myself back to the village of Langrish. My great grandfather George had a grandfather called - in my version - John Langrish.

We now have two versions of a tree, both connecting my immediate Langrish family with people who lived in the village of Langrish. Which one is the correct version? Does it matter? Ancestry does seem to matter to those who construct their own trees. It has mattered to the Irish Langrishe family who have continued to use the name Hercules. They have also celebrated their descent from French aristocracy in the person of Olympe du Plessis, married to the Hercules who ended up in a debtors' prison. Olympe's father was Lucullus du Plessis and her mother was part of the aristocratic de Griffon family. This ancestry enabled Richard Langrish (born 1834) to name one of his sons, John du Plessis Langrishe (1883 - 1947). Also, Richard researched his full family tree and was able to persuade the Ulster Herald to approve a splendid coat of arms with 42 quarterings, that is 42 small shields representing the arms of various ancestors starting with the four cups of the original Hercules.

Recording ancestry was important in ancient times. All those 'begats' in the Bible connect Adam with King David and then on to the family of Jesus. In America there are people who are very proud to be descended from someone who came over in the Mayflower. But what is it all FOR? All those births, marriages and deaths, is there any point to it all? Or, is it in the words of Ecclesiastes, "Vanity of vanities, saith the preacher; all is vanity".

What fascinates me is the numbers involved. Many people interested in their ancestors make use of modern sources found on web sites such as Ancestry dot com. A full family tree branches into two with every generation. Listed above we have eleven generations going back to the Nicholas baptised in 1473 and another ten Lords of the manor before that, making 21 generations back to the cupbearer Hercules. Two to the power of 21 is approximately two million. A few more doublings and you reach a number that is greater than the entire population. Obviously some of the same ancestors crop up on different sides of the tree. When Princess Elizabeth married Philip Mountbatten, it was pointed out that they were both related to the same great great-grandparents, namely Queen Victoria and Albert. Charles Darwin and his wife Emma were first cousins, sharing Wedgwood grandparents.

10.3 Talbot-Ponsonby

After the Langrish family had sold Langrish House and Bordean House, what happened to the village? I had discovered the village through finding Langrish Tooling Products Ltd and I became interested in how did such a firm exist in a small country village? The answer involved a family with the splendid name of Talbot-Ponsonby. In 1894, a new Local Government Act made Langrish into a civil parish. The first chairman of the Parish Council was Mr C W Talbot-Ponsonby who lived in Langrish House and was known locally as The Squire.

The village of Langrish has a Parish Church. Its notice board is headed 'St John, Langrish'. In 1979 some church members produced a booklet, "We Love Langrish" and this contains an article by Anne Morris writing about Tooling Products and how it came to be situated in what had been the stables and coach house of Langrish House. Originally the buildings had contained a landau, two broughams and horses. In her own words,

> It all began before the last war when Mr Edward Talbot-Ponsonby, the son of the Squire of Langrish,

was a schoolboy on holiday from Harrow. His favourite pastime was using a lathe and drill, set up in the stable. During the war that hobby was to be put to splendid use in the manufacture of components for aircraft and radar installations. After the war the business was to continue and flourish. In 1947 there were 22 skilled engineers on the pay roll and £20,000 worth of precision machinery installed in what had been the coach house and stables.

With the growth of the plastics industry, the demand for moulds increased. By 1954, the stable block had been enlarged. The company had begun taking on apprentices and built ten company houses.

In 1961, Mr Talbot-Ponsonby sold the firm to John Brown Ltd. the engineering giant whose Clyde-side shipyards had built the Cunarders.

The firm continued to expand and Tooling Products capacity for the manufacture of large moulds to a very high standard was proven with the order of a nose cone mould for the Anglo-French Concorde.

In 1986, a Langrish resident, Evelyn Hickox, published a booklet, Some aspects of Langrish Life through the ages. This gives us more information about Tooling Products Ltd. Apparently, the stables at Langrish House did not have electricity until 1946; the village was not connected to the electric grid until 1949. This means that during the war, Mr Edward Talbot-Ponsonby was able to manufacture parts for aircraft and radar without the benefit of mains electricity. The growing firm had difficulty in finding workers and had to tempt people from elsewhere by building ten houses. It had an apprentice scheme and paid good salaries. By 1986 it was employing 140 people.

Another person to write about Langrish House was the gardener, Philip Voice. He describes the gardens as they were in the 1980s and mentions that executives from the Weir Group, the Scottish company who acquired Tooling Products, would come once a month for a meeting and always stopped to talk and admire the garden.

I find it rather fascinating that modern technology, as represented by the Concorde, should have a place in the former stables of a country mansion surrounded by well-kept gardens. Anne Morris writes that commercial vehicles trying to make a delivery to the firm often had difficulty in finding it. Sadly, Tooling Products Ltd was wound up in 2009.

Langrish House became a hotel and is presently (2020) occupied by Nigel Talbot-Ponsonby, the son of Edward. The hotel has won several awards, including Les Routiers national hotel of the year award. The hotel's website states that Langrish house has now been the family home for seven generations. These 'seven generations' include several from the Waddington family who owned Langrish House in Victorian times. The Talbot-Ponsonby family acquired Langrish House through marriage when Charles Talbot-Ponsonby married Constance Waddington who inherited Langrish House from her uncle.

John Waddington the co-founder of Waddingtons, a publisher of card and board games in the 19th century, had purchased farmland in Langrish along with Langrish House in 1840. The firm became famous through acquiring the British rights to the Monopoly board game and subsequent games, enjoyed by four generations of my family who in addition to Monopoly have played Totopoly (first appeared in 1938) and Cluedo (1949). The Waddington firm was eventually sold to Hasbro. An earlier Waddington, Edward, was bishop of Chichester around 1710.

After the Langrishe branch had left for Ireland, the other large house in the area, Bordean House, belonged to several people but played a part in the development of the village. In 1871 Langrish became an ecclesiastical parish with its own parish church of St John and Mrs Nicholson of Bordean House laid the foundation stone for the new church. The house was leased to the Sue Ryder foundation for one of their hospices between 1975 and 1997 when it was sold to a property developer.

That is enough about Langrish village and its families. The next chapter returns to my own story with the years in LSS.

Chapter 11. LSS: 1967-1970

11.1 LSS and F R Jevons

This chapter continues the story from Chapter 9 with my leaving ICI to join a new university department. What was this Liberal Studies in Science? I discovered that the new department with a strange name was the brainchild of F R Jevons, born in Austria and originally known as Frederic Raphael Bettelheim. He had been a successful biochemist gaining a DSc degree from Manchester and producing an interesting book, The Biochemical Approach to Life.

In the 1960s, universities had expanded and several had created biochemistry departments that required professors as heads. F R Bettelheim was well qualified for this role but unsuccessful in his applications. It was rumoured that his wife persuaded him to change his name and he decided on Jevons, the name of his housemaster at his school in England and a good name in Manchester where Stanley Jevons had been Professor of Political Economy and founder of the so called Manchester School of Economics.

The 1960s expansion had seen an increase in the number of places available for science students and at Manchester, Physics and Chemistry had acquired new buildings. However, the number of students wanting to study science had not kept pace with the expansion in places. Chemistry had considered a course called Molecular Design but it feared that this would be regarded as inferior to 'proper' chemistry. The two senior heads in the science faculty, Brian Flowers from physics and Geoffrey Gee from chemistry then set up a faculty sub committee to look at new degrees that might attract more students.

The committee was chaired by F R Jevons who proposed a new science degree, originally called Science Greats. The aim of this new course was to produce interdisciplinary scientists who would counter C P Snow's claim that British education promoted two cultures. The inspiration was the Oxford degree, known as Greats, an interdisciplinary classics course combining the detailed study of the Roman and Greek languages together with their history and philosophy.

The Faculty of Science discussed the proposal when it became clear that 'Greats' could be misunderstood. R O Colclough (my post graduate supervisor) objected to the study of 'great' scientists.

His mistake was understandable because the Cambridge philosophy department provides a course on the Cambridge Greats, philosophers of renown including Russell, Wittgenstein, Whitehead, McTaggart and going back to Francis Bacon. To avoid confusion, the name was changed to Liberal Studies in Science (LSS for short) and the proposal approved. I tried to use the shorter LSS wherever possible. "Liberal Studies" had low prestige, being associated with vain attempts to add some 'culture' to technical students. High prestige interdisciplinary degrees had three letters in their titles - PMH and PPE - so why not LSS - similar to LSE (the prestigious London School of Economics).

In September 1966, the new department had opened with thirteen first year students housed in a small building on Coupland Street. This building had been the home of the University's computer and part of the physics department. Physics had been moved to its new building and the old Victorian physics building taken over by the Psychology Department, leaving the computer building vacant.

Jevons had managed to obtain some research funds from the Council for Scientific Policy (CSP). The funding was for a study of decision-making that was supposed to show that interdisciplinary people in industry made important contributions to the arrival of new products. G Williams had been appointed to carry out the study but family circumstances prevented him from continuing and the post was re-advertised, leading to my appointment. In Jan 1967 I arrived at the small building in Coupland Street to join Prof Jevons in the new LSS department. I was on secondment from ICI to do a study of decision-making and technological innovation.

My years with ICI had made me very curious about how new products appeared. ICI only continued to exist as long as it could keep on producing new products. Once they were established and out of patent protection then other firms could make them more cheaply. ICI Dyestuffs in Blackley, where I had worked, had produced a brand new class of dye - the Procions - that made a lot of money. Dyestuffs Division had also moved into the production of chemicals for making polyurethanes - used as flexible foams and as more rigid structures in building construction.

I had once found myself in the presence of the ICI Research Director and I had asked him about ICI's policy for finding new products. I also asked him if there were any books and he said that the only one that he knew was Jewkes, Sawers and Stillerman's The Sources of Invention. John Jewkes had been Manchester's Stanley Jevons Professor of Political Economy before being tempted away from the north by Oxford. He was regarded as a right wing economist, being against government planning. Macmillan had published his 1948 book, Ordeal by Planning. The preface to this book praises Hayek's Road to Serfdom. Both books claim that life is too complex for centralised planning to work. The only way that central plans can work is by forcing people to follow the plan rather than having policies that follow the people.

The Sources of Invention looked at fifty inventions and claimed that most of them depended on lone inventors rather than teams in R&D labs. In other words invention is not the result of planning. However, critics of the book claimed that the authors had selected their examples to fit the conclusion. Also, I knew from experience with ICI that some of their stories ignored what I saw as the commercial reality around successful invention. For example, their account of DuPont's synthetic rubber, Neoprene, emphasised the role of Julius Nieuwland, a priest and Professor of chemistry whose research into the chemistry of acetylene was made use of by DuPont's team. DuPont had invested in acetylene production from calcium carbide because they mistakenly had thought that acetylene lighting represented the future of illumination. They had neglected to see the future of battery-powered electric lights. As a result they employed a creative chemist, Walter Carothers, to find uses for acetylene. He created a team that not only produced the first successful synthetic rubber, Neoprene, but also created Nylon, the first successful synthetic fibre. (The book did not mention that Carothers committed suicide.)

The moral that I drew from this was that strategic planning on its own would not get you anywhere but creativity on its own was not enough either. Innovation needed a combination of the two. Two things coming together to make a different kind of thing is part of the way that chemists see the world. Table salt is made from sodium and chlorine but sodium is an explosive metal and chlorine a poisonous gas. The emergence of new properties out of the interaction of two different things is so ingrained in chemical thinking that it doesn't need to be mentioned after the first year of school chemistry where it crops up as part of the difference between mixtures and compounds.

When I got to work in LSS I discovered that there were other books on innovation by Manchester economists, Carter and Williams. Like Jewkes, Charles Carter had been the Stanley Jevons Professor of Political Economy (the title of the head of Manchester's Economics Department.). In those days Bruce Williams was a young Australian who liked to destroy the various myths that passed for knowledge about innovation and this made him an entertaining lecturer and supplied their books with a healthy scepticism. Charles Carter became vice chancellor of Lancaster University and then Williams grew up to become Sir Bruce, Vice Chancellor at Sydney. Some years later, Prof F R Jevons continued this tradition by becoming VC of Deakin University in Australia. I did not make VC myself but one of my PhD students, Bashir Makhoul, became VC of the University for the Creative Arts.

My position in LSS was Senior Research Fellow and the money came from the Council for Scientific Policy via the Department of Education and Science (DES). I was instructed to visit the DES with Prof Jevons and we agreed to meet on the train to London. This was when I realised that life in universities was rather different from industry. I could not find Jevons on the train. This was because I was travelling first class and he wasn't. Before we got to the DES, which in those days still had the remains of wartime blast protection, we had lunch. Much to my surprise I was taken to a milk bar frequented by office workers - rather a contrast to the expense account lunches I was used to with ICI. My experience in various organisations had convinced me of the importance of knowing 'the rules'. I had checked my conditions of service and found that the rules for Senior Research Fellow were the same as for Senior Lecturer. This meant that I was entitled to first class rail fare and a better lunch than that provided by a milk bar. Jevons had not yet become aware of how to be a university professor.

In 1967 LSS was a rather magical place. It occupied its own building - previously the home of Manchester's famous computer and Alan Turing's office. The first thirteen students were looked after by Jevons and two lecturers, Mike Gibbons and Bill Evans. There was also the departmental secretary, Margaret Bruce(not to be confused with a PhD student of the same name who became a Professor at UMIST). There were some researchers on temporary contracts such as Harry

Rothman who joined the department shortly after me. The entire department could sit down in a small room and - for example - listen to Harry talking about a new book, Marcuse's One-Dimensional Man. Some years later, when the department moved into the new maths tower (since demolished) it lost something - rather like the difference between living in your own home and living in a hotel.

11.2 The Queen's Award for Innovation

I occupied a large office and worked on files gathered by G Williams who had decided that the Queen's Award to Industry for Innovation offered a sample of innovations to study. The Queens Awards were first given in 1966. There were two categories, for innovation and for exports. The innovation awards had two advantages. They were selected by an independent body (Unlike the inventions in 'Sources' that seemed to have been selected by the researchers to fit their conclusion) and the winning firms provided publicity material describing their innovations.

My early research into the circumstances behind firms' being awarded the Queens Award for innovation led me to submit an entry into a competition organised jointly by the British AAS - the British Association for the Advancement of Science - and Shell Chemicals. I shared first prize and gained some publicity. Part of the prize was free attendance at the annual meeting of the British Association, held that year (1967) in Leeds. I had to present a paper and I found that this was scheduled for the sociology section.

In the 1960s, the sociology of science was a fairly new topic and people were talking about what for me was a new word - the paradigm. I only knew of this word as used in 'a paradigm of virtue' where it meant a model to be imitated. How was it to be pronounced? I though it rhymed with dim but the sociologists at Leeds rhymed it with dime.

I eventually discovered that an American called Thomas Kuhn had written a book, The Nature of Scientific Revolutions in which he introduced the concept of scientific paradigms. Kuhn had started by thinking that there were 'model experiments' in science - paradigms not of virtue but of how science was done. He subsequently enlarged this idea to include the basic assumptions, theories and questions that characterised a branch of science.

The paradigm became shorthand for the mental atmosphere around a subject at one time and place. This caused a lot of confusion between paradigm as something you did and something you thought. Further confusion was caused by some people seeing a controversy between Kuhn's view of science that seemed to make it subject to fashion and that of Karl Popper who was claiming that scientists should test their ideas by falsification, There is no way of reliably 'proving' something to be true but you can prove it to be false.

The so-called controversy was really a matter of different perspectives - like arguing over a penny being heads or tails - it's both. Kuhn was a sociologist. It seemed to me that some branches of sociology had been taken up by frustrated anthropologists. If you couldn't get funding to study some interesting people in Africa, New Guinea or Pacific Islands then you could make do with some home grown tribes with strange customs. Scientists could be studied as a group with their own rituals, totem poles and values. Kuhn was writing about how people called scientists seemed to do things. Popper was writing about how he thought they ought to do things.

Kuhn (1962) saw two kinds of science - normal and revolutionary. Normal science involved a group of scientists who shared a paradigm - a set of questions and how to answer these questions in a way that would satisfy the other scientists. After a time the paradigm would cease to work and there would be a period of competing ideas - revolutionary science - before things settled down again with a new paradigm. The process was not as reasonable as one might think. It was more in line with Bohr's claim that Physics did not advance through reason - it advanced because old physicists died.

Karl Popper was a philosopher, not a sociologist. He was not too concerned with what real scientists did. He was looking for a way to tell the difference between truth and falsehood. He had escaped from Nazi Austria to England and in modern terms he wanted to know how to spot false news. The traditional view that science found 'the truth' by induction would not do. The black swan syndrome meant that statements such as 'all swans are white' could not be proved to be true. They could, however, be proved to be false. In later life, this led Popper (1972) into a Darwinian view of science. Not so much the survival of the fittest - more the elimination of the false. Such ideas were to influence my thinking about technological change. Were there technological paradigms? Was change best described in Darwinian terms? If so, what was the replicator?

My paper presented in Leeds had at least three direct effects. One was a report that appeared on the front page of the Daily Telegraph. This was good publicity but unfortunately completely misunderstood my paper. A more important result was that my winning a prize impressed the two LSS lecturers, Bill Evans and Mike Gibbons and they decided to join me in covering all the innovations that had won the Queen's award in 1966 and 1967. Bill covered the ones that could be described as engineering; Mike looked at those that were vaguely physics and I did those that were chemical or craft. Viv Seal (later to become Walsh) did some and later Prof Jevons attempted to stick it all together.

The most important result of the Leeds paper was that it impressed R W Cahn of Sussex University who mentioned it in a paper in Nature (Vol 225 - Feb 21, 1970.} This included a summary of my award-winning essay. Cahn claimed that my paper "represents a new standard in this form of analysis". This comment impressed Tim Farmiloe, senior editor at Macmillan, the publisher of Nature and Sources of Invention. Farmiloe, who was looking for a replacement for Sources, wrote to say that he would publish any book that came out of the Manchester study. So the book Wealth from Knowledge had a publisher before it was written - before it had a title and without a proposal.

11.3 The Sussex Study SAPPHO

The LSS team looking at innovation found themselves in competition with a team in the Science Policy Research Unit (SPRU) at Sussex University. These two studies took innovating firms as the focus of study, a more manageable approach than focussing on the total innovation in the manner of American studies Hindsight and TRACES. The SPRU study was designed by R C Curnow in 1968 and known as project SAPPHO. (The acronym was supposed to stand for Scientific Activity Predictor from Patterns with Heuristic Origins but this full title was quietly dropped.) It was a systematic attempt to discover differences between successful and unsuccessful attempts at technological innovation. The method used was matched pair comparison. A successful innovation was compared with an unsuccessful attempt at the same innovation so that differences between the two could be noted. Success was defined as obtaining a profitable market share. Comparison was based on 122 factors covering information on the firm, its marketing, R&D, management and production methods and its interactions with external establishments. Comparisons were noted simply as greater than, equal to or less than. Data collection for the comparisons relied heavily on interviews with several people including, in some cases, interviews with customers. The first stage involved 29 matched pairs - 12 in scientific instruments and 17 in the chemical industry.

The two groups met for a discussion at SPRU. The Sussex team made two criticisms of the Queen's Award (QA) study. These were:

1. Just studying success told you nothing. Some of the factors that promote success might also promote failure under different circumstances. For example, an obsessive individual, determined to make something work, could be a success factor but more likely would lead to frustration and failure.

2. In any case, how did we know that Queen's Award winners formed a 'representative sample'?

My response to these questions was to claim an analogy with the discovery of an island with some very strange animals visible on the beach. Zoologists would want to visit the island to find out more about these strange creatures. In effect, I was agreeing with the economist, Robert Solow who claimed that "asking, just what is going on here?" was an important method.

The ancestors of these animals had been successful in surviving under the conditions of that island. So the zoologists would be studying reasons for success/survival - as well as other matters. The creatures on the beach might not be representative of other animals living inland in a dense jungle but they were there and worth looking at. My response was met with polite incomprehension. They did not understand what I was saying. The unstated implication seemed to be that zoology was not a proper science.

Turning to a discussion of the SPRU matched pairs method, I suggested the following problem. Categorising innovations into failed and successful was too simplistic. Some so-called failures might be a stepping-stone to future success. Success might hamper other attempts at innovation and ultimately lead to failure. In fact, at least one of their failures turned out to be a 'success' and vice versa. Their reply was that they had taken great care in the selection of their sample. Again they did not seem to understand the nature of the criticism, really a criticism of the Physics view of the world (P for short) and its belief in consistent causation (i.e. if you repeat the causal conditions, you repeat the successful result) Success in being an animal cannot be described in simple causal terms. Change in Physics is consistent but change in biology is evolutionary, contingent and unpredictable (B for short)

The two studies are discussed in Chapter 12 of a book, Critical Studies of Innovation, edited by Benoît Godin, and Dominique Vinck, (2017) and published by Edward Elgar. The main difference is claimed to be due to assumptions about causation - linear, consistent P type versus complex, contingent B type.

The SAPPHO project continued into a phase two with more matched pairs. For the later part of its existence, the project was directed by Roy Rothwell and in conversation with him some time later, he told me that he was unhappy with the way the project was carried out. There was supposed to be a significant difference in the level of authority between success and failure with the successful attempts having a higher level of authority in the person leading the project. Roy said that some of the people carrying out the study were expecting to find this difference but in fact, it was not always clear who had been 'in charge' of the project. In the case of failure, senior managers would not be keen to claim responsibility but for success, senior managers would try and claim responsibility.

This was certainly the case with one of the Queen's Award winners where L.F. Rose, the research director of ICI Dyestuffs Division, claimed that he was responsible, when in fact the highly successful Procion reactive dyes for cotton were discovered by two people who were not supposed to be working on reactive dyes and were involved with dyes for wool not cotton. However, once he had been convinced, Rose was able to make things happen in a way that would not have happened without his involvement. He had access to the necessary resources to get the Procions into production. If the initial attempts at finding new dyes had not been successful, Rose would never have been involved. It can be concluded that claiming level of authority to be a significant factor is far too simplistic. The real world is far too complex to be understood by a P strategy.

A report on SAPPHO phase two appeared in 1974 (Rothwell et al., 1974) Phase II extended the project to include a new total of forty-three pairs, twenty-two in chemical processes and twenty-one in scientific instruments. The results of phase I were confirmed with the same five underlying factors emerging as strongly differentiating between success and failure. These five main areas of difference between successful and unsuccessful innovators were stated as 'being related to' 1. The innovator's understanding of user needs. 2. Efficiency of development. 3. Characteristics of managers. 4. Efficiency of communications and 5. Marketing and sales efforts.

The big problem with these five factors is that they look like descriptions of the difference between so-called success and failure rather than causal factors that might be imitated by an aspiring innovator. If one criteria of success is that in one case something sold well and in another case it did not, then after the event it will seem that the sales efforts and the understanding of users must have been better in the successful case. Similarly, where success depends on finding the resources to make something happen, the successful case will depend on its managers' success in gaining resources. The five factors are not causative events; they are descriptions of outcomes.

A similar problem occurs with 'survival of the fittest' to describe biological innovation. (This phrase was first used by Herbert Spencer. Charles Darwin was aware that it did not describe what was really going on.) To many, it seems a tautology because survival is a definition of fitness (numerically inclined evolutionary biologists use a measure - inclusive fitness - the number of surviving offspring) but if this is so then the above five factors for innovation success are also tautologies.

11.4 Strange animals and evolution

In the early discussions with SPRU, I had been driven to use the analogy with strange animals on an island. Go and see what's happening seemed a good research method for looking at examples of innovation or examples of anything else that was complex. New kinds of animals come about via mutational changes. Most mutations are harmful and die out. A very small number provide an advantage and get carried on to future generations, giving the opportunity for more mutations to add further advantages.

Back in the 1960s I knew little about biology and next to nothing about evolution. I did, however, have a feeling for the power of large numbers, acquired from physical chemistry. I knew that a large number of gas molecules operating with random velocities could produce an overall pattern that was consistent. The macro effects of large numbers of random molecular movements were known as the Gas Laws and named after their discoverers - Boyle's Law and Charles' Law. It seemed to me that there was some similarity here with technological change and I came up with the idea of "the nutty inventor". In this theory there were large numbers of inventors coming up with large numbers of new things. I knew from ICI experience with patents that most patents were never used and therefore they might be analogous with genetic mutations.

The popular literature had a soft spot for people who invent things that are different but not really useful. The cartoons of Heath Robinson that became popular during the 1914-18 war are good examples of 'silly' inventions. The patent literature provides examples of inventions that are at least as silly as those of Heath Robinson. One of my favorites is a Victorian patent for a device to enable a handicapped gentleman to raise his hat in the presence of a lady. This has an illustration of a top-hated gent with both his arms in slings. He has a device beneath his armpit that releases a spring propelling his hat upwards.

With the power of large numbers embodied in my thinking systems, it seemed obvious that if you have a large number of nutty inventions then one of them will turn out to be useful. The lucky one will not have characteristics that are clearly identifiable as being different from the others. There is nothing special about a winning raffle ticket except that it won and winning comes after it has been bought. This led to the idea that evolution seemed to work the wrong way round. Out of a large number of mutations, only a small number get replicated and carried into the future. The reasons for survival could only be determined after the event. This began to look like teleological causation - the outcome being the cause of the start. That is not possible and so I was driven to find out about evolution.

I started by buying a copy of Darwin's Origin. This turned out to be no help at all! The book does not mention evolution and it starts by going on about pigeons. There were a few paper back books on biology that I owned. These had something to say about evolution but not much. There was a Pelican book by Julian Huxley and this revealed that he seemed to have failed to understand the nature of natural selection.

Another Pelican book, by Sir Charles Sherrington, seemed rather dated. It did not say that proteins were polymers and the word polymer was not in the index. I realized that although the book was published in 1952, it was based on the Gifford Lectures given by Sherrington in 1937 when he was aged 80. I also discovered a book, called An Introduction to Biology. This was in the Benn's Sixpenny Library series and published in 1928. The author of this book seemed to have some doubts about Darwin but not about the fact of evolution. He went to some length to describe the fact of evolution being known before Charles Darwin and agreed by scientists since then although there could be some dispute about its mechanism. Darwin's natural selection might be only part of the story. (I later discovered that it was not until the 1930s that the modern theory arrived and textbooks from the 1920s are a rich source of alternative theories for the mechanism of evolution.)

I then had to find other books. This was in the days before home computers. There was no Google and no Wikipedia. In those days, finding out involved going to the library, using the subject index to find the Dewey number (evolution is 576.8) and then finding where that number was kept in the library.

I suppose that most people who think of technology evolving know about biological evolution first and then transfer ideas into their thoughts on technological change. In my case it was the other way round. Studying technological innovation showed me that there was much contingency in the history of innovation, many chance encounters and lots of new things that got nowhere. This seemed to support the idea that studying innovations could be like studying animals and I should read some modern stuff about biological evolution. Unfortunately, there was not much in the library that seemed relevant. There was clearly an interest in our ancestors and much writing about the different kinds of homo - Neanderthal, Erectus, Peking Man, Cro Magnon man etc. but little about the mechanism. Evolution had happened but how it did it was rather vague.

A good example of what was available in the 1960s is a large tome, entitled, History of Mankind: Scientific and Cultural Development. The 'scientific and cultural' in the title stem from the fact that the book was published 'under the auspices of a UNESCO Commission'. Part One of this undertaking was simply, "Prehistory", a term that meant 'before writing was invented'. Its author was Jacquetta Hawkes a woman who succeeded in a men's world. Jacquetta Hawkes reminded me of two other women, Marie Stopes and Jane Goodall. All three managed to succeed in a male dominated world.

This offers an opportunity for a diversion.

11.5 Three remarkable women

Marie Stopes (1880 - 1958) was the first woman to be a lecturer in the University of Manchester where she was Lecturer in Palaeobotany and famous for advocating birth control, setting up clinics for women and chaining her book, Married Love, to the altar rail in Westminster Cathedral. As described in an earlier chapter, I heard her lecture to medical students. A heroine of the women's movement, in more recent times her reputation has been tarnished by her support for eugenics. Was she motivated by compassion for workingwomen or did she just want to stop them from breeding? In her defence, it is worth pointing out that she opposed abortion and she gave positive advice in her book, Married Love.

Jane Goodall (1934 -) and Jacquetta Hawkes (1910 - 1996) have one thing in common. They both had childhoods that foreshadowed later events. Jane Goodall was given a toy chimp instead of a teddy bear. She grew up to be the authority on how wild chimps behave. The desire to see for herself was present as a child when she caused alarm by going missing; she was eventually discovered in a hen house where she was hoping to watch a hen laying an egg. The desire to see just what was going on can be a powerful driver for research. She told this story during a lecture in Cambridge that I was fortunate to attend. She also described how she would only be allowed to study the chimps if she were accompanied. So she managed to persuade her mother to come to Africa with her.

Her observations showed that two commonly accepted beliefs were wrong. Many books proclaimed that only man made tools; vegetarian chimps might use tools but they did not make them. Jane showed that chimpanzees in the wild could make tools. She also showed that chimps were not vegetarian. They killed and ate other animals. Her results impressed Louis Leakey, the Kenyan paleoanthropologist who used his influence to get funds for her work and eventually to persuade Newham College, Cambridge to take her on as a post grad even though she had no first degree. In 1966 she successfully obtained a PhD for her thesis, Behaviour of free-living chimpanzees.

Like Goodall, Jacquetta Hawkes showed early signs of her future career. As a child, she was told that the family house was built on a spot where a Roman road and an Anglo Saxon cemetery had been discovered. She crept out at night and began digging up the lawn, hoping to find some ancient treasure but without success.

Her father, Sir Frederick Hopkins, was awarded a 1929 Nobel Prize for his work on vitamins but Jacquetta did not excel in biochemistry. Instead, she became the first woman to obtain a Cambridge degree in archaeology. During a dig at a Celtic site near Colchester, she met her future husband, Christopher Hawkes, an established archaeologist. She became a civil servant, the UK's representative on a UNESCO committee and advisor on archaeology to the 1951 Festival of Britain. She wrote some popular books, the most successful being A Land (1951) and The World of the Past (1963).

Her second marriage was with J B Priestley and together they wrote Journey Down a Rainbow (1955). In 1957 the Priestleys were involved in founding the Campaign for Nuclear Disarmament (CND). When writing, Jacquetta kept her Hawkes name. Her 1963 book on prehistory has a chapter with the title, The Evolution of Man, (In those days, the word 'man' was thought of as short for mankind i.e. both male and female.) This chapter goes into some detail in describing the different types of human ancestors known as hominoidae with illustrations of different kinds of skulls and suggestions as to their dates. Beyond some mention of different environments, there is no discussion of mechanism. Why or how creatures like the Australopithecus evolved into Homo sapiens is not discussed. Another chapter in the book is devoted to 'Material Culture'. In the 1960s this was a new expression for me.

11.6 What is culture?

In the Hawkes book, the chapter on material culture turned out to be about things that had been made and later discovered in the ground. These included tools, weapons, traps, nets, boats, lamps, pottery, clothes and ornaments. Again, the chapter is mainly descriptive; there is little discussion of how or why these objects changed over time. I was somewhat puzzled by the word, 'culture'. In the 1960s, cultural studies had not yet become popular and that word meant either a microorganism growing in a Petri dish or it meant knowledge about elite stuff to do with opera, Victorian literature, how to pass the port and so on. Culture as used in the prehistory book seemed to mean two things, a group of humanoids and the things that they made. The book's discussion includes statements of the form, "the Oldowan culture with its pebbles ..." or, "The lower Paleolithic flake cultures, best represented by the Clactonian ..."

It seemed to me that culture as used by archeologists was one of those words like science that represented both a process and the outcome of that process. Science is a way of adding to knowledge. It is also the cumulative result of many such additions. Similarly, culture seemed to mean a process of socialisation leading to a group of people with a shared knowledge but also the results of that knowledge in the form of artifacts and customs.

Culture is also one of those words that has different meanings in the singular and the plural. For example, singular language is an ability. Homo sapiens acquired language. But there are many languages in the plural. Similarly, culture can mean something that a society acquires but there are many cultures and 'a culture' is different from 'culture'.

By delving into dictionaries and encyclopedias, I discovered that the word culture was descended from a Latin verb meaning to cultivate. Over time, it had turned into a noun. Again, we have a process, 'to culture' and the result of that process, 'a culture'.

Further confusion is caused by the names of early cultures being used to name time periods. In another old book, Men of the Dawn by Dorothy Davison (published in 1934), we read, "The Solutrean period is followed by the Magdalenian ... Magdalenian culture was very localized ..." The same adjective is used to describe both the people and the products of those people. There is mention of both the Magdalenian skeletons and the Magdalenian industry. Despite the sub title, the Story of Man's Evolution to the End of the Old Stone Age, there is little discussion of evolution in this 1934 book; the word is missing from the index. Change is linked to the climate. Ice ages and floods accompany changes in skeletons and tools. It is claimed that the earliest pots found in Africa resemble the ostrich shells used to carry water but the idea that nature provides the inspiration for design is not explored.

Back in 1969 there was little written about the mechanism of evolution. Unfortunately, I missed Maynard Smith's 1958 book on evolution. (This book was republished in 1993 with a foreword by his pupil, Richard Dawkins.) It was not until 1974 that Peter Medawar, assisted by his wife, claimed that culture and technology evolved or rather, the design ideas evolved.

What I didn't know back then was that many years later I would find myself on a family holiday in France, at Le Paradis camp site in the Vézère valley, near to Le Moustier, source of the Mousterian culture and not far from the La Madeleine rock shelter where the remains of the Magdalenian culture were first discovered.

Whilst enjoying a family holiday at Le Paradis, I found that I could walk to Le Moustier and the Madeleine rock shelter. These visits turned out to be rather disappointing. La Madeleine told me nothing about evolution. It had last been inhabited by people known as troglodytes, people who lived under the ground. They were compared to the people of Cappadocia but years later I found the Turkish underground city to be much more impressive. The small village of Le Moustier is just that - a small village. It has a very small, very old church, evidence that no wealthy landowner had been around to modernise it. There is a small plaque to celebrate the discovery of the Mousterian skeleton by Otto Hauser in 1908. A small cast iron sign led to the hill overlooking the village with three caves or shelters on top of each other.

In the words of one of the many guidebooks to the area, (Lee 1996) "The Mousterian shelter will remain famous for having lent its name to the Mousterian culture." The guidebook also tells me, "Genetically speaking, Mousterian man is not our direct ancestor but from the cultural and technological viewpoint, we are his heirs." I still did not know how being the heir to culture and technology actually worked.

The Vézère valley between Les Eyzies and Montignac is full of the remains of ancient cultures including the famous Lascaux caves with those amazing paintings of animals. In one small museum, I saw a demonstration of the use of a spear thrower. The so called hand axes or scrapers are on sale from the front rooms of farmhouses, shops and small museums.

The Vézère runs into the Dordogne River near the town of Les Eyzies, a tourist centre with a prehistory museum. This museum also turned out to be rather disappointing because it did not tell me what I wanted to learn about the mechanism of technological evolution.

There were seven rooms in the Prehistory Museum, containing artifacts and bones dug out of caves and rock shelters in the region. In the 1990s when I went there, little in the way of interpretation was available. Reindeer bones seemed to have been popular, perhaps because they could be worked into tools. Some bones had holes drilled in them and were described as 'spear throwers' though to me they looked more like supports for rods going across a fire or some kind of early loom.

Guessing what things were used for can produce odd results. Early discoveries of crude spherical stone objects led to the idea that early humans had used bolas to capture running animals. In fact, the 'balls' were the residue from flaking off scrapers from larger rocks.

The front of the museum has a terrace with a famous statue, the Cro Magnon man. Produced in 1931 by a French sculptor, the statue is based on a skeleton discovered in the village of Cro Magnon during railway construction in 1868 and taken to the archaeology museum in Paris. Unfortunately, the skeleton was that of someone with a diseased spine, creating the round-shouldered appearance of the statue.

In the 1930s, when the statue was first seen, the evolution of our ancestors was thought of as a linear progression with an ape-like creature gradually becoming more upright in the manner of many cartoons. A round-shouldered semi-human fitted this image perfectly. Cro Magnon man could be seen as our immediate ancestor. However, there was a rival candidate for this place in our family tree. The Neanderthals seemed to be our nearest ancestor.

Some French scientists solved the problem by thinking that Cro Magnon and Neanderthal were the same species but others claimed that Cro Magnon had succeeded Neanderthal in Europe. After the Franco Prussian war of 1870, anti German feeling led the French to prefer their own origin story instead of seeing the German Neanderthals as our ancestor.

The more recent view is that modern humans, Homo sapiens sapiens, are not descended from either Cro Magnon or Neanderthals. Instead they are the result of a second exit from Africa by a new species that took over Europe. But back in my days in LSS, I was confused. How did evolution work and what did human evolution have to say that might help with understanding the evolution of technology?

The environment - climate, geology, other life forms etc, influenced biological evolution. This thing called culture might have a similar role in technological evolution but in LSS I could not develop these ideas when it came to writing the book, Wealth from Knowledge. The index to the book does not contain the words culture or evolution.

11.7 Wealth From Knowledge and Causation

Macmillan wanted a book about technological innovation. The title, Wealth from Knowledge, was meant to encompass the idea that economic growth came from new knowledge. Both governments and industrial management wanted the answers to two questions - what sort of knowledge and how to get it.

Studying the award winning innovations involved time spent in libraries and time spent visiting the award winning firms and other relevant organisations. Finding the background to technical advances could involve Manchester's Central Reference Library with its superb patent library (Austerity forced Manchester to sell its patent library). As an example, the background to the case study of shuttleless looms involved both a patent survey and the discovery of a privately printed book by the inventor,

It seemed to me that causal thinking was the cause of confusion. The debate at SPRU had shown me the perils of the P view in which every event had a cause and if you repeated the causes then you got the same result. My experience at ICI had shown me that the real world was not always like that. The properties of paint are not easily describable in terms of cause and effect. Paint is more like a magic black box into which you put things and other things pop out. We don't say that eggs 'cause' an omelette and we don't say that the ingredients of paint 'cause' it to stick to the wall.

Looking for causes has led to the undoubted success of physics but there are other ways of thinking about the world. Matt Ridley, in his 2003 book, Nature via Nurture, has a chapter called "The Madness of Causes". This starts with a quote from William James' Principles of Psychology, 'The word cause is an altar to an unknown god'. Ridley points out that causal thinking can produce chains of cause and effect so that which is which becomes uncertain. This can lead to 'circular causality' (p 273) - when each cause is the effect of a previous cause and the chain of cause and effect goes round in a circle, with no 'first' cause. But a circle is still a line even if it's a line without ends.

The real world of life is better described as complex. Thinking of technological change in linear terms did not work and thinking of human evolution as a linear progression did not work either. If you tried to put things into a causal chain, then you ran into trouble. What came first? Samuel Butler put this in his memorable claim, "a chicken is just an egg's way of making more eggs". Thinking along these lines led me to develop what I called 'The theory of wrong way round evolution'.

11.8 Wrong way round evolution

If Darwinian change had proceeded in an orderly step-by-step fashion, like a factory assembly line (which it didn't) then it would have had to move 'the wrong way round'. Before we acquired large brains, we would have needed large heads to fit them in. But before that, we would have had to solve the problem of how to give birth to large heads. The birth problem was solved by the trick of large headed babies being born early whilst they still had small heads. But that meant that the babies had to be looked after for a long time before they finished their early development. That was only possible because we had a system of family and tribal support to provide food for the adult carers of the babies and if such systems need larger brains then what came first?

It seems that we like to think in terms of lines of cause and effect. Narrative accounts are popular but where is the start? It is possible to start at the end. Joseph Wambaugh's 1973 book, The Onion Field, starts with someone being murdered in an onion field. The rest of the book covers the lives of the people involved in the killing, leading to the event in the field. More often, narratives begin in the past. Samuel Butler's novel, The Way of All Flesh, starts with the great grandparents of its hero, Ernest Pontifex. Similarly with technological change, it is possible to construct accounts that start at the end, at some arbitrarily chosen 'start' or somewhere in the middle. Chains of cause and effect can be constructed in many ways, including a circle with no first cause. For example, take the use of fire by our ancestors. Fire led to cooking and a better diet so that less time needed to be spent in chewing. Also, the large teeth and jawbones of Homo erectus were no longer needed. This caused more space to be available inside the skull. There was then room for larger brains and the larger brains began to be creative, leading to fire, cooking and larger brains? In fact, it makes no sense to ask which came first, the large head, the delayed development, the social support, the blood supply, cooking etc. Larger brains could only arrive in very small steps, each step being accompanied by other small steps involving the blood supply to the brain, what the larger brains actually did, larger heads, earlier births, family support systems etc. So all evolution has to happen bit by bit and the bits have to become coordinated. (Bit by Bit is the title of Stan Augarten's history of computing. Pebbles in the sand led to pebbles on a wire. Put in a frame and you have an abacus, then the slide rule. - add clockwork and you have Babbage's engine - combine with Boolean algebra, logic gates, numbers to base 2 plus electricity etc.)

Which is cause, which is effect and what came first are the kind of questions that pop out of linear thinking. To make things slightly more complicated, we can have causal chains going side by side with different things evolving together. So instead of asking which came first, larger skulls or larger brains, we can think of them as becoming larger together. This is known as co-evolution. Darwin called it, 'correlation of parts'. He wrote, (In Descent) "When one part is modified, other parts will change through the principle of correlation".

Correlation of Parts

Several observers before Darwin had noticed the fact that different parts of bodies seemed to have been designed to work together. The anatomist Baron Cuvier claimed that Lamarck's theory of evolution would not work because no part of the body could change in isolation. Everything was connected to everything else. He claimed that from one part of a body he could deduce what the rest would look like. The Rev William Paley in his 1802 Natural Theology (which the young

Charles Darwin had to study) claimed that the intricate ways in which things fitted together were evidence for the existence of God. He wrote, "There cannot be design without a designer; contrivance, without a contriver; order without choice; arrangement, without anything capable of arranging". One of the ways in which things were fitted together was what Paley called compensation. This happened "when the defects of one part, or of one organ, are supplied by the structure of another part". Animals that were not good at fighting were good at running away. His first example was - "the short unbending neck of the elephant is compensated by the length and flexibility of his proboscis. He could not have reached the ground without it". Compensation is a special case of what Paley called 'correspondence of parts'. He claimed that living things provided better evidence for a creator than did the moon and planets which did not have parts. Paley claimed that Lamarck was wrong. Elephants would have died waiting for their trunks to grow. A similar problem crops up with the evolution of land animals Land animals are supposed to have descended from sea animals. Land animals need legs to move about. But if some entrepreneurial fish jumped from a river on to the land it could not afford to wait for the legs to grow - the Paley knock out - It must have had legs first but what use would legs be to a fish? It seems the wrong way round. In fact we now know that there were fishes with 'legs'.

As Henry Gee (2000) puts it "That vertebrates came ashore and then evolved limbs is far from a foregone conclusion. On the evidence of Acanthostega, what seems to have happened is that tetrapods evolved limbs before they came ashore, for reasons unconnected with walking on land." Acanthostega is an ancient fossil tetrapod with internal gills and a big fish's tail. It must have been fully aquatic and yet it has limbs with eight digits. What it did with its 'fish fingers' is a mystery.

In fact, there are several creatures that 'walk' on the seabed or on both sea and shore. The Asian climbing perch is able to flop out of the sea and scurry across land. It is capable of killing large birds. A similar fish is the lionfish in the Caribbean. The advent of deep-sea exploration has revealed strange creatures that move along the sea floor. A mile below the sea near Australia's Great Barrier Reef has revealed a species of scorpion fish called rhinopias agroliba. It walks on its pectoral fins like a set of hands.

At a different level, the molecular basis of life, we can find other examples of wrong way round evolution. All life is based on chemical replicators, the most well known being RNA and DNA, though there could have been other earlier forms of replicating molecules. These molecules go around in pairs and in order to replicate, the pairs have to separate into their two strings, each of which then acts as a template for the creation of a new second string. In this way, one pair of molecules becomes two that become four and so on.

For this to happen, there has to be a way of unzipping the pair to make two single strings. This is achieved through the action of enzymes. So where do the enzymes come from? Well, from DNA of course. So you can't have replicating DNA molecules without enzymes to unzip them and you can't have enzymes without DNA to 'code' for them. So which came first?

At first sight, it doesn't seem possible that such a system could have happened. But we wouldn't be here if it had not happened. It is most unlikely to have resulted from some chance occurrence with all the necessary steps happening simultaneously. There must have been a series of small steps with each step having some survival advantage.

We cannot know what actually happened all those millions of years ago but we can show that there are small steps that could have happened. For example, laboratory experiments by L E Orgel and his students have shown that fairly simple molecular replicators (known as oligonucleotides) can be made to separate and act as templates without the action of enzymes. One very significant difference between this enzyme free replication and the system that exists in DNA based life is the amount of error in copying. Orgel's model replicators made errors of about one in ten whereas the error rate for DNA replication is one in some millions.

Given some kind of primordial alphabet soup with billions of possible chemical reactions between millions of possible organic chemical molecules, then those molecules that can replicate themselves will 'feed' on those that can't. At the stage when there are several different competing replicators, those that are better at replicating will 'feed' on the others. All sorts of small improvements become possible and eventually lead to complex systems with interacting parts built up gradually.

This is the only way that new complex systems can come into being. You can't start from nothing and make New

York or an aircraft carrier or an animal. These things have arisen in small steps allowing time for the different parts to change in step with each other i.e. all evolution is co-evolution.

11.9 The Reverse Paley Argument

Land animals are supposed to have descended from sea animals. Land animals need legs to move about. But if some entrepreneurial fish jumped from a river on to the land it could not afford to wait for the legs to grow - the Paley knock out - It must have had legs first but what use would legs be to a fish? It seems the wrong way round. In fact we now know that there were fishes with 'legs'. As Henry Gee puts it "That vertebrates came ashore and then evolved limbs is far from a foregone conclusion. On the evidence of Acanthostega, what seems to have happened is that tetrapods evolved limbs before they came ashore, for reasons unconnected with walking on land." Acanthostega is an ancient fossil tetrapod with internal gills and a big fish's tail. It must have been fully aquatic and yet it has limbs with eight digits.

What it did with its 'fish fingers' is a mystery.

Paley today is best remembered for his watch argument. Paley discussed crossing a heath and finding a stone that could have been the result of an accident. He contrasted this with finding a watch, suggesting "that the watch must have had a maker who comprehended its construction and designed its use". By analogy, Paley argued the same for the "works of nature" - "every manifestation of design which existed in the watch, exists in the works of nature". In effect, Paley claimed that a watch is complex with many parts fitting together and must therefore have been designed. So eyes and things in nature, which are much more complex than watches, must also have been designed and you can't have design without a designer.

Sat in my office in LSS, I realized that there was a huge flaw in Paley's argument and I produced an idea that I called, 'the reverse Paley argument'. My reversal of Paley's argument is to claim that if very complex living things like eyes, can result from a long series of accidents operating in a selection system that favours each one of the steps in that series then why can't real watches have come about by a similar evolutionary process? In a world without watches, no one sat down and said, 'I think I will invent a time keeping device small enough to fit in my pocket.' Watches emerged from the workplaces of clock makers. Following the invention of spring clocks, portable timekeepers became possible and a process of miniaturization led eventually to clocks that could be worn. The word, watch, emerged perhaps from the use of portable clocks by the night watchmen or by seamen timing the end of their watch at sea. I was convinced that technological change was an evolutionary process but I was still looking for a mechanism. At that time, academic debate seemed to be limited to questioning the impetus behind innovation. This was a policy issue. Both governments and industry believed that innovation was a 'good thing'. But what did you have to do to get it? There were two schools of thought. One saw invention as the start of a linear process leading to innovation and economic growth. The other saw the identification of a need or opportunity as the start. Was innovation pushed by discoveries or was it pulled by the need for change?

11.10 The pushmi-pullyu debate

The pushmi-pullyu is an imaginary gazelle-unicorn cross which has two heads (one of each) at opposite ends of its body as described in Hugh Lofting's novels (made into films) about Dr Dolittle. It provides a convenient name for the debate over whether innovation is pushed by discovery and invention or pulled by some kind of necessity. In economics, this is the debate about innovation being due to either supply or demand. "Either or" is typical of a P view (imitating classical physics). But in a world of complexity it is usually either and or, with a bit of something else as well. In biology, debates about nature versus nurture are based on a false premise. Both are needed to obtain the development of life. The modern term 'evo devo' is a reflection of the need to have both, as is the title of Matt Ridley's book, 'Nature via Nurture' (2003). However, those economists who stick to a P view don't seem able to appreciate the false nature of the demand v supply argument. The QA study did not claim that innovation was the result of market demand. Physical scientists in a faculty of science wrote it and they avoided economic terms such as market demand, using words like 'need' instead. It was claimed that discovery and need were too simple and both were subdivided into two, giving science push, technology push, customer need and internal need. Even then, it was stated in italics, "very few of them (Award winning innovations) fit any one of the above models in a clear and unambiguous manner". The study, however, did claim that if the question were restricted to "What stimulated the firm into the activity that led to the successful innovation?" then some cases could be categorized as push or pull and there were more pulls than pushes except in those cases involving a high degree of novelty where technology push described the majority. The 'degree of novelty' - 'how new is new?' turns out to be of crucial importance in any attempt at comparing pushes and pulls. How new is new? For the QA study, I invented a five-point scale of novelty, based on what happens to the standard textbook for a specific technology. A five meant that a new book would be needed. Four meant a new chapter in the textbook. When computers were added to machine tools to give numerically controlled machine tools, a new chapter in the book on machine tools was needed - a four. The four and fives were more likely to seem to be pushed than the others were. The term market demand cannot apply to a really new something. If we use a standard economics textbook definition then there is no demand for something that does not yet exist. As Nathan Rosenberg (1976) pointed out, there is a demand for better health but no demand for a particular innovation that does not yet exist. He collected examples of innovations whose origins demonstrated uncertainty and risk because their potential was yet to be realized - people often don't know what to do with a new invention when it's a four or five. He liked the example of the laser, once known as the invention in search of a use. Charles Townes (1968) who won the Nobel for research on the laser, claimed, "Bell's patent department at first refused to patent our amplifier or oscillator for optical frequencies because, it explained, optical waves had never been of any importance to communications and hence the invention had little bearing on Bell's System interests.

    The Queen's Award study provided many examples of the innovation process being more complex than described by a simple linear model. There were several cases of two or more separate developments having to come together before commercial success could be achieved.

    Biological evolution is not just like a tree. The combination of two separate branches is known as symbiosis and technological symbiosis is very common. The laser plus fibre optics or machine tools plus computers are obvious examples of two technologies combining. However, two is far too simple. The American study of the origins of new weapon systems (known as Project Hindsight) found an average of 35 research events as being crucial to the development of one new weapon system. In all, 710 events were identified in a 20-year retrospective framework and only 21 events were classed as undirected science as opposed to mission oriented.

Unsurprisingly, the Hindsight conclusion upset the American university science community who organised a rival study, TRACES, looking back over a longer time period and concluding in 1968 that 70% of key events were non-mission oriented.

Push or pull; curiosity or mission; policy makers needed to know which button to press. It seemed that the answer depended on the degree of novelty involved. It also might depend on how well things were going. In good times, business as usual seems to work but in hard times, there is a need for novel solutions.

The late 1960s was a period of change. It was like the morning after a good party. The party had begun with the festival of Britain in 1951, leading to a belief that science was a 'good thing' making discoveries that led to better health and brighter environments. Even my mother was affected. She wrapped up her red rose decorated tea set and replaced it with a modern abstract pattern in yellow and black.

Around 1967, things began to change. Pesticides that had increased food production were found to be dangerous. Synthetic insulin had turned a bedridden diabetic child into a happy child playing in the garden but later it was found to cause blindness. This meant that conditions producing good results could also produce harmful results. The pushmi-pullyu debate was really a debate about causation and causation was not consistent. The same set of causes could produce varying results.

P v B: As discussed above, the research strategies of classical physics (P) and biology (B) are different. Are individual innovations at the level of the firm best studied as though they were individual animals and different (B) or should the researcher be seeking some generalisations similar to the 'laws' of physics? (P). Protests against the search for general laws in economics go back to Veblen, who in 1898 criticised his contemporaries, such as Walras, who saw economics as imitating thermodynamics.

A chemical or C worldview is more complicated than a P view. It has some variety but not so much as to merit the label complex. It sees things in terms of interactions rather than causes. In the C world, there are so many examples of emergent properties that people don't even notice the phenomenon of emergency. For example, take sodium chloride, common salt, NaCl. As its name suggests, the white crystalline stuff that we sprinkle on our food is made from sodium and chlorine BUT sodium on its own is a shiny metal that explodes when it meets water. Chlorine on its own is a poisonous gas. Sodium chloride, however, is not a gas; it does not explode when mixed with vinegar and in small quantities it is not poisonous.

The properties of sodium chloride are emergent, they are quite different from the properties of its separate constituents. These emergent properties are describable in terms of the interaction between the atoms of sodium and chlorine. Using the terminology of a school textbook, an atom of sodium donates one electron to an atom of chlorine. As an electron is negatively charged, the chlorine atom becomes a negatively charged ion .... The story goes on but the point is that it is a story about interaction rather than causation. Chemists don't ask questions like, 'What are the relative contributions of the sodium and the chlorine to the properties of sodium chloride?' They know that you have to have both and that the emergent properties come from the way that the two interact.

Thinking in terms of interactions and emergent properties is an important way of viewing things other than chemicals. For example, the so-called nature/nurture question is not a question when viewed through C spectacles. It just does not even make sense in a C world to ask what are the relative contributions of nature and nurture to, say intelligence. You have to have both. What goes on in a human brain is the outcome of a series of interactions. It is not 'caused' in the P sense; it emerges.

All three ways of looking at things have their proper place. If someone's brain stops working because a bullet from a gun has recently passed through it, then a P view is appropriate - simple cause followed by simple effect. It might even be possible to work out where the bullet came from. On the other hand, if someone asks, 'where did brains come from in the first place?', there is no simple causal answer.

The brain likes consistent causation. If something bad or something good is noticed then the brain asks what caused it. Obviously there is survival value in knowing causes and it helps if the causes are consistent, so that the good something can be made to happen again and the bad something avoided.

Consistent causation is P type thinking. The activity of physics is an endless search for causes. But biology being complex doesn't lend itself to this way of viewing the world. This is put very well by Matt Ridley who did research in zoology at Oxford before becoming a science writer. In his 2003 Nature via Nurture, he has a chapter 4, "the madness of causes". This starts with a quote from William James' Principles of Psychology, 'The word cause is an altar to an unknown god'.

My thinking about innovation, how it happened and how to study it, resulted in two main out puts, writing parts of the book, Wealth from Knowledge, and giving some lectures to the second year of LSS.

Lectures

The original thirteen students in the new department all carried on into a second year. The original plan was for energy to be a crucial part of the second year teaching. With an interdisciplinary emphasis, energy enabled contributions to be made from the departments of physics, economics and government regarding the science, the money and government policy for energy. Although employed as a researcher, I was allowed to develop some lectures. These used rubber, both natural and synthetic, as an illustration of issues to do with science, technology, innovation, government policy and industrial management. These were set against a background of a four-sided triangle.

The four sides stand for science, technology and society with time as the fourth side. These ideas grew out of a conversation with Harry Rothman round a blackboard in LSS. We agreed that science and technology were different activities with technology concerned with making things happen and science concerned with understanding how they happened. The two both changed over time and interacted with each other in a two way process whilst remaining separate - technology in industry and science in universities and government laboratories. We also agreed that both these activities were part of a wider system that for lack of a better term could be called society - though Harry perhaps would have preferred 'capitalism'.

I developed these ideas into some lectures given to LSS students and one of them made a model of a four-sided triangle using a Toblerone bar. (Toblerone is a Swiss chocolate bar with a triangular cross section.) The idea that three things could influence each other and yet remain separate seems to surprise some people. For example, C K Maisels (1993) writing about the emergence of civilisation, claims three factors as important but puts stress on their interactions. He writes (p 126) "population density, technology and social organization are so interactive that each is a function of the other with population density not itself an independent variable or prime mover."

11.11 Research Funding

When I had been in LSS for nearly a year, I was contacted by Eric Packer from ICI and reminded that I was on twelve months unpaid leave of absence. The message was that if I returned to ICI there were good prospects. I would be part of a 'Prince Consort' scheme for training future senior managers. However, if I wanted this opportunity it had to be now. If I delayed it would be too late. At 32 I would be getting too old!

I declined but I realised I needed some thought about my future. The present research grant that paid my salary would expire and then what? I began to search for research opportunities and discovered an advert for the British Academy Research Grant Scheme. I submitted an application and was invited for interview.

The British Academy was housed in a Georgian building near London's Piccadilly. The interview was timed for after lunch so I took myself into a nearby pub for a pint and a pie. Whilst I was reading my application and drinking my pint, I noticed two well-dressed ladies entering the pub and heading for the stairs that led to an upstairs restaurant where waiter service was available. Much to my surprise, one of the ladies turned out to be my mother's sister, my Aunt Molly. She worked for Cartier, once known as 'jewellers for the crowned heads of Europe' and owners of an enormous diamond, the Cartier diamond (sold to Richard Burton and Elizabeth Taylor for over a million dollars.). Cartier's London office was nearby at 175, New Bond Street.

Molly spent most of her working life with Cartier. Her father - my grandfather - had enabled her entry to this unusual firm in the 1930s when he was a salesman for Roneo who made office equipment. Diamonds, being small are easy to steal. They have even been swallowed by people anxious to conceal stolen diamonds. This meant that Cartier had to be very careful who they employed. My grandfather had gained a contract to supply Cartier with a new filing system and got to know Jacques Cartier (1884 - 1941) who was in need of an office junior. So Molly was recruited and stayed with Cartier until she retired after working for Jean-Jacques Cartier (1919-)

After lunch I made my way to the imposing British Academy building. I was shown into a waiting area and then into the interview. Four or five people were sat with their backs to a fireplace facing a chair for me. This seemed to me to be a remnant of the days before central heating when important people sat near a fire and everyone wore hoods and gowns to keep warm.

The central figure of my inquisitors turned out to be Sir Mortimer Wheeler, a famous archaeologist and TV figure. He had been voted TV personality of the year in 1954 after successful appearances on Animal, Vegetable, Mineral? a programme in which experts had to identify strange objects mainly brought in from museum collections. The BBC had been a monopoly supplier of television until the 1956 advent of commercial television financed by adverts. (1956 was also the year I graduated.) The chairman of Animal, Vegetable, Mineral was another archaeologist, Glyn Daniels, who became TV personality of the year in 1955. Public interest in archaeology has remained a source of TV programmes such as Time Team, a Channel 4 series presented by Sir Tony Robinson.

I had come across Mortimer Wheeler some years earlier when he gave a public lecture at Manchester University. The only thing I remember from his talk was an account of an experiment in alchemy. It had been known for thousands of years that the colour of paintings was destroyed by sunlight. (Was that why the ancients painted in caves? Or is it that they painted all over the place but only those in the dark have survived) If sunlight had an effect then maybe the light from the planets could be detected.

Some curious investigators with knowledge of chemical analysis had spread sheets out in a field and left them overnight when a clear sky allowed the stars to shine. The next day the sheets were wet with dew and the water was analysed, showing the presence of organic matter including alcohol. Did this show that the alchemists were on to something? No, said Wheeler. It showed that the sheets had not been washed before use; the organic matter was sweat!

Wheeler's father had been a Bradford journalist and I suspect that the idea that a good story was more important that the 'truth' had passed from father to son. His early archaeological expeditions made important finds and he developed a matrix method of recording the presence of objects in a dig but Wheeler's imaginative interpretations of life in ancient times were - well - imaginative. His success in identifying unusual objects in the TV series also led to some doubts. It was rumoured that one of his assistants went to the museum that was supplying the objects and found which ones had been removed from their usual glass case. He had been born in 1890, which meant that for my interview in 1969 he was 79 years old. The records state that he stopped being secretary of the British Academy in 1968 but he must have continued to take part in meetings like this one. He had been in great demand as a speaker including cruise ship lectures and he had written several popular books but on that day he was old and had partaken of a good lunch. The room was warm and the effect of the lunchtime wine was beginning to affect the interviewing committee, with some members seeming to be falling asleep.

My research proposal aroused no interest at all and I departed to the underground station at Piccadilly and then to Euston and back home. I did not obtain a research grant from that meeting but I did learn a useful lesson, namely that meetings after lunch can be interesting. I later used this knowledge when organising PhD oral exams. The exams were set for 2.30 and the examiners were plied with as much alcohol as I could persuade them to drink.

Scientific techniques

I then had to find a future source of funding and I began to work on the idea that the benefits of university science might not flow from 'discoveries' or new theories but from its new techniques. Technology is about doing things. Science is about explaining things. University science sometimes comes up with new ways of doing things and these might be more useful than the explanatory outputs. As mentioned above, I had been involved in thinking about 'the economic benefits of curiosity oriented science'. An Australian publication (Brown 1969) in this area had been an attempt to show the economic benefits of atomic absorption spectroscopy (AAS) as used for metal analysis. Before the development of AAS, metal analysis as needed in quality control and prospecting, took a few hours of work by a skilled chemist. Using AAS meant that a machine did the hard work with obvious savings in time and cost.

Several new analytic techniques had emerged after the war. The standard story was that university scientists had been recruited into research for the war effort and had experienced new electronic capabilities, things like RADAR, code breaking computers and separating isotopes. They had then taken these new possibilities back to their universities and developed new techniques - some of which gained Nobel prizes. However, I was aware that it was not just university scientists who had participated in the development of new techniques. One of my favourite stories was that of the discovery and development of vapour phase chromatography by James Martin and others.

The initial work was carried out in the 1940s BY the Wool Industries Research Association (WIRA) in Leeds. Rumour has it that Martin had tried to interest various universities in his ideas without success - mainly because he wanted to use tall columns that would require holes in floors to accommodate them. One of the claimed potential advantages of chromatography was its ability to separate mixtures of amino acids and WIRA had obtained money to do just that. The finance came from the Australian Wool Growers' Association who had been persuaded that it would be useful to know the chemical structure of wool. In 1940 Nylon had become available and it was thought that other synthetic fibres would follow. Wool might need to become more 'scientific' and it would help if its chemical structure were known. The wool fibre is a protein, made up of different amino acids. When hydrolysed, wool gives a mixture of amino acids. Chromatography enables the separation and identification of these acids. Whether this knowledge helped the Wool Growers is doubtful but it helped Martin and his partner, Richard L.M. Synge, to gain a Nobel Prize.

In his acceptance speech at the 1952 Nobel Prize ceremony, Martin made some interesting points. He stated that his interest in columns started when he was at school. He used the cellar in his home to build a five foot high fractional distillation column, made from coffee tins, soldered together with their bottoms removed and filled with coke of graded size.

His description of the origins of partition chromatography demonstrates how a new technique can emerge without an input from so called curiosity-oriented science. Martin claimed that partition chromatography was the result of the marrying of two techniques, chromatography and counter current solvent extraction. This is another example of technological symbiosis. Martin further claimed that this combination could have happened many years before if laboratory scientists had been interested in counter current techniques developed in industry. In other words, far from this being an example of university discovers - industry applies, it was industry develops - Research Association makes use of.

Martin claimed to have made use of what he called Martin's principle of scientific research, "Nothing is too much trouble if somebody else does it". 'Somebody else' can become a machine and Martin realised that lengthy laboratory procedures could be replaced by ingenious machines. The separation of two substances can be achieved by partition between two different solvents but to make this work, as many as 200 different separating flasks would be needed. He worked out that 200 separate partitions could be replaced by one continuous counter current separation but this would need a column some 60 metres long. A 60-metre tube is obviously too long and so he devised a way of breaking it up into 45 smaller tubes joined together.

The Prize for Martin and Synge was for partition chromatography, that is for separating two substances by partition between solvents but at the end of his speech Martin announced a further development that was to prove of greater importance. This was what he called gas chromatography. Instead of partition between two liquid solvents, gas chromatography used a gas and a liquid. Scientists and instrument makers were quick to see the advantages of this new method. But first, they needed to make it sound more 'scientific'. And so, what Martin had called gas chromatography became known as vapour phase chromatography, VPC for short.

As a research student in the late 1950s, I was able to see VPC at work in the laboratory of a fellow PhD student. The VPC machine occupied a metal container about the size of one of those early top loading washing machines. A sample of liquid was injected into the side of this contraption and a whirring noise suggested that something was happening inside. Then a piece of paper emerged from the machine, revealing a graph. Comparison of this graph with similar ones in a book provided clues to the nature of the liquid.

Some time later, I attended the oral exam of the student whose VPC machine I had watched. PhDs in English chemistry departments conclude with an oral exam or viva voce, attended by other PhD students to experience what happens in one of these rather frightening experiences. On this occasion, I experienced a very useful lesson. The external examiner asked the candidate to explain how VPC worked and what it meant.

This came as a shock to me. VPC was something you used; you didn't have to understand it any more than you needed to know about internal combustion in order to drive a car. On reflexion, I realised that for research purposes, you had to know what was happening when you collected some data. How accurate was the data? Did it really measure what you wanted? Would someone else get the same result?

What I then realised was the difference between a technician and a research scientist. The technician knew how to do something. The scientist was supposed to understand what was going on. Doing and understanding are different. Research is an activity; it is something that you do. Doing something needs a method, how it is done. Understanding the method is known as methodology and a methodology chapter is an essential part of a PhD thesis.

The VPC apparatus inside a box became a symbol for science itself. Reality can be viewed as a set of black boxes with things going in and out of the boxes with their workings concealed inside. Technology tried to find boxes with desirable outputs and then find the optimum inputs for obtaining these outputs. The scientist tried to find out what went on inside the box.

Thinking about black boxes fed into my lecture in LSS. I used the rubber tree as an example of a natural black box. The owners of rubber plantations wanted to know about inputs. How far apart should you plant rubber trees? How often could you extract the rubber latex? How deep should you make the cut when extracting latex? What fertiliser should you use for feeding the rubber trees?

Scientists were curious about what happened inside the tree. Ordinary vegetable chemicals are converted into rubber latex. This is then extracted and used to make things. The tree makes latex at plantation temperature so why couldn't we do the same in a factory?

Whilst I was thinking about future funding, there were exciting developments in the University of Manchester. A government report had decided that the apparent superiority of American manufacturing was due to better management and that this was due to better management education. As a result the report had recommended the setting up of two English Business Schools, one in London and one in Manchester.

The new Manchester Business School (MBS) had been created as a faculty within the university. It was meant to provide teaching and research at postgraduate level. Its students needed a degree and some experience. On the research side it had a number of research groups, one of which was the R & D Research Unit, headed by an entrepreneurial academic, Alan Pearson.

I gained his interest in a study of scientific techniques and he supported my application for funding. This was successful and in October 1970 I joined the Business School as a Senior Research Fellow on a two years' contract funded by the CSP (Council for Science

References Chapter 11.
Brown, A W. 1960. The Economic Benefits to Australia from Atomic Absorption Spectroscopy. Economic Record, vol. 45, pp 159 - 180.
Davison. Dorothy. 1934. Men of the Dawn: the Story of Man's Evolution to the End of the Old Stone Age. The Thinker's Library. London: Watts and Co.
Dawson. 2013. Paul Lauterbur and the Invention of MRI. MIT Press.
Gee, Henry. 2000. The Deep Time: the Cladistics Revolution in Evolution. London: Harper Collins.
Godin, Benoit. Vinck, Dominique, eds. 2017, Critical Studies of Innovation, London: Edward Elgar.
Jewkes J. 1948, Ordeal by Planning. With Sawers and Stillerman, 1958, Sources of Invention. London: Macmillan.
Kuhn, Thomas S. 1962. The Structure of Scientific Revolutions. Chicago U P.

Lohrmann, R, Bridson, P K and Orgel, L E. 1980. Efficient metal-ion catalyzed template-directed oligonucleotide synthesis. Science 208, 1464-5.

Maisels C. K. 1993. The Emergence of Civilization: From Hunting and Gathering to Agriculture, Cities, and the State in the Near East. Routledge.

Medawar PB and JS, 1977, The Life Science, Wildwood House, London, Chapter 6, p52

Popper, Karl. 1972. Objective Knowledge: An Evolutionary Approach. Oxford:

Ridley, Matt. 2003. Nature via Nurture: Genes, experience and what makes us human. London: Harper.

Van Roode, J H G and Orgel, L E. 1980. Template-directed synthesis of oligoguanylates in the presence of metal ions. J. Mol. Biol. 144, 579-585.

Chapter 12. MBS: 1970-1974.

12.1 Manchester Business School

In 1970, I moved from LSS to join Alan Pearson's R & D Research Unit in the newly created Manchester Business School (MBS). Alan had been born in 1934 in Liverpool, where his father died when he was only two years old. Growing up with a with a widowed mother in the 1930s was a difficult experience, made worse by their house being destroyed in wartime bombing. He was not financially able to be a full-time student and worked in industry whilst studying part time at Liverpool Technical College and London University, who awarded him a first-class degree in maths and physics.

In 1964, Alan had applied for a job with the Centre for Business Research within Manchester University's Economics Faculty but he subsequently became a lecturer in statistics. His detractors would claim that he was employed to teach some maths to arts graduates who were hoping to learn some economics and that Alan was not an academic. He was, however, a brilliant facilitator who could make things happen and when parts of the economics faculty joined the new Business School, Alan was recruited by its first Director, Grigor McClelland, to teach Operations Research.

By the time I came across Alan, he had managed to obtain funding for research into the management of industrial research. His new venture, the R & D Research Unit, was supported by a group of industrialists in an advisory committee. In addition, he had persuaded a publisher that there would be a market for a new journal and so Alan had become the editor of the R & D Management Journal.

Wiley issued the first edition of the journal in October 1970. Money from the journal helped to support a secretary for Alan and still produce a surplus, eventually used to finance a charity, the Research and Development Management Association (RADMA), providing funds for research.

Alan liked talking and he sounded convincing to some people. One of his favourite expressions was, "We have evidence that ..." followed by an idea that he had heard earlier. This would be said in a very earnest manner and I never heard anyone challenge him by asking for this evidence.

The 1963 Franks Report had resulted in the foundation of Business Schools in London and Manchester but in 1970, Manchester was still waiting for its new building to be completed. When I joined MBS, it was housed in temporary premises near Piccadilly rail station not far from the end of the Rochdale canal. The school's building looked as though it had been designed as a car showroom with large glass windows on the ground floor, offices above and an underground car park below. It was not large enough for all the staff and the R & D Unit was housed in a Victorian building in Back China Lane.

12.2 Scientific Techniques

My position as Senior Research Fellow was funded by a grant to investigate the idea that new scientific techniques could produce economic benefits. The grant included money to pay for a research assistant and my first task involved recruiting a suitable person. I was fortunate to find Bernard Leach, a sociologist who had just completed a study of Shell tanker drivers. At interview he impressed me with his ability to understand my explanation of the study and leap to the end of a sentence before I had got there myself.

I had produced a list of techniques capable of providing case studies of how new techniques arise and what benefits ensue. Bernard decided to start with a study of the electron microscope. The conventional description of the origin of the electron microscope, as given in textbooks, says that when it was discovered that electrons travelled in waves, it was obvious to try to focus these waves in a microscope, analogous to the focusing of light waves. Since the wavelength of electron waves is less than the length of light waves, it should be possible to 'see' smaller things than could be seen with the most powerful light microscope. You can't use light to see something smaller than the wavelength of light.

Bernard tracked down the original papers for the first description of an electron microscope. The result was very surprising. It turned out to be an example of the confusion between causality and sequencing. Just because A happens before B, it must not be assumed that A causes B. De Broglie published his ideas on the wavelength of electron beams in 1924 and Ernst Ruska produced an electron microscope in the early 1930s, gaining him the 1986 Nobel Prize. However, the assumption that de Broglie's theory was 'applied' by Ruska turns out to be false. The original 1931 paper by Ruska and Knoll does not mention wavelength.

The idea that a practical instrument was the result of applying a theory is a 'neat' idea. It fits neatly into various assumptions about how things happen; it is copied but, in this case, it is wrong.

In 1968, the American report TRACES (Technology in Retrospect and Critical Events in Science) sought to show that research events in science came before practical applications, known as mission-oriented events. The electron microscope was included as one of the studies, but causality was not demonstrated. It is not enough to show that some events came after some other events.

TRACES lists several 'non-mission' events involving the discovery and investigation of electrons and their properties. These events became known as 'curiosity-oriented' and in the report they are followed by a list of 'mission-oriented' events involving the solution of practical problems. It is implied that the mission events are the 'result' of the earlier events.

However, there is no evidence for this assumed causality. In fact, there is evidence that the so-called applications came first, followed by attempts to explain what was going on. Even in the year 2020, the neat idea persists. The Encyclopaedia Britannica's 2020 entry for Ernst Ruska states that it was established in the 1920s that electrons had the properties of waves that were much shorter than light waves. This is followed by the claim that Ruska "posited that if electrons could be focused … they would yield greater detail than would conventional light microscopes." This seems an obvious thing to 'posit', but this is with the advantage of hindsight.

Ruska's career started in industry. He was a practical electrical engineer. In their early days, electrons were known as cathode rays. For practical purposes, it did not matter whether the rays were composed of particles or waves. The cathode rays were negatively charged and could be focussed by positive fields. A stream of electrons (waves or particles; it didn't matter) could be directed at a fluorescent screen, giving off light. This led eventually to television. Before that, cathode rays were used in oscilloscopes, devices for displaying the voltage of a signal.

In the 1930s, various workers were investigating practical uses of cathode rays. In Berlin, Ruska joined a Technical University team in the Institute for High Voltage Technology, working on oscilloscopes for studying voltage surges in power lines. Ruska's PhD supervisor was Max Knoll who also had industrial experience.

In 1930, Ruska wrote a university diploma project, entitled Untersuchung elektrostatischer Sammelvorrichtungen als Ersatz der magnetischen Konzentrierspulen bei Kathodenstrahl-Oszillographen (Investigation of electrostatic collection devices as a substitute for the magnetic concentrating coils in cathode ray oscillographs). Clearly, Ruska was trying to improve oscillographs and he was still using the term 'Kathodenstrahl' (cathode ray). In fact, in his Nobel speech, Ruska claimed that in 1930, they had not even heard of de Broglie's electron theory. The 'concentrating device' became a lens before several lenses put together made a microscope.

In 1931, Ruska and Knoll published a paper on the design of an electron lens. This was an electromagnet that could focus a cathode ray. Knoll moved on to work on the development of television and Ruska on his own, developed a series of lenses into a microscope. He then had to leave university to develop his idea in industry where, in 1939, Siemens produced the first commercial instrument.

Some accounts of the invention of the EM imply that Ruska was its inventor in the heroic mould of history being the result of smart individuals. However, the EM turned out to be an example of simultaneous discovery. Tom Mulvey's 1962 book on the history of EM claims that "every part of this first electron microscope, except for the electrostatic lens, was known before 1900". Mulvey sees EM as an example of simultaneous discovery, with teams in German, England, Switzerland and America all doing development work without being aware of each other.

Having established that the early electron microscope was not an 'application' of de Broglie's theory and not the result of invention by a lone genius, Bernard Leach moved on to examine later developments. These included scanning and high voltage microscopes.

There are two types of electron microscopes, transmission and scanning, TEM and SEM. As with light and X rays, electron beams can pass through an object (transmission, like light through a window) or they can be reflected (like light bouncing back from a mirror or X-ray diffraction). When an electron beam hits an object, there is an emission of electrons and photons from the object. These secondary emissions can be captured and processed to give information about the surface of the object. In order to view the inside of an object, high voltage is needed and that is expensive.

In order to justify the expense of high-voltage electron microscopes (HVEM), scientists claimed considerable benefits could be obtained from their use. Bernard was surprised to find that the supposed benefits were mainly fictional, but this was no surprise to me. I had long been aware that scientists were very good at arguing a case for more money and I had developed a talk for non-academic audiences called 'The Scientific Confidence Trick'.

12.3 The Scientific Confidence Trick

In 1956, when I started research for my MSc, I overheard an organic chemist boasting how he had got some money out of the British Empire Cancer Campaign. (It was not until 1970 that the charity dropped the 'Empire' from its title.) He claimed that he knew almost nothing about cancer but had still got finance for equipment that he needed by claiming that his line of research could help us understand what went on in cancer growth.

Since then, I had acquired many examples of the way that scientists bent the truth in the pursuit of funding. I had published some of my thoughts in a paper, Does Industry Need Science? This concluded that what industry got from university science was not understanding; not science, but scientists who would than develop industry's own knowledge base.

I had supervised research by Carol Goldstone who had looked at a report by the Polymer Panel. This was a report by a subcommittee of the Science Research Council arguing the case for more money being spent on Polymer research. Five examples of basic discoveries in polymers producing benefits were provided to support the argument that basic research produces benefits. Universities do basic research; therefore give money to universities for polymer research. Unfortunately for the argument, only one of the examples was based on university research. This was the so-called 'living polymers'. The other examples were due to industrial research.

At the bar in a conference, I happened to meet the chair of the Polymer Panel and suggested that even a car salesman would not argue the merits of car A in order to justify buying car B. He just gave me one of those looks that imply you don't know how the world works. He did get more money for polymers.

One of my talks on the confidence trick was a memorable occasion. This was an after dinner talk to the Round Table, held in the Ram's Head, Disley. In those days, people still smoked in restaurants but the Table tradition was no smoking until after the Royal Toast at the end of the meal. The chair of the Disley Table was a chain smoker, so the royal toast took place after the soup course and smoking accompanied the rest of the dinner.

A more recent example of the use of strong arguments for research is the claim for the benefits of sorting out the human genome. Our genetic makeup has now been unravelled but we are still waiting for the promised benefits.

Bernard's investigation of the HVEM provided another example of the confidence trick. Bernard, without discussion with me, published a paper in volume 2 of a new journal, Research Policy. Entitled, 'Decision making in big science - the development of the high-voltage electron microscope'. The paper was critical of the way that government funding had been obtained for the purchase of highly expensive new HVEM. Bernard Leach's paper concluded that:

> The scale of such "Big Science" developments in this country, as the HVEM may well prove unjustifiable in relation to achieved or anticipated research and other benefits, and that in the future closer public scrutiny needs to be made of alternative funding policies in relation to anticipated benefits.

Bernard's results, together with my own findings, formed the basis of a report to the Council for Science Policy (CSP), which had funded the study. The terms of the grant that had funded the study stated that permission from the CSP was needed before anything could be published. Permission was not granted so there is no public record of this study apart from Bernard's paper.

Bernard then had to find new employment and to my surprise he failed to find a university position. Instead, he became a lecturer in general studies in the Technology Faculty of Manchester Polytechnic. I have no evidence, but I do believe that he was blackballed by the scientific establishment, who can be quite vicious.

Mike Gibbons recalls being approached in a London Club and asked, 'So and so; is he sound?' Someone who turned out not to be sound was Chris Freeman of SPRU fame. When he applied for the position of director of a new Technical Change Centre, I assumed he would be successful but the job went to Sir Bruce Williams, returning from Australia. I happened to meet a member of the appointment committee, who told me that Freeman had been in the Communist Party. I knew from talking to people in Manchester that in the 1930s people who wanted to oppose the rise of Moseley's Fascist thugs often joined the CP, but years later that meant not being 'sound'.

I assumed that Bernard had been classified as lacking in soundness because of his public criticism of the finance system. In addition, he was a member of an organisation set up for joint meetings between sociologists and trades unions. In some eyes this was seen as troublesome. Nonetheless, many years later, Bernard Leach did succeed in becoming head of the department of social studies in the Polytechnic's new guise as Manchester Metropolitan University.

12.4 The Saver Seven

Back in 1970 I was still driving to my office in Back China Lane in the maroon Cortina Estate that I had acquired along with the house in the Square. The places in the underground car park were fully allocated but I managed to park in some waste ground opposite the entrance to Back China Lane. Eventually I realised that being near a railway station offered an alternative form of transport and I became a rail commuter. There was a special weekly ticket called the Saver Seven and this provided one of my many ideas for producing a book that never happened.

The breathalyser fines for drinking and driving had produced a different attitude to driving. The Saver Seven ticket could be used as many times as you wanted within one week. This made it possible to go on a pub-crawl by train without having to pay train fares. A book listing pubs near to a rail station, together with details of last trains home, nearby fish and chip shops etc., sounded a good idea.

At lunchtime if I had nothing better to do, I could search for potential pub-crawls along the many lines going from Piccadilly station. One day, I decided to visit a station in Trafford Park. I had a mental picture of chemical works, warehouses, factories and busy streets but when I arrived, I discovered that Trafford Park rail station was in the middle of a field. I was told that the railway had been built before the park had been turned into a huge industrial estate following the construction of the Manchester Ship Canal. The rail company had refused to sell its land to the estate and so Trafford Park industrial estate had been built round it, leaving a vacant field. My exploration of the rail lines from Piccadilly was cut short by the opening of the new Business School building in Booth Street West.

12.5 The New Building

I was one of the first people to occupy the new Business School building. I found that I had a desk in the open-plan top floor. This was a large space, later to be humanised by the addition of partitions, dividers, posters, plants and other signs of life. I found myself alone in this huge space with no one else around. It was eerie and I had the strange impression that the ceiling was moving downwards in the manner of the film industry's idea of a torture chamber. I fled.

After I arrived at the new MBS building, people were reading "The Beer Report". I thought this was about the liquid. As a supporter of the Campaign for Real Ale, I was pleased that MBS could be interested in beer. But, of course, the beer was Professor Stafford Beer, whose ideas about the School were attracting interest. Beer was a large man, both physically and influentially. Many years later, in 2019, a book appeared that described him as the 'father of Management Cybernetics'. (Beer, V. & Leonard, A. 2019).

To me, cybernetics is about control and communication. It sees the world in terms of systems connected by circular causality. Life causes breath, but breath causes life. His report on the Business School described various systems that made up MBS. One description saw MBS as 'an hotel with educational attachments'. The school managed to persuade large organisations to send some of their middle management on a three-month residential executive course. The residence was a tower block with rooms, well furnished with Parker-Knoll reclining chairs.

Beer left Manchester to advise the socialist government of Salvador Allende, on applying cybernetic theories to the management of the state-run sector of the Chilean economy. As a result, his office became available for me to move from the open plan into my own office.

Some of the early lecturers were American, recruited on the principle that only Americans knew how to run a business school. The famous Harvard Business School had been founded in 1908 and in the 1920s it had pioneered the use of case studies as a training aid.

To me, case studies as teaching aids seemed to resemble flight simulators, both being based on the idea of learning by mistakes. Two more American institutions were imported. One was the matrix style of management. There were different activities and different subject areas, so it made sense to have someone in charge of the first year of the MBA course whilst someone else would oversee teaching economics.

An important American innovation was the working breakfast. Given the school's hotel function, breakfast was of a high standard and some meetings were arranged over breakfast. The catering facilities included private dining rooms with waitress service for important visitors to the school. On one occasion, two visitors from Brazil were meeting the R & D Unit to find out if it could be copied in Brazil. Someone was needed to take them to lunch and I volunteered. I was missing the sort of business lunches that I enjoyed with ICI. This lunch became one of those contingencies that determine the course of individual histories.

Because the Brazilians got to know me, I was invited to participate in a session held in Rio, where amongst other people I met an American who was responsible for making me a visiting professor at Iowa State University (ISU).

Going to Iowa led to an invite to visit Nathan Rosenberg at Stanford and that led to a meeting with NASA, the American Space Agency. All this from a chance lunchtime meeting, supporting the idea that history is just one darned thing after another.

12.6 The MSc. in Structure and Organisation of Science and Technology.

12.6.1 Modules

Although I had left LSS, connections still existed. The book Wealth from Knowledge had not yet been finished and it was 1972 before Macmillan finally published the book. I was also involved in a plan to produce an edited collection of papers and I contributed a chapter on the Pushmi-pullyu debate. This did not see the light of day then, but an updated version of it appeared years later in an edited book (Langrish, 2017).

Another connection was a new MSc course, entitled The Structure and Organisation of Science and Technology. LSS and the R&D Research Unit ran this course with joint Directors from the two units. I became the MBS half and the LSS Course Director was Jarlath Ronayne, a new lecturer who now occupied the office that I had vacated when I left LSS.

The bookcase in that office still held my 22-volume set of history books that I had not got round to moving. Jarlath had a science degree from Trinity College Dublin and a Cambridge PhD. He was working on the health benefits of biomedical innovation. This was seen as a parallel study to the Wealth from Knowledge study and was nicknamed 'Health from Porridge". Eventually, Jarlath went to Australia where he became the first vice-chancellor of a new university, Victoria University, formed from older establishments in Melbourne.

The MSc course document for 1974-5 states "Enquiries to Dr J Ronayne or to Dr J Langrish" and lists 13 modules from which students had to select five. The list, given below, demonstrates the interdisciplinary ethos of LSS, with staff from three different faculties being involved.

The modules were:

Introductory Module – Jarlath Ronayne.
Sociology of Science – Richard Whitely
Structure and Ideology of Science – Ron Johnston
Technology: Processes of Assessment and Choice - Harry Rothman
Science, Technology and Innovation – J Langrish

Science and Technology in the Corporation and the Economy
– P C Stubbs
R & D Management – Alan Pearson
Science, Technology and Government – Phil Gummett
Science Policy and Biomedical Research – J Ronayne.
Science and Utopia - Mike Gibbons
Internal and External Factors in the Development of Science – F R Jevons
Science Technology and Underdevelopment – Ken Green
The Sociology of Organisations – A MacAlpine

    The breadth of the topics covered by the MSc reflects the philosophy of the original LSS first degree. I was responsible for adding the study of technological innovation to the mix. The near absence of technological change from the descriptions of the other modules is evidence for my claim.
    Jarlath Ronayne's introductory module has a mention – "relationship between science and technology and the linear model of innovation." Harry Rothman has 'technological innovation may be a mixed blessing' and 'protest movements of the 1960s were protests against the development and use of particular technological innovations…' but it was only my module that got to grips with innovation.
    As a framework, I used the four-sided triangle of science, technology and society, changing through time. This became developed by others into STS, a suitable interdisciplinary subject, capable of being taught at many levels so that for example, in 2019 you could have studied an MSc in STS at University College London or its sister course, the MSc in History and Philosophy of Science.
    At Manchester, the history of science, technology and medicine became a new centre (CHSTM), originally headed by Michael Worboys, who was one of the many graduates from the MSc course. The history of medicine grew in importance because of generous financial support from the Wellcome Foundation.
    Another person who benefitted from the MSc is Robert Bud who became senior curator at the Science Museum, London. In one of my talks with the students, I got drawn into a discussion of interdisciplinarity and I trotted out my usual spiel about how interdisciplinary degrees existed with the name of a school subject. These were regarded as 'proper' degrees. New interdisciplinary degrees, on the other hand,

were regarded with suspicion as 'Mickey Mouse' degrees, Green Shield Stamps degrees or worse. So, geography was OK, even though it could cover almost anything from economics to sociology and geology to conservation.

In support of my thesis, I claimed that chemistry was an ideal interdisciplinary degree, giving different ways of viewing the world that were transferable into other areas. For example, a Manchester chemist, Chaim Weizmann, made developments in fermentation chemistry that were important in the First World War. He then used his skills in a new area – as first President of the State of Israel. Robert Bud remembered this and a picture of Weizmann appears in his book on the history of biotechnology (1993). This picture had been hanging on the walls of the chemistry department when I was a student.

12.6.2 Dissertations - Taxonomy

A major part of the MSc was the dissertation or thesis, based on an original piece of research, supervised by an appropriate staff member. I enjoyed supervising dissertations. They were sources of new ideas without the trouble of digging them out. The student did the hard work and I benefitted from the result.

One of these dissertations was on numerical taxonomy. I had heard about this from Harry Rothman and it fitted into my fascination with the way that apparent randomness could result in predictable order. The classic case is, of course, the fact that tossing a coin randomly 100 times produces nearly 50% heads. At a more complicated level we get statistical thermodynamics, the properties of molecules moving randomly to produce regular and predictable behaviour.

Ronnie Fisher, in the 1930s, took the idea of statistical thermodynamics from chemistry into biology to show how random mutations in a population could have interesting results. When you have large numbers of events, some are more probable than others – as with the continuous tossing of a coin. This offers a way out from the snare of determinism. The classical physics view of things is that everything happening now is determined by the previous state of things. If the future is determined by the past, there is not much point in being human. Choice becomes an illusion.

When the future becomes a matter of probability rather than being determined, there seems to be room for choice.

God can do miracles without offending the laws of Nature. This idea led Einstein to write, 'God does not play dice with the universe' (in a 1926 letter to Max Born). So how did large numbers get together with taxonomy to give us numerical taxonomy?

Ever since there were people with the opportunity to think and write about things, there have been systems for sorting things into kinds of things, classes, or taxa. Aristotle's 'Physics' is a taxonomy of types of motion. (It includes twirling and aging as kinds of motion). For centuries, 'The Great Chain of Being' provided a structure for putting things in their place. The chain extended from rocks to God, passing through plants, animals, humans and angels. Then Linnaeus produced his system, still in use today.

All these systems used observations, put together in groups. The groups were based on what some people thought was reasonable but they might not represent reality. They could be based on human ideas and prejudices.

Numerical taxonomy avoided this criticism by counting differences and similarities in a systematic manner. Some complicated maths showed that if you could obtain measures of fifty attributes then it was possible to compare the different values and group them into sets and subsets by using techniques such as cluster analysis to work out the taxonomic distance between the things being classified. If you had fifty different things and each one had fifty measurements, then comparing them required much computation, so it is not surprising that this approach was not fully developed until the 1960s when computers were becoming freely available. (Though it should be noted that William Petrie (1853-1942) tried to use a pencil and paper method of classifying his Egyptian pots.)

I knew that there were interesting differences between technological innovations. I had shown that large changes in technology tended to happen in a different way from less novel innovations and there should be other differences waiting to be documented. I found a student who was interested in numerical taxonomy and he applied the method of taxonomic distance to some of the Queen's Award winners. He managed to produce a 'tree' resembling an evolutionary arrangement but with no obvious meaning to the different subgroups.

Instead of thinking of reasons for assigning things to particular groups, numerical taxonomy relied on the concept that large numbers could produce interesting results. However, there is a danger of slipping into a logical fallacy. Just because some interesting patterns have emerged from large numbers, it does not follow that all large number systems will produce results. In this case, they didn't.

Numerical taxonomy remained one of those 'might have beens' that I did not develop. In academia, it became cladistics, classifying plants and animals into branching hierarchies with possible evolutionary significance.

12.6.3 Dissertations - Industrialised building

Another MSc thesis threw light on how national and local housing policies interacted with new building systems. As part of the Queen's Award study, I had investigated the Bison Wall Frame system, developed by Concrete Ltd in response to the post-war need for new housing and the shortage of steel. As the name suggests, the system used factory made concrete wall panels that could be assembled on site to produce multi-storey blocks of flats. Manchester, like most cities, had lost houses to wartime bombing and it had had an energetic slum clearance system in place. This, together with soldiers returning home to start families, meant that new housing was needed.

The rise of factory-based housing systems in England is usually associated with Harold Wilson's Labour government, elected in 1964 on a platform of the 'white heat of new technology'. In fact, the first Bison block of flats was opened in 1963 by Sir Keith Joseph, the Tory Minister of Housing, who declared it to be the first fully industrialised building in the UK.

The MSc Thesis included a comparison of the costs of building tower blocks and the costs of providing the same number of homes on the ground. It claimed that traditional brick semi-detached housing came out cheaper than industrialised concrete structures. Also. factory-based panels in low-rise buildings were cheaper than in towers. Why then were local authorities building tower blocks? It wasn't for lack of space. Building regulations meant that towers had to be a good distance apart, with public space in between; so the same amount of housing could have been placed on the ground.

It was a desire to be 'modern' that pushed housing upwards. This desire took over local councils and the national government, with the Wilson government giving financial assistance for the use of industrialised building. The partial collapse of the Ronan Point tower in east London in 1968 allowed criticism of the towers to seem sensible and housing systems stayed nearer the ground in England, though in other parts of the world the desire to gain prestige from having the tallest building has carried on.

I continued to be interested in local authority attempts at providing houses. This area provided examples of the way that large-scale plans could go wrong and that Darwinian change (i.e. a bit at a time in a selection system) might be better. Both the grand plan and the detailed design turned out to have many problems.

In Manchester and its neighbouring city, Salford, a huge area was filled with council housing. This had the obvious danger of producing a working-class ghetto and it was suggested that there should be some housing for retired professional people. It had been the case that several forms of employment provided living accommodation. From heads of independent schools through bank managers and railway station masters to ministers of religion, there were professional people needing somewhere to live after their retirement.

The idea of giving council houses to such people was supported by some schoolteachers who liked to ask their pupils to bring in different daily newspapers to school so that different ways of reporting the news could be compared. In some places, this was not possible. Local shops did not sell the Times – too posh – or the Daily Telegraph – too Tory. Widening the social mix was clearly a good idea, but in Manchester it did not happen until the workers decided that they did not wish to live in what the council provided, and accommodation became available for anyone, including army officers with families and post-grad students.

I knew some Manchester councillors and I was told that the original lack of middle-class people in the new estates was a deliberate policy of the left-wing-controlled housing committee. It was claimed that the romantic left still believed in the revolution and that it was important to develop class-consciousness amongst the workers by housing them together in the absence of bourgeois influence.

It wasn't just the left that had romantic phantasies. The architects who designed the new blocks laboured under the idea that the demolished slums had produced a strong communal feeling of togetherness, generated by the long streets of houses opening directly on to the street. They thought they were recreating this togetherness by having 'streets in the sky' - long walkways with individual doors opening on to the walkway. But they got it wrong. In a slum street of terraced houses there were two sides to the street so that anything that happened on one side of the street was visible from the opposite side. In the new blocks there was no other side to keep an eye on things. Noise from returning revellers and, even worse, the occasional burglar testing the windows caused problems that were made worse by having the children's small bedroom next to the front door where the children could be woken and frightened.

In addition to the social problems, the new systems had technical defects. Traditional building techniques have flexibility. Where one wall meets another, bricks can be shortened to make them fit and any small gap is filled with mortar or sealant. When factory made panels are joined together at the corners of a building, they might not fit. Ground is never truly horizontal and units do not fit together exactly. The result was buildings that let in water or draughts. To make things worse, tall buildings need lifts and these tended to break down.

Another problem was caused by cellars. The new housing estates were mostly constructed on sites that had been prepared from slum clearance. The cellars of some Victorian buildings were still lurking underground waiting for an excuse to collapse, causing havoc with the new construction sitting on top of them.

The Hulme area of Manchester became home to a huge housing development. Manchester Council built homes for 13,000 residents in 1972 but the technical and social problems led to its demolition in 1993.

The economics of industrialised building like that of assembly line manufacture, depend on large throughput. To reduce the cost per item you need to make a lot of items and that requires a demand for this large number of items. The large market for industrialised buildings was supplied by large-scale slum clearance. Whole swathes of cities were demolished.

In Manchester, I watched this process with some fascination. There were many people involved in clearing the slums. The process started with planners drawing lines on maps. The maps were given to valuers, who produced estimates of the cost of CPOs (compulsory purchase orders). I knew a valuer who claimed that on one occasion he had returned to report that the area that he had surveyed would cost several million pounds to purchase. Why? Because it included the headquarters of ICI Dyestuffs Division.

Not too much thought went into the initial surveys. This could be seen in the area surrounding the university. Block by block the old terraced houses disappeared, leaving the odd, church and pub surrounded by fields. Before new building arrived, in one place the map lines had left a hole, with the result that a building was saved from demolition. This had been a small factory with an entrance wide enough to take a horse-drawn vehicle, leading into a central courtyard. This was eventually transformed into an unusual pub with a side door containing the number '27' as evidence that it had once been part of a no longer-existing street. Nearby there were two Victorian houses that escaped demolition, and these became another pub, the Sand Bar.

The army of people involved in slum clearance included Harold Tinker, a member of the Reform Club who lived opposite me. His job was to pay out the compensation owing to the owners of property that had been compulsory purchased. He had to make sure that the paperwork was in order, write out a cheque and then send off the cheque and letter to the mailroom. He said to me that this was so boring that he enlivened things a little by sorting the receivers of compensation into deserving and grasping.

The grasping ones were landlords who owned several properties and had spent nothing on repairs, allowing their properties to let in rain and in some cases, rats. The cheques for these were placed at the bottom of a drawer and left until complaints were made.

The slum clearance machine gradually became a slum-creating machine. The first rule of any organisation is survival. A slum clearance machine survives by creating more slums to clear. As slum clearance moved out from the centre of Manchester, property owners realised that it was about to be their turn to be demolished so there was no point in repairing their property, and new slums were created. The process, however, stopped in Levenshulme, formerly a proud borough with its own Town Hall, absorbed into the city of Manchester in 1909. This area had several large Victorian buildings, formerly family houses converted into bedsits and smaller homes.

Being near to the university and to the Royal Infirmary, Levenshulme had many educated and vocal occupants who objected to the area being demolished. Many people were surprised by the opposition and by the election of three Liberal councillors to oppose the Labour party's grip on Manchester Council. Manchester's housing policy changed gradually. No more blanket demolitions of large areas. No more 'streets in the sky'. Traditional building techniques – bricks and mortar – came back into fashion. It was not until the year 2011 that Labour regained the Levenshulme Ward in the local elections.

12.7 Contract Research
12.7.1 Zero growth and new idea points

The continuity of the R & D Unit depended on a flow of research contracts. These came from various agencies and were the result of successful applications. Shortly after I had joined the unit, Alan Pearson made three applications for future funds. He had decided that he had a one in three chance of being successful so three applications might produce the one that he needed.

As it happened, all three were successful and room had to be found for three more people. I realised that this was like a more general problem facing small organisations with varying income flows. The problem was that zero growth is only one point on a line stretching from plus a large number to minus a large number. Achieving zero growth is almost impossible.

I had a friend, Arthur Mellor, who ran a one-man solicitor's practice with the aid of a part-time secretary. He made a comfortable living from house conveyance and writing wills. He was able to support a family and still have time to play golf twice a week.

However, he acquired more clients and was forced to take on another solicitor to cope with the increased work. This meant that he could no longer play golf in the afternoon. Growth had meant a reduction in his freedom and in his income as money was diverted to the new solicitor.

Similar problems face small firms. Builders, electricians, plumbers etc. survive by gaining contracts. Finding a steady supply of work is often just a dream. One way of smoothing the gaps between contracts is to have some other source of more regular income. That's why maintenance contracts are so popular.

The R&D unit had a source of income from Alan Pearson's editorship of the journal R & D Management. It was also possible to raise money by persuading industrialists to pay for the privilege of attending special events. I was asked to put on such an event, "The First British Seminar on Technology Assessment". I was not too keen on doing this. It reminded me of having to help with jumble sales in Eccles, where organisations such as the Scouts and Sunday School had raised money through selling things that were no longer wanted. The Liberals in Crumpsall had also relied on jumble.

Some of the research contracts came from the Programmes Analysis Unit (PAU), a branch of the UKAEA (Atomic Energy). The PAU was using theoretical physicists to develop quantitative techniques that might be useful in policy making. One of the PAU funded projects that attracted my attention was a study of 'New Idea Points', carried out by Clive Morphet.

The conventional view of innovation was a three-stage process – invention, innovation and diffusion. The latter stage required the innovation to be adopted and the project looked at the idea that people only adopted something new when they needed something new. So, if you found a firm with a problem, then it would be receptive to a new idea that solved that problem.

I was reminded of this some years later when a research student was looking at the Red Ring kettle, the first successful electric jug kettle in the UK. A young designer was having no success in trying to persuade manufacturers that electric kettles should be a different shape from the traditional flat-bottomed kettles that acquired heat from an outside source through their wide base. If the heat came from an inside electric heater, they could be jug-shaped, avoiding heating too much water.

However, established kettle manufacturers had rejected the jug shape because market research found people saying, 'it doesn't look like a kettle". The firm, Red Ring, were heating engineers seeking to diversify. They wanted to be involved with energy saving and when approached by a designer with a plan for an energy saving kettle, they said 'come in'.

There were several occasions when I had use of the idea that some people only do new things when they need to, which, of course, is why I remember this project out of the many that were carried out by the unit.

A basic principle of contract research is to try and obtain funding for something that you had done already. As part of my MSc course on Production Policy there had been lectures on 'how much?' These had included my Pythonesque 'Macro Silly Thing' as mentioned above. I was able to turn these ideas into a proposal, 'diseconomies of scale', gaining financial support from the PAU as described below (12.7.3)

12.7.2 Small Ideas

After the techniques project had finished, I carried out a series of short projects that brought an income into the unit. The Wealth from Knowledge study had produced the apparent conclusion that ideas from British Universities had little effect on British industrial innovation. To counteract this conclusion, there was always money available for anything that might show university science to be useful. I was funded to look at the idea that industrial growth rested on research and development carried out in industry, not university, but the day-to-day progress of industrial research depended on university research in lots of small ways rather than on big discoveries. For example, industrial chemists spend some time reading the results of university chemistry.

In order to test this 'small ideas' claim, I devised a method that looked at reviews of advances in certain fields and discovered the origins of these advances. An annual publication, Reviews of Progress in Applied Chemistry, had chapters by industrial specialists describing events in their field of expertise. A typical chapter had about 60 references, with half of these being patents and about a quarter references to journals in the industrial literature. For example, the Journal of the Oil and Colour Chemicals Association (JOCCA) published papers about advances in dyes and paints.

Seven review articles written by British industrial chemists were examined. These reviews contained 567 references to other publications, including patents. The institutional origins of 396 of the references were identified. References do not state where the authors come from; this requires finding the original publication. The grant included money for an assistant and I was able to employ a very unusual person, Trevor Parkinson. He showed considerable ingenuity in tracking down the institutional origins of publications. Patents are granted to people and some names are accompanied by enigmatic descriptions such as 'Gentleman' or in an old patent, 'Citizen of the Czar'.

The 396 institutions that had provided ideas of interest to British industrial chemists were categorised into university, industry or government, and UK or abroad. It was found that only 6% came from UK universities, with 21% from foreign universities. This was not much support for those people who thought that university science provided the new ideas for industry.

Another source of ideas for the chemical industry came from a series of abstracts published by the Journal of the Society of Chemical Industry. This showed even less attention being paid to the output of universities. Only 1% of these abstracts came from a UK university, with 5% from other universities (see column 3 in Table 1). This research into 'small ideas' gave similar conclusions to the findings from Wealth from Knowledge, looking at the key technical concepts involved in Award-winning innovations. This study of Queen's Award-winning innovations (Langrish et al 1972) showed that out of 158 key technical ideas made use of in innovation, 56 originated within the innovating firms and, of the remaining 102, 7 came from a British university and 19 from a British government laboratory (including Research Associations). (See the first column of Table 12.1)

Table 12.1 gives the data from three studies. The first column is the data for 102 key concepts from outside the Award-winning firms. The second column of Table 12.1 gives the percentage breakdown of the institutional origins of the 'small' ideas, considered worthy of mention by industrial chemists writing a review of progress. The figures are very similar to those in column 1, representing the 'big ideas'.

Table 12.1
Institutional Origins of Knowledge Inputs to British Industry.

Origins	% of 102 Ideas abstracts	% of 396 references	% of 452
UK Industry	22	10	19
UK University	7	6	1
UK Government	19	11	1
Other Industry	40	40	68
Other University	3	21	5
Other Government	9	12	6

From Langrish, 1978. The Changing Relationship Between Science and Technology, in Bradbury ed. Transfer Processes in Technical Change. Netherlands: Sijthoff & Noordhoff, 171 - 17

Column three of Table 12.1 gives the figures for the study of 452 abstracts published by the Journal of the Society of Chemical Industry which showed even less attention being paid to the output of Universities. In other words, the evidence does not support the claim, often made by university scientists, that industrial advance rests on the back of university research

12.7.3 Small is Beautiful

One of the small PAU funded contracts that I obtained was on diseconomies of scale.

The argument in favour of smaller scale manufacture was put by Schumacher (1973) in his Small Is Beautiful: A Study of Economics As If People Mattered. The opposing argument in favour of economies of scale used maths and geometry to demonstrate that making more lowered the cost per unit. The so called two thirds power rule seeks to shoe that when you double the size of a manufacturing unit the cost increases by 2 squared and the capacity by 2 cubed so the cost per item is halved (4/8), (Think of a cubic oven. Its material cost is proportional to its surface area. Also, its running costs are due to heat loss through its surface and therefore proportional to surface area. The number of items you can put in the oven is proportional to its volume - a cubic function.)

Things can go wrong, however. The 2/3 rule only works if you can sell the increased output. If you have a larger oven but you cannot sell a larger output, then you are losing money. An unexpected increase in some other cost can also produce a loss. That is what happened in the brewing industry. In the 1950s fuel was cheap and the cost of transporting beer was not too important. Then the price of fuel shot up. The industry had gone for economies of scale by closing small breweries and concentrating production in a small number of centres. This meant that the distance between the large breweries and their customers increased. Increased distance plus increased fuel cost caused problems. One smaller brewer who survived the transport problem was Boddingtons. In the days of horse drawn drays, they had adopted a policy of buying pubs within a horse drawn distance. The horses were long gone but the distance from brewery to customer remained small.

There were other diseconomies of scale and the contrast between the rule and reality reminded me of the contrast between a P view of the world and a B view. This contrast can be illustrated by the cricket ball example. If you fire a cricket ball (or a baseball) from a machine that tells you its speed and direction, then physics can work out its trajectory and predict where it will land. However, if you add a human with a bat into the picture, then you have no idea where the ball will land.

P relies on consistent causation – if you replicate the settings of the ball firing machine, you will get the same result. But when you add a human, the B view applies and the ball could end up anywhere. Rocket science is in fact very simple. It is making a rocket to work reliably that is the problem.

12.8 Visitors.
The R&D Unit attracted visitors from many parts of the world.
12.8.1 Derek Medford
A memorable feature of the PAU connection was Derek Medford. He had been a theoretical physicist working for the AERE and then moved to the PAU to develop techniques of cost-benefit analysis. When the USA began to discuss Technology Assessment, he worked on techniques for doing assessments. The basic idea was that before introducing some new technology, there should be a careful

assessment of its possible effects. The USA came up with an Office of Technology Assessment and a law that made it compulsory for any agency of the government to carry out assessments before introducing something new such as a new highway.

Medford saw that this was a new kind of law, one that said you had to be careful. This was different from existing laws that said you must do something or not do something. This law said you had to think about it first. Medford came up with a book, Environmental Harassment or Technology Assessment (1973). He persuaded Alan Pearson to organise an event that would publicise his book. That is how I came to organise The First British Seminar on Technology Assessment.

Medford was nearly responsible for changing my life and that of my family. He managed to become Head of Department at the new International Institute for the Management of Technology (IIMT) in Milan. I was invited to visit IIMT and found it fascinating. Situated in a former convent on the other side of the road from Leonardo's The Last Supper, it had simultaneous translation into English, German, French and Italian, the four countries who were financing this venture. Inside its mediaeval buildings, it had the latest design for study bedrooms and the latest technology for teaching.

The staff of the Institute was paid in Euro currency and were promised that no country would charge them with income tax. There was a possibility that I would be offered a position there and I discussed the chance of moving to Italy with Sandra. She was excited by the idea of moving. There was an English language school in Milan that would be good for Nina and Suzanne. The money looked good. Then it all fell apart.

IIMT put on one course. It must have been the most costly management course ever and the German government decided to withdraw its financial backing. When the British discovered that the Germans were withdrawing, they said, 'me too' and the Institute folded. The "Teach Yourself Italian" course was placed in a drawer and forgotten.

12.8.2 Ken Hill

Another visitor from the PAU was Ken Hill. He was one of the few to challenge the notion that something called basic research, in the words of the Council for Science Policy, provided "most of the original discoveries from which all other progress flows".

The UKAEA, in addition to working on the development of atomic energy for military and peaceful uses, was carrying out basic research. (When established in 1954, The UKAEA had included a physics research section, headed by Brian Flowers who later became head of Physics at Manchester University and one of the supporters of the new LSS Department. Later, Flowers became Lord Flowers, Rector of Imperial College.)

Ken Hill, with two colleagues (1969), was responsible for a report into the UKAEA's funding of basic research. They referred to "the remote possibilities of making scientific discoveries" and suggested that the most important function of basic research was its interaction with the rest of the organisation.

12.8.3 The Sloan

Internal communication within large laboratories became a topic of interest in the Sloan school of Management at MIT. Three professors from the Sloan visited Manchester on different occasions. These were Tom Allen, Jim Utterback and Eric von Hippel. Tom Allen was an American who like me, went from industry on secondment to university for a year but then stayed after completing a PhD. In his case he left Boeing to develop research and teaching in the Management School of MIT. He visited the R & D Research Unit and had a paper in the very first edition of Alan Pearson's R & D Management journal.

This 1969 paper was headed 'Communication networks in R & D Laboratories'. In 1977 Allen's research led to a book, 'Managing the Flow of Technology'. This book included Allen's ideas on the gatekeeper, a person who had access to external information and brought it in to the attention of others.

Another visitor from MIT was Jim Utterback, who published on communication in research and management of innovation. He pushed the idea of dominant design. When bicycles, aeroplanes and motorcars first appeared, there were many versions until one design became dominant. Further innovation is then often focussed on manufacture rather than product design.

Eric von Hippel made a name for himself by pushing the notion that new product innovation could stem from customers as well as producers. His 1988 book, Sources of Innovation, extended this notion to include suppliers as well as customers. He showed that the process of innovation could be kick started almost anywhere in the complex mixture of different organisations.

I agreed with this conclusion and had some good examples from the Queen's Award study. For example, routine physical testing of plastic sheets produced a surprising result, leading to fibrillation, a new way of making plastic fibres. Another example came from Imperial Metals who claimed that successful titanium alloys were the result of their customer being able to specify the properties that they needed for aircraft manufacture.

The American studies of communication of ideas led Alan Pearson to obtain funding for a British study. This was carried out by Penny Frost and an earnest young sociologist, Richard Whitley. (1971). One conclusion of the British study was that our research labs did not have individual gatekeepers on Allen's American model. The role of external communication seemed to be carried out by people in authority.

12.8.4 Mensch Cycles

An important visitor to the R & D Unit was Gerhard Mensch, a German economist. He gave a lecture claiming that major technological innovations came in cycles after economic depressions. The idea that every fifty years or so there was a depression was associated with the name of Kondratiev. In the 1930s, Kondratiev had made himself unpopular with the Soviet authorities by claiming that the panic in the USA was not the downfall of capitalism as predicted by Marx, but simply the latest in a series of depressions. Kondratiev divided his 50-year cycles into four periods in which prosperity went into decline and then depression, to be followed by recovery and more prosperity

Kondratiev was arrested and died in the purge of 1938, but his idea of business cycles – boom followed by bust – was taken up in the West, where Joseph Schumpeter described innovation as causing "gales of creative destruction". Mensch was claiming that innovation ended depressions, rather than being their cause. He had compiled lists of major technological innovations between 1750 and 1960. The dates ascribed to these events clustered in four bunches, roughly fifty years apart and corresponding to the agricultural revolution, the industrial revolution, electricity and synthetic chemicals at the end of the nineteenth century and a host of innovations between 1935 and 45 – television, atomic power, computers, rockets etc.

Mensch had also collected data on the dates of the primary inventions that he regarded as the origins of his innovations. These inventions were evenly scattered through time and did not fit into a cyclical view. In discussion with Mensch, after his talk, I was able to convince him that the simple linear idea of invention, followed by development and innovation, was wrong. The cyclical nature of innovation was not due to a cyclical invention cycle. It was the result of a cycle of need.

In 1975, Mensch turned his ideas into a book, Das technologische Patt. The English version of his book was published as Stalemate in Technology: Innovations Overcome the Depression. Mensch mentioned me to Hayek, the Austrian economist who was famous for being against central planning. His post war book, The Road to Serfdom had claimed that the only way for a national plan to work was through force. This was regarded as right-wing extremism until people like Margaret Thatcher and G W Bush claimed he was right. Born in 1899, Hayek was still active and he sent me a message suggesting that we meet at London airport on his way from Germany to the USA. This was another of those 'might have been' moments of my personal history. I was not able to meet Hayek and I never found out what he wanted.

The 50-year Kondratiev/ Mensch cycle etched a pattern in my mind and was to produce some interesting research later, when Cycles of Optimism in Design became a top paper of mine.

12.9 The Lloyds Arms.

At lunch times I sometimes escaped from the Business School to eat a pie in the nearby Lloyds Arms, an old pub in what was Higher Ormond Street. The Lloyds was destined for demolition, to make way for phase two of the new Royal Northern College of Music building. (The RNCM had been formed in 1972 as an amalgamation of two previous colleges.

the Royal and the Northern. The Royal connection was continued through its president, the Duchess of Kent.)

The shadow of demolition had meant that the Lloyds avoided the 'modernisation' afflicted on most pubs. As a result, it was still selling 'real ale' and displaying a Manchester dart board. (The Manchester 'log end' board has no trebles and the doubles are small - only 3.2 mm wide. It has a 4 at the top where the standard board has 20) The Landlord and his wife, Vera, had been there since before the demolition of the terraced housing, now replaced by the new educational buildings.

On one occasion, I got chatting to a woman who was on a trip down memory lane. She said she had lived in Ormond Street, gone to school at All Saints and worked in a factory on Booth Street. The Lloyds Arms was the last remnant of her growing up. This reminded me that not all change is good. The demolition of large areas destroyed existing communities of real people. The area round All Saints had been a separate township, the Borough of Chorlton on Medlock, with its own Town Hall. (In the present centaury, the frontage of the Town Hall is still there as part of MMU)

Next door to the Town Hall had been the School of Art and Design, established in 1838 and now part of the Faculty of Art and Design School in MMU. The old Art Colleges has included groups of staff responsible for 'Complementary Studies'. The Manchester group had been absorbed into a new department of General Studies but part of them kept together and used to lunch in the Lloyds.

The elder statesman of this group was Peter Ferriday, known as the editor of a collection of papers (1963), claimed to be the first book on Victorian architecture. In the 1960s, things Victorian were regarded as old, dirty and best got rid of. Ferriday had been one of the founders of the Victorian Society, dedicated to saving buildings from destruction by modernist town planners and developers.

Rumour had it that Nicholas Pevsner had told Ferriday that he could get him a job in any university. But being a romantic socialist, Ferriday had said 'how about a Polytechnic?'. So he joined Manchester Poly as an art historian. Rumour also had it that he had given a lecture on Victorian pornography and claimed that the largest collection of this was in Buck House's cellar. Present at that lecture was Sir Anthony Blunt, Keeper of the Queen's paintings. Blunt claimed that Ferriday was mistaken. When Blunt was exposed as a spy, Ferriday was delighted. "I knew he was a liar. Who's for another pint?"

Ferriday had convinced the Polytechnic art historians that it was not a good idea to be part of a department existing by providing service teaching. They needed their own degree and this meant getting approval from the CNAA (Council for National Academic Awards). The conversation in the Lloyds sometimes turned to the progress of the large number of documents required to obtain approval. This could lead to jokes about how many taxis would be needed to carry the documentation to the CNAA office near Kings Cross station.

One member of the Lloyds group was Richard Tilston who lived near me and went to the Crown on Heaton Moor Road where Ferriday, and others would meet in the evenings. Tilston had published a book on Seurat.

At that time, I had no idea that one day I would be working for the Poly. The Lloyds provided a useful introduction to life in a different section of higher education. It also provided a useful space away from the pressures of contract research. Once a month the R & D Unit was visited by Tony Hamlin from the PAU, checking that their money was being well spent. Ferriday spotted that I was rather concerned about these visits and he invented the image of Ham Lin, the evil villain.

My joining the Poly as a Dean is described in Part Two of my autobiography. Before that happened, I spent a few years in UMIST as described in the next chapter.

References Chapter 12.

Beer, Vaniila & Leonard, Allenna. 2019. Stafford Beer The Father of Management Cybernetics: Big Data Analysis.
Bud, Robert and Cantle Mark F. 1993. The Uses of Life: A History of Biotechnology. Cambridge U. P.
Ferriday, Peter ed. 1963.Victorian Architecture: An Age Revisited, with contributions by Nikolaus Pevsner and others.
Frost, P.A. & Whitley, R.D. 1971. Communication patterns in a research laboratory. Journal of R & D Management 1, 71-79.
Hayek, F A. 1944. The Road to Serfdom, London: Routledge.
Hill, K. 1069 How much basic research is enough? Long Range Planning, Volume 1, Issue 3, Pp. 38-43

Langrish, J. Gibbons, M. Evans W. and Jevons F R. 1972. Wealth from Knowledge: Studies of Industrial Innovation. London: Macmillan.

Langrish, J. 1971. "Technology Transfer; Some British Data", R & D Management, 1, 134-135.

Langrish, J. 1972. University Chemistry Research: Any Use to Industry? Chemistry in Britain.

Langrish, J. 1974. "The Changing Relationship between Science and Technology", Nature, vol 250 No 5468, August

Langrish, J. 1978. The Changing Relationship Between Science and Technology, in Bradbury (ed.) Transfer Processes in Technical Change. Netherlands: Sijthoff & Noordhoff. pp 171 - 179.

Langrish J. 2017. Physics or biology as models for the study of innovation. Chapter 15 in Benoît Godin and Dominique Vinck (eds.) Critical Studies of Innovation: Alternative Approaches to the Pro-Innovation Bias. Edward Elgar Publishing).

Medford, D. 1973. Environmental Harassment or Technology Assessment? Amsterdam; Elsevier Scientific Publishing.

Mulvey, T.1962, Origins of the Electron Microscope, British Journal of Applied Physics, vol 13.

Schumacher, E F. 1973. Small Is Beautiful: A Study of Economics As If People Mattered London: Blond & Briggs

Chapter 13. UMIST Man. Sciences 1974-1977

13.1 Technical Colleges

Following my recruitment by Malcolm Cunningham, I found myself in the Department of Management Sciences, in charge of a new degree. The Department was situated in a concrete tower overlooking the 1960s UMIST campus, a sprawling concrete village that had emerged from the red brick technical college.

UMIST (University of Manchester Institute of Science and Technology) liked to trace its origins to the founding of the Manchester Mechanics' Institution in 1824 but this was a slight exaggeration. The 'Mechanics' was used by factory workers but also by office workers and shop assistants who were seeking to improve their literacy and numeracy. In addition, its Princess Street building was used for meetings and in1868 the TUC (Trades Union Congress) was founded there. It was not until 1883 that the 'Mechanics' was turned into the Manchester Technical School ('the tech'), an education and training establishment. This was achieved by a Manchester shoemaker, John Henry Reynolds (not to be confused with the Reynold, without an s, who had a building named after him).

In the 1890s, Reynolds was able to take advantage of government money being provided for technical education in an attempt to keep up with Germany. Government support led to the establishment of technical colleges in major cities including Salford and Manchester. These were housed in rather splendid new buildings. The Manchester Tech absorbed the existing school into its new building in Sackville Street and became the Manchester Municipal College of Technology.

The technical colleges were mainly centres for part time education, particularly in the evening. They offered courses leading to professional qualifications and those of examining boards such as the Union of Lancashire and Cheshire Institutes and the London Institute's City and Guilds. My brother, Peter, became a trainee gardener when he left school. He studied in the evening at Manchester Tech for the junior qualifications of the Royal Horticultural Society. (He gained a distinction.)

The 1890s technical colleges developed through various changes over seventy years until they became universities. Salford Tech acquired the adjective Royal. Then it became a College of Advanced Technology and finally, the University of Salford, where I was to become a Visiting Professor.

An agreement was reached in 1905 for the professors at the Manchester College of Technology to constitute the Faculty of Technology of the Victoria University of Manchester. Students at 'Tech' could take Victoria University degrees

To become part of higher education, the colleges had to lose their lower level courses. For example, Manchester's Department of Printing Technology was moved from the Tech to the Manchester College of Art which itself became part of the Polytechnic and then the Metropolitan University (MMU).

Removing the low level courses from Salford Tech required the creation of a new technical college to house them. The new technical college then gave degrees validated by the CNAA (Council for National Academic Awards) These degree level courses allowed the new tech to become a university college, offering degrees of the University of Salford.

This left the lower level courses in Limbo and they were housed by another City of Salford technical college, acquired from Worsley in the 1970s reorganisation of local government.

In 1956 the Manchester College of Technology gained independent status as a university college. In 1966, during a period of rapid expansion, the College of Technology was renamed the University of Manchester Institute of Science and Technology (UMIST) but remained largely independent of the Victoria University.

Both Salford and Manchester Techs were part of the local community in the sense that most people knew someone who had been there. My brother had attended courses at Manchester Tech and my daughter, Nina, did her A levels in theatre studies at Salford before becoming Assistant Stage Manager at Wythenshawe Theatre. And of course, I was to become a visiting Professor at Salford, something that did not enter my head when I joined Management Sciences at UMIST

13.2 Management Sciences

In 1955, the formal teaching of Management arrived in Manchester with the creation of a Department of Industrial Administration in the Manchester Municipal Technical School. Part of the funding for this new department came from the third (Sir) Samuel Turner (1878–1955) who had acquired his money from Turner Bros Asbestos Co. My mother had worked as a secretary for Turners in Trafford Park. Turners became Turner and Newall and then ran into trouble with asbestos. (There is a book on its history, Magic Mineral to Killer Dust, Tweedale and Hanson, 2000)

The thinking behind this new department was partly provided by Charles Garonne Renold (son of Hans Renold of Renold's Chains with a factory two miles from where I now live. Its site is now a Tesco car park.) Reginald Revans, the pioneer of action learning, provided academic insight.

In 1955 Revans had become the first professor of industrial management at UMIST. Revans did not believe in experts. He pushed the idea of learning by doing, i.e. Action Research. This was one of those opportunities that I did not follow. I could have combined the ideas of Revans with my thoughts on evolution, starting with Thorstein Veblen (1898) who saw the routines of technology as analogous to biological genes including their mutation. It was actions/routines that were passed on from one generation to the next. Such ideas had to wait until memes appeared.

The Management Sciences Department that I joined was the largest department in UMIST. It took 110 students a year on to its three-year BSc in Management Sciences degree course. It also provided a one-year full time master's degree and had an impressive research activity. It was multicultural in the sense that both staff and students came from many different backgrounds.

The staff included some Americans and a visiting Brazilian psychologist who was a very good-looking redhaired woman. She came from a wealthy family and arrived in Manchester accompanied by her child and a maid. One weekend, feeling a little bored she went on a shopping expedition to Milan. If you have enough money you can fly from Manchester to Milan, take in the shops and a restaurant and fly back. Later, we were astonished to hear that she had developed a nervous breakdown. How could someone, so attractive and so wealthy acquire a breakdown?

An American member of staff, psychologist Cary Cooper, claimed that in the US, this problem was known as the Californian syndrome. If you could do anything that you wanted to do, you have no way of deciding what to do and this causes a breakdown. (More on Cary later; he became Sir Cary).

In addition to overseas students, the English students came in two main groups. There were people from northern grammar schools and an unexpected number of students from Home Counties' public schools. The public school entry had come about because of a piece in the Financial Times recommending the degree. This had been noted by careers advisors and passed on to anxious parents.

The MSc in Management Sciences course had even greater diversity including some army officers. The section of the army that was responsible for weapons and equipment was known as REME (Royal Electrical and Mechanical Engineers). Its responsibilities included running factories and workshops with civilian workers. Since the army relied on obedience and training, organising civilians was outside normal experience, hence the need for some training for officers. The UMIST Masters included options on production management and was therefore judged suitable for REME officers who were going to oversee civilian workers.

Two of the officers attending the course stand out in my memory. One was a German, Eric von Zugbach De Zugg. He was a cavalry officer with a duelling scar and a horse. He rode into UMIST in the morning and stabled his horse under a railway arch. The other officer travelled on a motorbike and was reading Zen and the Art of Motorcycle Maintenance.

He was responsible for getting me to give a talk to a group of army people. This put me in good company; Lord Longford who was notorious for trying to defend the Moors murder, Myra Hindley, had given an earlier lecture. By the time I came to deliver my talk, I had left UMIST and become a Dean. Army protocol requires that someone of equivalent rank should greet a visitor. Professors as heads of department rate as Colonel. Since a Dean is higher than a Professor, it was decided that I needed a Brigadier but there wasn't one available. However, just down the road was an American base with a one star general. So, he and his wife turned up to greet me and enjoy the hospitality of the Officers' Mess where a jolly evening was held after my talk on The Scientific Confidence Trick. (See Section 12.3)

My involvement with the MSc had come about through a series of contingencies. The department had built up a strong commitment to production management. The head of the production team had published a textbook but was then tempted away through being offered a chair in another university. He had taken most of the team with him, leaving the department without the staff to fill its published commitments. Existing members of staff were asked to help, and I volunteered to run a module on production policy.

These days, 'production' implies theatre, film or TV productions. In those days, production took place in factories. I decided that production policy was what, how, where, when and how much to manufacture. This gave me the opportunity to talk about economies of scale and to use beer as a case study. Years later I discovered that von Mises, the Austrian economist and sociologist, had claimed that only free market competition produced the data needed for economic decision making. He claimed that the main data required for economic calculation were "What to produce? How much to produce and in what manner?"

Shortly after I started teaching production, some senior REME people inspected the MSc course and I found myself having coffee with the Major General who was head of REME. He questioned the relevance of teaching sociology to army officers. I suggested that motivation was crucial to a disciplined army. Why did soldiers charge out of their trenches in the First World War? The General replied, "Leadership of course."

Years later I bumped into a chap who claimed to remember me from his doing the MSc. He said he had enjoyed my 'Macro Silly Thing'. When Monty Python's Flying Circus had first appeared on TV, the catch phrase, "This is very silly" had been popular, and I used it to describe what happened when an industry had several firms who all tried to gain advantage from economies of scale. This had happened in the brewing and petrochemical industries where rival firms aiming at economies of scale had resulted in massive over capacity in the total industry - a 'macro silly thing'.

A student from overseas approached me after a lecture and said, "I like to consult the books after your lectures but I cannot find a reference to the "macro silly". I replied that I had not yet written the book. My point was that universities should be places where you get new ideas before they have reached the books.

In addition to the MSc, I taught a module in the final year of the main three years degree. In their third year, students could pick modules from a large number, made available by the varied staff. Malcolm Cunningham's marketing option was the most popular but my Management of Innovation module attracted about seventy takers. Some of my ideas on innovation are given later after discussing my main role in the department viz Director of the MACS Course.

13.3 The MACS Course

This new degree (BSc in Management and Chemical Sciences) had been approved in outline and my job was to make it work. The course had a novel structure known as 'the leg of lamb'. This had a lot of chemistry in the first year but tapering off so that most of the final year was management. UMIST was familiar with the problems that could be caused by joint degrees involving two departments. Instead of floating between departments, students belonged to the first named department. Students on the degree in Maths and Management were looked after by Maths but a similar degree in Management and Maths was the opposite.

My son Tom had experience of a joint degree. He joined York University to take a degree in Politics and History but he found that the two departments had different approaches to essay writing including different reference systems. Politics used the Harvard citations but history used footnotes. He transferred from a joint degree to a history degree and had practical experience of politics through involvement with the Students' Union.

I tried to give the course an identity by describing it as 'Men, Molecules and Money: the three things that everyone should know about'. This was the time when it became unacceptable to use 'man' as short for mankind or human. Man was not pc (hence jokes about Manchester becoming Peoplechester and what about manhole covers?). I therefore changed my description of the new degree to 'People, Particles and Profits: the three things that everyone should know about'.

'People' was psychology and sociology. 'Particles' was chemistry and 'profits' 'was economics and accountancy.

One of the problems of joint degrees is that they end up being one and a half degrees i.e. trying to cover too much. Since the majority of the first year was chemistry, I hoped to compress the management inputs. For the money part of the MACS course, I was fortunate in finding two members of staff who were interested in exploring the relationship between economics and management accounting. I was less fortunate with the people input. I found a psychologist, Mike Smith, who had taught sociology. He was keen to do a people course but departmental politics reared its head.

The Management Sciences Department was large enough to contain sub-groups including a team of sociologists who were of the 'politics is power' chain of thought. They were familiar with Trades Union restrictive practises and protested against a psychologist teaching sociology. This resulted in half the people course being taught by a sociologist with the other half by Mike Smith.

The responsibilities of course director included overseeing admissions. When I had been at school, studying for 'A' levels, applications to university were made directly to a university and there was no limit to the number of different applications. This system became unwieldy and in 1964 applications in England were made via the Universities Central Council on Admissions (UCCA).

Admissions tutors had a thankless task. Too few new students and there was not enough money to pay the staff. Too many students meant no room to fit them in and the possibility that government funding would not be available for the extra students. In the summer after A level results had been published, those students who had failed to gain admission to their chosen courses, entered the UCCA clearance system. I had to rely on clearance to find enough students to keep the MACS course going. This meant that when my colleagues were enjoying their summer vacation, I was at the end of a phone hoping to find anxious students with A level chemistry and a desire to study something that was not just a chemistry degree. Such people included applicants to medical schools with good science A levels but not good enough to enter medicine.

I was struck by the difference in student preference between 1953 when I left school and the late 1960s. In my day, science degrees were highly prized and difficult to enter. The year I started, there were 650 applications for

Manchester's chemistry degree and only 60 places in the Victorian chemistry building. In my science sixth form there was a boy who was not too good at science but he got a place in medical school. He went on to be Professor of Ophthalmic Optics and earn more money than those of us with science careers.

In the 1960s there was a massive expansion of university science. Both the university and UMIST acquired brand new chemistry buildings but then had difficulty in finding students to occupy them. That is why the heads of chemistry in both places supported new science degrees: LSS in the University and MACS in UMIST.

In the months before Christmas, admission tutors were trying to persuade A level students to apply for their course. This involved open days, interviews etc. On one occasion, I received a phone call from a potential applicant. She was at the stage of choosing what subjects to study at A level and she wanted to study history and chemistry but her School would not let her combine those two. She had been told that such a combination would not lead to anything. I was able to tell her two things. First, chemistry and history was an ideal combination for the MACS course. Chemistry being obvious and history because it involved discursive essays, a good foundation for some management courses. Secondly, I could claim that there were many job opportunities for people who knew the language of science but did not wish to be scientists.

I suppose that in creating a degree that encouraged people to study both chemistry and history, I was creating something that would have been ideal for myself. I did obtain 80% for my O level history as well as 80% for A level chemistry. Both subjects require a deep level of understanding - Chemistry is more than cookery and history is more than just one thing after another.

Some of my ideas provided inputs into the second and third years of the MACS Course. Science policy, technological innovation and synthetic rubber were developed into short teaching modules. At the same time, I was developing material for my innovation course in the main Management Sciences degree and for this I attempted to have a team project.

13.4 Interdisciplinary Team Projects

My experience in ICI had taught me that the academic way of organising things was a poor preparation for working in industry. Academia places people in disciplines and rewards individual efforts. Industry places people in interdisciplinary teams. Making science students spend three years working on their own to get a degree, followed by three more years pursuing a PhD was a poor preparation for working in industry.

Someone persuaded the Science Research Council (SRC) that it would be a good idea to give PhD students some experience of team working. As a result, the SRC offered Science PhD students the opportunity to join a one-week's residential course with all expenses paid. One of these courses was offered by a team from Liverpool University, organised by Jack Blears and I was invited to join the team.

The students were organised into groups of four or five and given problems to work on collectively. Jack Blears had designed a waste disposal project. This started with a booklet containing a vast amount of data. The group had to design a system for the collection and disposal of domestic waste, involving transport it to a transfer site where some recycling might take place and then transporting the remaining waste to its final destination, land fill, incineration or pyrolysis (heating in the absence of air).

Groups met and divided the task into separate problems so that each student could work on a problem on their own as they were used to doing. However, they soon found that they did not have all the information. For example, the student trying to design a transfer station needed to know the quantity of waste arriving every day. Another student was calculating that quantity. And that was the point of the exercise.

I attempted to include a team project in my innovation module. I did this by forming groups of four or five and asking them to collectively select an innovation and study it. The assessed output was a joint report describing how changes in science, technology and society had led to the innovation. The report also had to discuss the effects of the innovation and include an attempt at describing the group dynamics of writing a joint report.

Assessment of the group project caused a few problems. I wanted everyone in the group to gain the same mark for the project. Some people thought this was outrageous. What happens if you have a free loader in the group? My response was to allow the group to get rid of someone who was not contributing. To do this, they had to follow the standard procedure of giving written warning before dismissal. Some good reports were produced and several students said that there should be more group activity in university education.

13.5 Publications

In addition to developing teaching material, I was putting my ideas into print. My main outlet at that time was three chapters published in books of edited collections. The first of these was a chapter written at the request of Dick Ottoway, an American member of staff in Management Sciences who was publishing a book with the title, Humanising the Workplace (Ottoway 1977). My contribution was called Technological Determinism and was based on ideas I had used in my Ames public talk, Technology: Servant or Master. The basic idea was that our freedom to choose a humanised workplace was limited by the demands of the technology.

Two other chapters were "The Changing Relationship between Science and Technology" published in Bradbury ed. (1978) and "The Effects of Technological Change" in Baker, ed. (1979). The changing relationship chapter was an update to a paper published in Nature, using citation data to show how in the early days of something new, university and industry cited each other but once things were established, science (university) and technology (industry) parted company. The effects paper combined data from Carol Goldstone's thesis on the effects of innovation with a discussion of technological determinism.

In addition to the published chapters, I tried to put my ideas together in the form of a book called, The Four Sided Triangle. This was the title of a book that Macmillan paid me to write but I never finished. One day, for reasons that are lost in the mists of fading memory, I was walking alone in north London, near Kenwood House. I was worried about money. At that time, Sandra was not working and the bills kept arriving. Direct Debits had not yet been invented. Standing orders for fixed amounts existed but most monthly bills were variable and had to be paid by cheque in the post. Monthly salary payments arrived on the last Thursday of the month, so money tended to be in short supply towards the end of the month. I had avoided this problem by obtaining an overdraft but now the bank was suggesting that I should reduce my overdraft. How could I get some more money? Then it came to me - write a book or rather write a book proposal for Tim Farmiloe at Macmillan.

Macmillan accepted my proposal and agreed to pay me advance royalties. This solved my immediate financial problem but there was no urgency to actually write the book. Over the next few years, I wrote first drafts of several chapters and then I discovered memes. Macmillan was taken over by Palgrave and I wrote to the new editor, saying I needed to change the book into one about memetics. I got a reply asking for a proposal. So I produced an outline that converted the original four sides (science, technology, society, time) into different kinds of memes. Technology became recipemes. Science became explanemes and society became selectemes. Time became Darwinian change.

Palgrave had not heard of memes but they discovered that a philosopher, Dan Dennett, had written about memes so the proposal was passed to the philosophy editor who sent it to the most junior member of the team, a young woman responsible for textbooks used on postgrad philosophy courses. She wrote a report saying that my book was not suitable for postgrad philosophy. I quite agreed. It was never intended to be a philosophy book. Publishers and booksellers must organise things in simple categories, which is why Wealth from Knowledge became listed under economics - wealth is money, isn't it? - And money is economics.

The Four Sided Triangle never got published but some of the draft chapters found their way onto my present computer. It was a long journey. First versions were written and then typed by my secretary. At some stage they were on a university computer and then my own LC Apple Mac. In those far away days, Mac used Claris Works software. This combined word processing, spreadsheets and drawing programs. However, the rival software for so called IBM compatibles won the day and everyone was stuck with Microsoft. So, the chapters had to be converted to Word for

Mac, a version of Word, designed to run on Macs. As computers improved, they could no longer run the early Word programs and my chapters went through various conversion until they became available in Word.doc.

The draft chapter 7 of the Four Sided Triangle just happens to contain a good summary of my ideas on innovation before I left UMIST and is therefore a good end to this part of my mental journey.

13.6 The Four Sided Triangle

As explained above, this section is chapter 7 from the draft of a book that was never finished. It is in two halves, a discussion of technological determinism leading to the idea of technological Darwinism and a second section outlining my views on technological innovation as requiring three necessary conditions. The chapter is presented as it stood without corrections.

Technological Determinism.
The core content of technological determinism is that the nature of technology so controls the rest of society that the idea of free choice between different kinds of technology with different kinds of effects is an illusion. Many factors stand in the way of using technology to improve the quality of life [whatever that means]. These include the social, political and economic systems within which the technology is used. Technological determinism considers that such factors are themselves the product of the technology so that a major change in the structure of society or how we organise our workplaces is impossible without a change in technology.

Examples from the past have been used to support the idea of technological determinism. Thus Lynn White [1962] has attempted to demonstrate that the entire feudal system was the result of one technological change viz the stirrup. [The stirrup made cavalry a superior fighting unit to Roman style foot soldiers. This meant that a society wishing to survive needed horses. Horses must be fed in winter. This needs land which was parcelled out in return for military service with the horse soldier knight becoming a key figure in society.]

White makes the even more startling claim that the Renaissance was due to a technological change in the method of food production, increasing the protein content of European diet and giving people enough mental energy to be creative in addition to just surviving. In White's words, Europe at the time of the Renaissance was 'full of beans'.

Less spectacular claims for technological determinism are such ideas as the destruction of the feudal system by gunpowder and the cannon, railways causing the modern city, the steam engine and coal leading to a factory based society and so on.

These ideas represent a very simple form of technological determinism in which inventions or groups of inventions result directly in massive changes in social, political and economic systems. This simple technological determinism may be countered by a variety of arguments: Where do the inventions come from? The use of inventions is determined by other systems - the Chinese did not use their gunpowder. Or today we can say that inventions now come from science so we can choose what inventions we want.

A more sophisticated view of technological determinism that is much harder to refute is Technological Darwinism. According to this view, inventions occur in large numbers by a random process analogous to gene mutation in biological evolution. Most inventions are never used. Those that are used survive because they impart some survival value to the users. Eventually, everyone who is in competition with the users of the new technology must follow suit or cease to survive. If using the new technology means changing social, political or economic systems there is no choice, the new technology and all its consequences are adopted or extinction follows.

Thus, the English cottage weavers had no choice when the factory-based textile industry emerged; they either starved or went to work in the factory. Even if they could have burned down the factories, this would only have delayed things until some other factory-based system overcame them either through the strength of a factory-based army or through the commercial strength of cheaper goods.

It is not fashionable these days to pay serious attention to this concept of technological determinism but any discussion of the effects of technological change must answer the question, just how free is man to alter his technology? David Dickson [1974] dismisses technological determinism. He has two main arguments against it, which may be described as 'the Greeks knew about steam' argument and the Marxist view.

Such facts as the ancient Greeks knowing about steam engines, or the Chinese knowing about gunpowder, are quoted to show that inventions by themselves do not necessarily lead to the use of inventions and that some other factor determines whether the invention is used or not. This other factor then becomes the determinant of technology and technological determinism can be forgotten about. In the theory of technological Darwinism, however, most inventions are never used; those that are used become developed because they convey some advantage to the users. Labour saving inventions, for example, convey little advantage in societies with a plentiful supply of slaves or other cheap labour. In the same way that white bears had to wait the arrival of climatic changes before being white was an advantage, so many inventions have remained unused until a set of conditions gave them some survival value or advantage.

The conditions that decide whether a particular invention has an advantage are complex and varied, including not just economic factors but also strategic, political and social factors. Within this complex advantage system, it is possible for technology to evolve in a manner which leaves little room for free will within the process.

Dickson's second objection to technological determinism takes the conventional Marxist approach that is to stress the economic causes of technological change. Although Marx was very much aware of how the nature of technology [means of production] can have a profound effect on the structure of society [relations of production] Dickson claims that Marx was not a technological determinist. Marx 'repeatedly stresses that it is not technology which makes it necessary for the capitalist to accumulate, but the need for accumulation which makes him develop the powers of technology'.

One of the problems of saying that the need for something led to a technical change is that the need corresponds to the advantage. Any surviving technology must have some advantage. After the event, that advantage can be interpreted as a need which was present before the technology and which led to the development of the technology. This is a classic Adam's navel or chicken and egg dichotomy. Does the need for the advantage produce the technology or does the technology produce the advantage and hence the awareness of a need for that advantage?

Fortunately, [for the purposes of this discussion that is] Dickson's objection to technological determinism can be refuted without getting involved in chicken and egg arguments. Quite simply, Dickson does not appreciate the nature of Technological Darwinism which does not claim that new technology made it necessary for the capitalist to accumulate.

Technological Darwinism, which Dickson does not refute, regards the early beginnings of both the factory system and the capitalist system as arriving by quite independent mechanisms. Once the two systems coincided, the survival value of factory technology became apparent. Other societies, in order to survive, found that they must have factories. In order to get factories, they found they needed capital accumulation as well, to gather the resources necessary for the technology.

Once this happened, societies in competition with others ceased to have freedom of choice. In order to compete, they needed the technology with survival value and if this technology requires capital accumulation for its functioning, they must be that sort of society. This is not the same as saying that technology made the capitalist accumulate in the first place, but once the two have come together, the effect is the same, the nature of society cannot easily be changed; it is 'determined' by the technology. Associated with the rise of factories is the development of the division of labour which made factory-based technologies more competitive. Again, societies in competition had no alternative;

they were forced to adopt the division of labour and its consequences.

A good illustration of the way that the nature of a society is more in the grip of its technology of production than any other factor is provided by the way in which the societies of USA and USSR are moving closer together in certain important aspects. In order to compete successfully, both societies have found it necessary to move away from their original conceptions towards a direction in which they become more like each other.
[Remember, this was written in the late 1970s.]

Several writers have expressed this 'convergence' view of American and Russian societies. WS Buckingham [1958], from the point of view of economics, concluded that the two economic systems were growing more similar. PA Sorokin [1964], the American sociologist, concluded that future society and culture are likely to be neither capitalist nor communist but a new type, intermediary between the two existing forms.

Galbraith's [1967] view of industrial society was well known. He considered that the demands made by technology are more important than the concepts of capitalism and socialism. He has described how decision-making in both systems is becoming a similar process, with more decentralisation in Russia and more centralisation in the States producing the 'technostructure' required to maintain modern technological society. If societies as apparently dissimilar as those of Russia and America [not to mention many others throughout the world] are evolving in a similar direction, it seems reasonable to look for a common factor. There is such a factor, namely their technology, which is capital intensive and based on the division of labour. Galbraith claims that 'nearly all the consequences of modern technology ... derive from this need to divide and sub-divide tasks'.

One of the consequences of the division of labour is the so-called dehumanisation of the workplace. If the workplace needs humanising because it has been dehumanised through the division of labour, the central question becomes why did this process of dehumanisation take place? The technological determinist answer is that societies in competition had no choice; division of labour and dehumanisation were required for a more competitive technology. Alternative answers are that dehumanisation was caused by capitalist society or that it happened because no one bothered to stop it, i.e., that no one was very worried about it until recently.

The latter alternative is just not true. Even Adam Smith predicted that the division of labour would make life more boring for the workers. Marx wrote about the alienation of the workers and the following quotation from the Shop Stewards Movement of 1919 shows that at least some workers have been resisting dehumanisation for a long time:

Under the guise of scientific management, the Capitalists are introducing into industry schemes for dividing operations and making labour more automatic. The result of this tendency is to deny the worker responsibility, rob him of initiative and reduce him to the level of some ghastly inhuman, mechanical Puppet. - from Elliott & Elliott (1976)

Thus, as long ago as 1919, workers were objecting to 'inhuman' practices and blaming them on 'the Capitalists'. However, the 'nasty Capitalist' hypothesis is not a good one. Lenin made a study of the 'scientific management' techniques of FW Taylor which were based on work-study and the sub-division of manual tasks. Lenin's conclusion in 1918 was, 'We must organise in Russia the study and teaching of the Taylor system'. Being in a state of competition with the rest of the world, Russia had to use the most efficient form of technology available to it; if this meant dehumanising the workplace, there was not much choice. Even though Lenin was theoretically opposed to the accumulation of capital and the division of labour, he was forced through fear of war to adopt not only the machines of modern technology but also those social forms of Western Capitalism required to support the machines.

Similarly India, even with politicians theoretically in favour of industrial development at village level, has been forced to adopt ways of doing things developed by Europeans and North Americans, not noted for their belief in the importance of villages.

Thus, a case can be made for saying that technological change is not a controlled process; rather it is like the weather - something we have to learn to live with. Such a conclusion can be used however to support opposite policies for controlling the effects of technology.

Assuming the concepts of Technological Darwinism, it is possible to claim either that we don't have to worry about the effects of technological change as long as we encourage free market competition [because those changes with harmful effects will be destroyed through free competition - including consumers having a choice of alternative technologies plus the ability to sue for damages and workers having the ability to force up the cost of unpleasant forms of technology, like working on an assembly line, until other forms of technology become more competitive]; or, alternatively, that what we must do is find ways of having less competition since it is competition that forces people to do things that they don't want to do, and if competition could be reduced we could get on with doing things that a majority found desirable.

The United States seems to be attempting both policies for the control of technological effects. Their product liability legislation with high penalties for harmful effects is the market competition approach and their central control of standards [e.g. auto safety] is the opposite approach.

America has also witnessed the growth of pressure groups concerned with technological effects and the arrival of Technology Assessment, that is the attempt to encourage decision makers to think of possible consequences before harmful effects of new technology are detected instead of relying on "post disaster" legislation and the "technological fix".

Such concepts have spread to other countries. In other words, many people are not prepared to accept Technological Darwinism; there must be ways of controlling technology.

In fact, there are three arguments that can be used to restrict the power of Technological Darwinism. First, it seems likely that this lack of choice only applies to a small number of unusually important technological changes. For the large number of small changes that constitute much of technological change, those who make technological decisions do choose between alternatives and their decisions can be influenced by such mechanisms as legislation, pressure groups and fear of future penalties.

However, there may be limits to this degree of choice. If one country, on its own, decided to improve conditions both inside and outside of factories without changing the technology, such factories may not be able to compete with factories from other countries. [This need not be so if the technology is changed e.g. the move from batch to continuous production in the chemical industry led to better working conditions, less pollution and greater efficiency, but the reason for this change was greater efficiency, the other effects were almost accidental.]

The problem of international competition leads to the second possible argument against Technological Darwinism namely the possibility of international agreement to restrict competition. Such agreement can be by Government e.g. agreement to control fishing; by industries e.g. cartels or it can arrive by diffusion i.e. by the citizens of one country pressing for benefits enjoyed by the citizens of another country [e.g. the spread of clean air legislation]. However, such agreement may be confined to areas that have only a minor effect on a country's survival. Attempts at international agreement on disarmament have failed and the diffusion approach [i.e. unilateral disarmament] seems so risky that no country has yet been prepared to try it.

The third possible way out of Technological Darwinism is concerned with a breakdown in the analogy between biological and technological evolutions. Both systems of evolution can be seen as resulting from

competition taking place within a set of circumstances [such as the climate] which can be called the advantage system. A change in this system alters the competitive advantage of one entity over another leading to the dominance of new entities. In biological evolution, the advantage system which determines which species has an advantage over another is not controllable by the species in question [e.g. white bears had no way of producing snow and black moths had no way of producing soot to make trees black] but the human animal is maybe able to adjust the advantage system to make one form of technology more competitive than another.
To explore this possibility further requires a digression to discuss the role of this advantage system in technological change.

A new look at technological change: three necessary conditions.

This section seeks to show that there are three necessary conditions which have to be met before some new technology can survive the competition with other ways of doing things. The existence of three necessary conditions enables technological change to be viewed as the product of three interacting systems each contributing one of the conditions.

The three conditions which must all be fulfilled before a technological change survives are:
1] a technical concept capable of being developed to the stage of achieving
2] an advantage over alternative technical concepts; and
3] the capability of developing [1] to the stage of achieving [2]

The technical concept may be a brand-new idea or discovery, a new combination of ideas [old and or new] or an old concept not previously developed because of lack of [2] or [3].

The advantage can take a variety of forms. The capability also has different aspects including money, skills or the availability of some form of organisation necessary to achieve the development of the technical concept.

The three conditions can be illustrated by reference to examples in which one of the conditions is missing. A cure for cancer is an example of condition 1 being missing. There are lots of advantages awaiting such a cure and no shortage of money or skills for development. What is missing is the concept of what to develop.
It can be argued that the hovercraft is an example of condition 2 being missing. Here we have a new technical concept, government money for development though NRDC, some very skilled design effort and yet firms have gone bankrupt attempting to manufacture Hovercraft, as described by Johnson (1974). The problem with the hovercraft is the absence of any real advantage over alternative ways of travelling from A to B. The helicopter can also travel over land and water and the hydrofoil is increasingly being used for short-distance water transport. The Concorde might also fit into this category of having no advantage.
Examples of the third condition being absent are frequent in development countries, where technical concepts may be prevented from providing an advantage through lack of money and technical skills.

The three conditions have to co-exist in the same place and time. For example, when the US army was in Vietnam, many soldiers contracted malaria and several pharmaceutical firms started programmes aimed at the development of new improved antimalarial compounds. Although some potentially important discoveries were made, the American withdrawal from Vietnam led to the dropping of development work on antimalarials. So, we now have the situation where conditions 3 and possibly 1 exist in one place and condition 2 somewhere else. This is not to say that the pharmaceutical firms are deliberately withholding some new wonder drug from those parts of the world where malaria is common. It means that the pharmaceutical firms do not see any net advantage to themselves in spending a lot of money on testing new compounds in the hope of finding a better drug which even if it existed would not produce enough financial return to pay for the development costs.

This situation also illustrates the point that whether a new technical concept possesses an advantage or not is usually a matter of speculation until it has been tested. Finding out if an advantage exists or not can be very expensive so it is necessary to state that innovation is attempted when there exist a 'perceived net advantage' to be gained from the use of a 'capability' in developing a 'technical concept' that is considered capable of development to the stage of obtaining the advantage.

If the attempt fails, it could be that the perception of the advantage was incorrect, the technical concept was in fact not capable of development to the advantage stage or the capability of carrying out the development did not exist. [An example of the latter is the case of an electronics firm that attempted to develop the concept of numerically controlled machine tools to the stage where it would make a profit from selling them. The attempt failed because the firm lacked capability in the design of machine tools.]

The relationship between the three factors is not static. The three factors can be thought of as three systems, continually changing and interacting. There is the technical system, which mainly consists of the conventional history of technology. There is the perceived advantage system, which describes why anyone allocates resources to specific technological changes at a particular point in time; and there is the capability system, which consists of a developing set of resources, money, skills, availability of energy, access to raw materials and so on.

All the three systems interact with each other and also with other systems of society. For example, the technical system interacts with an independent scientific system; the perceived advantage system with political economic and marketing systems and the capability system interacts with financial and educational systems.

At first sight, the above description of interacting systems seems to support Technical Darwinism. Once a set of conditions appear that enable the successful development of a new technology, competitors who are forced to adopt that technology are also forced to adopt the conditions, which in the case of international competition has meant the appearance all over the world of those educational, financial and social systems which are thought necessary for the support of 'advanced' technology. It does rather look as though man is not in control of technology and its effects.

However, it is possible that control of the advantage system offers an element of choice. An example may help to explain what this means. Synthetic rubber was first produced in a small factory in 1912 by a group of Manchester chemists who developed the so-called Buna rubber (polybutadiene catalysed by sodium). However, this development did not survive because it had no advantage over natural rubber obtained from plantations. In particular, the price of the synthetic material was about fifteen shillings per pound when the price of the natural product, although fluctuating, remained below two shillings per pound and the technical properties at that time were slightly inferior to those of the natural product.

There was no advantage, therefore, to any company in developing synthetic rubber; nor was there any advantage to the British nation. As the majority of the rubber plantations were owned by Britain there was no national advantage to be gained from developing a rival product.

The situation in Germany, however, was different. Under the Nazi government of the late 1930s, it was realised that Germany at war would need considerable supplies of rubber. There was, therefore, an advantage to be gained from the development of synthetic rubber and the capability existed in the German chemical industry. The main problem was how to persuade private-enterprise peacetime German industry to use expensive synthetic rubber in the national interest. This problem was solved by manipulating the advantage system as perceived by private industry.

The German government imposed an import tax on natural rubber so as to make it more expensive than synthetic rubber, which then had an advantage in the eyes of German industrialists. It was not until the Japanese took over the natural rubber plantations that the rest of the world saw an advantage in synthetic rubber. A massive investment programme, involving government-owned factories in the USA, Canada and Russia was able to supply the wartime needs of the Allied nations.

This example illustrates the fact that in a conflict between national interests and the interests [perceived advantages] of individual firms in a private-enterprise system, there exist two alternative ways for government to control the introduction of new technology. The first can be seen as direct control of the capability system [e.g. government-owned factories] and the second as manipulation of the advantage system [e.g. differential taxation]. As the first alternative is not very popular in some countries, more attention needs to be given to the possibilities of the second.

Control of the advantage system offers a possibility for nation states to indulge in competition and also to produce more beneficial effects at the same time.

For example, the British Government is worries about the imports of foreign cars. It does not wish to impose controls of a conventional nature as it fears retaliation against our own exports. It could however use the desire to obtain beneficial effects as a way of controlling imports. It could say, for example, that all cars sold in Britain must conform to some standard of safety where this standard involved some new British technology which otherwise would have no competitive advantage. [It might even say that in order to protect the quality of working life, all cars sold in Britain must be manufactured under working conditions approved of by British trades union]

This technique was used by the USA to restrict Concorde through anti-noise regulations. A whole new vista of international technological competition could emerge. Individual firms could see an advantage in developing 'nice' technology if they thought that their government would bring in regulations insisting that new standards of 'niceness' were obligatory or at least carried some tax advantage.

Because the present structure of the advantage system is economic, countries and firms are forced to become more efficient, which in the long run means that people must be either subjected to greater stress or be unemployed. Under these conditions there is no escape from Technological Darwinism. A way out is to change the rules of the game in such a way that technology capable of improving the quality of human life is given some advantage.

The above ideas on technological determinism were used in a public talk, Technology, Servant or Master, given in Ames, Iowa during a visit to the USA.

13.7 Iowa State University (ISU)
As mentioned in the MBS chapter, a lunch time meeting with two Brazilians led to my being invited to Rio where I met an Egyptian American, Professor Aziz Fouad (1928 - 2017) who later invited me to go to Ames, Iowa as a Visiting Professor. Fouad had graduated in Cairo, gained a Masters at UoI and PhD at ISU. He had used a fund from the League of Mid-West Universities to make me a Distinguished Foreign Scholar and Visiting Professor.

Fouad's main claim to fame was his expertise in electric power systems but he had also been attempting to develop courses in science as an activity. This is what had led him to give a paper at the Rio conference and to invite me to Ames. Aziz and his wife, Maria, were very hospitable and looked after me during my stay in January 1977.

This turned out to be a freezing January. The residents of that part of the world were accustomed to temperatures unknown in England (In 1996 the January temperature in Ames was -33C). People travelling through the Mid-West took sleeping bags with them. If transport broke down, there was a risk of freezing to death.

Whilst I was there, I was invited to visit Nat Rosenberg in Stanford. This involved flying from Chicago to San Francisco and from the plane I could see the rivers Mississippi and Missouri, both frozen -a spectacular sight. Stanford, being in California was much warmer and I remember sitting outdoors, drinking Anchor Steam Bitter with a one of Rosenberg's assistants, David Mowery. (Later, I was very surprised when Mowery and Rosenberg (1977) published a paper, claiming that existing studies of innovation, including W f K, were 'flawed')

The visit to Stanford was memorable for three reasons, a book in the library, a bird in a garden and a talk I gave to a group in NASA. The book was Social Evolution: A study of the evolutionary basis of the science of society. (Keller, 1915) Keller was the second person to be described as Professor of the Science of Society at Yale. His book turned out to be unusual in two respects. It was based on the evolutionary ideas of Wallace and he stressed that he was not using analogy. He wrote, (1915): -

"If social scientists use the terms variation, selection and so on, they mean   nothing definite and actual by them; their usage of these terms is vaguely analogical and does not help them to get anywhere. ... they received the idea from Darwin, Wallace and others. I find a something in the social field, which IS variation, whether or not it may be like what is called variation in the organic field; similarly social selection IS selection and not merely like it." (And so on through transmission and adaptation to cover the four main features of Wallace's version of evolution).

In the Stanford campus I sat in a small garden at the back of a café bar enjoying a beer when I noticed a bird about the size of an English starling. This bird was jumping up and down. I don't think I had ever seen a bird do this before. Birds normally jump up and then fly away. This one was not flying anywhere. I then spotted that there was a water pipe sticking out of a wall, about four feet above the ground. Water was accumulating slowly at the open end of this pipe. The bird was jumping up, sticking its beak in the end of the pipe, grabbing some water, falling back to the ground and then waiting for more water to appear before jumping up again. The bird was using its wings to jump. One downward push from its wings was enough to propel the bird upwards.

One of the standard criticisms of Darwinian gradual change is "What use is half a wing?". It seemed to me that the jumping trick offered one way in which a simple wing could be useful. The ability to jump onto the back of a possible meal would be helpful to a predator.

Years later, I discovered that the jumping bird idea was a serious contender to be one way in which flight evolved gradually. Pouncing was presented as an alternative to the gliding theory in which predators glided from the tops of trees. (It was not too clear how they got back up the trees again). The theory of a pouncing proavis was first proposed by Garner, Taylor, and Thomas (1999) (proavis is a term for a speculative ancestral bird). I had this idea in 1977 and recorded it in my notebook.

My third memory is a visit to a NASA laboratory, organised by Nat Rosenberg who received funding from NASA. The National Aeronautics and Space Administration organised some very expensive projects, including the Apollo moon landings and the space shuttle. NASA had been established by US President Eisenhower in 1958` as a response to the Russian artificial satellite, Sputnik.

The original justification for the expense of space research had been in terms of national prestige and security but after the moon landing of 1969, NASA increasingly relied on more industrial justifications. Nat Rosenberg was the leading academic supporter of what became known as the discovery-push model of industrial innovation. (See the Pushmi-Pullyu debate in section 10.10)

As Nathan Rosenberg (1976) pointed out, there is a demand for better health but no demand for a particular innovation that does not yet exist. He collected examples of innovations whose origins demonstrated uncertainty and risk because their potential was yet to be realized - people often don't know what to do with an invention when it's really new. He liked the example of the laser, once known as the invention in search of a use and he quoted Charles Townes (1968) who won the Nobel for research on the laser, "Bell's patent department at first refused to patent our amplifier or oscillator for optical frequencies because, it explained, optical waves had never been of any importance to communications and hence the invention had little bearing on Bell System interests". The Laser needed another technology - fiber optics - before optical communication could become important.

Rosenberg's support of the discovery push argument won him finance from NASA who were arguing in support of curiosity-oriented research against its alternative, mission-oriented research. I was not able to discover which came first, Rosenberg's views or NASA finance.

I met a group of NASA scientists for a discussion. They agreed that the moon landing success had followed a clear mission statement by President Kennedy but it was also true that the basic discoveries had already been made. I trotted out the data form Wealth from Knowledge. (Langrish et al. 1972) It became clear to me that this was one of those either/or debates where the answer was 'both'.

When I returned to Iowa, it was still cold. The ISU university campus had kiosks scattered around and I discovered their purpose when walking to a distant building. When my trousers began to freeze, I ventured into one of the kiosks and discovered a heater and a supply of hot coffee. (In 1996 the Iowa temperature had fallen to -33 C)

The city of Ames had started life as a communication centre where a railroad crossed the Skunk River. It had grown round the university, originally an agricultural college (a so-called land-grant college). It had established a School of Veterinary Science that grew into a major research centre. I visited Vet Sci and was fascinated by its facilities, including an animal operating theatre. This had a rotating table so that a horse could be fastened to the table in a vertical position and then rotated into a horizontal position.

I gave a few lectures including one offered to the public. I also appeared on local lunchtime TV where I was shown how to talk to the camera with a red light. (There were three cameras covering different angles. The red light showed which one was transmitting.) Walking down a corridor later, I was stopped by a woman who said she had seen me on TV. 'Fame at last' I thought but it turned out that she had been watching the interviewer, her daughter.

I met some interesting people and one of them (Pat Hill) was responsible for inviting me to Wisconsin in 1985, thus completing the chain of consequences that had started with a lunch at MBS.

On my way back from the States, flying over the Atlantic and listening to a Mozart piano concerto in my earphone, I was overcome by a feeling of disbelief. This wasn't just Magic Carpet travel. Carpets did not carry a symphony orchestra.

I was reminded of when I was young, meeting a cousin of my mother who lived in the USA. She had said that when I was in the States, I must visit her. She was not pleased with my lack of response. This was because I could not imagine ever visiting America. My parents had never left the UK and I thought that only rich people engaged in foreign travel. In those days, people went across the Atlantic by sea.

13.8 The Swinging Sporran

When the new UMIST campus sprang up in the 1960s, it included a multi storey car park. In the corner there was a pub, The Swinging Sporran, occupying three floors at 78 Sackville Street. It was run by a Greek Cypriot, Costas, who provided interesting lunches. It was used by several members of UMIST staff and others who worked in the area. In the evenings, licensing law required that the pub closed but the basement then became a night club with a supper licence.

I enjoyed several sessions there. At lunch time I became familiar with the juke box playing Kate Bush. In 1978, she topped the charts with a strange single, Wuthering Heights, based on the Emily Bronte novel. To rhyme with Heights, Bush goes into the singular and rhymes with 'lost in the night', 'put it right' and 'lose the fight'. (Back then, I could not have imagined that Kate Bush would top the UK chart again in 2022 with a repeat of her 'Running up the Hill')

In the evenings, licensing law required the pub to stop serving alcohol at 10.30. However, people wishing to continue drinking simply moved downstairs to the Basement Club which had a supper licence, allowing for the consumption of alcohol as an accompaniment to food. This arrangement gave me an opportunity to see the law inaction.

In 1976, Greater Manchester acquired a new chief constable, Sir James Anderton, known as 'God's Copper' because of his belief that he had a direct line to God. He saw the police as a means of providing moral enforcement against "social nonconformists, malingerers, idlers, parasites, spongers, frauds, cheats and unrepentant criminals", (1987) and he was a vocal opponent of gay rights, illegal activities, feminism, pornography and those who "openly hankered after total debauchery and lewdness" (1987).

More realistically, Anderton waged a war against corruption in the police. In what was known as the Vackers Club case, police were shown to have been receiving brown envelopes in return for turning a blind eye against illegal activities.

He assumed that clubs with no police record were paying the police. This led him to investigate the Swinging Sporran by sending a young policewoman to visit the night club. She reported that there was no sign of food in the club. Costas was summoned to appear before the licensing magistrates and I agreed to appear as a witness.

The policewoman claimed that no food was visible and that when she asked for some chips, she was told to go to a chip shop.

In the witness box, Costas was superb. He demolished the police case. From memory, he said something like, "I am a chef. My food is in the 'fridge, the oven or in my customers. It is not lying about. I do not sell chips on their own. I sell meals." He then produced some files showing his VAT returns. This was proof that he sold many meals and paid tax on their cost. (What the magistrates did not realise was that most of his food income came from lunch time trade, not from the night club).

There was no need for further witnesses. The magistrates threw out the police case with a complaint against wasting the court's time.

I was also involved in another Anderton case that went against him. Running through the centre of Manchester was the Junction Canal that connected the Rochdale northern canal system with the Bridgewater canal system, leading to Liverpool. With visions of a Manchester Venice, the Victorians built a Canal Street next to this canal (In more recent times, Canal St. became the centre of Manchester's Gay community.)

Near the canal and not far from UMIST was an establishment known as The Queen's Club. This opened when the pubs were closed i.e. in the late afternoons and late evenings. It was run by a retired burglar.

Anderton believed that burglars were 'unrepentant criminals' who never retired and the fact that the Queens Club had not been in trouble made him suspicious. He orders an investigation.

The law required that clubs must maintain a register of members. The Queen's Club register was found to contain some well-known names including Alex Ferguson, the manager of Manchester United, and Graham Stringer, the leader of Manchester City Council. My name was also on the members' list. I used to have chats with PhD students in the Queens and on one occasion we talked to Graham Stringer who turned out to know about the Kuhn - Popper debate. (Stringer had a chemistry degree from Sheffield and in 1997 he replaced Paul Rose as MP for Blackley)

I was visited at home by a uniformed police officer. He inquired if I knew of the Queen's Club and was I a member. He sighed when I said yes and crossed my name off a list. Anderton's idea that the members' register contained false names turned out to be a mistake. The Queen's club kept strictly to the law.

13.9 Institute of Advanced Studies (IAS)

In 1977, after my American trip, I saw an advert for an interesting opportunity, Dean of the Institute of Advanced Studies at Manchester Polytechnic. The Poly had recently been formed by amalgamation of three existing Manchester colleges, The John Dalton College of Science and Technology, the Manchester College of Commerce and the Manchester Regional College of Art and Design.

The John Dalton claimed its origin to be in the Manchester Mechanics' Institute. The Art College claimed to be older than London's Royal College of Art. Manchester's most famous student was L S Lowry who was taught by a French impressionist, Adolphe Valette.

The Principal of the Polytechnic was Alex Smith. (After being chair of the Schools' Council, he became Sir Alex. His autobiography, Lock up The Swings on Sunday, revealed his Scottish origin).

Alex Smith had been Head of Research at Rolls-Royce and we knew each other from being at conferences on science policy and innovation. He owned a copy of Wealth from Knowledge.

IAS had started life as the School of Advanced Studies in the Art College. In those days there were no degrees in art colleges so there was no postgraduate work. John Holden, the last Principal of the college had dreamed up the idea of the equivalent of a postgrad year with the opportunity to become an Associate of the School of Advanced Studies. (ASAS). When Alex Smith had become the head of the new Poly, he had taken Advanced Studies out of Art and Design and turned it into an interdisciplinary extra-faculty unit to encourage research in the Polytechnic.

I sent off an application and was duly invited for an informal chat with Alex Smith and a few others. Various UMIST people told me that I must be mad thinking of going to the Poly. If I stayed at UMIST, there was every chance that I would become a professor. This reminded me of leaving ICI when people had said I could become a manager if I stayed. Eventually, a shortlist of four was picked for formal interview. One of these was Roy Bradshaw who expected to become the new Dean. He was a member of IAS and had pulled in external funds for research. The retiring Dean, Ray Howarth, had already introduced Roy to others as his successor. This was another reason why people were telling me I was being silly.

I turned up for the formal interview and was shown into a room with about twenty people waiting to interview me. This was my first experience of Manchester Education Committee. The interviewing crowd contained councillors, Union reps and academics who bombarded me with questions. There were people there who had said the Institute should be closed because it was a waste of money and others who thought it was a bunch of Holden's cronies, nicknamed advanced buddies. Then there was a group who were supporting Roy Bradshaw.

However, it happened to be one of those occasions when everything turned out right. It was like a tennis match where all the returns went two inches to the winning side of the line. A councillor asked me what use was research for those trying to teach West Indian children in Moss Side. I was able to reply that some recent American research had shown that the test scores of black children were higher when a black teacher administered the test. The implication was that Manchester needed to recruit more West Indian teachers.

The Dean of Science and Technology asked a question designed to favour Roy Bradshaw. This was did I know about the Joint Committee. I was able to reply that I was familiar with the work of the Joint Committee of the SRC and the SSRC. Furthermore, I had obtained funding from that source and there was now a PhD student at UMIST funded by the Committee as a Research Assistant. I coped with more questions and then waited for the others to be interviewed.

There was a long wait whilst the committee deliberated. Eventually Alex Smith turned up and said that they were having difficulty making a decision. He suggested that we went home and he would let us know the result by 'phone. So, more waiting and eventually I had a call from Alex Smith saying that the job was mine if I still wanted it. I was told later by Dr Hamer, the Poly's number two, that Smith thought I would leave when I found what the Poly was like. He was wrong; I stayed as Dean of the Institute until I was forced to retire at age 65. But that is a subject for part 2.

References Chapter 13.
Anderton, James. 1987. "God may be using me, says Anderton". BBC 4 Radio interview reported in The Glasgow Herald. 19 January 1987. p. 3.
Buckingham W S 1958 Theoretical Economic Systems. New York.
Cardwell, D. S. L. (ed.) (1974) Artisan to Graduate: Essays to Commemorate the Foundation in 1824 of the Manchester Mechanics' Institution Manchester UP
Dickson D. 1974. Alternative Technology. Glasgow: Fontana.
Elliott D & Elliott R.1976.The Control of Technology London: Wykeham.
Galbraith J K. 1967. The New Industrial State. Boston
Garner, J. P.; Taylor, G. K.; Thomas, A. L. R. 1999. "On the origins of birds: the sequence of character acquisition in the evolution of avian flight". Proceedings of the Royal Society B: Biological Sciences. 266 (1425): 1259–1266
Hodgson, G. 2012. Thorstein Veblen: The Father of Evolutionary and Institutional Economics. In E. Reiner & F. Viano 2012. pp. 283-296.
Johnson P S. 1974.The Development of Hovercraft, Three Banks Review, Dec. 1974.
Keller, Albert G. 1915. Social Evolution: A study of the evolutionary basis of the science of society. New York, Macmillan.

Langrish, J. Gibbons, M. Evans, W. Jevons, F R. 1972. Wealth from Knowledge: Studies of Innovation in Industry. London: Macmillan.

Langrish, J. 1977. "Technological Determinism" in Ottoway, R N ed. "Humanising the Workplace". Croom Helm 1977

Langrish, J. 1978. "The Changing relationship between Science and Technology" in Bradbury ed. "Transfer Processes in Technical Change. Setoff and Noordhoff.

Langrish, J. 1979. "The Effects of Technological Change" in Baker, M ed. "Industrial Innovation". London: Macmillan 1979

Mowery, D and Rosenberg, N. 1979. Th Influence of Market Demand on Innovation: A critical Review. Research Policy, April 1979.

Pirsig, R. 1974. The Art of Motor Cycle Maintenance. New York: William Morrow.

Reinert E S & Viano F L (Eds.), 2012.Thorstein Veblen: Economics for an Age of Crises. Anthem Press

Sorokin P A. 1964. The Basic Trends of Our Times. Yale U P

Rosenberg, N. 1976. Perspectives on Technology. Cambridge U P.

Townes, Charles. 1968, p701. "Quantum Mechanics and Surprise in the Development of Technology." Science, Feb 16.

Tweedale, G and Hansen, P. 2000. Magic Mineral to Killer Dust, Oxford U. P.

White L. 1962. Medieval Technology and Social Change. Oxford U P

UMIST MAN SCIENCES 1974-1977

Chapter 14. From Darwin to Dawkins

14.1 Darwinian Change

This chapter provides a link between the two parts of my autobiography. Part one ends in December 1977 with my leaving UMIST to join Manchester Polytechnic. I moved from a science and technology background into an Art and Design background. 1977 was also a year of change for my family. My daughters left Bramhall High School to pursue their A levels at colleges in Manchester and Salford. This change was accompanied by a change of residence. We moved from Bramhall to 9 Parsonage Rd, Heaton Moor, Stockport, just round the corner from the Reform Club and near to St Paul's church.

My work on innovation had convinced me that change in science and technology could best be described as evolutionary. Involvement with design added another item to the list of things that could be said to evolve. A fascination with evolutionary change provides a link between the two halves.

A clue to finding a satisfactory account of descent in technological change came from Sam Butler's 1872 Erewhon (almost 'nowhere' backwards). This book has a debate between two professors in an imaginary country where new technology has been banned.

One professor argues that machines evolve with the help of humans and this will lead to the enslavement of humans by machines
(Butler uses 'machines' to mean what we now call technology). Hence the need to ban any newer stuff.

The opposite view was that machines are simply an extension of human ability. A spade is like an improved arm and the evolution of machines is exosomatic (outside the body). These ideas first appeared in print in a New Zealand newspaper, The Press, under the heading 'Darwin amongst the Machines' (1863)   People who objected to the idea of technological evolution used to say, "machines don't mate". Butler's response is

Does anyone say that the red clover has no reproductive system because the humble bee must aid and abet it before it can reproduce? No one.

Machines use humans to aid and abet them, which is why the people of Erewhon were persuaded to get rid of them.

The solution to the problem of how an object could evolve into a different object came to me from Peter Medawar (1977), who claimed that instruments could be viewed as evolutionary, undergoing a slow systematic change, provided of course one realises that it is the design of these instruments that undergoes the evolutionary change and not the instruments themselves.

In other words, objects don't change into new objects but ideas about objects can lead to new ideas.

I discovered that there were several theories of evolution: not just Charles Darwin and Lamarck. There were ideas from Erasmus Darwin, Samuel Butler and Herbert Spencer. Thomas Munro (1961 p416) discussed different meanings of 'evolution' in art and concluded,

> If the term 'evolution in art' is so ambiguous, so loaded with inconsistent meanings, is it usable at all in scholarly discussion? Would it be better to find another term, or a set of them?

My answer is yes, it would be much better if we stopped using 'evolution' and used terms like Darwinian change, Lamarckian change, Spencerian progress, incremental change, trial and error, unfolding, emergence, cosmic force, etc. to distinguish between the many versions of 'evolution'.

My new post as Dean of the Institute of Advanced Studies (IAS) placed me in an environment that had emerged from the Manchester College of Art and Design and I decided it was time to explore the notion of evolutionary design in some detail. However, other things took priority and it was some years before I asked Nigel Cross, the editor of Design Studies, what books there were about evolution outside biology.

He recommended two books, George Basalla's The Evolution of Technology (1988) and Philip Steadman's The Evolution of Designs (1979). Basalla's evolution is of the strong variety. He claimed, "Any new thing that appears in the made world is based on some object already in existence". However, we are not told what 'based' means. He does not have a mechanism to produce new things (neither did Darwin). Like Basalla, Steadman offers no theory to account for design evolution. The subtitle to his book, biological analogy in architecture and the applied arts, shows that he ducks the mechanism question by calling it an analogy.

Steadman's scholarly work introduced me to various Victorian writers who had thought about evolution outside biology. These included Pitt Rivers whose collection of objects from around the world became a museum attached to the Natural History Museum in Oxford. Pitt Rivers arranged objects to show an evolutionary progression. One of his illustrations has a stick in the centre surrounded by gradual changes to lead to spears in one direction and axes in another. A special line leads to the boomerang. Since the objects come from different parts of the world, there is no suggestion of how one object leads to another.

Ironically, the entrance to the Pitt Rivers Museum was next to the horse display in the Natural History Museum. This was supposed to show the evolution of the horse from something the size of a dog through stages into a modern horse. However, the different animals in the display came from different continents. So again, we have no clue as to how a proto horse turned into a modern horse.

In the present century, the horse display was changed and the curators of the Pitt Rivers collection decided that evolution was not pc and downplayed its evolutionary significance. The curators were not alone in backing away from evolution. Philip Steadman told me that he had been warned off doing any more work on evolution. Employed as a lecturer in architecture, his next publications were about house plans in Victorian London.

It was not until 2008 that Steadman managed to return to evolution. He published a revised edition that had an added chapter – "An Afterword".

In the 2008 version, he included a mention of my ideas but he still thought in terms of analogy and failed to understand the nature of complex systems. He wrote –

The difficulty, it seems to me, is that if all thoughts, ideas and beliefs are memes, does this not mean that memes are being selected by other memes? Langrish (1999) seems to imply this when he introduces a distinction, in the context of design history, between what he calls 'recipemes' (instructions for how to do things, recipes) and 'selectemes' (values, criteria for choice). But does this not lead to an infinite regress? (2008 p. 244)

Well, no it doesn't. In a complex system anything can interact with anything else, and this does not have to lead to neat chains of linear causality. Complexity is not deterministic; it is not physics.
(Despite this, Steadman's book is highly recommended.)

The cover illustration to Basalla's book follows the tradition of a line of things without a causal connection. It has stones leading to hand axes, leading to hammers and finally a steam hammer. The assumption that technological change involves a linear progression does not stand up to scrutiny. The major ancestors of a stream hammer are not hand axes; they are earlier steam engines and gravity powered heavy tilt hammers.

The steam hammer emerged in the mind of James Nasmyth (1808-1890). In 1828 he designed a steam carriage that ran a mile carrying 8 passengers. In 1839 he made detailed drawings for a steam hammer designed to be an improvement on earlier tilt hammers.

A visiting French engineer who built the first steam hammer copied Nasmyth's design. In 1842 Nasmyth was able to patent his design and build his first hammer at his factory in Patricroft (a suburb of my birthplace, Eccles, with its coat of arms containing a symbolic representation of a steam hammer).

The mind of Nasmyth produced another first, the steam powered pile driver. It seemed clear that Medawar's claim about the evolution of designs could be a fruitful start. Steam engines had not evolved. It was ideas about how to make them and what to do with them that had evolved.

14.2 Salford Conference, 1995

An opportunity to test my ideas about evolution on a design audience was provided by the inaugural conference of the European Academy of Design (EAD). The EAD was the brainchild of Rachel Cooper, formerly Rachel Davies, a PhD student in IAS. I had introduced Rachel to Cary Cooper who subsequently left his wife and married Rachel. (Many years later, Cary was knighted and Rachel then became Lady Cooper. She also became President of the Design Research Society (DRS). For 24 years I was Treasurer of the DRS, complaining that it did not spend enough of its money.)

My paper (1995) for the EAD conference included the following model, meant to be a model for a general theory

covering the evolution of humans, animals, vegetables, science, technology, society and design.
A basic Darwinian evolutionary model has 4 main requirements:

1]   The existence of variety - different kinds of things having mixtures of differing properties held in varying amounts.
2]   A competitive selection process which picks certain things, properties or amounts of properties as 'winners'.
3]   A reproductive system which leads to the replication of the 'winners' and the disappearance of the 'losers'.
4]   Since the above three on their own lead simply to a steady state, there has to be a mechanism for the generation of new varieties which takes us back to 1] and the continuation of the process.

    To which it is necessary to add a fifth: -
5]   Even with the addition of 4] the system of change would slow down through diminishing returns, unless we have a fifth feature viz a mechanism for changing the rules of the selection process. Without changes in the environment, evolution would stop.

The EAD conference was held in Salford with the conference dinner on the set of Coronation Street (the UK's longest running soap) to the puzzlement of some overseas speakers. After presenting the paper, I had a conversation with a former PhD student, Chris Rivlin, in the Salford University campus pub, the Waldorf Tavern. He said that I should read Dawkins' Blind Watchmaker (1986). I was aware of the Selfish Gene but had obviously not got as far as the last chapter on memes and cultural evolution (Dawkins 1976). At that time, I ignored anything that mentioned 'culture', so my mind was not prepared. However, when I read about memes and about Dawkins' discussion of Lamarckism, it struck me that these made sense of some problems with the model presented above.

14.3 Dawkins
Following the advice from Chris Rivlin, I read The Blind Watchmaker. Its title suggests an argument that I

already knew as the reverse Paley argument. Instead of saying a watch shows evidence of human design so a much more complex living thing must have been designed intentionally, the reverse says if a complex living thing can arrive via a long series of small changes, then a watch could have arrived by a similar process.

The most important result of reading Watchmaker was my rediscovery of Dawkin's major book, The Selfish Gene (1976). This book has been widely misunderstood. Philosopher, Mary Midgley, published an attack in the Journal, Philosophy, in which she claimed that genes could not be selfish because they were not sentient. She was not aware that Charles Darwin had suffered similar criticism. 'You cannot have selection without the presence of a selector' is a criticism that is still around in the form of so-called intelligent design, needing an intelligent designer.

Other critics were confused by the way that biologists write. 'The gene for blue eyes' is mistaken to mean that this gene 'causes' blue eyes. In fact, it means that the absence of this gene prevents blue eyes from forming. Critics thought that 'selfish gene' meant a gene that makes people selfish. It doesn't. It means that genes behave as though they were selfish, only interested in their own survival and replication.

A better tile for The Selfish Gene would have been The Selfish Replicator. Dawkins' book provides a general evolutionary account in which an imperfect replicator is essential. In an evolutionary process, something must be passed on. Dawkins calls this something a replicator. This something must make errors when it is copied. It becomes an 'imperfect replicator'. In biological evolution, the replicators are genes and the errors are mutations. The genes exist as chemical structures strung together in giant molecules of DNA.

Before DNA could become the biological replicator, there had to be an evolutionary process that resulted in DNA. Some simple ancient molecules had stumbled on a way of being copied. As well as speculating on replicators before DNA, Dawkins has a chapter on replicators after DNA and he invented a new word, 'meme', to describe a cultural replicator. Dawkins says memes are ideas about pots, arches, clothing and also religion, fashion etc. They are 'replicated' by passing from one human to another. These replicating ideas get copied, modified and stuck together with other ideas and can form the basis of a memetic theory of change. Since Dawkins originated the word 'meme', it has displaced a rival word, culturgen, and moved into popular usage as something that cries out to be passed on in the sense of 'going viral'.

Charles Darwin saw two problems with his theory. He was not sure what was passed on and he wondered where novelty came from. Genes and their mutation solved these two problems but Darwin did not know about genes. When it comes to human evolution, there is another problem. Biological evolution has no preset direction but humans have choice and intention; technological change is directed.

Dawkin's answer to this problem is simple; there is no way of predicting the future; choosing technology speeds things up but our choices evolve and are subject to natural selection. Many choices are just wrong and do not survive. As described in an earlier chapter, the builders of the East Lancs Road, put water pipes in lay-bys to supply the steam lories of the future but they were wrong. Similarly, the post WWII choice of seaplanes to be the future was wrong. Concrete runways turned out to be a better choice.

In The Blind Watchmaker, Dawkins (1986 p288) gives arguments against Lamarck's theory being correct. He states,

> Lamarckism is not just something that might be; it actually couldn't be ... the theory is in principle incapable of explaining the evolution of serious adaptive complexity not just on this earth but anywhere in the universe.

Lamarck saw change resulting from striving to meet needs (les besoins) leading to the acquisition of improvements that could be inherited. Dawkins states,

> Suppose the skills acquired during life by animals could be translated into DNA and get passed on. They would be one jump ahead and evolution would be speeded up". However, "this all presupposes that the changes in behaviour that we call learning are, indeed, improvements. Why should they necessarily be improvements?... there must be a Darwinian underpinning to ensure that acquired characteristics are advantageous.

14.4 Different kinds of memes

In practice, Dawkins' memes have not proved to be very useful. This is partly through thinking of them as 'units of culture'; culture is not chemistry or physics; it is not analysable into units; memes are not units - they are patterns of ideas. Another reason for memetics (the study of memes) not proving very useful has been an over concentration on memes as mental 'viruses', infectious ideas that pass from one human to another like an epidemic.

In 1998 I discovered that there was a Journal of Memetics. I went to the library to look at its list of journals and where they could be found. There was no record of this journal but I subsequently discovered that it was an electronic journal, a new kind of entity, pointing to a future with the Internet replacing the library as the main source of information.

In a paper for this new journal (Langrish 1999), I claimed that the way forward for memetics was to recognise that there are different kinds of memes that do different sorts of things and are replicated by different mechanisms. That paper suggested that three types of memes are particularly important. These are:

1. Recipemes - ideas about how to make things or do things
2. Selectemes - ideas about what sorts of things we actually want to make or do i.e. ideas of betterness and
3. Explanemes - ideas which are used to answer 'why' questions.

Recipemes, such as solutions to design problems, compete within an environment of selectemes that range from ideas of what a client wants, existing in the mind of an individual designer, to societal norms enshrined in laws and regulations. This 'climate' of selectemes within which the recipemes compete is different from the climate that selects some genes to survive and others to become rare. It is different because it is to some extent controllable; we can tax or ban some things and give rewards for others. The problem is that in the long term we have no idea of what is going to become 'better'.

This means that this climate of values is itself part of a Darwinian natural selection system. Some selectemes survive and others don't. This means that the value climate becomes the 'Darwinian underpinning' of the competing ideas.

It turned out that the electronic Journal of Memetics was not a harbinger of the future. Electronic journals need stable sites and this journal lost its home.

I returned to a conventional journal, the American Journal of Design Issues, to publish a paper (Langrish 2004) on the memetic evolution of design ideas. By 2004 I had retired from full time work at MMU but I continued to supervise PhD students.

The description of explanemes, given above, as 'ideas which are used to answer 'why' questions' turned out to be confusing for students attempting to use memetics. This confusion was a good example of the logical fallacy known as the excluded middle (A Victorian example: All sailors are men. Fred is a man. Therefore, Fred is a sailor. FALLACY.)

Explanemes are answers to 'why?' But not all such answers are explanemes. The answers to 'Why did you buy that one?' are usually selectemes such as 'it was mor reliable'. In a later paper (Langrish 2014) I wrote,

> memes are patterns of thought and there are three kinds of memes, recipemes (how to do things), selectemes (what sort of things you want to do, notions of 'betterness' and desirability) and **explanemes that explain how recipes produce their results**.

My thoughts on explanemes had emerged from thinking about science and technology. If technology is a black box with inputs and out puts then science is an attempt to explain what happens inside the box. Such attempts are explanemes.

Explanemes range from scientific theories to ancient myths and need a language for their reproduction. Newton's law of gravity is an explaneme. It is passed on using maths and words. It is not imitated.

14.5 Purposive Pattern Recognition (PPR)

The University of Salford invited me to be a Visiting Professor in their Design Research Unit, headed by Rachel Cooper and I was also involved with students in other universities. Details of these activities are mentioned in Part Two if this autobiography but one of them is worth a mention here, I was joint supervisor to three PhD students at the De Montfort University, Leicester. One of these, Maria Abu-Risha, was from Jordan and she produced an excellent thesis on visual choice. This led to the idea of Purposive Pattern Recognition - PPR and a joint paper (2008) for a DRS) conference in Sheffield.

Maria asked practicing designers how they made visual choices. "Why an elephant on the front cover?" "Why that particular elephant?" Relies, such as "it's intuitive". "You just know it's right". 'it's not scientific" suggested to us that the design process involved the comparison of two patterns.

The visual alternatives are compared with the need pattern until there is a mental 'click' that is the brain's way of telling our conscious mind that we have a match between two circuits or patterns. The concept of two thought patterns coming together in a moment of creativity is well known. The moment when insight occurs was described by Arthur Koestler (1964) as 'bi-sociation' - two areas of thought becoming so integrated into one that it is difficult to imagine how these previously existed separately.

This 'click' is an example of a wider phenomenon, the recognition of a pattern that tells you what to do next. Hence PPR. (See Chapter 5)

When designers say that their 'click' is not scientific, they mean, 'it's not physics'. Biology is a science; it deals with variety and complexity. It is not consistent; it changes. It is not physics.

It is not just designers who have realized that the physics way of viewing the world is not always the best. Francis Crick was a physicist before he changed biology by helping to discover the double helix. He then moved on to study neurobiology and the problem of consciousness.

Since this chapter is meant as a bridge, it seems appropriate to end with an account of Ronnie Fisher who like me, started in physical chemistry and moved on. He studied mathematical physics at Cambridge and then moved into statistical mechanics. He saw the usefulness of having large numbers and used this to devise a new way of looking at evolution. He saw evolution as a change of frequency in populations. He then went on to devise new statical methods for plant breeding. (A biography of Fisher was written by his niece, Joan Fisher Box, and given to me by Fisher's granddaughter, Emma Posey, a PhD student.)

Like Fisher, I was fascinated by statistical mechanics and like him I am an Anglican with a belief in the Social Gospel (Thy Kingdom come on earth …) Fisher's involvement with politics was much more successful than mine. In pursuit of a way of encouraging the middle class to have more children, he persuaded the government to introduce a tax rebate for a second child. When I became the father of twins, I was grateful for my income tax being reduced.

Fisher's evolutionary theory influenced my finances. But it didn't have to; it was not deterministic; it was not consistent; it was not physics.

My brain is telling me that I am straying into topics meant for Part Two. So, what I need to do next is to get Part One published. But, the opera isn't over until the fat lady sings: -

14.6 So, what's it all about?

> "All the world's a stage,
> And all the men and women merely Players,
> They have their exits and their entrances,
> And one man in his time plays many parts,"
> - Shakespeare, As You Like It.

The trouble with the play pattern is that plays have an author. The apparent lack of meaning in life as a stage is replaced by the intentions of the author.

Charles Darwin had a similar problem. You can't have selection without a selector. Design implies a designer. But Darwinian change is blind; it has no aim. Could life be a play without an author?

The human brain is constructed so that it can detect boundaries. It separates its surroundings into different kinds of things. It then decides the value of these things; good, desirable or bad and to be avoided.

The higher brain tries to determine causes. How to get more of the desirable things and how to avoid the dangerous things. This involves the notion of change. Things then get very complicated but the brain has various devices for making things seem simpler than they are. The ultimate device is Physics with its apparent simplicity. Th brain then looks for meaning and constructs meanings that exist in the brain but not in reality.

The lack of objective meaning was detected by ancient thinkers as expressed in a biblical quote (Ecclesiastes 1. New International) The words of the Teacher, son of David, king in Jerusalem:
"Meaningless! Meaningless!"
   says the Teacher.
[The traditional translation starts –
   "Vanity, Vanity!" saith the Preacher.]

"Utterly meaningless!
   Everything is meaningless."
[3] What do people gain from all their labors
   at which they toil under the sun?
[4] Generations come and generations go,
   but the earth remains forever.
[5] The sun rises and the sun sets,
   and hurries back to where it rises.
[6] The wind blows to the south
   and turns to the north;
round and round it goes,
   ever returning on its course.
[7] All streams flow into the sea,
   yet the sea is never full.
To the place the streams come from,
   there they return again.
[8] All things are wearisome,
   more than one can say.
The eye never has enough of seeing,
   nor the ear its fill of hearing.
[9] What has been will be again,
   what has been done will be done again;

there is nothing new under the sun.
[10] Is there anything of which one can say,
"Look! This is something new"?
It was here already, long ago;
it was here before our time.

14.7 Newton and the Secret

This book starts with Newton, and it ends here with some thoughts about Isaac Newton. He can be thought of as the inventor of Physics. His Laws of motion and the Law of gravity started a new way of thinking that provided a model for future natural philosophers.

And yet, there is a problem: when others saw the power of Newton's Laws they used the word, Newtonian, to describe a deterministic view of things. When Newton realised this, he declared, "I am not a Newtonian". When asked how gravity worked, he replied, "I make no hypothesis" (Hypotheses non fingo).

He knew that mathematical equations were not enough, and he searched ancient documents in the hope of uncovering secret knowledge, including alchemical secrets and the key to biblical prophesies.

When I was young, libraries caused a strange feeling. I thought that the ultimate secret might be hidden somewhere in the library. This feeling was particularly strong in libraries with old documents like Manchester's John Rylands. Somewhere, there must be the answer to, "What's it all about, then?"

Newton's anti-Trinitarian views were considered heretical and his alchemical studies eccentric. So, his extensive writings on non-physics type matters were hidden for years but purchased for the nation by John Maynard Keynes, the 1930s leading economist.

These papers have been described in a book by Sarah Dry (2014). A paper describing how to treat the plague includes hanging a frog upside down in a chimney for three days until it vomits.

In other words, the founder of physics, when thinking about the ultimate knowledge, believed that -

It's Not Physics.
Or as Douglas Adams put it in Hitchhiker's,

"The answer to the ultimate question of life, the universe and everything" - is - 42.

THE END

References Chapter 14.
Basalla, George. 1988. The Evolution of Technology. Cambridge U P.
Butler, Samuel. 1863. Darwin amongst the Machines. Letter to The Press. New Zealand.
Butler, Samuel, 1872. Erewhon: or Over the Range. London: Jonathan Cape.
Dawkins, Richard. 1976. Memes: the new replicators, chapter 11 in The Selfish Gene, Oxford U P. pp189 - 201.
Dawkins Richard. 1986. The Blind Watchmaker. Longmans, London. p. 288.
Dry, Sarah. 2014.The Newton Papers: The Strange and True Odyssey of Isaac Newton's Manuscripts. Oxford U P.
Koestler, A. 1964, The Act of Creation. London: Hutchinson
Langrish, J. 1995. Evolutionary Design. EAD Inaugural Conference. Salford.
Langrish, J. 1999 "Different Types of Memes: Recipemes, Selectemes and Explanemes" Journal of Memetics Vol. 3,1999.
http://www.cpm.mmu.ac.uk/jom-emit/1999/vol 3/langrish_jz.html
Langrish, J, 2004. "Darwinian Design: The Memetic Evolution of Design Ideas." Design Issues, Nov. pp 4-19.
Langrish, J. 2005. Evolutionary Design - Ten years on:memes and natural selection. Proc. EAD 6 Conference, University of the Arts, Bremen, Germany.
Langrish, John Z and Abu-Risha, Maria. 2008. Purposive Pattern Recognition: The Nature of Visual Choice in Graphic Design. In: Undisciplined! Design Research Society Conference 2008, Sheffield Hallam University. Available from Sheffield Hallam University Research Archive (SHURA) at: http://shura.shu.ac.uk/461/
Langrish J Z. 2014. Darwinian Design in an Era of Disruption. in DMI Conference, London 2014
Medawar PB and JS, 1977, The Life Science, London: Wildwood House p. 52.

Munro, Thomas. 1961. Do the Arts Evolve? Some Recent Conflicting Answers. Journal of Aesthetics and Art Criticism; 1961. 407-417.

Steadman, Philip.1979. The Evolution of Designs: Biological analogy in architecture and the applied arts. Cambridge U P. 2008. Revised edition with added chapter. Abingdon and New York: Routledge.

INDEX

USE WITH CONTENTS

Abu Risha
   Maria, 96, 397
Adams
   Douglas, 401
Adler
   Larry, 75
Airport Hotel, 202, 204
Albert St Church School, 44, 190
   Chess Club, 74
   Cubs, 18, 30, 44, 45, 55, 67
   Scouts, 18, 45
   Sunday school, 18, 44, 55, 57, 73, 147, 156, 171, 326
   Youth Club, 18, 156, 190, 218
Alexander
   Samuel, 119
Allen
   Tom, 334, 335
Allende
   Salvador, 314
Anderson
   Perry, 97
Anderton
   James, Sir, 377, 378, 379
Anglican Fellowship, 158
Anglican Pacifist Fellowship, 114
Aristotle, 72, 83, 319
Art & Design, viii, 380, 385, 387
   Faculty. See MMU
   School, 338
Ashworth
   John, 189
Asquith
   Herbert H, 186
Assistant Masters Association, 197, 240
Atkinson
   Peter, 216
Attlee
   Clement, 175, 176, 180, 185, 220
Augarten
   Stan, 285
Austin
   A35, 242
   A40, 100
   Mini, 100

Bacon
   Francis, 264
Bailey
   H J, 14
Baker
   Hilda, 30
Balcombe
   Fred, 221
Ball
   Johnny, 112
Bannerman
   Campbell, xi
Barker
   David, 85
Barnes
   Luke, 110, 125
Barton Aerodrome, 203
Barton swing bridge, 15, 44, 57, 59, 79
Basalla
   George, ix, 388, 389
Baxendale
   Dr, 168
Bayer Peacock, 252, 255
Beer
   Stafford, 313, 314
Beilstein
   F K, 165
Bell
   Captain and Mrs., 25
Belle Vue, 28
Benson
   Bernice, 171
   Izzy, 171, 203, 219
   Phil, 171, 219
   Ralph, 171, 219
Bentley
   Dick, 49, 75
Bernstein
   Leonard, 171
   Mick, 169, 170, 210
   Sadie. See Clyne
   Sidney, 171
Berry
   Miss, 60
Bettelheim
   F R. See Jevons
Bilko
   Sergeant, 236
Birch
   Arthur, 133

Blackley, 208, 213, 219, 222, 223, 226, 227, 231, 233, 239, 243, 265, 379
Blears
 Jack, 352
Blunt
 Anthony, Sir, 338
Bonham Carter
 Mark, 186
 Voilet, Lady, 186
Booth
 Webster, 75
Bor
 Daniel, 89, 91
Bordean House, 253, 254, 257, 260
Born
 Max, 319
Bradburn's 'Original Eccles Cake Shop, 41
Bradshaw
 Roy, 381
Brains Trust, 82, 105
Bramall Hall, 159
Bramhall High School, 385
Bramhall Urban District Council, 189
Bren guns, 115
Brenda, iii, 84, 85
Bridgewater canal, 31, 44, 57, 58, 63, 77
British Academy, 296, 298
British Dyestuffs Corporation, 213
British Gaumont, 46
British Rail, 176, 241
British Rubber Producers Research Association, 131
British Society for the History of Science, ix
Bruce
 Margaret, 267
Buckingham
 W S, 361
Bud
 Robert, 317, 318
Buist
 Jack, 228, 229
Burket
 Rev, 47
Burnage Grammar School, 113, 114
Bush
 G W, 337
Butler
 Samuel, 83, 122, 123, 284, 285, 385, 386, 387
Byrne
 Richard, 97
Cahn
 R W, 270
Cajal
 Santiago Ramon y, 98
Cambridge University, 69, 108, 133, 193, 278, 398
 Trinity College, 120
Campenot
 R B, 82
Cannon, 233
 H Graham, 126, 127
 Walter Bradford, 128
Carothers
 Walter, 266
Carter
 Charles, 266
Cartier, 296
 Jacques, 296
 Jean-Jacques, 296
Catholic Truth Society, 146
Cheetham Town Hall, 202
Chemical Society, 161
Chetham
 Hospital, 215
 Humphrey, 214
 Library, 215
Chicks' Own, 30, 39
Chitnis
 Pratap, 223
Chomsky, 89
Church of England, 17, 53, 122, 144, 145, 146, 147, 148, 149, 190
Churchill, 173, 175, 183, 184
Ciba-Geigy, 208
Clapton
 Mr, 197
Clarendon Road Primary School, 35, 36
Clean Air Acts - 1956 and later, 13, 104, 365
Clyne
 Kitty, 203
 Maurice, 170
 Sadie, 170, 210
 Sandra. See Langrish
 Sid, 203
CNAA, 339
CND, 156, 186, 188, 195, 247, 279
 Swaffham Rocket Site, 188

INDEX

Colclough
 Richard O, 150, 151, 159, 200, 263
College Arms, 157
Collins
 Cannon, 187
Compton
 Richmal, 29
Conservative Club, 18
Conservative Party, 175, 182
Co-op Biscuit Works, 213
Co-op Dairy, 79
Cooper
 Alan, 184, 190
 Cary, Sir, 345, 390
 Rachel, Lady, 168, 390, 397
Council for Science Policy (CSP), 311
Cravenwood Road Primary School, 239, 246
Crescent Road, 159, 215
Crick
 Francis, 398
Crips
 Stafford, Sir, 176
Cross
 Nigel, 388
Crowley
 Gerry Dr, 235
Crown cinema, 173
Crumpsall, 159, 169, 170, 188, 193, 205, 206, 207, 208, 210, 211, 212, 213, 214, 215, 217, 219, 222, 224, 242, 243, 246, 326
Crumpsall Hall, 214
Cunningham
 Malcolm, 341, 348
Curnow
 R C, 271
Cuvier
 Baron, 286
Cyril Lord carpets, 226
Daniels
 Glyn, 297
Darwin
 Charles, 20, 72, 122, 257, 274, 276, 286, 386, 387, 388, 392, 393, 399
 Emma, 104, 257
 Erasmus, 387
Davies
 Clement, 186
 Rachel. See Cooper

Davison
 Dorothy, 280
Davy
 Humphry, 235
Dawkins
 Richard, ix, 20, 105, 281, 391, 392, 393, 394, 395
de Broglie, 307, 308, 309
de Trafford
 John Humphrey, Sir, 59
de Waal
 Frans, 57
Delaunay
 Angel, 213
Dennett
 Daniel, 28, 354
Derbyshire
 Dickey, 71
Design
 History Society, ix
 Management Institute, ix
 Research Society, ix, 158, 168, 391, 397
Dick Barton, Special Agent, 76
Dickson
 David, 358, 359
Didsbury Road School, 246
Dimbleby
 Richard, 185
Donegan
 Cedric, 70
Dos Passos
 John, 52
Dry
 Sarah, 401
Dunlop Rubber Company, 234
 Dunlopillo, 234
Dunne
 J W, 124
DuPont
 Acetylene, 266
Dyer
 Alan, 80
East Lancashire Road, 70, 71
Eccles and Patricroft Hospital, 152
Eccles and Patricroft Journal, 45, 56, 85, 154, 175, 182
Eccles Grammar School, 61, 63, 65, 78, 81, 176
Eccles Library, 42
Eccles Secondary School, 60, 65, 176
Eccles Technical School, 155, 171
Eccles Town Hall, 14, 43

Education Offices, 14
Treasurer's Department, 14, 43, 50, 177
Eden
    Anthony, Sir, 184, 185
Edward VIII
    King, 175
Edwards
    Jimmy, 49, 75
Einstein, 199, 319
Eisenhower
    Dwight D, 85, 375
Elections, 177, 223
    General, 182, 183, 185, 220, 222
    Local, 221, 223, 324
Elgar
    Edward, 273
Elizabeth II
    Queen, 85, 257
Ellesmere Avenue, 19, 20, 22, 25, 27, 28, 31, 33, 40, 47, 76, 145, 154, 175
Ellesmere Park, 42, 70, 77, 154, 155
Elliott & Elliott, 362
Elmore
    Mabel and Winnie, 25
Empedocles, 84
Engels, 185, 215
Epictetus, 106
European Academy of Design (EAD), 390
Evans
    Bill, ix, 267, 270
Evens-Bramwell
    George, 72
Eysenck
    Hans, 181
Faculty of Science, vi, 126, 168, 263
Fairbanks
    Arthur, 84
Fairclough
    Grace, 26
    John Scarisbrick, ix, 16, 45
    Marjorie. See Langrish
    Molly, 16, 17, 18, 22, 296
Farmiloe
    Tim, 270, 354
Ferguson
    Alex, Sir, 379
Ferriday
    Peter, 338, 339

First World War, 12, 37, 48, 60, 225, 275, 318, 347
Fisher
    Ronnie, 130, 318, 398
Fisher Box
    Joan, 398
Flat Earth Society, 200
Flowers
    Brian, 333
Ford
    100E Popular, 100
    Consul, 128
    Cortina, 242, 312
Fouad
    Aziz, ix, 372
    Maria, 373
Franklin
    Rosalind, 141
Free Church of England, 17
Free Trade Hall, 186, 187
Freeman
    Chris, 312
    Paul, 113, 114, 116, 120
Friends Meeting House, 187
Frost
    Penny, 335
Gaitskell
    Hugh, 186
Galbraith
    J K, 361
Garner
    J P, 374
Gas Laws, 275
Gee
    Geoffrey, 131, 132, 162, 262
    Henry, 287, 289
General Strike, 16
George
    Lloyd, xi
George V
    King, 70
George VI
    King, 51
Ghazi
    Arif, 215, 216
Gibbons
    Mike, 248, 267, 270, 311
Gill
    Eric, 221
Glaser
    Barney G, 163
Glasstone
    Samuel, 165

INDEX

Godin
  Benoît, 273
Goldstone
  Carol, ix, 310, 353
Golgi
  Camillo, 98
Goncharov
  Vadim, ix
Goodall
  Jane, 277, 278
Goon Show, 118
Gram. Soc, 157, 186
Grasmere Crescent, 13
Green
  Daisy, vi, 173
Greenwood
  June, 69
Grimond
  Jo, 181, 186, 219, 220, 222
Hall
  Mike, 120, 158, 203
  Patsy, 203
Hamer
  Dr, 382
Hamlin
  Tony, 339
Hammond
  R Michael, 222
Hancock
  Tony, 50, 74
Handley
  Tommy, 49
Harcourt Road, 205, 206
Harrison
  Eileen May, 74
Hauser
  Otto, 281
Hawkes
  Christopher, 279
  Jacquetta, 277, 278, 279
Haworth
  Walter, 108
Hayek
  A, 134, 179, 180, 265, 336, 337
Heaton Moor Congregational church, 189
Heaton Moor Infants, 246
Hill
  Christopher, 103
  Ken, 333
  Pat, 376
Hindle
  Stan, 156

Hindsight
  Project, 271, 292
Hinnels
  Mark, ix
Hippel
  Eric von, 334, 335
Hitler, 35, 51, 70, 80, 104, 173, 175
Holden
  John, ix, 380, 381
Holt
  Arthur, 184
Hope Hospital, 85
Hopkins
  Frederick, Sir, 279
Horne
  Kenneth, 49, 75
Howard
  Frankie, 50, 74
Howarth
  Elgar, 94
  Ray, 381
Huxley
  Julian, 276
Hyde
  Tony, 195
ICI, vi, 117, 177, 208, 209, 213, 214, 217, 221, 224, 226, 228, 229, 230, 231, 233, 234, 236, 237, 238, 240, 241, 248, 262, 264, 265, 267, 275, 284, 295, 314, 352, 380
  Daltoflex, 236, 238
  Dyestuffs, 93, 113, 208, 211, 213, 214, 223, 265, 273, 323
  Hexagon House, 208, 214
  Polymer Lab, 235, 236
  Research Department, 208, 230
  Surface Coatings, 224
  Vulcaprene, 237, 238
Imperial Legislative Council, 183
International Union of Pure and Applied Chemistry, (IUPAC), 129
Iowa State University, 315, 372, 376
Jackson
  Brian, 167
Jagger
  Tony, 164, 165
James
  Sid, 74
  William, 284, 294

Jepson
  Mike, 246
Jevons
  F R, ix, 248, 262, 264, 267, 270
  Stanley, 262
Jewish Chronicle, 210
Jewish Telegraph, 210
Jewkes
  John, 179, 180, 181, 265, 266
Joad
  C E M, 82, 106, 119
John Brown Ltd, 258
John Rylands Library, 251, 400
Johnson
  P S, 367
Jones
  E R H, 132
  Mr, 41
Joseph
  Keith, Sir, 320
Joule
  James, 112
Just William, 29, 68, 180, 185, 214
Kahneman
  Daniel, 96
Kanizsa triangle, 95
Keller
  Albert G, 373
Kerr
  Bill, 50, 74, 75
Keynes
  John Maynard, 401
Kidd
  Colin, 102
King Edward VII School, vi, 168, 193, 202, 245
Knoll
  Max, 307, 308
Knowles Greengrocers, 28
Kocabiyik
  Elif, ix
Koestler
  Arthur, 397
Kondratiev, 335, 336, 337
Korean War, 115
Kuhn
  Thomas, 268, 269
Kurzweil
  Ray, 94
Labour Party, 175, 177, 182, 222, 324
Lamarck
  Jean-Bapiste, 126, 127, 286, 287, 387, 394
Lambert
  Mr, 43
Lancashire's county cricket, 47
Lancaster bomber, 16, 48, 59
Langrish
  Alice Mary, 12
  Brian, 12, 18
  Edna, 12
  Elsie, 12
  George, 252, 255
  George Arnold, xi, 12, 32, 251
  George William, 12, 252
  Helen, viii, ix
  House, 231, 232, 253, 254, 257, 258, 259
  Irene, 252
  June, 31, 83
  Marjorie, 12
  Michael Rev, 255
  Nina, viii, x, 207, 210, 239, 245, 246, 333, 343
  Norman, 12, 18, 252
  Paul, 252, 253, 254
  Peter, 14, 17, 18, 22, 30, 44, 55, 57, 70, 178, 342
  Sandra, ix, 158, 159, 168, 170, 188, 195, 202, 205, 206, 207, 210, 215, 219, 223, 224, 240, 242, 243, 245, 248, 332, 354
  Suzanne, viii, ix, 188, 207, 210, 239, 245, 246, 333
  Tom, viii, x, 348
  Tooling Products Ltd, 231, 232, 257, 258, 259
  Vernon, 30
  Village, 232, 260
Langrishe
  Carolyn, 251
  Hercules, Sir, 251, 252
  John du Plessis, 256
Larkin
  John, 154
Laser, 291, 375
Lavoisier
  Antoine, 198
Leach
  Bernard, 306, 309, 311, 312
Lenin, 363
Lesser, 157
Leverhulme

INDEX

Lord, 123
Levinstein
    Herbert Dr, 213
    Ivan, 213
Levi-Strauss
    Claude, 163
Lewis
    Geraint F, 110, 125
Liberal Club, 18, 184, 185, 217, 218, 221, 223, 237
Liberal Democrats, 239
Liberal Party, 175, 184, 186, 189, 190, 218, 219, 220, 223, 237, 239, 243, 324, 326
    Young Liberals, 156, 184, 185
Library Theatre, 129, 157
Limestead Avenue, 159, 170, 171, 208, 210, 217, 218, 219, 239, 246
Linnaeus, 319
Linstead
    Patrick, Sir, 241
Litolff, 75
Litt
    Morton, 137
Lloyds Arms, 337, 339
Lofting
    Hugh, 290
London Midland and Scottish Railway Co, 176
Longford
    Lord, 346
Lord
    Cyril, 226, 227, 228
Lorenz
    Konrad, 52
Lowry
    L S, 380
LSS, 249, 260, 264, 266, 267, 270, 271, 283, 289, 294, 295, 301, 304, 315, 316, 333, 350
Lubbock
    Eric, 220, 221, 223
Lucretius, 84
Lysenko
    Trofim, 185
Mackay
    G, 194, 195
Main, 157
Maisels
    C K, 295
Makhoul
    Bashir, 267

Management Sciences, 341, 344, 345, 349, 351, 353
Manchester Cathedral, 187
Manchester Evening News (MEN), 244
Manchester Grammar School, 61, 217
Manchester High School for Girls, 215
Manchester Liverpool railway, 54
Manchester Polytechnic, vi, 311, 338, 379, 385
Manchester Ship Canal, 15, 31, 40, 44, 57, 204, 313
Manchester United, 47, 379
Manchester University, 13, 238, 244, 277, 302
Mann
    Eileen, 55
    Peter, 54, 55
Margaret
    Princess, 100
Marsden
    Mr, 42
Martin
    James, 299, 300
Marx, 122, 215, 336, 359, 362
Maslen
    Elizabeth, 121
MBS, vi, 302, 304, 306, 313, 314, 315, 372, 376
McCauley
    Dr, 35
McClelland
    Grigor, 304
McDougal Centre, 125
McGrail
    Nellie, 138
McLeod
    Herbert, 136
McTaggart
    John, 120, 264
Meadowcroft
    Stella, 78
Medawar
    Peter, 281, 387, 390
Medford
    Derek, 331, 332
Mellor
    Arthur, 325
Men's Debating Hall, 118, 157
Men's Student Union, 118
Mendeleev
    Dmitri, 112

Mensch
  Gerhard, 335, 336
Metrovicks, 143
Meyer
  Lothar, 111
Midgley
  Mary, 392
Midland Railway Co., 228
Milan Polytechnic, 162
Miller
  Stanley, 86, 166
Ministry of Supply, 131
Mises
  Ludwig von, 134, 347
MIT, 334
  IIMIT, 332, 333
  Management School, 334
  Sloan School of
  Management, 334
MMU, vi, 312, 338, 343, 396
Montecatini, 151, 161, 162
Monty Python, 119, 347
Moores
  John, 137
Morley
  Edward Williams, 108
  Paul, 35
Morphet
  Clive, 326
Morrison
  Herbert, 176
Morse code, 48, 87
Mosco
  Maisie, 170
Moseley, 170, 312
Moss
  Candida R, 105
Mowery
  David, 373
Mulvey
  Tom, 309
Munro
  Thomas, 387
Murdoch
  Richard, 49, 75
Myles
  Eleanor, 25
Nagle
  Mrs, 145
NASA, 315, 373, 374, 375
Nasmyth
  James, 63, 390
National Coal Board, 177
Natta
  Giulio, 151, 161, 162
Neoprene. See Carothers,Walter
Nether Edge Hospital, 207
Neville Road School, 246
Newman
  Jeremy, 216
  Monte, 215
  Pat, 206, 207, 215, 216
  Stephen, 216, 217
Newton, i, 14, 141, 199, 396, 400
Nichols
  Joy, 49, 75
Nieuwland
  Julius, 265
Nobel Prize, 98, 108, 110, 114,
  141, 151, 162, 167, 279, 291,
  299, 307, 308, 375
O'Donnell
  Anne, 244
  Mike, 244
Okanoya
  Kazuo, 102
Old Rectory Diners Club, 247
Oliver
  Philip M, 223
Orgel
  L E, 288
Ottoway
  Dick, 353
Owen's College, 13, 108, 157, 161
Oxford University, 69, 132, 193,
  221, 252, 253, 265
P v B views, 292
Packer
  Eric, 295
Page
  Cyril, 73
Paley
  William, Rev, 286, 289
Parkhurst Prison, 35
Parkinson
  Trevor, 328
Parsonage Rd, 385
Pathé News, 46
Pearson
  Alan, 302, 304, 305, 325,
  332, 334, 335
Pedley
  Brian, 136
Pendlebury
  Tom, 70
Pendleton High School for Girls, 16
Perkin
  Henry, 108, 241, 242

INDEX

Petrie
  William, 319
Pevsner
  Nicholas, 338
Pinker
  Steven, 27
Pitman's shorthand, 14
Planck
  Max, 99
Plato, 121
Plaza Stockport, 159
Polanyi
  John, 110
  Karl, 110
  Michael, 109, 110
Polytechnic Institute of Brooklyn, 137
Popper
  Karl, 53, 200, 269, 270
Porter
  George, 112
Posey
  Emma, 130, 398
Powell
  Enoch, 228
Poznanski
  Kazimir, ix
Priestley
  J B, 279
Pritchard
  Huw, 131, 141, 150
Programmes Analysis Unit (PAU), 326, 327, 330, 332, 333, 339
Queen Mary College, 121
Queen's Award, 268, 271, 273, 291, 320, 328, 335
Queen's Club, 379
Quincke
  Heinrich, 111, 112
R & D
  Management, 325
  Management Journal, 304, 334
  Research Unit, 302, 304, 306, 315, 324, 325, 331, 334, 335, 339
Rawicz & Landauer, 75
Read
  Mrs, 145
Reagan
  Ronald, 180
Redmans Grocery Store, 84
Redring, 100, 326
Reform Club, 323

Heaton Chapel, 156, 248, 385
Regent cinema, 27
REME, 346, 347
Renold
  Charles Garonne, 344
Research and Development Management Association (RADMA), 305
Revans
  Reginald, 344
Reynolds
  John Henry, 341
Ridley
  Matt, 199, 284, 290, 294
Rigby
  David, x
Ringway, 204, 229
Rivers
  Pitt, 388, 389
Rivington, 123
Rivlin
  Chris, ix, 391, 392
Robinson
  Heath, 275
  Robert, 108
  Tony, Sir, 297
Rolls Royce, 16, 221, 228, 380
  Merlin engines, 16, 59
Ronayne
  Jarlath, 316, 317
Roneo Office Equipment Supplier, 16, 296
Roosevelt, 173
Roscoe
  Henry, Sir, 108, 109, 112
Rose
  L F, 273
  Paul, 379
Rose's sweet shop, 211
Rosenberg
  Nathan, 291, 315, 373, 374, 375
Rothman
  Harry, ix, 268, 294, 317, 318
Rothwell
  Evelyn, 157
  Roy, 273
Rousseau, 121
Royal Northern College of Music (RNCM), 337
Royal Society, ix, 127, 139
Royal Society of Arts (RSA), 15
Ruska

336

Ernst, 307, 308, 309
Russell
　Bertrand, 119, 187, 264
SAPPHO Project, 271, 273, 274
Schopenhauer
　Arthur, 81, 119
Schorlemmer
　Carl, 108, 111
Schrödinger
　Erwin, 110, 167
Schumacher
　E F, 330
Schumpeter
　Joseph, xi, 336
Schunck
　Edward, 108, 112
Science Policy Research Unit (SPRU), 271, 272, 274, 284, 312
Science Research Council (SRC), 352
Scottish Dyes, 241, 242
　Monastral Fast Blue CR, 241
Scouts, 67, 73, 200, 206, 325
SDP, 239
Secombe
　Harry, 118
Second World War, xi, 14, 16, 131, 166
Shambles, 187
　Sinclair's Oyster Bar, 187
　Wellington Inn, 187
Shaw
　George Bernard, 83
　Miss, 35, 40
Sheffield University, 112, 196
　Student union, 206
Sherrington
　Charles, Sir, 276
Shop Stewards Movement of 1919, 362
Sijthoff & Noordhoff, 330
Silvers
　Phil, 236
Sisters of the Cross and Passion, 124
Slater
　N.B., 97, 139, 140, 141, 143
Smith
　Adam, 362
　Alex, Sir, 380, 382
　Cairns, 167
　Maynard, 281
　Mike, 349

Snow
　C P, 263
Snowdon
　Anthony, Lord, 100
Solow
　Robert, 272
Sorokin
　P A, 361
Spencer
　Herbert, 274, 387
Spitfire, 16, 48, 59
Spring
　Howard, 170
St Gabriel's Hall, 124
St Paul's church, 385
St. Andrew's church, 190
Stafford
　Ron, 233, 234, 235, 236, 237
Stalin, 85, 173, 185
Stanford University, 315, 373, 374
Steadman
　Philip, ix, 388, 389
Steel
　David, 239
Sten guns, 115
Stephenson
　Manchester Liverpool railway, 204
　Robert, 41, 204
　The Rocket, 41
Stockport Convent High School for Girls, 244, 245, 246
Stone
　Laurence, 220
Stopes
　Marie, 125, 277
Strangeways, 36, 170
Stringer
　Graham, 379
Students' Union, 119, 157, 196, 348
Sullivan
　Tony, 219, 221
Swinging Sporran, 377, 378
　Basement Club, 377
Sykes
　Mark, 46
Synge
　Richard L.M., 299, 300
Szilárd
　Leó, 109
T Seymour Meads, 28
Talbot-Ponsonby

INDEX

C W, 257, 259
Edward, 258
Nigel, 259
Taylor
   A J P, 187
   Bill, 186
   F W, 362
   G K, 374
Technology
   Science, Technology and Society (STS), 294, 317, 352
Territorial Army, 114, 115, 116, 125
   Ashton barracks, 117
   Holcombe, 116
Thatcher
   Margaret, 180, 337
The Square, 240, 243, 244, 246, 247
Thomas
   A L R, 374
Thorpe
   William, 101
Tilston
   Richard, 339
Times Educational Supplement, 168, 193
Tinker
   Harold, 323
Tithe Barn School, 246
Tito, 86
Todd
   Alexander. Lord, 108
Torricelli
   Evangelista, 135
Townes
   Charles, 291, 375
Trafalgar Street, 170
Trafford Park, 15, 16, 40, 42, 44, 58, 59, 142, 143, 152, 208, 313, 344
Trevor Roper
   Hugh, 103
Trinity College Dublin, 133
Truman
   Mr, 196
Turner
   Samuel, Sir, 344
Turner Brothers Asbestos Co, 15, 16, 59, 344
UKAEA, 326, 333

UMIST, vi, 267, 339, 341, 343, 344, 345, 346, 348, 350, 355, 377, 379, 380, 381, 385
Uncle Chic, 202
Union of Lancashire and Cheshire Institutes, 15, 341
University of Glasgow, 102
University of Salford, 343, 391, 397
University of Tübingen, 132
Utterback
   Jim, 334
Vackers Club, 378
Valette
   Adolphe, 380
Veblen
   Thorstein, 238, 292, 344
Vernon
   Mr, 197
Victoria
   Queen, xi, 44, 148, 251, 257
Victoria University, 69, 108, 111, 343
Viking Engineering, 233
Viking Pumps, 234
Vinck
   Dominique, 273
Waddington
   John, 259
Walras, 293
Wambaugh
   Joseph, 52, 285
Warhurst
   Ernest, 110
Watson and Crick, 86, 141
Wealth from Knowledge, 270, 283, 294, 315, 316, 327, 328, 355, 376, 380
Webster
   Beryl, 73
Wedgwood
   Thomas, 89
Weir Group, 259
Weizmann
   Chaim, 108, 318
Weldon
   Fay, 13, 52
Wesley College, 202
Westinghouse, 15, 59, 143
Wheeler
   Mortimer, Sir, 297
Whewell
   William, 72
White
   Lynn, 356

Whitehead, 264
Whitley
    Richard, 335
Wiley, 304
Williams
    Bruce, Sir, 266, 267, 312
    G, 264, 268
    Shirley, 220
Wilson
    Harold, 320
Wilson's brewery, 16
Winton Senior School, 60
Wislicenus
    Johannes, 111
Wittgenstein, 264
Women's Student Union, 118
Wood Jones
    Frederic, 127
Wool Industries Research Association (WIRA), 299
Worboys
    Michael, 317
Worden
    Blair, 104
Wright
    Jeanne, 123, 125, 128, 143, 144, 146, 150, 156
    Mr and Mrs, 128, 146
    Sewall, 102
Yagou
    Artemis, x
Yates
    Julia, x
York University, 348
Young Communists, 185
Zeitgeist, xi
Ziegler
    Anne, 75
    Karl, 162
Zoo
    Belle Vue, 28, 127
    London, 127
Zugbach De Zugg
    Eric von, 346

Printed in Great Britain
by Amazon